THE LAKE REGIONS OF CENTRAL AFRICA
VOLUME I

FROM ZANZIBAR TO LAKE TANGANYIKA

By Sir Richard F. Burton
Capt. H. M. I. Army: Fellow and Gold Medallist
of the Royal Geographical Society

THE NARRATIVE PRESS
TRUE FIRST PERSON ACCOUNTS OF HIGH ADVENTURE

"Some to discover islands far away."

- Shakespeare

To My Sister Maria Stisted,
These Pages are
Affectionately Inscribed

The Narrative Press
P.O. Box 2487, Santa Barbara, California 93120 U.S.A.
Telephone: (805) 884-0160 Web: www.narrativepress.com

ISBN 1-58976-062-X (Paperback)
ISBN 1-58976-063-8 (eBook)

Produced in the United States of America

TABLE OF CONTENTS

PREFACE

I had intended this record of personal adventure to appear immediately after my return to Europe, in May 1859. The impaired health, the depression of spirits, and worse still the annoyance of official correspondence, which to me have been the sole results of African Exploration, may be admitted as valid reasons for the delay.

In April, 1860, the Royal Geographical Society of Great Britain honoured me by publishing a detailed paper, forming the XXIXth Volume of their Journal, from which the topographical descriptions contained in the following pages have, with their kind permission, been extracted. I have now attempted to combine with geography and ethnology, a narrative of occurrences and an exposition of the more popular and picturesque points of view which the subject offers.

When I communicated to my friends the publishers certain intentions of writing an exclusively "light work," they protested against the project, stating that the public appetite required the addition of stronger meat. In compliance, therefore, with their suggestion, I have drawn two portraits of the same object, and mingled the gay with the graver details of travel, so as to produce an antipathetic cento.

Modern "hinters to travellers" direct the explorer and the missionary to eschew theory and opinion. We are told somewhat peremptorily that it is our duty to gather actualities not inferences – to see and not to think, in fact, to confine ourselves to transmitting the rough material collected by us, that it may be worked into shape by the professionally learned at home. But why may not the observer be allowed a voice concerning his own observations, if at least his mind be sane and his stock of collateral knowledge be respectable?

I have not attempted to avoid intruding matters of a private and personal nature upon the reader; it would have been impossible to avoid egotism in a purely egotistical narrative. The official matter, however, has been banished into Appendix II. In publishing it, my desire is to avoid the possibility of a charge being concealed in the pigeon-holes of the India House, to be produced, according to custom, with all the effect of a surprise whenever its presence is convenient. I know the conditions of appealing from those in office to a higher tribunal – the Public. I well know them and I accept them. Avant tout, gentilhomme!

I have spoken out my feelings concerning Captain Speke, my companion in the Expedition which forms the subject of these pages. The history of our companionship is simply this: – As he had suffered with me in purse and person at Berberah, in 1855, I thought it but just to offer him the opportunity of renewing an attempt to penetrate into Africa. I had no other reasons. I could not expect much from his assistance; he was not a linguist – French and Arabic being equally unknown to him – nor a man of science, nor an accurate astronomical observer. The Court of Directors officially refused him leave of absence; I obtained it for him by an application to the local authorities at Bombay. During the exploration he acted in a subordinate capacity; and as may be imagined amongst a party of Arabs, Baloch, and Africans, whose languages he ignored, he was unfit for any other but a subordinate capacity. Can I then feel otherwise than indignant, when I find that, after preceding me from Aden to England, with the spontaneous offer, on his part, of not appearing before the Society that originated the Expedition until my return, he had lost no time in taking measures to secure for himself the right of working the field which I had opened, and that from that day he has placed himself en evidence as the primum mobile of an Expedition, in which he signed himself "surveyor," – cujus pars minima fuit?

With deference to the reader's judgment, I venture to express a hope that whatever of unrefinement appears in these pages, may be charged to the subject. It has been my duty to draw a Dutch picture, a cabaret-piece which could not be stripped of its ordonnance, its boors, its pipes, and its pots. I have shirked nothing of the unpleasant task, – of recording processes and not only results; I have entered into the recital of the maladies, the weary squabbles, and the vast variety of petty troubles, without which the coup d'oeil of African adventure would be more like a Greek Saint in effigy – all lights and no shade – than the chapter of accidents which it now is.

The map and the lists of stations, dates, &c., have been drawn upon the plan adopted by Mr. Francis Galton, F.R.G.S. The outline of Africa, the work of Mr. Weller, F.R.G.S., contains the latest and the best information concerning the half-explored interior of the Continent. The route-map has been borrowed by permission from the laborious and conscientious compilation of Mr. Findlay, F.R.G.S., accompanying the paper forwarded by me to the Royal Geographical Society. The latter gentleman has also kindly supplied a profile of the country traversed, showing the Eastern limits of the Great Depression, and the "elevated-trough formation" of Central Africa.

In conclusion, I would solicit forbearance in all that concerns certain errors of omission and commission scattered through these pages. The migratory instinct is now hurrying me towards the New World: I have, therefore, been obliged to content myself with a single revise.

10th April,
E.I.U.S. Club, 14 St. James's Square.

Table 1: DATES OF JOURNEYING

1856	September	Left England.
	2nd December	Sailed from Bombay.
	19th December	Arrived at Zanzibar Island.
1857	6th January	Left Zanzibar the first time.
	14th June	Left Zanzibar the second time.
	27th June	Set out from Kaole on the coast.
	7th November	Arrived at Unyanyembe of Unyamwezi.
1858	14th February	Reached Ujiji on the Tanganyika Lake.
	26th April	Arrived at Uvira on the North of the Tanyanyika Lake.
	26th May	Left Ujiji.
	19th June	Returned to Unyanyembe.
	25th September	Left Unyanyembe.
1859	3rd February	Reached Konduchi on the coast.
	4th March	Landed at Zanzibar Island.
	4th May	Left Aden.
	20th May	Landed at Southampton.

LIST STASIMETRIC AND HYPSOMETRIC. NAMES OF THE KHAMBI OR STAGES MADE BY THE EAST AFRICAN EXPEDITION, AND HEIGHTS OF THE SEVERAL CRUCIAL STATIONS.

Table 2: FIRST REGION

	FROM KAOLE ON THE COAST TO ZUNGOMERO, CHIEF DISTRICT OF K'HUTU.	H.	M.
1	Kaoli to Mgude or Kuingani	1	30
2	Kuingani to Bomani	1	30
3	Bomani to Mkwaju la Mvuani	0	30
4	Mkwaju to Nzasa (of Uzaramo)	3	20
5	Nzasa to Kiranga-Ranga	6	0
6	Kirnaga-Ranga to Tumba Ihere	3	30
7	Tumba Ihere to Muhonyera	4	40
8	Muhonyera to Sagesera	2	45
9	Sagesera to Tunda	7	0
10	Tunda to Dege la Mhora	2	30
11	Dege la Mhora to Madege Madogo	3	0
12	Madege Madogo to Kidunda	3	0
13	Kidunda to Mgeta Ford	7	0
14	Mgeta Ford to Kiruru in K'hutu	6	0
15	Kiruru to Dut'humi	6	40
16	Dut'humi to Bakera	2	0
17	Bakera to Zungomero	7	0
¤17		67	55

	Kaole, Latitude, South 6° 25', Longitude, East 38° 51' Zungomero, Lat. South 7° 27', Long. East 37° 22' Altitude of Zungomero, 330 feet above sea level. Average altitude of First Region, by B.P. Therm., 230 feet.	

Table 3: SECOND REGION

	FROM ZUNGOMERO, OVER TO MOUNTAINS OF USAGARA, TO UGOGI.	H.	M.
1	Zungomero to Mzizi Mdogo (in Usagara)	5	0
2	Mzizi Mdogo to Chya K'henge	4	30
3	Chya K'henge to Rufuta River	4	30
4	Rufuta River (up the Goma Pass) to Mfu'uni	1	50
5	Mfu'uni to "Overshot Nullah"	6	10
6	"Overshot Nullah" to Zonhwe	2	0
7	Zonhwe to Muhama	4	45
8	Muhama to Makata	6	30
9	Makata to Myombo River	4	30
10	Myombo River to Mbumi	4	30
11	Mbumi to Kadetamare	5	55
12	Kadetamare to Muinyi	8	10
13	Muinyi to Nidabi	4	50
14	Nidabi to Rumuma	5	30
15	Rumuma to Marenga Mk'hali	3	30
16	Marenga Mk'hali to ¤ in Jungle	5	0
17	Jungle to Inenge	4	0

18	Inenge to first gradient of Rubeho Pass	6	30
19	First gradient to second gradient ditto	2	0
20	Second gradient to summit of Rubeho	1	45
21	Summit to ¤ one quarter of the way down the counterslope	3	0
22	From ¤ on slope to ¤ below half-way	5	0
23	From ¤ below half-way to Ugogi at the base	4	0
¤ 23 + 27	(carried forward) = 33 ¤'s Carried forward,	103 25 67 55	
	Total hours from the coast to Ugogi	17 120	
	Rubeho Pass, (about) Latitude, South 6° 38' Longitude, East, 36° 19' Ugogi, Lat., South 6° 40' Long. 36° 6' Altitude of Rubeho summit, 5700. Altitude of Ugogi at Western Counterslope, by B.P. Therm. 2770.		

Table 4: THIRD REGION

	FROM UGOGI, THROUGH MARENGA MK'HALI, UGOGO, AND MGUNDA MK'HALI, TO TURA OF UNYAMWEZI	H.M.	
¤ 1	Ugogi to ¤ in Jungle	4	0
2	Jungle to Marenga Mk'hali (second of that name)	4	40
3	Marenga Mk'hali to ¤ in Jungle	4	10
4	¤ in Jungle to ¤ in Jungle	5	0
5	¤ in Jungle to Ziwa or tank (on frontier of Ugogo)	2	0
6	Ziwa to Kifukuru	3	0
7	Kikufuru to ¤ in Jungle	5	40
8	¤ in Jungle to Kanyenye	1	25

9	Kanyenye to Kanyenye of Magomba	2 45
10	Kanyenye of Magomba to ¤ in Jungle	5 0
11	¤ in Jungle to K'hok'ho	7 40
12	K'hok'ho to Mdaburu	6 20
13	Mdaburu to ¤ in Jungle of Mgunda Mk'hali	6 30
14	Mgunda Mk'hali to Mabunguru	6 0
15	Mabunguru to Jiwe la Mkoa	7 0
16	Jiwe la Mkoa to Kirurumo	3 10
17	Kirurumo to Jiweni of Uyanzi	4 30
18	Jiweni to Mgongo Thembo	2 20
19	Mgongo Thembo to ¤ Tura Nullah	7 0
20	¤ Tura Nullah to Tura in Unyamwezi	5 30
¤ 20 + 33	(carried forward) = 53	93 40
	Carried forward	17120
	Total hours from the coast to Tura	26 50
	Eastern limit of Tura, Latitude, South, 5° 27' Longitude, East, 34°. Altitude, by Bath, Thermometer, 4125 feet.	

Table 5: FOURTH REGION

	THROUGH UNYAMWEZI, UGARA, UWENDE, AND UVINZA, TO FORD OF MALAGARAZI RIVER.	H.M.
1	Eastern limit of Tura to Western Tura	1 30
2	Western Tura to Kwale Nullah	6 30
3	Kwale Nullah to Eastern Rubuga	5 45

4	Eastern Rubuga to Western Rubuga	2 40
5	Western Rubuga to Ukona	2 15
6	Ukona to Kigwa	5 5
7	Kigwa to Hanga village	6 30
8	Hanga to Kazeh (Arab ☿)	5 0
9	Kazeh to Zimbili Hill	1 40
10	Zimbili to Yombo	2 0
11	Yombo to Pano (clearing in jungle)	4 0
12	Pano to Eastern Mfuto	1 40
13	Eastern Mfuto to Western Mfuto	2 0
14	Western Mfuto to Eastern Wilyankuru	6 30
15	Eastern Wilyankuru to Central Wilyankuru	2 50
16	Central Wilyankuru to Western Wilyankuru	2 0
17	Western Wilyankuru to Masenge	2 30
18	Masenge to Eastern Kirira	2 0
19	Eastern Kirira to Western Kirira	3 0
20	Western Kirira to Eastern Msene	4 0
21	Eastern Msene to Western Msene (Arab ☿)	2 0
22	Western Msene to Mbhali	1 30
23	Mbhali to Sengati	2 0
24	Sengati to Sorora or Solola	4 5
25	Sorora to Ukungwe	2 15
26	Ukungwe to Panda	1 50
27	Panda to Kajjanjeri	1 30
28	Kajjanjeri to Eastern Usagozi	3 45
29	Eastern Usagozi to Western Usagozi	1 0

30	Western Usagozi to Masenga of Wagara	2 0
31	Masenga to Mukozimo of Wawende	2 45
32	Mukozimo to Uganza of Wanyamwezi	3 15
33	Uganza to Usenye of Wavinza	4 0
34	Usenye to Rukundu	2 20
35	Rukundu to Wanyika	3 0
36	Wanyika t Unyanguruwwe	4 50
37	Unyanguruwwe to Ugaga on the Malagarazi River	3 0
¤ 37 + 53	(Carried over) = 90 Carried forward Total hours from coast to Malagarazi River	110 30 26 50 375 30
	Kazeh Latitude, South 5° 1', Longitude, East 33° 3'	
	Malagarazi Ferry, Lat., South 5° 7', Long., East 31° 13'	
	Altitude of Kazeh, by Bath Therm. 3490 feet.; altitude of Usenye, by Bath Therm, 3190 feet.	

Table 6: FIFTH REGION

	FROM THE MALAGARAZI FERRY TO UKARANGA ON THE TANGANYIKA LAKE	H.M.
1	Ugaga on left to Mpete on right hand	0 25
2	Mpete to Kinawani	5 20
3	Kinawani to ¤ in jungle	5 25
4	¤ in jungle to Jambeho	1 40
5	Jambeho to Salt pans of Rusugi	5 15
6	Salt pans to ¤ in jungle	4 20
7	¤ in jungle to Ruguva River	3 30

8	Ruguva River to Unguwwe River	4 40
9	Unguwwe River to ¤ in Jungle	7 35
10	¤ in Jungle to Ukaranga on Lake	6 35
¤ 10 + 90	(carried forward) = 100	44 45
	Carried forward	37 530
	Total hours from the coast to the Tanganyika Lake	420 25
	Ukaranga, Latitude, South 4° 58', Longitude, East, 30° 3' 30". Altitude by Bath Therm. 1850.	

The distance from Kaole to Ujiji is of 540 rectilinear geographical miles: or in statute miles, allowing one for windings of the road, thus:

From Kaole to Kazeh, statute miles 520
From Kazeh to Ujiji, statute miles..............276
....796
Add one-fifth for detour – 159 miles..........159
Total of statute miles 955

Assuming the absolute time of travelling to be 420 hours, this will give a marching time of 2.27 miles per hour.

Chapter 1

WE QUIT ZANZIBAR ISLAND IN DIGNIFIED STYLE

At noon, on the 16th of June, 1857, the corvette Artémise, after the usual expenditure of gunpowder which must in Eastern lands announce every momentous event, from the birth of a prince to the departure of a bishop, slowly gliding out of Zanzibar harbour, afforded us a farewell glance at the white-washed mosques and houses of the Arabs, the cadjan-huts, the cocoa-grown coasts, and the ruddy hills striped with long lines of clove. Onwards she stole before a freshening breeze, the balmy breath of the Indian Ocean, under a sun that poured a flood of sparkling light over the azure depths and the bright green shallows around, between the "elfin isles" of Kumbeni, with its tall trees, and Chumbi, tufted with dense thickets, till the white sandstrip mingled with the blue ocean, the gleaming line of dwarf red cliff and scaur dropped into the water's edge, the land faded from emerald to brown, and from brown to hazy purple, the tufts of the trees seemed first to stand out of, then to swim upon, the wave, and as evening, the serenest of tropical evenings, closed in over sky, earth, and sea, a cloud-like ridge, dimly discernible from our quarter, was all that remained of Zanzibar.

I will not here stay the course of my narrative to inform the reader that Zanzibar is not, as the Cyclopaedias declare, "an island of Africa, governed by a king who is subject to the Portuguese;" that it is not, as the Indian post-offices appear to believe, a part of the Persian Gulf; nor, as homekeeping folk, whose notions of African geography are somewhat dim and ill-defined, have mentally determined, a rock in the Red Sea, nor a dependency of the Niger, nor even an offshoot of the Cape of Storms.

The Artémise is a kind of "Jackass-frigate", an 18-gun corvette, teak-built in Bombay, with a goodly breadth of beam, a slow sailer, but a sure. In the days of our deceased ally, Sayyid Said, the misnamed "Imaum of Muscat," she had so frequently been placed by his Highness at the disposal of his old friend Lieut.-Colonel Hamerton, that she had acquired the sobriquet of "the Balyuz or Consul's yacht." On this occasion she had been fitted up for a cruise to the mainland; her yards, usually struck, had been swayed up and thrown across; her top spars had been transferred from the hold to their proper place; her ropes and rigging, generally hanging in tatters about her sticks, had been carefully overhauled; her old sails had been bent, and her usual crew, a few slaves that held their own with difficulty against a legion of rats and an army of cockroaches, had been increased to its full complement of twenty men. His Highness the Sayyid Majid, who after the demise of his father had assumed the title of "Sultan of Zanzibar and the Sawahil," came on board accompanied by his four brothers, of whom two – Sayyids Jamshid and Hamdan – died of small-pox before our return, and one – Sayyid Barghash – has lately become a state prisoner at Bombay, to bid what proved a last adieu to his father's friend. At the same time His Highness honoured me, through his secretary, Ahmed bin Nuuman, more generally known as Wajhayn, or "Two-faces," with three letters of introduction, to Musa Mzuri, the Indian doyen of the merchants settled at Unyamwezi, to the Arabs there resident, and to all his subjects who were travelling into the interior.

The Artémise conveyed the personnel and the materiel of the East African Expedition, namely, the two European members – my companion and myself – two Portuguese, or rather half-caste Goanese "boys," two Negro gun-carriers, the Seedy

Mubarak Mombai (Bombay), and Muinyi Mabruki, his "brother" and finally, eight so-called "Baloch" mercenaries, a guard appointed by the Sultan to accompany me. Lieut.-Colonel Hamerton, at that time Her Majesty's consul and Hon. East India Company's agent at Zanzibar, though almost lethargic from the effects of protracted illness – he lived only in the evening – had deemed it his duty to land us upon the coast, and to superintend our departure from the dangerous seaboard. He was attended by Mr. Frost, the apothecary attached to the consulate, whose treatment for a fatal liver-complaint appeared to consist of minute doses of morphia and a liberal diet of sugar.

By Lieut.-Colonel Hamerton's advice, I ventured to modify the scheme of the East African Expedition, as originally proposed by the Expeditionary Committee of the Royal Geographical Society of London. In 1855, M. Erhardt, an energetic member of the hapless "Mom-bas Mission," had on his return to London offered to explore a vast mass of water, about the size of the Casplan, which, from the information of divers "natives," he had deposited in slug or leech shape in the heart of Intertropical Africa, thus prolonging the old "Maravi," or "Moravim Lake" of Portuguese travellers and school atlases, to the north of the equator, and thus bringing a second deluge upon sundry provinces and kingdoms thoroughly well known for the last half century. He had proposed to land, with an outfit of 300 dollars[1], at Kilwa, one of the southern ports of the Zanzibar mainland, to hire a score of Wasawahili porters, to march with a caravan upon the nearest point of his own water, and to launch an adventurous canoe upon a lake which, according to his map, could not be traversed under twenty-five days. Messrs. Erhardt and Krapf, of the "Mombas Mission," spent, it is true, a few hours at Kilwa, where they were civilly entreated by the governor and the citizens; but they egregiously deceived themselves and others, when they concluded that they could make that place their ingress-point. Lieut. Christopher, I.N., who visited the East African coast in 1843, wisely advised explorers to avoid the neighbourhood of Kilwa. Wisely, I repeat: the burghers of that proud old settlement had, only a year before my arrival, murdered, by means of the Wangindo savages, an Arab merchant who ventured to lay open the interior.

At the same time I had laid before the Council of the Royal Geographical Society my desire to form an expedition primarily for the purpose of ascertaining the limits of the "Sea of Ujiji, or Unyamwezi Lake," and secondarily, to determine the exportable produce of the interior, and the ethnography of its tribes. I have quoted exactly the words of the application. In these days every explorer of Central Africa is supposed to have set out in quest of the coy sources of the White Nile, and when he returns without them, his exploration, whatever may have been its value, is determined to be a failure. The Council honoured my plans with their approval. At their solicitation, the Foreign Office granted the sum of 1000*l.* for the outlay of the exploration, and the defunct Court of Directors of the late East India Company, who could not be persuaded to contribute towards the expenses, generously allowed me two years' leave of absence from regimental duty, for the purpose of commanding the Expedition. I also received instructions to report myself to his Excellency the Lord Elphinstone, then

---

1.   The sum was wholly inadequate. M Erhardt has, I have been told, expended as much on a week's march from Pangani Town to Fuga. The smallest of Wasawahili pedlars would hardly deem an outfit of 300 dollars sufficient. M. Erhardt was, even according to his own reduced ideas of distance, to march with twenty followers 400 miles, and to explore a lake 300 miles in breadth and of unknown length. In 1802, when cloth and beads were twice their present value in Africa, the black Pombeiros sent by M. Da Costa, superintendent of the "Cassangi Factory," carried with them for the necessary expenses and presents, goods to the value of nearly 500*l.* M. Erhardt's estimate was highly injurious to future travellers: either he knew the truth, and he should have named at once a reasonable estimate, or he was ignorant of the subject, and he should have avoided it. The consequence of his proposal was simply this: – With 5000*l.* instead of 1000*l.* the limited sum of the Government grant, the East African Expedition could have explored the whole central area; nothing but the want of supplies caused their return at the time when, after surmounting sickness, hardship, and want of discipline amongst the party, they were ready to push to the extreme end.

Governor of Bombay, and to Lieut.-Colonel Hamerton, from whose influence and long experience much was expected.

When the starting-point came to be debated, the Consul strongly objected to an Expedition into the interior via Kilwa, on account of the opposition to be expected at a port so distant from the seat of government, where the people, half-caste Arabs and Wasawahili, who are under only a nominal control, still retained a strong predilection for protection, and a violent hostility to strangers. These reasons led him to propose my landing upon the coast opposite Zanzibar, and to my thence marching with a strong escort, despatched by the Arab prince, through the maritime tribes, whose cruel murder of M. Maizan, the first European known to have penetrated beyond the sea-board, was yet fresh in the memories of men. This notion was accepted the more readily, as during my short preliminary sojourn at Zanzibar, I had satisfactorily ascertained from Arab travellers that the Maravi or Kilwa Lake is distinct from the "Sea of Ujiji;" that the former is of comparatively diminutive dimensions; that there is no caravan route between the two; and therefore that, by exploring the smaller, I should lose the chance of discovering the larger water. Moreover, the general feeling of the Zanzibarites – of the Christian merchants, whom I had offended by collecting statistics about copal-digging, ivory, and sesamum – of the Bhattias or Hindus of Cutch, who systematically abuse the protection of the British flag to support the interest of the slave trade – of the Arabs, who remembered nothing but political intrigue in the explorations of the "Mombas Mission," and the lamentable result of Dr. Krapf's political intrigues – and of the Africans generally, who are disposed to see in every innovation some new form of evil – had been conveyed to my ears explicitly enough to warrant my apprehensions for the success of the Expedition, had I insisted upon carrying out the project proposed by M. Erhardt.

I must here explain, that before my departure from England, the Church Missionary Society had supplied me, after a personal interview in Salisbury Square, with a letter to their *employé*, M. Rebmann, the last remnant of that establishment at Mombasah, which had, it is said, expended about 12,000l. with the minimest of results. The missionaries had commenced operations with vigour, and to the work of conversion they had added certain discoveries in the unknown lands of the interior, which attracted the attention of European geographers. Unhappily Dr. Krapf, the principal, happened to commit himself by the following assertion: – "The Imaum of Muskat has not an inch of ground on the coast between the Island of Wassin and the Pangani River; this tract, in fact, belonging to King Kmeri of Usumbara, down from 4° 30' to 5° 30' S. The tract, which is very low, is inhabited by the Wasegua tribes, and is the chief slave-market for supplying Zanzibar."

This "information," put forth in the Journal of the Royal Geographical Society (vol. i. p. 203), was copied into the Proceedings (vol. xxiii, p. 106), with the remark, that the territory alluded to was a "supposed possession" of the Imaum. Orientals are thin-skinned upon questions of land; the assertion was directly opposed to fact, and the jealousy of the rival representatives at Zanzibar each on his own side, exaggerated its tendency. Lieut.-Colonel Hamerton, who felt his influence sapped by this error on the part of his protege, had reported the facts to his government. Dr. Krapf had quitted the scene of his labours and discoveries, but his Highness the Sultan and the sadat, or court, retained a lively remembrance of the regretable incident. Before the arrival of the Expedition, "Muhiyy-el-Din," the Shafei Kazi of the island, had called upon Lieut.-Colonel Hamerton, probably by direction of his superiors, and had received an answer, fortified by an oath, that the Expedition was wholly independent of "Dutchmen," as the missionaries were called by the Zanzibarites. I was compelled, somewhat unwillingly, to dispense with urging M. Rebmann's presence. By acting in any other way I should have lost the assistance of the consul, and the Arabs, with a ready display of zeal, would have secured for me an inevitable failure.

At six P.M. on Wednesday, the 17th of June, 1857, the Artémise cast anchor off Wale Point, a long, low bush-grown sandspit, about eighty-four miles distant from the little town of Bagamoyo. Our sailing-master, Mohammed bin Khamis, anchored in deep water, throwing out double the length of chain required. For this prudence, however, there was some reason. The roadsteads are open; the muddy bottom shelves gradually, almost imperceptibly; the tides retire ten or eleven feet, and a strong gale, accompanied by the dangerous raz de maree, or rollers from seaward, especially at the seasons of the syzygies, with such a shore to leeward, is justly dreaded by the crews of square-rigged vessels.

There is a something peculiarly interesting in the first aspect of the "Mrima," the hill-land, as this portion of the African coast is called by the islanders of Zanzibar. On one side lies the Indian Ocean, illimitable towards the east, dimpled with its "anerithmon gelasma," and broken westward by a thin line of foam, creaming upon the whitest and finest of sand, the detritus of coralline and madrepore. It dents the coast deeply, forming bays, bayous, lagoons, and backwaters, where, after breaking their force upon bars and black ledges of sand and rock, upon diabolitos, or sun-stained masses of a coarse conglomerate, and upon strong weirs planted in crescent shape, the waters lie at rest in the arms of the land like sheets of oil. The points and islets formed by these sea-streams are almost flush with the briny surface, yet they are overgrown with a profuse vegetation, the result of tropical suns and copious showers, which supply the want of rich soil. The banks of the backwaters are lined with forests of white and red mangrove. When the tide is out, the cone-shaped root-work supporting each tree rises naked from the deep sea-ooze; parasitical oysters cluster over the trunks at water-level, and between the adults rise slender young shoots, tipped with bunches of brilliant green. The pure white sand is bound together by a kind of convolvulus, whose large fleshy leaves and lilac-coloured flowers creep along the loose soil. Where raised higher above the ocean level, the coast is a wall of verdure. Plots of bald old trees, bent by the regular breezes, betray the positions of settlements which, generally sheltered from sight, besprinkle the coast in a long straggling line, like the suburbs of a populous city. Of these, thirteen were counted in a space of three miles. The monotony of green that clothes the soil is relieved in places by dwarf earth-cliffs and scaurs of rufous hue – East Africa is mostly a red land – and behind the foreground of littoral or alluvial plain, at a distance varying from three to five miles, rises a blue line of higher level, conspicuous even from Zanzibar Island, the sandy raised beach now the frontier of the wild men. To this sketch add its accompaniment; by day, the plashing of the wave, and the scream of the gull, with the perpetual hum and buzz of insect life; and, after sunset, the deep, dead silence of a tropical night, broken only by the roar of the old bull-crocodile at his resting-time, the qua-qua of the night-heron, and the shouts and shots of the watchmen, who know from the grunts of the hippopotamus, struggling up the bank, that he is quitting his watery home to pay a visit to their fields.

We were delayed ten days off Wale Point by various preliminaries to departure. Said bin Salim, a half-caste Arab of Zanzibar, who, sorely against his will, was ordered by the prince to act as Ras Kafilah, or caravan-guide, had, after ceaseless and fruitless prayers for delay, preceded us about a fortnight, for the purpose of collecting porters. The timid little man, whose nerves were shaken to weeping-point by the terrors of the way, and by the fancy that, thus cooperating with the exploration, he was incurring the hatred of his fellows, had "taken the shilling," in the shape of 500 dollars, advanced from public funds by the consul, with a promise of an ample reward in hard coin, and a gold watch, "si se bene gesserit:" at the same time Lieut.-Colonel Hamerton had warned me against trusting to a half-caste. Accompanied by a Cutch Banyan of the Bhattia caste, by name Ramji – of whom more anon – he had crossed over, on the 1st of June, to the mainland, and had hired a gang of porters, who, however, hearing that their employer was a Muzungu, a "white man," at once dispersed, forgetting to return their hire. About one hundred and seventy men were required; only thirty-six were procurable. The large amount of carriage was necessitated by the bulky and ponderous nature of African specie, cotton cloth, brass-wire, and beads, of which a total of seventy loads was expended in one year and nine months. Moreover, under the impression that "vert and venison" abounded in the interior, I had provided ammunition for two years, – ten thousand copper-caps of sizes, forty boxes, each restricted, for convenience of porterage, to forty pounds, and containing ball, grape, and shot, six fire-proof magazines, and two small barrels of fine powder, weighing in total fifty pounds, together with four ten-pound kegs of a coarser kind for the escort, – in all, two hundred rounds for each individual of the party. This supply was deemed necessary on account of the immense loss to which ammunition is subjected by theft and weather in these lands.

On the second day after anchoring off Wale Point, a native boat brought on board the Artémise Ladha Damha, the collector of customs at Zanzibar, who, in compliment to Lieut.-Colonel Hamerton, of old his friend and patron, had torn himself from his beloved occupations to push the departure of the Expedition. Ladha, hearing that the Arab merchants had hastened to secure their gangs before corrupted by the more liberal offers of the "white men," – "Pagazi," or porters, being at that time scarce, because the caravans from the interior had not yet reached the coast, – proposed to send forward the thirty-six fellows hired by Said bin Salim, with orders to await the arrival of their employer at Zungomero, in the land of K'hutu, a point situated beyond the plundering maritime tribes. These men carried goods to the value of 654 dollars German crowns (each 4s. 2d.), and they received for hire 124 dollars; rations, that is to say, 1'50 lbs. of grain per diem, not included: they preferred to travel with the escort of two slave-musketeers rather than to incur the fancied danger of accompanying a "Muzungu," though followed by a well-armed party. For the personal baggage and the outfit necessary for crossing the maritime region, which reached by waste the figure of 295 dollars, asses were proposed by Ladha Damha: Zanzibar and the mainland harbours were ransacked, and in a short time thirty animals, good, bad, and indifferent, were fitted for the roads with large canvas bags and vile Arab packsaddles, composed of damaged gunny-bags stuffed with straw. It was necessary to leave behind, till a full gang of porters could be engaged, the greater part of the ammunition, the iron boat which had proved so useful on the coasting voyage to Mornbasah, and the reserve supply of cloth, wire, and beads, valued at 359 dollars. The Hindus promised faithfully to forward these articles, and received 150 dollars for the hire of twenty-two men, who were to start in ten days. Nearly eleven months, however, elapsed before they appeared; caravan after caravan came up from the coast, yet the apathetic Bhattias pretended want of porters as the cause of their delay. Evidently my preparations were hurriedly made; strong reasons, however, urged me on, – delay, even for a few days, might have been fated.

During the brief detention off Wale Point, the latitudes and longitudes of the estuary of the Kingani, the main artery of these regions, and of the little settlements Bagamoyo and Kaole, – strongly against the advice of Lieut.-Colonel Hamerton, who declared that by such proceedings the Expedition was going to the bad, – were laid down by my companion: a novice lunarian, he was assisted by Mohammed bin Khamis, who had read his "Norie" in England. Various visits to the hippopotamus haunts produced little beyond the damaging of the corvette's gig, which, suddenly uplifted from the water upon the points of two tusks, showed two corresponding holes in her bottom. Nor did I neglect to land as often as possible at Kaole, the point of departure upon the mainland, for the purpose of making sketches with the pen and pencil, of urging on preparations, and of gathering those items of "bazar-gup," i.e., tittle-tattle, that represents the labours of the "fourth estate" in Eastern lands.

The little settlement of "Kaole" – an abbreviation of Kaole Urembo, meaning literally, in the ancient dialect of the coast, "to show beauty" – is the normal village-port in these regions, which, from Mombasah southwards to Kilwa, still ignore a town of masonry. You land, when the tide is out, upon half a mile of muddy sand, and if a "swell," you are carried by four men upon the Kitanda – cot or cartel – which is slung along the side of your craft. Arrived at the strip of dry ground that marks the limit of the tide, you are let down, and amidst the shouts of the men, the shrieks of the women, and the naive remarks of the juvenile population, you ascend by a narrow footpath, worn through the thick jungle and through the millet-fields which press upon the tattered palisade, a dwarf steep bank, on whose summit the settlement lies. Inside the fence are a dozen pent-roofed houses, claret-chests of wattle and dab, divided into three or more compartments by dwarf party-walls of the same material: each messuage is jealously separated from its neighbour by large enclosed "compounds" or court-yards appropriated to the women and children. The largest timber is that of the mangrove; the flying thatch-roof, so raised that, though windows are unknown, the interior enjoys tolerable ventilation, is of jauli, or rude cocoa-plaits, and under the long and projecting eaves, which rest upon strong perpendiculars, are broad earth-benches, divided by the entrance, and garnished with mats: these form the shops and sitting-rooms of the settlement. Some houses have a partial second story, like a ship's bunk, a planking supported by rafters, and used as a store-closet or a dormitory. Around the larger habitations cluster masses of hovels, and the characteristic African haycock-huts. With closed doors in still weather, these dens are unendurable to a European; the people, however, fearing thieves and wild beasts, never fail to barricade themselves within at night. The only attempt at masonry in the settlement is the "Gurayza," or fort, a square of lime and coralline, with store-rooms for the Banyan's goods below, and provided with a crenelled terrace for watch-men.

In the "garrison-towns" the soldiers and their families form the principal part of the population. These men, who call themselves Baloch, are, with few exceptions, originally from Mekran, and from the lowlands about Guadel. Many of them have been born and bred in Arabia. In former days their fathers migrated from their starving homes to Maskat, in the Arab dows which visited their ports, to buy horses, and to collect little cargoes of wheat and salt. In Arabia they were fakirs, sailors, porters, and day-labourers, barbers, date-gleaners, asinegos, beggars, and thieves. Sultan Bin Hamid, the father of the late Sayyid Said, first conceived the bright idea of putting matchlocks into their hands, and of dubbing them Askar, or soldiers, as a slight upon his less docile compatriots. The son of Sultan followed his site's plan, and succeeded in dividing and ruling by means of the antipathy prevailing between the more disciplinable mercenary and the unruly Arab subject. The Baloch are, however, rather hated than feared. They hang, say the Semites, their benefits behind their backs, whilst they wear their grievances in full view, woman-like, upon their breasts. Loud in debate, and turbulent in demeanour, they are called by the Arabs a "light folk," and are compared to birds fluttering and chirruping round a snake. Abject slaves to the Great Gaster, they collect in swarms round a slaughtered goat, and they will feast their eyes for hours on the sight of a rice-bag. When in cantonment on the island or the coast, they receive as pay from 2.50 to 5 dollars per mensem; when in the field or on outpost duty, a "batta" of 10 dollars; – a sensible system, which never allows them to become, like the Indian Sepoy, independent. They are not averse to active service, as, when so employed, they have full permission to "pill and poll." In camp they are commanded by a jemadar, who, assisted by a "moollah," – some wretch who has retained, as sole traces of his better days, a smattering of reading, writing, and arithmetic, – robs them and his government with the recklessness of impunity. Thus the jemadar, or C.O., who also dispenses promotion, is a man having authority. Similarly our colonels in India, by superior position and allowances, commanded the respect of their men before centralisation, falling upon the land like a pestilence, systematically monopolised all power, and then rained blame upon those who had lost it. These Baloch are a tame copy of the Turkish Bashi Buzuk, or "mad-cap," far inferior as desperadoes to the Kurd and Arnaut. They live the life of the Anglo-Indian soldier of the past generation, drinking beer when they can "come by it," smoking, chatting, and arguing; the younger wrestle, shoot, and exchange kit; and the silly babbling patriarchs, with white beards and venerable brows, tell wondrous tales of scenes long gone by, and describe to unbelieving cars the ice and snow, the luscious fruits and the sweet waters of the mountains and valleys of far Balochistan.

The other items of the population are the Wamrima[2] – Western Negroids of a mixed Arab and African descent, who

---

2. It must be borne in mind, that, in the Kisawahili and its cognates, the vowel u prefixed to a root, which, however, is never used without some prefix, denotes, through a primary idea of causality, a country or region, as Uzaramo, the region of Zaramo. Many names, however, exceptionally omit this letter, as the Mrima, K'hutu, Fuga, and Karagwah. The liquid *m*, or, before a vowel and an aspirated h, *mu*, to prevent hiatus, being probably a synaeresis of Mtu, a man, denotes the individual, as Mzaramo, a man or woman of Zaramo. When prefixed to the names of trees, as has been instanced, it is evidently an abbreviation of Mti, a tree. the plural form of *m* and *mu* is Wá, a contraction of Wátu, men, people; it is used to signify the population, as Wamrima, the "coast-clans," Wazaramo, the people or tribe of Zaramo, and Wasawahili (with a long accent upon the penultimate, consonant with the spirit of the African language, and contrary to that of the Arabic), the population of the Sawahil. Finally, the syllable *ki* – prefixed to the theoretical root – denotes anything appertaining to a country, as the terminating *ish* in the word English. It especially refers in popular usage to language, as Kizaramo, the language of Zaramo; Kisawahili, the language of the Sawahil, originally called Kingozi, from the district of Ngozi, on the Ozi River. It has been deemed advisable to retain these terse and concise distinctions, which, if abandoned, would necessitate a weary redundance of words.

fringe the shore in a thin line. These "coast-clans" support themselves in idleness and comparative luxury, by amicably plundering the down-caravans, and by large plantations of cereals and vegetables, with which they, or rather their slaves, supply the island of Zanzibar, and even the shores of Arabia. The Wamrima are an ill-conditioned race; they spend life in eating, drinking, and smoking, drinking and dancing, visits, intrigue, and low debauchery. They might grow cotton and coffee, and dig copal to almost any extent; but whilst a pound of grain remains in bin, no man will handle a hoe. The feminine part of the community is greatly superior in number to the masculine, and this leads to the usual result: on a "Siku ku" or fete-day, the ladies of the village, with yellow pigment over their faces and their woolly heads, perform in their cups impromptu-dances upon the open, enter a stranger's house as if it were. their own, and call for something to drink, as if they had been educated at Cremorne, or the Rue Cadet. The Wamrima are ruled by Diwans, or headmen, locally called "Chomwi;" these officials are subject to Zanzibar, and their numbers are everywhere in inverse ratio to the importance of the places. The Chomwi enjoys the privileges of "dash," fines and extortions; he has also certain marks of distinction. For instance, he is authorised to wear turbands and the wooden pattens called by the Arabs "kabkab;" he may also sit upon cots, chairs, and the mkeka, a fine dyed mat; whereas a commoner venturing upon such display would infallibly be mulcted in goats or cattle. At the Ngoma Ku or great dance, which celebrates every event in this land of revelry, only the Chomwi may perform the morris with drawn sword before the admiring multitude. A subject detected in intrigue with the wife of a headman must, under penalty of being sold, pay five slaves; the fine is reduced to one head in the case of a plebeian. With this amount of dignity the Diwan naturally expects to live, and to support his family with the fat of the land, and without sweat of brow. When times are hard, he organises a kidnapping expedition against a weaker neighbour, and fills his purse by selling the proceeds. But his income is derived chiefly from the down-caravans bringing ivory and slaves from Unyamwezi and the far interior. Though rigidly forbidden by the Prince of Zanzibar to force caravans to his particular port, he sends large armed parties of his kinsmen and friends, his clients and serfs, as far as 150 and 200 miles inland, where they act less like touters than highwaymen. By every petty art of mercantile diplomacy,-now by force, then by fraud, by promises, or by bribes of cloth and sweetmeats,-they induce the caravan to enter the village, when the work of plunder begins. Out of each Frasilah (thirty-five lbs. avoirdupois) of ivory, from eight to fourteen dollars are claimed as duties to the Government of Zanzibar; the headmen, then, demand six dollars as their fee, under various technical names, plus one dollar for "ugali" or porridge – the "manche," – and one dollar for the use of water – the "pour boire." The owner of the tusk is then handed over to the tender mercies of the Banyan, from whom the Diwan has received a bribe, called his "rice"; and the crafty Hindu buys for eighteen to twenty dollars an article worth, at Zanzibar, fifty. If the barbarian be so unwise as to prefer cash, being intellectually unfit to discriminate between a cent and a dollar, he loses even more than if he had taken in barter the coarse and trashy articles provided for him by the trade. An adept at distinguishing good from bad cloth and a cunning connoisseur in beads of sorts, he has yet no choice: if he reject what is worthless, he must return home with his ivory and without an investment. Such is an outline of the present system. It is nowhere the same in its details; but everywhere the principle is one – the loss is to the barbarian, and the profits are to the coast-clans, the Wamrima and their headmen. Hence the dislike to strangers and the infinite division into little settlements, where people might be expected to prefer the comfort and safety of large communities. The 10th article of the commercial treaty, concluded on the 31st May, 1839, between Her Majesty's Government and His Highness

Sayyid Said of Muscat and Zanzibar, secured to the possessors of the Mrima a monopoly in the articles of ivory and gum-copal on that part of the east coast of Africa from the port of Tangata (Mtangata), situated in about 5½° S. lat. to the port of Quiloa (Kilwa) lying in about 7° S. of the equator. It is not improbable that the jealousy of European nations, each fearing the ambitious designs of its neighbour, brought about this invidious prohibitionist measure.

Besides the Baloch and the Wamrima, the settlements usually contain a few of the "Washenzi" or barbarians from the interior, who visit them to act as day-labourers, and who sometimes, by evincing a little disrespect for the difference between the "mine" and the "thine," leave their heads to decorate tall poles at the entrance. The Wazaramo tribe send, when there is no blood-feud, numbers to Kaole, where they are known by their peculiar headdress, a single or a double line of pips or dilberries of ochre and grease surrounding the head. They regard the stranger with a wild and childish stare, and whenever I landed, they slunk away from me, for reasons which will appear in the course of this narrative. The list of floating population concludes with a few Banyans, – there are about fifty in Kaole and its vicinity – a race national as the English, who do their best to import into Eastern Africa the cows and curries, the customs and the costumes, of Western India.

The first visit to Kaole opened up a vista of unexpected difficulties. My escort had been allowed to leave the Artémise, and their comrades in arms had talked them half-crazy with fear. Zahri, a Baloch, who had visited Unyamwezi, declared that nothing less than 100 guards, 150 guns, and several cannon could enable them to fight a way through the perils of the interior. Tulsi, the Banyan, warned them that for three days they must pass amongst savages, who sit on trees and discharge poisoned arrows into the air with such dexterity that they never fail to fall upon the travellers' pate; he strongly advised them therefore, under pain of death, to avoid trees – no easy matter in a land all forest. Then the principal Chomwi assured them that the chiefs of the Wazaramo tribe had sent six several letters to the officials of the coast forbidding the white man to enter their country. Ladha Damha also obscurely hinted that the Wazaramo might make caches of their provisions in the jungle, and that the human stomach cannot march without feeding. Divers dangers of the way were incidentally thrown in: I learned for the first time that the Kargadan or rhinoceros kills 200 men, that armies of elephants attack camps by night, and that the craven hyaena does more damage than the Bengal tiger. In vain I objected that guns with men behind them are better than cannon backed by curs, that mortals can die but once, that the Wazaramo are unable to write, that rations might be carried where not purchaseable, and that powder and ball have been known to conquer rhinoceroses, elephants, and hyaenas. A major force was against me.

Presently the cause of intimidation crept into sight. The Jemadar and the eight Baloch detached by His Highness the Sayyid Majid of Zanzibar could not march without a reinforcement of four others, afterwards increased by a fifth in the person of an "Ustad," a tailor-boy. The garrison of Kaole having no employment, was ready, with the prospect of the almighty dollar, to march anywhere on this side of Jehannum. The perils of the path rendered it absolutely necessary that we should be escorted by a temporary guard of thirty-four men and their Jemadar Yaruk: and they did not propose to do the good deed gratis. Ramji, the Banyan clerk of the customs at Zanzibar, had a number of slaves whom he called his "sons;" they were "eating off their heads" in idleness at Zanzibar. He favoured me by letting out ten of these youths at the rate of thirty dollars ahead for a period of six months: for the same sum every man might have been purchased in the market. When asses were proposed ass-men were necessary; in the shortest space of time five were procured, and their pay for the whole journey was fixed at thirty dollars, about twice the sale-value of the article. I cannot plead guilty to not having understood the manoeuvre, – a commercial speculation on the part of the rascal Ramji. Yet at times, – need I say it? – it is good to appear a dupe. It is wise, when your enemies determine you to be that manner of sable or ermine contrivance into which ladies insert their fair hands, to favour the hypothesis. I engaged the men, I paid the men, and mentally I chronicled a vow that Ramji should in the long run change places with me.

Presently Mr. Frost with brow severe and official manner, informed me that the state of Lieut.-Colonel Hamerton's health forbade a longer stay near the coast. To this there was no reply: I contented myself with remarking once more that morphia appeared a curious cure for a confirmed liver complaint, and I made preparations for landing at once. Mr. Frost replied that the doses of morphia were very "little ones," – an excuse which, according to Capt. Marryat, has been urged under somewhat dissimilar circumstances by the frail ancilla. I confided to Mr. Frost's care two MSS. addressed through the Foreign Office, one to Mr. John Blackwood, the other to Dr. Norton Shaw, of the Royal Geographical Society. As the former arrived in safety, whilst the latter, – a detailed report concerning the commerce and capabilities of Zanzibar, – was lost, I cannot help suspecting that it came somehow to an untimely end. Lieutenant-Colonel Hamerton had repeatedly warned me that by making inquiries into the details of profit I was exciting the jealousy of the natives and the foreigners of Zanzibar. According to him the mercantile community was adopting the plan which had secured the foul murder of M. Maizan: the Christians had time and opportunity to alarm the Banyans, and the latter were able to work upon the Wasawahili population. These short-sighted men dreaded that from throwing open the country, competition might result: Oriental-like, thinking only of the moment, of themselves, they could not perceive that the development of resources would benefit all concerned in their exploitation. There were, however, honourable exceptions, amongst whom I am bound to mention M. Berard, agent to Mess. Rabaud, fréres, of Marseilles, who by direction of his employers offered me every manner of assistance; and the late M. Sam. Masury, a Salem merchant, to whose gratuitous kindness I was indebted for several necessaries when separated from civilisation by one half of Africa. They contrasted sharply with the rest of the community: in the case of a certain young gentleman, Lieut.-Colonel Hamerton was, – he informed me, – compelled to threaten a personal chastisement, unless he ceased to fill native ears with his malignant suspicions.

The weary labour of verifying accounts and of writing receipts duly concluded, I took a melancholy leave of my warm-hearted friend Lieut.-Colonel Hamerton, upon whose form and features death was written in legible characters. He gave me his last advice, to march straight ahead despising "walnut and velvet-slipper men," who afford opinions, and conciliating the Arabs as much as possible. Then he spoke of himself: he looked forward to death with a feeling of delight, the result of his religious convictions; he expressed a hope that if I remained at Kaole, he might be buried at sea; and he declared himself, in spite of my entreaties, determined to remain near the coast until he heard of our safe transit through the lands of the dreaded Wazaramo. This courage was indeed sublime! Such examples are not often met with amongst men!

After this affecting farewell, I took leave of the Artémise and landed definitively at Kaole. The Baloch driving the asses were sent off to the first station on the road westwards, headed by my companion, on the same evening, lest a longer sojourn in the lands of semi-civilisation should thoroughly demoralise them. The Wanyamwezi porters, whose open faces and laughing countenances strongly prepossessed me in their favour, had already passed beyond their centre of attraction, the coast. I spent that evening with Ladha Damha, inside the gloomy Gurayza. He lectured me for the last time upon my development of what the French cartomantiste calls "la bosse de la témérité" Might not the Sahib be a great Sahib in his own land – Cutch or Guzerat? Are there not other great Sahibs there, A – Sahib and B – Sahib, for instance, who only kill pigs and ignore the debtor and creditor side of an account in Guzeratee?

I must mention that, on the morning of the same day, I was present at a conversation held by the Ladha, the respectable collector of the customs, with the worthy Ramji, his clerk. I had insisted upon their inserting in the estimate of necessaries the sum required to purchase a boat upon the "Sea of Ujiji."

"Will he ever reach it?" asked the respectable Ladha, conveying his question through the medium of Cutchee, a dialect of which, with the inconsequence of a Hindu, he assumed me to be profoundly ignorant.

"Of course not," replied the worthy Ramji;" what is he that he should pass through Ugogi?" (a province about half way.)

At the moment I respected their "sharm," or shame, a leading organ in the oriental brain, which apparently has dwindled to inconsequential dimensions amongst the nations of the West. But when Ladha was alone, I took the opportunity to inform him that I still intended to cross Ugogo, and to explore the "Sea of Ujiji." I ended by showing him that I was not unacquainted with Cutchee, and even able to distinguish between the debits and the credits of his voluminous sheets.

During the conversation, the loud wail of death rang wildly through the grave-like stillness of night. "O son, hope of my life! O brother, dearest of brothers! O husband! O husband!" these were the cries which reached our ears. We ran to the door of the Gurayza. The only son of the venerable Diwan Ukwere, who had been ascending the Kingani river on a mercantile expedition, with five slaves, had been upset by a vengeful hippopotamus, and, with two of his attendants, had lost his life.

"Insaf Karo! be honest!" said the Banyan, with whom I had had many discussions as to whether it be lawful or unlawful to shoot the hippopotamus, "and own that this is the first calamity which you have brought upon the country by your presence."

I could only reply with the common-places of polemics. Why should Ladha, who by purchasing their spoils encouraged the destruction of herds of elephants, object to the death of a "creek-bull"? and why should the man who would not kill the "creek-bull" be ready to ruin a brother-man for making a better bargain about its tusks? Ladha received these futile objections contemptuously, as you would, right reverend father, were I to suggest that you, primate and spiritual peer, are not exactly following in the footsteps .of certain paupers whom you fondly deem to have been your prototypes, – your exemplars.

When Ladha left, my spirits went with him. In the solitude and the silence of the dark Gurayza, I felt myself the plaything of misfortune. At Cairo I had received from the East India House an order to return to London, to appear as a witness on a trial by court-martial then pending. The missive was, as usual, so ineptly worded, that I did not think proper to throw overboard the Royal Geographical Society – to whom my services had been made over – by obeying it: at the same time I well knew what the consequences would be. Before leaving Egypt, an interview with the Count d'Escayrac de Lauture, had afforded me an opportunity of inspecting an expedition thoroughly well organised by His Highness Said Pacha, of military predilections, and the contrast between an Egyptian and an English exploration impressed me unpleasantly. Arrived at Aden, I had enlisted the services of an old and valued friend, Dr. Steinhaeuser, civil surgeon at that station: a sound scholar, a good naturalist, a skilful practitioner, endowed, moreover, with even more inestimable personal qualities, his presence would have been valuable in a land of sickness, skirmishes, and sporting adventures, where the people are ever impressed with the name of "medicine-man," and in a virgin field promising subjects of scientific interest. Yet though recommended for the work by his Excellency the Governor of Bombay, Dr. Steinhaeuser had been incapacitated by sickness from accompanying me: I had thus with me a companion and not a friend, with whom I was "strangers yet." The Persian war had prevented the fitting-out of a surveying vessel, ordered by the Court of Directors to act as a base of operations upon the African coast; no disposable officer of the Indian navy was to be found at the Presidency; and though I heard in Leadenhall Street of an "Observatory Sergeant" competent to conduct the necessary astronomical and meteorological observations, in the desert halls of the great Bungalow at Colaba only a few lank Hindus met my sight. Nor was this all. His Highness the late Sayyid Said, that estimable ally of the English nation, had for many years repeatedly made the most public-spirited offers to his friend Lieut.-Colonel Hamerton. He was more than once upon the point of applying for officers selected to map the caravan routes of Eastern Africa, and he professed himself willing to assist them with men, money, and the weight of his widely extended influence. This excellent prince had died forty days before the Expedition arrived at Zanzibar. Lieut.-Colonel Hamerton, also, whose extraordinary personal qualities enabled him to perform anything but impossibilities amongst the Arabs, was compelled by rapidly failing health, during my stay at Zanzibar, to lead a recluse life, which favoured the plans of my opponents. Finally, as Indian experience taught me, I was entering the unknown land at the fatal season, when the shrinking of the waters after the wet monsoon would render it a hotbed of malaria.

The hurry of departure, also, had caused a necessary neglect of certain small precautions, which, taken in time, save much after trouble. I should have shunned to have laid down limits of space and time for the Expedition, whereas my friend and adviser had specified the "Sea of Ujiji." I intended to have drawn out every agreement in an official form, registered at the Consulate, and specifying all particulars concerning rations and presents for the escort, their ammunition, and their right of sporting – that is to say, of scaring the game before it could be shot – their reward for services, and their punishments for ill conduct. Lieut.-Colonel Hamerton's state of health, however, rendered him totally unfit for the excitement of business; and, without his assistance, a good result was not to be expected from measures so unfamiliar, and therefore so unpalatable, to the people whom they most concerned.

Excuse, amiable reader, this lengthy and egotistical preface to a volume of adventure. Do not think that I would invert the moral of the Frog-fable, by showing that what is death to you, may become fun to me. As we are to be companions – not to say friends – for an hour or two, I must put you in possession of certain facts, trivial in themselves, and all unworthy of record, yet so far valuable, that they may enable us to understand each other. Au reste, to quote the ballad so much admired by the Authoress of "Our Village": –

> *"The Pindar of Wakefield is my style,*
> *And what I list I write;*
> *Whilom a clerk of Oxenford,*
> *But now – a banished wight."*

Chapter 2

ZANZIBAR AND THE MRIMA EXPLAINED

The history of the word Zanzibar is curious. Its Persian origin proves that the Iranians were in early days a more maritime people than Vincent and other writers imagine. Zanzibar, signifying Nigritia, or Blackland, is clearly derived from the "Zang," in Arabic Zanj, a negro, and "bar," a region. This Zangbar was changed by the Arabs, who ignore in writing the hard g, into Zanjíbár; they still, however, pronounce Zangbar, and consider it synonymous with another popular expression, "Mulk el Zunuj," or "the Land of the Blacks." Thus the poet sings, –

"And it hath been called Land of the Blacks, all of it."

Traces of the word may be found in the earliest geographers. Ptolemy records a Zingis or Zingisa, which, however, with his customary incorrectness, he places north of the equator. According to Cosmas Indicopleustes, the Indian Ocean beyond Barbaria is called Zingium. "Sinus Barbaricus" seems to have been amongst the Romans the name of the belt of low land afterwards known as "Zanzibar," and it was inhabited by a race of Anthropophagi, possibly the fathers of the present "Wadoe" tribe. In more modern times the land of the Zunuj has been mentioned by a host of authors, E1 Novayri and others.

The limits of Zanzibar, – a word indiscriminately applied in former times to the coast, the island, and even to the principal town, – are variously laid down by geographers. Usually it is made to extend from Cape Delgado, in S. lat. 10° 41° to the equator, or more strictly to S. lat. 0° 15', at the mouth of the Vumbo, or the Webbe Ganana, which appears in our maps under the deceptive corruptions "Juba" and "Govind," from the Somali "Gob," a junction, and "Gob-wen," a large junction. Mr. Cooley (Inner Africa Laid Open, p. 111) corrects the great error of the Portuguese historian, de Barros, who has made the embouchure of the Obi – in Somali Webbe, meaning any river, – the demarcation line between "Ajan" on the north, and "Zanguebar" in the south, and has placed the mouth of that stream in 9° N. lat., which would extend Zanzibar almost to Cape Guardafui. Asiatic authors, according to M. Guillain, (Documents sur l'Histoire, &c. de l'Afrique Orientale. Premiere partie, p. 213) vary in opinion concerning the extent of the "land of the Zunuj" and its limits; some, as El Masudi, make it contain the whole country, including Sofala, between the embouchure of the Juba River (S. lat. 0° 15') and Cape Corrientes (S. lat. 23° 48'): others, like El Idrisi and Ibn Said, separate from it Sofala. In local and modern usage the word Zanjibar is generally confined to the chief town upon the island, the latter being called by Arabs, as well as by the Negroids, Kisiwa, "insula," in opposition to the Barr el Moli, a barbarised Semitic term for the continent.

As usual throughout these lands, where comprehensive geographical names are no longer required, there is no modern general word for East Africa south of the equator. The term "Sawahil," or "the shores," in present parlance is confined to the strip of coast beyond the half-Somali country, called from its various ports, – Lamu, Brava, and Patta, – Barr el Banadir, or Harbour-land. The "Sawahil" extend southwards to Mombasah, below which the coast suddenly falling flat, is known as Mrima or the Hill, and its people as Wamrima, the "hill-men." It is limited on the south by the delta of the Rufiji River, whose races are termed Watu wa Rufiji, Rufiji clans, or more shortly, Warufiji.

The country properly called the Mrima has no history beyond its name, whilst the towns immediately to the north and south of it, – Mombasah and Kilwa, – have filled many a long and stirring page. The Arab geographers preceding the Portuguese conquest mention only five settlements on the coast between Makdishu (Magadoxo) and Kilwa, namely, Lamu, Brava, Marka, Malindi (Melinda), and Mombasah. In Captain Owen's charts, between Pangani and the parallel of Mafiyah (Monfia Island) not a name appears.

The fringe of Moslem Negroids inhabiting this part of the East African coast is called by the Arabs Ahl Maraim, and by themselves Wamrima, in opposition to the heathen of the interior. These are designated in mass the Washenzi – conquered or servile – properly the name of a Helot race in the hills of Usumbara, but extended by strangers to all the inner races. The Wasawahili, or people of the Sawahil, Mulattos originally African, but semiticised, like the Moplahs of Malabar, by Arab blood, are in these days confined to the lands lying northwards of Mombasah, to the island of Zanzibar, and to the regions about Kilwa.

The Mrima is peopled by two distantly connected families, the half-caste Arabs and the Coast-Clans. The former are generally of Bayazi or Khariji persuasion; the latter follow the school of el Shafei; both, though the most imperfect of Moslems, are fanatical enough to be dangerous. They own a nominal allegiance to the suzerain of Zanzibar, yet they are autonomous and free-spoken as Bedouins, when removed a few miles from the coast, and they have a rooted aversion to the officials of the local government, whom they consider their personal enemies. Between them and the pure Arabs of Oman, who often traverse, but who now never settle upon the Mrima, there is a repugnance increased by commercial jealousy; they resent the presence of these strangers as an intrusion, and they lose no opportunity of thwarting and discouraging them from travelling into the interior. Like their ancestors, they dislike Europeans personally, and especially fear the Bent Nar, or Sons of Fire, – the English – "hot as the Ingrez," is in these lands a proverb. In their many Riwayat, Hadisi, and Ngoma – tales, traditions, and songs – they predict the eventual conquest of the country that has once felt the white man's foot.

The half-caste Arab is degenerate in body and mind; the third generation becomes as truly negroid as the inner heathen. Even Creoles of pure blood, born upon the island and the coast of Zanzibar, lose the high nervous temperament that characterises their ancestors, and become, like Banyans, pulpy and lymphatic. These mestizos, appearing in the land of their grandsires, have incurred thc risk of being sold as slaves. the peculiarity of their physiognomy is the fine Semitic development of the upper face, including the nose and nostrils, whilst the jaw is prognathous, the lips are tumid and everted, and the chin is weak and retreating. The cranium is somewhat rounded, and it wants the length of the Negroid's skull. Idle and dissolute, though intelligent and cunning, the coast-Arab has little education. He is sent at the age of seven to school, where in two or three years he accomplishes the Khitmah, or perlection of the Koran, and he learns to write a note in an antiquated character, somewhat more imperfect than the Cufic. This he applies to the Kisawahili, and as nothing can be less fitted for the Semitic tongues than the Arabic syllabarium, so admirably adapted to its proper sphere, his compositions require the deciphering of an expert. A few prayers and hymns conclude the list of his acquirements. His mother-tongue knows no books except short treatises on Bao, or geomancy, and specimens of African proverbial wisdom. He then begins life by aiding his father in the shop or plantation, and by giving himself up to intoxication and intrigue. After suffering severely from his excesses – in this climate no constitution can bear up against over-indulgence long continued – at the age of seventeen or eighteen, he takes unto himself a wife. Estranged from the land of his forefathers, he rarely visits Zanzibar, where the restraints of semi-civilisation, the decencies of oriental society, and the low estimation in which the black skin is held, weary and irritate him. His point of honour seems to consist chiefly in wearing publicly, in token of his Arab descent, a turban and a long yellow shirt, called El Dishdasheh.

The Wamrima, or coast-clans, resemble even more than the half-caste Arabs their congeners the Washenzi. The pure Omani will not acknowledge them as kinsmen, declaring the breed to be Aajam, or gentiles. They are less educated than the higher race, and they are more debauched, apathetic, dilatory, and inert; their favourite life is one of sensual indolence. Like the Somal, they appear to be unfitted by nature for intellectual labour; of the former people there is but one learned man, the Shaykh Jami of Harar, and the Kazi Muhiyy-el-Din of Zanzibar is the only literato amongst the Wasawahili. Study, or indeed any tension of the mind, seems to make these weak-brained races semi-idiotic. They cannot answer Yes or No to the simplest question. If, for example, a man be asked the place of his tribe, he will point to a distance, though actually living amongst them; or if questioned concerning some particular of an event, he will detail everything but what is wanted. In the earlier days of exploration, I have repeatedly collected the diwans, and, after a careful investigation and comparison of statements, have registered the names and distances of the stages ahead. These men though dwelling upon the threshold of the regions which they described, and being in the habit of traversing them every year, yet could hardly state a single fact correctly; sometimes they doubled, at other times they halved, the distance; they seldom gave the same names, and they almost always made a hysteron-proteron of the stations. The reader may gather from this sample some idea of the difficulties besetting those who would collect information concerning Africa from the Africans. It would not have happened had an Arab been consulted. I soon resolved to doubt for the future all Wasawahili, Wamrima,

Washenzi, and slaves, and I found no reason for regretting the resolution.

The Wamrima are of darker complexion, and are more African in appearance, than the coast Arabs. The popular colour is a dull yellowish bronze. The dress is a fez, or a Surat-cap; a loin-cloth, which among the wealthy is generally an Arab check or an Indian print, with a similar sheet thrown over the shoulders. Men seldom appear in public without a spear, a sword, or a staff; and priding themselves upon the possession of umbrellas, they may be seen rolling barrels, or otherwise working upon the sands, under the luxurious shade. The women wear a tobe, or long cloth, wrapped tightly round the body, and extending from beneath the arms to the ankles; it is a garb ungraceful as was the European "sacque" of bygone days. It spoils the figure by depressing instead of supporting the bosom, and it conceals none of its deficiencies, especially the narrowness of the hips. The Murungwana, or free-woman, is distinguished from the slave-girl, when outside the house, by a cloth thrown over the head. Like the women of the Bedouins and of the Persian Iliyat, even the matrons of the Mrima go abroad unmasked. Their favourite necklace is a string of shark's teeth. They distend the lobes of the ears to a prodigious size, and decorate them with a rolled-up strip of variously-dyed cocoa-leaf, a disk of wood, a plate of chakazi or rawgum-copal, or, those failing, with a betel-nut or with a few straws. The left wing of the nose is also pierced to admit a pin of silver, brass, lead, or even a bit of manioc-root. The hair, like the body, is copiously anointed with cocoa-nut or sesamum oil. Some shave the head wholly or partially across the brow and behind the ears; others grow their locks to half or full-length, which rarely exceeds a few inches. It is elaborately dressed, either in double-rolls rising like bear's ears on both sides of the head, or divided into a number of frizzly curls which expose lines of scalp, and give to the head the appearance of a melon. They have also a propensity for savage "accroche-coeurs," which stand out from the cheek bones, stiffly twisted like young porkers' tails. In early youth, when the short, soft, and crisp hair resembles Astrachan wool, when the muscles of the face are smoothly rounded, and when the skin has that life and texture, and the countenance has that vivacity and amiability which belong only to the young, many of the girls have a pretty piquancy, a little minois chiffonne, a coquettishness, a natural grace, and a caressing look, which might become by habit exceedingly prepossessing. In later life, their charms assume that peculiar solidity which is said to characterise the beauties of Mull-ingar, and as a rule they are shockingly ugly. The Castilian proverb says that the English woman should be seen at the window, the French woman on the promenade, and the Span-ish woman everywhere; – the African woman should be seen nowhere, or in the dark. The children mostly appear in the graceful costume of the Belvidere Apollo; not a few of them have, to the European eye, that amusing prettiness which we admire in pug-pups.

The mode of life in the Mrima is simple. Men rise early and repair to either the shop, the boat, or the plantation, – more commonly they waste the morning in passing from house to house "ku amkia," – to salute neighbours. They ignore "manners": they enter abruptly with or without the warning cry of "Hodi! Hodi!" place their spears in the corner, and without invitation squat and extend themselves upon the floor till wearied with conversation they take "French leave." Life, to the European so real and earnest, is with them a con-tinued scene of drumming, dancing, and drinking, of gossip, squabble, and intrigue. The favourite inebrients are tembu or cocoa toddy, and mvinyo, its distillation, pombe or millet-beer, opium, Bhang, and sometimes foreign stimulants pur-chased at Zanzibar. Their food is mostly ugali, the thick por-ridge of boiled millet or maize flour, which represents the "staff of life" in East Africa: they usually feed twice a day, in the morning and at night-fall. They employ the cocoa-nut extensively: like the Arabs of Zanzibar, they boil their rice in the thick juice of the rasped albumen kneaded with water, and they make cakes of the pulp mixed with the flour of various grains. This immoderate use of the fruit which, according to the people, is highly refrigerant, causes, it is said, rheumatic and other diseases. A respectable man seen eating a bit of raw or undressed cocoa-nut would be derided by his fellows. They chew tobacco with lime, like the Arabs, who, under the influence of Wahhabi tenets, look upon the pipe as impure, and they rarely smoke it like the Washenzi.

The Wamrima as well as the Wasawahili are distinguished by two national peculiarities of character. The first is a cautiousness bordering upon cowardice, derived from their wild African blood; the second is an unusual development of cunning and deceitfulness, which partially results from the grafting of the semi-civilised Semite upon the Hamite. The Arabs, who are fond of fanciful etymology, facetiously derive the race-name "Msawahili" from "Sawwa hilah,"[3] he played a trick, and the people boast of it, saying, "are we not Wasawahili?" that is "artful dodgers." Supersubtle and systematic liars, they deceive when duller men would tell the truth, the lie direct is no insult, and the offensive word "muongo!" (liar) enters largely into every dialogue. They lie like Africans, objectlessly, needlessly, when sure of speedy detection, when fact would be more profitable than falsehood; they have not discovered with the civilised knave, that "hon-

---

3.　　Dr. Krapf, in the Preface to his "Outlines of the Kisuahelí Language," deduces the national name from Síwá á hílah, which would mean exactly the reverse of astute – "without guile." He has made other curious linguistic errors: he translates, for instance, the "Quilimancy" River – the ancient name for the Ozi or Dana – "water from the mountain," after a Germanic or Indo-European fashion, whereas, in the Zangian languages, the compound word would, if admissible, signify "a mountain of water." It is curious that the learned and accurate Mr. Cooley, who has charged Dr. Krapf with "puerile etymologies," should have fallen into precisely the same error. In the "Geography of N'yassi," p. 19, "Mazingia" is rendered the "road or land along the water," but Májí Mjíá, if the elision of the possessive affix ya be allowed in prose as in poetry – Májí Mjíá for Májí yá Mjíá – would mean only the "water of the road." As a specimen of Dr. Krapf's discoveries in philology the following may suffice. In his vocabulary of the Engutuk Eloikob or Kikuafi dialect, he derives Olbitir, *a pig* from the Arabic El Batrah, *a young ass*, or from El Basir, *a sharp-seeing dog*.

esty is the best policy;" they lie till their fiction becomes subjectively fact. With them the lie is no mental exertion, no exercise of ingenuity, no concealment, nor mere perversion of the truth: it is apparently a local instinctive peculiarity in the complicated madness of poor human nature. The most solemn and religious oaths are with them empty words; they breathe an atmosphere of falsehood, manoeuvre, and contrivance, wasting about the mere nothings of life – upon a pound of grain or a yard of cloth – ingenuity of iniquity enough to win and keep a crown. And they are treacherous as false; with them the salt has no signification, and gratitude is unknown even by name.

Though partially Arabised, the Wamrima, as well as the Wasawahili, retain many habits and customs derived from the most degraded of the Washenzi savagery. Like the Wazegura heathen of Eastern Africa, and the Bangala of the Kasanji (Cassange) Valley, in the West, the uncle sells his nephews and nieces by an indefeasible vested right, with which even the parents cannot interfere. The voice of society even justifies this abomination. "What!" exclaim the people, "is a man to want when his brothers and sisters have children?" He is thus encouraged in doing, on the slightest pretext, that of which the heathen rarely approve, except to save themselves from starvation. At the same time the Wamrima, holding the unchastity of woman as a tenet of belief, consider the sister's son – the "surer side" – the heir, in preference to the son. They have many superstitions, and before all undertakings they consult a pagan Mganga or medicine-man. If the K'hunguru or crow caws from the house-top, a guest is coming; if a certain black bird cries "chee! chee!" in front of a caravan, the porters will turn back, saying that there is blood on the road, and they will remain four or five days till the "chika! chika!" of the partridge beats the "General." An even number of wayfarers met in early morning is a good omen, but an odd number, or the bark of the Mbweha – the fox – before the march, portends misfortune. Strong minds of course take advantage of these and a thousand other follies of belief, and when there is not, as in civilised countries, a counteracting influence of scepticism, the mental organisation of the people becomes a mass of superstitious absurdities.

The chief industry of the Mrima, namely the plundering of caravans, has already been alluded to; it will here be described with somewhat more of detail. The industrious and commercial nations near Kilwa and the southern regions delay but a few days on the coast; the Wanyamwezi, on the line now to be described, will linger there from three to six months, enjoying the dear delights of comparative civilisation. Many old campaigners have so far overcome their barbarous horror of water travelling, which has been increased by tales of shipwreck and drowning, as to take boat and carry their ivory to the more profitable market in this land of Zanzibar, where the Wanyamwezi occupy their own quarter. Arrived within two marches of the coast-town, the head of the caravan calls a halt till the presents promised by an escort of touters have arrived and have been approved of. He then delays as long as possible, to live gratis upon those with whom he proposes to deal. After a time, the caravan enters in stately procession, a preliminary to the usual routine of commercial operations. Having settled the exorbitant claims of the village headmen and the charges of the Zanzibar Government, which are usually levied in duplicate by the local authorities, the barbarian has recourse to the Indian Banyan. Bargains are usually concluded at night: to a civilised man the work would be an impossible trial of patience. A lot of two hundred tusks is rarely sold under four months. Each article is laid upon the ground, and the purchaser begins by placing handsome cloths, technically called "pillows," under the point and bamboo of the tusk, and by covering its whole length with a third; these form the first perquisites of the seller. After a few days, during which rice and ghee, sugar and sweetmeats, must be freely supplied, commences the chaffering for the price. The Banyan becomes excited at the ridiculous demand of his client, screams like a woman, pushes him out of doors, and receives a return of similar treatment with interest. He takes advantage of his knowledge that the African in making a bargain is never satisfied with the first offer, however liberal; he begins with a quarter of the worth, then he raises it to one-half, and when the barbarian still hesitates he throws in some flashy article which turns the scale. Any attempt at a tariff would be contemptuously rejected by both parties. The African delights in bargaining, and the Indian having brighter wits relies upon them for a profit, which the establishment of fair prices would curtail. It were in vain to attempt any alteration in this style of doing "business;" however despicable it may appear in the London market, it is a time-honoured institution in East Africa.

Chapter 3

TRANSIT OF THE VALLEY OF THE KINGANI AND THE MGETA RIVERS

It was a gallant sight to see the Baloch, as with trailed matchlocks, and in bravery of shield, sword, and dagger, they hurried in Indian file out of the Kaole cantonments, following their blood-red flag and their high-featured, snowy-bearded chief, the "Shaib Mohammed," – old Mohammed. The band, "like worms," as they expressed its numbers, which amounted to nearly a hundred, about one-third of the venerable Jemadar's command, was marching forth to bid us farewell, in token of respect, at Mgude or Kuingani, "the cocoa-plantation near the sea." It is a little settlement, distant an hour and a hall's walk from Kaole: hither my companion had preceded me, and hence we were to make our second departure. Accompanied by Said bin Salim, Valentine my Goanese servant, three Baloch, and two slaves, I followed in the wake of the main body, bringing up the rear of the baggage on three Unyamwezi asses bought that morning at the customhouse. The animals had been laden with difficulty: their kicking and plunging, rearing and pawing, had prevented the nice adjustment of their packs, and the wretched pads; which want of time had compelled me to take, instead of panels or pack-saddles, loosely girthed with rotten coir rope, could not support a heap of luggage weighing at least 200 lbs. per load. On the road they rushed against one another; they bolted, they shied, and they threw their impediments with such persistence, that my servant could not help exclaiming, "Unka nam gadha" –

"Their name is jackass." At last, as the sun neared the salt sea, one of these half-wild brutes suddenly sank, girth-deep, in a patch of boggy mire, and the three Baloch, my companions, at once ran away, leaving us to extricate it as best we could. This little event had a peculiar significancy to one about to command a party composed principally of asses and Baloch.

The excitement of finding myself on new ground, and the peculiarities of the scenery, somewhat diverted melancholy forebodings. Issuing from the little palisade of Kaole, the path winds in a south-westerly direction over a sandy soil, thick with thorns and bush, which in places project across the way. Thence ascending a wave of ground where cocoas and the wild arrow-root flourish, it looks down upon park land like that described by travellers in Kaffraria, a fair expanse of sand veiled with humus, here and there growing rice, with mangoes and other tall trees, regularly disposed as if by the hand of man. Finally, after crossing a muddy grass-grown swamp, and a sandy bottom full of water when rain has been heavy, the path, passing through luxuriant cultivation, enters Kuingani. Such is the "nakl," or preparatory-stage of Arab travellers, an invariable first departure, where porters who find their load too heavy, or travellers who suspect that they are too light, can return to Kaole and re-form.

The little settlement of Kuingani is composed of a few bee-hive huts, and a Bandani or wall-less thatched roof – the village palaver-house – clustering orderless round a cleared central space. Outside, cocoas, old and dwarfed, mangoes almost wild, the papaw, the cotton shrub, the perfumed Ray-han or Basil, and a sage-like herb, the sugarcane, and the Hibiscus called by the Goanese "Rosel," vary the fields of rice, holcus, and "Turiyan," or the Cajanus Indicus. The vegetation is, in fact, that of the Malabar coast; the habitations are peculiarly African.

The 28th of June was a halt at Kuingani, where I was visited by Ramji and two brother Bhattias, Govindji and Kesulji. The former was equipped, as least becomes the Banyan man, with sword, dudgeon, and assegai. But Ramji was a heaven-made soldier; he had taken an active part in the military operations directed by His Highness the late Sayyid Said against the people of the mainland, and about thirteen years ago he defended Kaole against a host of Wazaramo, numbering, it is said, 3,000 men, when, lacking balls, he had loaded his honeycombed cannon and his rusty matchlocks with pointed sticks. The Europeans of Zanzibar called him "Rush," – the murderer. His fellow-countrymen declared him to be a "sharp practiser," who had made a reputation by spending other people's money, and I personally had proofs which did not allow me to doubt his "savoir faire."

The nights at Kuingani were not pleasant. The air was stifling, the mosquitoes buzzed without intermission, and I had neglected to lay in "essence of pennyroyal" against certain other plagues. On the second evening, seeing by the hang-dog look of my Jemadar that he was travailing in mind, I sent for a Mganga or medicine-man, and having previously promised-him a Surat skull-cap for a good haul of prophecy, I collected the Baloch to listen. The Mganga, a dark old man, of superior rank, as the cloth round his head and his many bead necklaces showed, presently reappeared with a mat-bag containing the implements of his craft. After taking his seat opposite to me he demanded his fee – here, as elsewhere, to use the words with which Kleon excited the bile of Tiresias,

"Το μαντικον γαρ παν πηελαργυρον γενοσ; "

– without which prediction would have been impossible. When gratified he produced a little gourd snuff-box and indulged himself with a solemn and dignified pinch. He then drew forth a larger gourd which contained the great medicine, upon which no eye profane might gaze: the vessel, repeatedly shaken, gave out a vulgar sound as if filled with pebbles and bits of metal. Presently, placing the implement upon the ground, Thaumaturges extracted from the mat-bag two thick goat's horns connected by a snake-skin, which was decorated with bunches of curiously-shaped iron bells; he held one in the left hand, and with the right he caused the point of the other to perform sundry gyrations, now directing it towards me, then towards himself, then at the awe-struck bystanders, waving his head, muttering, whispering, swaying his body to and fro, and at times violently rattling the bells. When fully primed with the spirit of prophecy, and connected by ekstasis with the ghosts of the dead, he spake out pretty much in the style of his brotherhood all the world over. The journey was to be prosperous. There would be much talking, but little killing. – Said bin Salim, in chuckling state, confessed that he had heard the same from a Mganga consulted at Zanzibar. – Before navigating the sea of Ujiji a sheep or a parti-coloured hen should be killed and thrown into the lake. – Successful voyage. – Plenty of ivory and slaves. – Happy return to wife and family.

This good example of giving valuable advice was not lost upon Mr. Rush Ramji. He insisted upon the necessary precautions of making a strong kraal and of posting sentinels every night; of wearing a kerchief round the head after dark, and of avoiding the dangerous air of dawn; of not eating strange food, and of digging fresh wells, as the Wazaramo bewitch water for travellers; of tethering the asses, of mending their ropes, and of giving them three lbs. of grain per diem. Like the medical directions given to the French troops proceeding to China, the counsel was excellent, but impracticable.

The evening concluded with a nautch. Yusuf, a Baloch, produced a saringi – the Asiatic viol – and collected all the scamps of the camp with a loud scraping. Hulluk, the buffoon, acted dancing-girl to perfection. After the normal pantomime, somewhat broadly expressed, he did a little work in his own character; standing on his head with a peculiar tremulousness from the hips upwards, dislocating his person in a sitting position, imitating the cry of a dog, cat, ape, camel, and slave-girl, and finally reproducing me with peculiar impudence before my face. I gave him a dollar, when, true to his strain, he at once begged another.

All accounts and receipts being finally duly settled with the Hindus, the last batch of three donkeys having arrived, and the baggage having been laden with great difficulty, I shook hands with old Mohammed and the other dignitaries, and mounting my ass, gave orders for immediate departure from Kuingani. This was not effected without difficulty: every one and everything, guide and escort, asses and slaves, seemed to join in raising up fresh obstacles. Four P.M. sped before we turned out of the little settlement. Among other unpleasant occurrences, Rahmat, a Baloch knave, who had formed one of my escort to Fuga, levelled his long barrel, with loud "Mimi na piga" (I am shooting him), when his company was objected to. His Jemadar, Yaruk, seized the old shooting-iron, which was probably unloaded, and Rahmat, with sotto-voce snarls and growls, slunk back to his kennel. A turbaned Negroid, who appeared on the path, was asked to point out the way, and, on his refusal, my bull-headed slave Mabruki struck him on the face, when, to the consternation of all parties, he declared himself a Diwan. The blow, according to the Jemadar, would infallibly lead to bloodshed.

After a second short march of one hour and a half, we pitched tents and obtained lodgings in Bomani, "the Stockade," a frontier village, but within the jurisdiction of Bagamoyo. On this road, which ascended the old sea-beach, patches of open forest and of high rank grass divided cultivated clearings, where huts and hamlets appeared, and where modest young maidens beckoned us as we passed. The vegetation is here partly African, partly Indian. The Mbuyu, – the baobab, Adansonia digitata, monkey-bread, or calabash, the Mowana of the southern and the Kuka of the northern regions, – is of more markedly bulbous form than on the coast, where the trunk is columnar; its heavy extremities, depressed by the wind, give it the shape of a lumpy umbrella shading the other wild growths. There appear to be two varieties of this tree, similar in bole but differing in foliage and in general appearance. The normal Mbuyu has a long leaf, and the drooping outline of the mass is convex; the rarer, observed only upon the Usagara Mountains, has a small leaf, in colour like the wild indigo, and the arms striking upwards assume the appearance of a bowl. The lower bottoms, where the soil is rich, grow the Mgude, also called Mparamusi (*Taxus elongatus*, the Geel hout or Yellow-wood of the Cape?) a perfect specimen of arboreal beauty. A tall, tapering shaft, without knot or break, straight and clean as a main-mast forty or forty-five feet in height, and painted with a tender greenish-yellow, is crowned with parachute-shaped masses of vivid emerald foliage, whilst sometimes two and even three pillars spring from the same root. The Mvumo, – a distorted toddy tree, or Hyphaena allied to the Daum palm of Egypt and Arabia – has a trunk rough with the drooping remnants of withered fronds, above which it divides itself into branches resembling a system of Y's. Its oval fruit is of a yellowish red, and when full-sized it is as large as a child's head; it is eaten even unripe by the people, and is said to be the favourite food of the elephant. Pulpless, hard, and stringy, it has, when thoroughly mature, a slight taste of gingerbread, hence it is also called the Gingerbread-tree. The Ukhindu or brab, of whose fronds mats and the grass kilts worn by many of the tribes are made, flourishes throughout the country, proving that the date-tree might be naturalised. The Nyara or Chamae-rops humilis, the dwarf fan-palm or palmetto of Southern Europe, abounds in this maritime region. The other growths are the Mtogwe and the Mbungo-bungo, varieties of the Nux vomica; the finest are those growing in the vicinity of water. The fruit contains within its hard rind, which, when ripe, is orange-coloured, large pips, covered with a yellow pulp of a grateful agro-dolce flavour, with a suspicion of the mango. The people eat them with impunity; the nuts, which contain the poisonous principle, being too hard to be digested. The Mtunguja (the *Punneeria coagulans* of Dr. Stocks), a solanaceous plant called by the Indians Jangli bengan, or the wild egg-plant, by the South Africans Toluane, and by the Baloch Panir, or cheese, from the effect of the juice in curdling milk, is here, as in Somaliland, a spontaneous growth throughout the country. The same may be said of the castor plant, which, in these regions, is of two kinds. The Mbono (*Jatropha curcas*?) is the Gumpal of Western India, a coarse variety, with a large seed; its fetid oil, when burnt, fouls the lamp; yet, in Africa, it is used by all classes as an unguent. The Mbarika, or Palma Christi, the Irindi of India, is employed in medicine. The natives extract the oil by toasting and pounding the bean, adding a little hot water and skimming off what appears upon the surface. The Arabs, more sensibly, prefer it "cold-draw." These plants, allowed to grow unpruned, often attain the height of eighteen to twenty feet.

The 30th June was another forced halt, when I tasted all the bitterness that can fall to the lot of those who explore regions unvisited by their own colour. The air of Bomani is stagnant, the sun fiery, and clouds of mosquitoes make the nights miserable. Despite these disadvantages, it is a favourite halting-place for up-caravans, who defer to the last the evil days of long travel and short rations. Though impressed with the belief, that the true principle of exploration in these lands is to push on as rapidly and to return as leisurely as possible, I could not persuade the Baloch to move. In Asia, two departures usually suffice; in Africa there must be three, – the little start, the great start, and the start χατ εζοχην. Some clamoured for tobacco – I gave up my cavendish; others for guitar-strings – they were silenced with beads; and all, born donkey-drivers, complained loudly of the hardship and the indignity of having to load and lead an ass. The guide, an influential Mzaramo, promised by the Banyans Ladha and Ramji, declined, after receiving twenty dollars, to accompany the Expedition, and from his conduct the Baloch drew the worst of presages. Much ill-will was shown by them towards the European members of the Expedition. "Kafir end, mara bandira na khenen" (they are infidels and must not carry our flag) – it was inscribed with the usual Moslem formula – was spoken audibly enough in their debased Mekrani to reach my ears: a faithful promise to make a target of the first man who might care to repeat the words, stopped that manner of nuisance. Again the most childish reports flew about the camp, making these jet-bearded and fierce-eyed hen-hearts faint with fears. Boxes had been prepared by the barbarians for myself, and gates had been built across the paths to arrest my party. P'hazi Mazungera, M. Maizan's murderer, had collected a host that numbered thousands, and the Wazaramo were preparing a levee en masse. To no purpose I quoted the Arab's proverb – "the son of fifty dieth not at thirty"; all would be heroic victims marching to gory graves. Such reports did real damage: the principal danger was the tremulous alacrity with which the escort prepared upon each trivial occasion for battle and murder, and sudden death. At one place a squabble amongst the villagers kept the Baloch squatting on their hams with lighted matches from dusk till dawn. At another, a stray Fisi or Cynhyaena entering the camp by night, caused a confusion which only the deadliest onslaught could have justified. A slave hired on the road, hearing these horrors, fled in dismay; this, the first of desertions, was by no means the last. The reader may realise the prevalence and the extent of this African traveller's bane by the fact that during my journey to Ujiji there was not a soul in the caravan, from Said bin Salim the Arab, to the veriest pauper, that did not desert or attempt to desert.

Here, at the first mention of slaves, I must explain to the reader why we were accompanied by them, and how the guide and escort contrived to purchase them. All the serving-men in Zanzibar Island and on the coast of E. Africa are serviles; the Kisawahili does not contain even a word to express a hired domestic. For the evil of slave-service there was no remedy: I therefore paid them their wages and treated them as if they were freemen. I had no power to prevent Said bin

Salim, the Baloch escort, and the "sons of Ramji," purchasing whomever they pleased; all objections on my part were over-ruled by, "we are allowed by our law to do so," and by declaring that they had the permission of the consul. I was fain to content myself with seeing that their slaves were well fed and not injured, and indeed I had little trouble in so doing, as no man was foolish enough to spoil his own property. I never neglected to inform the wild people that Englishmen were pledged to the suppression of slavery, and I invariably refused all slaves offered as return presents.

The departure from Bomani was effected on the 1st of July with some trouble; it was like driving a herd of wild cattle. At length, by ejecting skulkers from their huts, by dint of promises and threats, of gentleness and violence, of soft words and hard words, occasionally backed by a smart application of the "Bakur" – the local "cat" – by sitting in the sun, in fact by incessant worry and fidget from 6 A.M. to 3 P.M., the sluggish and unwieldy body acquired some momentum. I had issued a few marching orders for the better protection of the baggage: two Baloch were told off for each donkey, one to lead, the other to drive; in case of attack, those near the head of the file, hearing the signal, three shots, were to leave their animals and to hurry to the front, where my companion marched, whilst the remainder rallied round my flag in the rear: thus there would have been an attacking party and a reserve, between which the asses would have been safe. the only result of these fine manoeuvres was, that after a two-mile tramp through an umbrageous forest in which caravans often lose the way, and then down an easy descent across fertile fields, into a broken valley, whose further side was thick with luxuriant grass, tall shrubs, and majestic trees, a confused straggling line, – a mere mob of soldiers, slaves, and asses, – arrived at the little village of Mkwaju la Mvuani, – the "Tamarind in the rains."

The settlement is composed as usual of a few hovels and a palaver-house, with a fine lime-tree, the place of lounging and gossip, grain-husking, and mat-weaving, in the open centre. Provisions and rough muddy water being here plentiful, travellers often make a final halt to polish their weapons, and to prepare their minds for the Wazaramo. It is the last station under the jurisdiction of Bagamoyo; from Changahera, the crafty old Diwan, I obtained the services of his nephew Muinyi Wazira, who received seventeen dollars as an inducement to travel in the interior, and was at once constituted linguist and general assistant to Said bin Salim. The day passed as usual, a snake was killed, and a gun-shot heard in the distance supplied conversation for some hours. The "sons of Ramji" carefully lost half a dozen of the axes, bill-hooks, and dibbles, with which they had been supplied, fearing lest they might be called upon to build the Siwta or Boma, the loose thorn-fence with which the halting-place ought to be surrounded before the night, and 7 P.M. had passed before I could persuade the Baloch to catch, tether, and count the asses. One of the escort, Ismail, was attacked with dysentery and required to be mounted, although we were obliged by the want of carriage to wend our way on foot. During the last night, Said bin Salim had taken charge of three Wanguru porters, who, freshly trapped by Said el Hazrami, had been chained pro tempore to prevent desertion. The Arab boasted that he was a bad sleeper, but bad sleepers are worse watchers, because when they do sleep they sleep in earnest. The men were placed for the night in Said's tent, surrounded by his five slaves, yet they stole his gun, and carrying off an axe and sundry billhooks, disappeared in the jungle. The watchful Said, after receiving many congratulations on his good fortune – fugitive slaves sometimes draw their knives across the master's throat or insert the points into his eyes – sent off his own attendants to recover the fugitives. In the jungle, however, search was of scant avail: the Wanguru feared that if caught by the Baloch, they would lose their ears; three days would enable them to reach their own country; and their only risk was that if trapped by the Washenzi before their irons – a valuable capture to the captors – could be removed, they might again be sold to some travelling trader. As the day wore on, Said's face assumed a deplorable expression: his slaves had not appeared, and though several of them were muwallid or born in his father's house, and one was after a fashion his brother-in-law, he sorely dreaded that they also had deserted. He was proportionably delighted when in the dead of the night, entering Mkwaju la Mvuani, they reported ill-success; and though I could little afford the loss, I was glad to get rid of this chained and surly gang.

On the next day we began loading for the third and final departure, before dawn, and at 7.30 A.M. were on the dew-dripping way. Beyond the settlement a patch of jungle led to cultivated grounds belonging to the villagers, whose scattered and unfenced abodes were partially concealed by dense clumps of trees. The road then sweeping parallel with the river plain, which runs from N.W. to S.E., crossed several swamps, black muddy bottoms covered with tall thick rushes and pea-green paddy, and the heavily laden asses sunk knee-deep into the soft soil. Red copalliferous sand clothed the higher levels. On the wayside appeared for the first time the Khambi or substantial kraals, which evidence unsafe travelling and the unwillingness of caravans to bivouac in the villages. In this region they assumed the form of round huts and long sheds or boothies of straw or grass supported by a framework of rough sticks firmly planted in the ground and lashed together with bark-strips. The whole was surrounded with a deep circle of thorns which – the entrance or entrances being carefully closed at nightfall, not to reopen until dawn – formed a complete defence against bare feet and naked legs. About half-way a junction of the Mbuamaji road was reached, and the path became somewhat broader and less rough. Passing on the right a hilly district, called Dunda or "the Hill," the road fell from the ancient sea-beach into the alluvial valley of the Kingani River; presently rising again, it entered the settlement of Nzasa, a name interpreted "level ground."

Nzasa is the first district of independent Uzaramo. My men proceeded to occupy the Bandani, in the centre of the hamlet, when Said bin Salim, discovering with the sharp eye of fear a large drum, planted in readiness for the war-signal or the dance-signal, hurried about till he had turned all hands out of the village into a clump of trees hard by, a propitious place for surprise and ambuscade. Here I was visited by three P'hazi or headmen, Kizaya, Tumba Ihere or the "poison gourd," and Kombe la Simba or the "lion's hide." They came to ascertain whether I was bound on peaceful errand or – as the number of our guns suggested – I was marching to revenge the murder of my "brother" Muzungu. Assured of our unwarlike intentions, they told me that I must halt on the morrow and send forward a message to the next chief. As this plan invariably loses three days, – the first being a dies non, the second being expended in dispensing exoteric information to all the lieges squatting in solemn conclave, whilst on the third the real message is privily whispered into the chieftain's ear, – I replied through Said that I could not be bound by their rules, but was ready to pay for their infraction. During the debate upon this fascinating proposal for breaking the law, Yusuf, one of the most turbulent of the Baloch, drew his sword upon an old woman because she refused to give up a basket of grain. She rushed, with the face of a black Medusa, into the assembly, and provoked not very peaceable remarks concerning the peaceful nature of our intentions. When the excitement was allayed, the principal P'hazi began to ask what had brought the white man into their country, and in a breath to predict the loss of their gains and commerce, their land and liberty. "I am old," pathetically quoth the P'hazi, "and my beard is grey, yet I have never beheld such a calamity as this!" "These men," replied Said, "neither buy nor sell; they do not inquire into price, nor do they covet profit. Moreover," he pursued, "what have ye to lose? The Arabs take your best, the Wasawahili your second best, and your trifling tribute is reduced to a yoke of bullocks, a few clothes, or half a dozen hoes." An extravagant present – at that time ignorance of the country compelled me to intrust such matters to the honesty of Said bin Salim – opened the headmen's hearts: they privily termed me Murungwana Sana, a real free-man, the African equivalent for the English "gentleman," and they detached Kizaya to accompany me as far as the western half of the Kingani Valley. At 4 P.M. a loud drumming collected the women, who began to perform a dance of ceremony with peculiar vigour. A line of small, plump, chestnut-coloured beings, with wild beady eyes, and a thatch of clay-plastered hair, dressed in their loin-cloths, with a profusion of white disks, bead necklaces, a little square bib of beads called a t'hando, partially concealing the upper bosom, with short coils of thick brass wire wound so tightly round the wrists, the arms above the elbows, and the fat ankles, that they seemed to have grown into the flesh, and, – hideous perversion of taste! – with ample bosoms tightly corded down, advanced and retired in a convulsion of wriggle and contortion, whose fit expression was a long discordant howl, which seemed to

"Embowel with outrageous noise the air."

I threw them a few strings of green beads, which for a moment interrupted the dance. One of these falling to the ground, I was stooping to pick it up when Said whispered hurriedly in my ear, "Bend not; they will say 'he will not bend even to take up beads!'"

In the evening I walked down to the bed of the Kingani river, which bisects a plain all green with cultivation, – rice and holcus, sweet potato and tobacco, – and pleasantly studded with huts and hamlets. The width of the stream, which here runs over a broad bed of sand, is about fifty yards; it is nowhere fordable, as the ferry-boat belonging to each village proves, and thus far it is navigable, though rendered dangerous by the crocodiles and the hippopotami that house in its waters. The colour is tawny verging upon red, and the taste is soft and sweet, as if fed by rain. The Kingani, like all streams in this part of the continent, is full of fish, especially a dark-green and scaleless variety (a Silurus?) called Kambari, and other local names. This great "miller's thumb" has fleshy cirri, appears to be omnivorous, and tastes like animal mud. The night was rendered uncomfortable to the Baloch by the sound of distant drums, which suggested fighting as well as feasting, and by the uproar of the wild men, who, when reconnoitred by the scouts, were found to be shouting away the hippopotami.

In the hurry and the confusion of loading on the next morning one ass was left behind, and the packs were so badly placed that the fatigue of marching was almost doubled by their repeated falls. Whilst descending the well-wooded river terrace, my portion of the escort descried an imaginary white flag crossing the grassy valley below. This is the sign of a Diwan's expedition or commando: it is unwisely allowed by the Arabs, whose proper colours are a plain blood-red. After marching a few miles over undulating ground, open and park-like, and crossing rough and miry beds, the path disclosed a view verging upon the pretty. By the wayside was planted the peculiarly African Mzimu or Fetiss hut, a penthouse about a foot high, containing, as votive offerings, ears of holcus or pombe-beer in a broken gourd. There, too, the graves of the heathen met the eye. In all other parts of East Africa a mouldering skull, a scattered skeleton, or a few calcined bones, the remains of wizards and witches dragged to the stake, are the only visible signs of man's mortality. The Wazaramo tombs, especially in the cases of chiefs, imitate those of the Wamrima. They are parallelograms, seven feet by four, formed by a regular dwarf paling that encloses a space cleared of grass, and planted with two uprights to denote the position of head and feet. In one of the long walls there is an apology for a door. The corpse of the heathen is not made to front any especial direction; moreover the centre of the oblong has the hideous addition of a log carved by the unartistic African into a face and a bust singularly resembling those of a legless baboon, whilst a white rag tied turbanwise round the head serves for the inscription "this is a man." The Baloch took notice of such idolatrous tendency by spitting and by pronouncing certain national anathemas, which literally translated might sound unpleasant in Europeans' ears. The abomination of iconism is avoided in the graves of Moslem travellers: they are usually cleared ovals, with outlines of rough stone and a strew of smooth pebbles, according to the custom of the Wasawahili. Several stumps of wood planted in the earth show that the corpse faces Mecca, and, as amongst the Jinga of Western Africa, the fragments of a china bowl or cup lying upon the ground are sacred to the memory of the departed. In Zanzibar Island, also, saucers, plates, and similar articles are mortared into the tombstones.

The number of these graves made the blackness of my companions pale. They were hurrying forward with sundry "la haul!" and with boding shakes of the head, when suddenly an uproar in the van made them all prepare for action. They did it characteristically by beginning with begging for ranjak – priming powder. Said bin Salim, much excited, sent forward his messmate Muinyi Wazira to ascertain the cause of the excitement. One Mviraru, the petty lord of a neighbouring village, had barred the road with about a dozen men, demanding "dash," and insisting that Kizaya had no right to lead on the party without halting to give him the news. My companion, who was attended only by "Bombay," his gun-carrier, and a few Baloch, remarked to the interferers that he had been franked through the country by paying at Nzasa. To this they obstinately objected. The Baloch began to light their matches and to use hard words. A fight appeared imminent. Presently, however, when the Wazaramo saw my flag rounding the hill-shoulder with a fresh party, whose numbers were exaggerated by distance, they gave way; and finally when Muinyi Wazira opened upon them the invincible artillery of his tongue, they fell back and stood off the road to gaze. The linguist returned to the rear in great glee, blowing his finger tips, as if they had been attached to a matchlock, and otherwise deriding the overboiling valour of the Baloch, who, not suspecting his purport, indulged in the wildest outbreak of boasting, offering at once to take the whole country and to convert me into its sultan. Towards the end of the march we crossed a shallow, salt, bitter rivulet, flowing cold and clear towards the Kingani River. On the grassy plain below noble game – zebra and koodoo – began to appear; whilst guinea-fowl and partridge, quail, green-pigeon, and the cuculine bird, called in India the Malabar-pheasant, became numerous. A track of rich red copalliferous soil, wholly without stone, and supporting black mould, miry during the rains, and caked and cracked by the potent suns of the hot season, led us to Kiranga-Ranga, the first dangerous station in Uzaramo. It is the name of a hilly district, with many little villages embosomed in trees, overlooking the low cultivated bottoms where caravans encamp in the vicinity of the wells.

Before establishing themselves in the kraal at Kiranga-Ranga, the two rival parties of Baloch, – the Prince's permanent escort and the temporary guard sent by Ladha Damha from Kaole – being in a chronic state of irritability, naturally quarrelled. With the noise of choughs gathering to roost they vented their bile, till thirteen men belonging to a certain Jemadar Mohammed suddenly started up, and without a word of explanation set out on their way home. According to Said bin Salim, the temporary guard had determined not to proceed beyond Kiranga-Ranga, and this desertion was intended as a preliminary to others by which the party would have lost two-thirds of its strength. I at once summoned the Jemadars, and wrote in their presence a letter reporting the conduct of their men to the dreaded Balyuz, the consul, who was supposed to be still anchored off Kaole. Seeing the bastinado in prospect, the Jemadar Yaruk shouldered his sabre, slung his shield over his arm, set out in pursuit of the fugitives, and soon succeeded in bringing them back. He was a good specimen of the true Baloch mountaineer – a tall, gaunt, and large-boned figure, with dark complexion deeply pitted by small-pox, hard, high, and sun-burnt features of exceeding harshness; an armoury in epitome was stuck in his belt, and his hand seemed never to rest but upon a weapon.

The 4th of July was a halt at Kiranga-Ranga. Two asses had been lost, the back-sinews of a third had been strained, and all the others had been so wearied by their inordinate burdens, to which on the last march the meat of a koodoo, equal in weight to a young bullock, had been superadded, that a rest was deemed indispensable. I took the opportunity of wandering over and of prospecting the country. The scene was one of admirable fertility; rice, maize, and manioc grew in the rankest and richest crops, and the uncultivated lands bore the Corindah bush (*Carissa Carandas*), the salsaparilla vine, the small whitish-green mulberry (the Morus alba of India), and the crimson flowers of the Rosel. In the lower levels near the river rose the giants of the forest. The Mparamusi shot up its tall head, whose bunchy tresses rustled in the breeze when all below was still. The stately Msufi, a Bombax or silk-cotton tree, showed as many as four or five trunks, each two to three feet in diameter, rising from the same roots; the long tapering branches stood out stiffly at right angles from the bole; and the leaves, instead of forming masses of foliage, were sparsely scattered in small dense growth. The Msukulio, unknown to the people of Zanzibar, was a pile of dark verdure, which dwarfed the finest oaks and elms of an English park. No traces of game appeared in the likeliest of places; perhaps it preferred lurking in the tall gross grass, which was not yet in a fit state to burn.

At Kiranga-Ranga the weather began to be unpropitious. The Mcho'o, the heavy showers which fall between the Masika or vernal, and the Vuli or autumnal rains, set in with regularity, and accompanied us during the transit of the maritime plain. I therefore refused to halt more than one day, although the P'hazi or chiefs of the Wazaramo showed, by sending presents of goats and grain, great civility – a civility purchased, however, by Said bin Salim at the price of giving to each man whatever he demanded; even women were never allowed to leave the camp unpropitiated. I was not permitted in this part to enter the villages, although the Wazaramo do not usually exclude strangers who venture upon their dangerous hospitality. Girls are appointed to attend upon them, and in case of sickness or accident happening to any one in the settlement, they are severely interrogated concerning the morality of the guest, and an unfavourable account of it leads to extortion and violence. The Wazaramo, like the Wagogo, and unlike the other East African tribes, are jealous of their women; still "damages" will act, as they have acted in other lands, as salve to wounded honour and broken heart.

On the 5th of July we set out betimes, and traversing the fields around Kiranga-Ranga, struck through a dense jungle, here rising above, there bending into the river valley, to some stagnant pools which supply the district with water. The station, reached in 3hrs 30', was called Tumba Ihere, after the headman, who accompanied us. Here we saw cocos emerging from a fetid vegetation, and for the last time the Mwembe or mango, a richly foliaged but stunted tree which never attains the magnificent dimensions observed at Zanzibar. Several down-caravans were halted at Tumba Ihere; the slaves brought from the interior were tied together by their necks, and one obstinate deserter was so lashed to a forked pole with the bifurcation under his chin, that when once on the ground he could not rise without assistance. These wretches scarcely appeared to like the treatment; they were not, however, in bad condition. The Wanyamwezi porters bathed in the pools and looked at us without fear or shame. Our daily squabble did not fail to occur. Riza, a Baloch, drew his dagger on one of Said bin Salim's "children," and the child pointed his Tower-musket at the Baloch; a furious hubbub arose; the master, with his face livid and drawn like a cholera patient's, screamed shrilly as a woman, and the weapons returned to their proper places bloodless as those wielded by Bardolph,

Nym, and ancient Pistol. My companion began to suffer from the damp heat and the reeking miasma; he felt that a fever was coming on, and the fatigue of marching under these circumstances prevented our mustering the party. The consequence was, that an ass laden with rice disappeared, – it had probably been led out of the road and unburdened by the Baloch; – whilst axes, cords, and tethers could nowhere be found when wanted.

On the next morning we left Tumba Ihere, and tramped over a red land through alternate strips of rich cultivation and tangled jungle, which presently opened out into a forest where the light-barked Msandarusi, or copal-tree, attains its fullest dimensions. This is one of the richest "diggins," and the roadsides are everywhere pitted with pockets two or three feet deep by one in diameter. Rain fell in huge drops, and the heaviness of the ground caused frequent accidents to the asses' loads. About noon we entered the fine grain-fields that gird the settlements of Muhogwe, one of the most dreaded in dreaded Uzaramo. In our case, however, the only peril was the levee en masse of the fair sex in the villages, to stare, laugh, and wonder at the white men. "What should you think of these whites as husbands?" asked Muinyi Wazira of the crowd. "With such things on their legs? – Sivyo! – not by any means!" – was the unanimous reply, accompanied with peals of merriment.

Beyond Muhogwe all was jungle and forest, tall trees rising from red copalliferous sand, and shading bright flowers, and blossoming shrubs. After crossing a low mud overgrown with rush and tiger-grass, and a watercourse dotted with black stagnant pools, we ascended rising well-forested ground, and lastly debouched upon the kraals of Muhonyera.

The district of Muhonyera occupies the edge of the plateau forming the southern terrace of the Kingani River; and the elevated sea-beach is marked out by lines of quartsoze pebbles running along the northern slope of the hill upon which we encamped. Water is found in seven or eight reedy

holes in the valley below; it acquires from decomposed vegetation an unnaturally sweet and slimy taste. This part of the
country, being little inhabited by reason of its malarious climate, abounds in wild animals. The guides speak of lions, and
the cry of the Fisi or Cynhyaena was frequently heard at
night, threatening destruction to the asses. The Fisi, the
Wuraba of the Somal, and the Wilde Honde of the Cape, is
the wolf of Africa, common throughout the country, where it
acts as scavenger. Though a large and powerful variety, it seldom assaults man, except when sleeping, and then it snatches
a mouthful from the face, causing a ghastlier disfigurement
even than the scalping of the bear. Three asses belonging to
the Expedition were destroyed by this beast; in all cases they
were attacked by night with a loud wrangling shriek, and the
piece of flesh was raggedly torn from the hind quarter; after
affording a live rumpsteak, they could not be driven like
Bruce's far-famed bullock. These, however, were the animals
brought from Zanzibar; that of Unyamwezi, if not tied up,
defends itself successfully against its cowardly assailant with
teeth and heels, even as the zebra, worthy of Homeric simile,
has, it is said, kept the lion at bay. The woods about Muhonyera contain large and small grey monkeys with black faces;
clinging to the trees they gaze for a time at the passing caravan imperturbably, till curiosity being satisfied, they slip
down and bound away with long plunging leaps, like a grey-
hound at play. The view from the hill-side was suggestive.
The dark green plain of sombre monotony, with its overhanging strata of mist-bank and dew-cloud, appeared in all the
worst colours of the Oude Tirhai and the Guzerat jungles. At
that season, when the moisture of the rainy monsoon was like
poison distilled by the frequent bursts of fiery sunshine, it was
a valley of death for unacclimatised travellers. Far to the
west, however, rose Kidunda, "the hillock," a dwarf cone
breaking the blurred blue line of jungle, and somewhat northward of it towered a cloud-capped azure wall, the mountain-

crags of Duthumi, upon which the eye, long weary of low levels, rested with a sensation of satisfaction.

It was found necessary to halt a day at Muhonyera: according to some authorities no provisions were procurable for a week; others declared that there were villages on the road, but were uncertain whether rations could be purchased. Said bin Salim sent Ambari, a favourite slave, back to buy grain at Muhogwe, whence he had hurried us on in fear of the Wazaramo; and the youth, after wasting a day, returned on the evening of the 2nd July with about sixty lbs., – a poor supply for eighty-eight hungry bodies. This proceeding naturally affronted the Baloch, who desired for themselves the perquisites proceeding from the purchases. Two of their number, Yusuf and Salih Mohammed, came to swear officially on the part of their men that there was not an ounce of grain in camp. Appearing credulous, I paid them a visit about half an hour afterwards; all their shuffling and sitting upon the bags could not conceal a store of about 100 lbs. of fine white rice, whose quality, – the Baloch had been rationed at Kaole with an inferior kind, showed whence it came.

After repairing the "boma," or fenced kraal, – it had been burnt down, as often happens, by the last caravan of Wanyamwezi, – I left my companion, who was prostrate with fever, and went out, gun in hand, to inspect the country, and to procure meat, that necessary having fallen short. The good P'hazi, Tumba Ihere, accompanied me, and after return he received an ample present for his services, and departed. The Baloch employed themselves in cleaning their rusty matchlock-barrels with a bit of kopra, – dried cocoa-nut meat, – in weaving for themselves sandals, like the spartelle of the Pyrenees, with green palmetto-leaves; in preparing calabash fibre for fatilah or gun-matches, and in twisting cords for the asses. The best material is supplied by an aloetic plant, the Hig or Haskul of Somaliland, here called by the Arabs Bag, and by the natives Mukonge. The Mananazi, or pine-apple, grows wild as far as three marches from the coast, but its fibrous qualities are unknown to the people. Ismail, the invalid Baloch, was the worse for remedies; and two other men gave signs of breaking down.

During the first week, creeping along at a slug's pace, we heard the booming of the Artémise's evening gun, an assurance that refuge was at hand. Presently these reports ceased. Lieut.-Colonel Hamerton, seized with mortal sickness, had left Kaole suddenly, and he died on board the Artémise on the 5th July, shortly after his return to Zanzibar. The first letters announcing the sad event were lost: with characteristic African futility the porter despatched with the parcel from the island, finding that the Expedition had passed on to the mountains of Usagara, left his charge with a village headman, and returned to whence he came. Easterns still hold that

> *"Though it be honest, it is never good,*
> *To bring bad news."*

The report, spread by a travelling trader, was discussed throughout the camp, but I was kept in ignorance of it till Khudabakhsh, a Baloch, who had probably been deputed by his brethren to ascertain what effect the decease of the consul would have upon me, "hardened his heart," and took upon himself the task of communicating the evil intelligence. I was uncertain what to believe. Said bin Salim declared, when consulted, that he fully trusted in the truth of the report, but his reasons were somewhat too Arabo-African to convince me. He had found three pieces of scarlet broadcloth damaged by rats, – an omen of death; and the colour pointed out the nationality of the departed.

The consul's death might have proved fatal to the Expedition, had its departure been delayed for a week. The court of Zanzibar had required the stimulus of a strong official letter from Lieut.-Colonel Hamerton, before it would consent, as requested by the Foreign Office, "to procure a favourable reception on the coast, and to ensure the protection of the chiefs of the country" for the travellers. The Hindus, headed by Ladha Damha, showed from first to last extreme unwillingness to open up the rich regions of copal and ivory to European eyes: they had been deceived by my silence during the rainy season at Zanzibar into a belief that the coast-fever had cooled my ardour for further adventure; and their surprise at finding the contrary to be the case was not of a pleasant nature. The home-sick Baloch would have given their ears to return, they would have turned back even when arrived within a few marches from the Lake. Said bin Salim took the first opportunity of suggesting the advisability of his returning to Zanzibar for the purpose of completing carriage. I positively refused him leave; it was a mere pretext to ascertain whether His Highness the Sayyid Majid had or had not, in consequence of our changed position, altered his views.

Lieut.-Colonel Hamerton's death, however, was mourned for other than merely selfish considerations. His hospitality and kindness had indeed formed a well-omened contrast with my unauspicious reception at Aden in 1855, before my departure to explore the Eastern Horn of Africa, when the coldness of some, and the active jealousy of other political authorities, thwarted all my projects, and led to the tragic disaster at Berberah.[4] Lieut.-Colonel Hamerton had received two strangers like sons, rather than like passing visitors. During the intervals between the painful attacks of a deadly disease, he had exerted himself to the utmost in forwarding my views; in fact, he made my cause his own. Though aware of his danger, he had refused to quit, until compelled by approaching dissolution, the post which he considered his duty to hold. He was a loss to his country, an excellent linguist, a ripe oriental scholar, and a valuable public servant of the old Anglo-Indian school; he was a man whose influence over Easterns, based upon their respect for his honour and honesty, his gallantry and determination, knew no bounds; and at heart a "sad good Christian," – the Heavens be his bed!

On the 8th of July we fell into what our Arab called Wady el Maut and Dar el Jua – the Valley of Death and the Home of Hunger – the malarious river-plain of the Kingani River. My companion was compelled by sickness to ride, and thus the asses, now back-sore and weak with fatigue, suffered an addition of weight, and a "son of Ramji" who was upon the point of deserting openly required to be brought back at the muzzle of the barrel. The path descending into a dense thicket of spear grass, bush, and thorny trees based on sand, with a few open and scattered plantations of holcus, presently passed on the left Dunda Nauru, or "Seer-fish-hill," so called because a man laden with such provision had there been murdered by the Wazaramo. After 2hrs. 45' a ragged camping-kraal was found on the tree-lined bank of a half-dry Fiumara, a tributary of the neighbouring Kingani: the water was bad, and a mortal smell of decay was emitted by the dark dank ground. It was a

---

4.   Capt. R. L. Playfair, Madras Artillery and First Assistant Pol. Resident, Aden, in a selection from the records of the Bombay Government, (No. 49, new series, Bombay, printed for Government, at the Education Society Press, Byculla, 1859,) curiously misnamed "A History of Arabia Felix or Yemen," transports himself, in a "supplementary chapter," to East Africa, and thus records his impressions of what happened in the "Somali Country:" –

1855. – "During the afternoon of the same day (the 18th of April), three men visited the camp, *palpably as spies*, and as such, *the officers of the Expedition were warned against them by their native attendants.* Heedless of this warning, they retired to rest at night in the fullest confidence of security, and without having taken any extra, or even ordinary means, to guard against surprise."

The italics are my own: they designate mistatements unpardonable in an individual whose official position enabled him to ascertain and to record the truth. The three men were represented to me as spies, who came to ascertain whether I was preparing to take the country for the Chief Shermarkay, then hostile to their tribe, not as spies to spy out the weakness of my party. I received no warning of personal danger. The "ordinary measures," that is to say, the posting of two sentinels in front and rear of the camp during the night were taken, and I cannot blame myself because they ran away.

I will not stop to inquire what must be the value of Capt. Playfair's 193 pages touching the history of Yemen, when in five lines there are three distinct and wilful deviations from fact.

I am well aware that after my departure from Aden, in 1855, an inquiry was instituted during my absence, and without my knowledge, into the facts of the disaster which occurred at Berberah. The "privileged communication" was, I believe, in due course, privily forwarded to the Bombay Government, and the only rebuke which this shuffling proceeding received was from a gentleman holding a high and honourable position, who could not reconcile himself to seeing a man's character stabbed in the back.

wild day. From the black brumal clouds driven before furious blasts pattered rain-drops like musket-bullets, splashing the already saturated ground. The tall stiff trees groaned and bent before the gusts; the birds screamed as they were driven from their perching places; the asses stood with heads depressed, ears hung down, and shrinking tails turned towards the weather, and even the beasts of the wild seemed to have taken refuge in their dens. Provisions being unprocurable at "Sagesera," the party did what men on such occasions usually do – they ate double quantities. I had ordered a fair distribution of the rice that remained, consequently they cooked all day. Yusuf, a Jemadar of inferior rank, whose friends characterised him as "sweet of tongue but bitter at heart," vainly came to beg, on plea of hunger, dismissal for himself and his party; and another Baloch, Wall, reported as uselessly that a sore foot would prevent him advancing.

Despite our increasing weakness, we marched seven hours on the 9th of July, over a plain wild but prodigiously fertile, and varied by patches of field, jungle and swamp, along the right bank of the Kingani river, to another ragged old kraal, situated near a bend in the bed. This day showed the ghost of an adventure. At the "Makutaniro," or junction of the Mbuamaji trunk-road with the other lines branching from various minor sea-ports, my companion, who was leisurely proceeding with the advance guard, found his passage barred by about fifty Wazaramo standing across the path in a single line that extended to the travellers' right, whilst a reserve party squatted on the left of the road. Their chief stepping to the front and quietly removing the load from the foremost porter's head, signalled the strangers to halt. Prodigious excitement of the Baloch, whose loud "Hai, hui!" and nervous anxiety contrasted badly with the perfect *sang froid* of the barbarians. Presently, Muinyi Wazira coming up, addressed to the headman a few words, promising cloth and beads, when this African modification of the "pike" was opened, and the guard moved forward as before. As I passed, the Wazaramo stood under a tree to gaze. I could not but admire the athletic and statuesque figures of the young warriors and their martial attitude, grasping in one hand their full-sized bows, and in the other sheaths of grinded arrows, whose black barbs and necks showed a fresh layer of poison.

At Tunda, "the fruit," so called from its principal want, after a night passed amidst the rank vegetation, and within the malarious influence of the river, I arose weak and depressed, with aching head, burning eyes, and throbbing extremities. The new life, the alternations of damp heat and wet cold, the useless fatigue of walking, the sorry labour of waiting and re-loading the asses, the exposure to sun and dew, and last, but not least, of morbific influences, the wear and tear of mind at the prospect of imminent failure, all were beginning to tell heavily upon me. My companion had shaken off his preliminary symptoms, but Said bin Salim, attacked during the rainy gusty night by a severe Mkunguru or seasoning-fever, begged hard for a halt at Tunda – only for a day – only for half a day – only for an hour. Even this was refused. I feared that Tunda might prove fatal to us. Said bin Salim was mounted upon an ass, which compelled us to a weary trudge of two hours. The animals were laden with difficulty; they had begun to show a predilection for lying down. The footpath, crossing a deep nullah, spanned a pestilential expanse of spear-grass, and a cane, called from its appearance Gugumbua, or the wild sugar plant, with tinge calabashes and natural clearings in the jungle, where large game appeared. After a short march I saw the red flag of the vanguard stationary, and turning a sharp corner found the caravan halted in a little village, called from its headman Bana Dirunga. This was premature. I had ordered Muinyi Wazira to advance on that morning to Dege la Mhora, the "large jungle-bird," the hamlet where M. Maizan's blood was shed. Said and Wazira had proposed that we should pass it ere the dawn of the next day broke; the advice was rejected, it was too dangerous a place to show fear. The two diplomatists then bethought themselves of another manoeuvre, and led me to Bana Dirunga, calling it Dege la Mhora.

We halted for a day at the little hamlet, embosomed in dense grass and thicket. On our appearance the villagers fled into the bush, their country's strength; but before nightfall they took heart of grace and returned. The headman appeared to regard us with fear, he could not comprehend why we carried so much powder and ball. When reassured he offered to precede us, and to inform the chief of the "large jungle-bird" that our intentions had been misrepresented, – a proposal which seemed to do much moral good to Said, the Jemadar, and Wazira.

On the eleventh day after leaving Kaole I was obliged to mount by a weakness which scarcely allowed me to stand. After about half an hour, through a comparatively open country, we passed on the left a well-palisaded village, belonging formerly to P'hazi Mazungera, and now occupied by his son Hembe, or the "wild buffalo's horn." Reports of our warlike intentions had caused Hembe to "clear decks for action;" the women had been sent from the village, and some score of tall youths, archers and spearmen, admirably appointed, lined the hedges, prepared, at the levelling of the first matchlock, to let loose a flight of poisoned arrows, which would certainly have dispersed the whole party. A halt was called by the trembling Said, who at such conjunctures would cling like a woman to my companion or to me. During the few minutes' delay the "sons of Ramji," who were as pale as blacks could be, allowed their asses to bump off half a dozen loads. Presently Hembe, accompanied by a small guard, came forward, and after a few words with Wazira and Said, the donkey from which I had not dismounted was hurried forward by the Baloch. Hembe followed us with a stronger escort to Madege Madogo, the next station. Illness served me as an excuse for not receiving him: he obtained, however, from Said a letter to the headmen of the coast, bespeaking their good offices for certain of his slaves sent down to buy gunpowder.

An account of the melancholy event which cut short at Dege la Mhora the career of the first European that ever penetrated beyond this portion of the coast may here be inserted.

M. Maizan, an *enseigne de vaisseau*, and a pupil of the Polytechnic School, after a cruise in the seas off Eastern Africa, conceived, about the end of 1843, the project of exploring the lakes of the interior, and in 1844 his plans were approved of by his government. Arrived at Bourbon, he was provided with a passage to Zanzibar, in company with M. Broquant, the Consul de France, newly appointed after the French Commercial Treaty of the 21st Nov. 1844, on board the corvette Le Berceau, Capitaine, afterwards Vice-Admiral, Romain Desfosses, commanding. At the age of twenty-six M. Maizan had amply qualified himself by study for travel, and he was well provided with outfit and instruments. His "kit," however, was of a nature calculated to excite savage cupidity, as was proved by the fact that his murderer converted the gilt knob of a tent-pole into a neck ornament, and tearing out the works of a gold chronometer, made of it a tobacco-pouch. He has been charged with imprudence in carrying too much luggage – a *batterie de dejeuner*, a *batterie de diner*, and similar superfluities. But he had acted rightly, when bound upon a journey through countries where outfit cannot be renewed, in providing himself with all the materials for comfort. On such explorations a veteran traveller would always attempt to carry with him as much, not as little as possible, – of course prepared to abandon all things, and to reduce himself, whenever the necessity might occur, to the *"simple besace du pelerin."* It is easy to throw away a superfluity, and the best preparation for severe "roughing it," is to enjoy ease and comfort whilst attainable.

But M. Maizan fell upon evil times at Zanzibar. Dark innuendos concerning French ambition – that nation being even suspected of a desire to establish itself in force at Lamu, Pangani, and other places on the coast of East Africa – filled Hindu and Hindi with fear for their profits. These men influenced the inhabitants of the island and the sea-coast, who probably procured the co-operation of their wild brethren in the interior. For the purpose of learning the Kisawahili, M. Maizan delayed nearly eight months at Zanzibar, and, seeing a French vessel entering the harbour, he left the place precipitately, fearing a recall. Vainly also M. Broquant had warned him against his principal confidant, a noted swindler, and Lieut.-Colonel Hamerton had cautioned him to no purpose that his glittering instruments and his numerous boxes, all of which would be supposed to contain dollars, were dangerous. He visited the coast thrice before finally landing, thus giving the Wasawahili time and opportunity to mature their plans. He lowered himself in the eyes of the Arabs by "making brotherhood" with a native of Unyamwezi. Finally, fearing Arab apathy and dilatoriness, he hastened into the country without waiting for the strong armed escort promised to him by His Highness the late Sayyid Said.

These were grave errors; but they were nothing in comparison with that of trusting himself unarmed, after the fatal habit of Europeans, and without followers, into the hands of an African chief. How often has British India had to deplore deaths "that would have dimmed a victory," caused by recklessness of danger or by the false shame which prevents men in high position from wearing weapons where they may be at any moment required, lest the safe mediocrities around them should deride such excess of cautiousness!

After the rains of 1845 M. Maizan landed at Bagamoyo, a little settlement opposite the island of Zanzibar. There leaving the forty musketeers, his private guard, he pressed on, contrary to the advice of his Mnyamwezi brother, escorted only by Frederique, a Madagascar or Comoro man, and by a few followers, to visit P'hazi Mazungera, the chief of the Wakamba, a subtribe of the Wazaramo, at his village of Dege la Mhora. He was received with a treacherous cordiality, of which he appears to have been completely the dupe. After some days of the most friendly intercourse, during which the villain's plans were being matured, Mazungera, suddenly sending for his guest, reproached him as he entered the hut with giving away goods to other chiefs. Presently working himself into a rage, the African exclaimed, "Thou shalt die at this moment!" At the signal a crowd of savages rushed in, bearing two long poles. Frederique was saved by the P'hazi's wife: he cried to his master to run and touch her, in which case he would have been under her protection; but the traveller had probably lost presence of mind, and the woman was removed. The unfortunate man's arms were then tightly bound to a pole lashed crosswise upon another, to which his legs and head were secured by a rope tied across the brow. In this state he was carried out of the village to a calabash-tree, pointed out to me, about fifty yards on the opposite side of the road. The inhuman Mazungera first severed all his articulations, whilst the war-song and the drum sounded notes of triumph. Finding the sime, or double-edged knife, somewhat blunt, he stopped, when in the act of cutting his victim's throat, to whet the edge, and, having finished the bloody deed, he concluded with wrenching the head from the body.

Thus perished an amiable, talented, and highly educated man, whose only fault was rashness – too often the word for enterprise when Fortune withholds her smile. The savage Mazungera was disappointed in his guest's death. The object of the torture was to discover, as the Mganga had advised, the place of his treasures, whereas the wretched man only groaned and implored forgiveness of his sins, and called upon the names of those friends whose advice he had neglected. The P'hazi then attempted to decoy from Bagamoyo the forty musketeers left with the outfit, but in this he failed, tie then proceeded to make capital of his foul deed. When Snay bin Amir, a Maskat merchant, – of whom I shall have much to say, – appeared with a large caravan at Dege la Mhora, Mazungera demanded a new tribute for free passage; and, as a threat, he displayed the knife with which he had committed the murder. But Snay proved himself a man not to be trifled with.

Frederique returned to Zanzibar shortly after the murder, and was examined by M. Broquant. An infamous plot would probably have come to light had he not fled from the fort where he was confined. Frederique disappeared mysteriously. He is said now to be living at Marungu, on the Tanganyika Lake, under the Moslem name of Muhammadi. His flight served for a pretext to mischievous men that the prince was implicated in the murder: they also spread a notoriously false report that Mazungera, an independent chief, was a vassal of the suzerain of Zanzibar.

In 1846 the brig-of-war Le Ducouedic, of the naval division of Bourbon, M. Guillain, Capitaine de Yaisseau, commanding, was charged, amongst other commercial and political interests, with insisting upon severe measures to punish the murderers. In vain His Highness Sayyid Said protested that Mazungera was beyond his reach; the fact of the robber-chief having been seen at Mbuamaji on the coast after the murder was deemed conclusive evidence to the contrary. At length the Sayyid despatched up-country three or four hundred musketeers, mercenaries, and slaves, under command of Juma Mfumhi, the late, and Bori, the present, Diwan of Saadani. The little troop marched some distance into the country, when they were suddenly confronted by the Wazaramo, commanded by Hembe, the son of Mazungera, who, after skirmishing for a couple of days, fled wounded by a matchlock-ball. The chief result of the expedition was the capture of a luckless clansman who had beaten the war-drum during the murder. He was at once transferred to Zanzibar, and passed off by these transparent African diplomatists as P'hazi Mazungera. For nearly two years he was chained in front of the French Consulate; after that time he was placed in the fort heavily ironed to a gun under a cadjan shed, where he could hardly stand or lie down. The unhappy wretch died about a year ago, and Zanzibar lost one of its lions.

After the slaughter of M. Maizan the direct route through Dege la Mhora was long closed, it is said, and is still believed, by a "ghul," a dragon or huge serpent, who, of course, was supposed to be the demon-ghost of the murdered man. The reader will rejoice to hear that the miscreant Mazungera, who has evaded human, has not escaped divine punishment. The miserable old man is haunted by the P'hepo or spirit of the guest so foully slain: the torments which he has brought upon himself have driven him into a kind of exile; and his tribe, as has been mentioned, has steadily declined from its former position with even a greater decline in prospect. The jealous national honour displayed by the French Government on the occasion of M. Maizan's murder has begun to bear fruit.

Its sensitiveness contrasts well with our proceedings on similar occasions. Rahmat, the murderer of Captain Milne, still wanders free over the hills in sight of Aden. By punishing the treacherous slaughter of a servant of Government, the price of provisions at the coal-hole of the East would have been raised. Au Ali, the murderer of Lieut. Stroyan, is still at large in the neighbourhood of Berberah, when a few dollars would have brought in his head. The burlesque of a blockade, – Capt. Playfair, in a work previously characterised, has officially mistermed it, to the astonishment of Aden, "a rigid blockade," a "severe punishment," and so forth, – was considered sufficient to chastise the Somal of Berberah for their cowardly onslaught on strangers and guests; and though the people offered an equivalent for the public and private property destroyed by them, the spirit of Centralisation, by an exercise of its peculiar attributes, omniscience and omnipresence, decided that the indemnity, which in such cases is customary throughout the East, must not be accepted, because – forsooth! – it was not deserved by the officers. This is a new plan, a system lately adopted by the nation once called "la plus orgueilleuse et la plus perilleuse" – to win and preserve respect in lands where prestige is its principal power. The Arabs of Yemen have already learned from it to characterise their invaders as Sahib Hilah, – a tricky, peddling manner of folk. They – wiser men than we – will not take upon themselves the pains and penalties of subject-hood, without its sole counterweight, the protection of their rulers, in cases where protection is required.

At Madege Madogo, the "little birds," so called in contradistinction to its western and neighbouring district, Madege Makuba, the "great birds," we pitched tent under a large sycamore; and the Baloch passed a night of alarms, fancying in every sound the approach of a leopard, a hippopotamus, or a crocodile. On the 13th July, we set out after dawn, and traversing forest, jungle, and bush, chequered with mud and morass, hard by the bending and densely-wooded line of the Kingani River, reached in three hours' march an unwholesome camping-ground, called from a conspicuous landmark Kidunda, the "little hill." Here the scenery is effective. The swift, yellow stream, about fifty yards broad, sweeps under tall, stiff earth-works, ever green with tangled vegetation and noble trees. The conical huts of the cultivators are disposed in scattered patches to guard their luxuriant crops, whilst on the northern bank the woody hillock, and on the southern rising ground, apparently the ancient river-terrace, affect the sight agreeably after the evergreen monotony of the river-plain. A petty chief, Mvirama, accompanied by a small party of armed men, posted himself near the cantonment, demanding rice, which was refused with asperity. At this frontier station the Wazaramo, mixed up with the tribes of Udoe, K'hutu, and Usagara, are no longer dreaded.

From Kidunda, the route led over sandy ground, with lines and scatters of water-worn pebbles, descended the precipitous inclines of sandstone, broken into steps of slabs and flags, and crossed the Manyora, a rough and rocky Fiumara, abounding in blocks of snowy quartz, grey and pink syenites, erratic boulders of the hornblende used as whetstones, and strata of a rude sandstone conglomerate. Thence it spanned grass, bush, and forest, close to the Kingani, and finally leaving the stream on the right hand, it traversed sandy soil, and, ascending a wave of ground, abutted upon the Mgeta or rivulet, a large perennial influent, which, rising in the mountains of Duthumi, drains the head of the River-valley.

This lower portion of the Mgeta's bed was unfordable after the heavy rains: other caravans, however, had made a rude bridge of trees, felled on each side, lashed with creepers, and jammed together by the force of the current. The men perched upon the trunks and boughs, tossed or handed to one another the loads and packages, whilst the asses, pushed by force of arm down the banks, were driven with sticks and stones across the stream. Suddenly a louder cry than usual arose from the mob; my double-barrelled elephant-gun found a grave below the cold and swirling waters. The Goanese Gaetano had the courage to plunge in; the depth was about twelve feet; the sole was of roots and loose sand, and the stream ran with considerable force. I bade farewell to that gun; – by the bye it was the second accident of the kind that had occurred to it; – the country people cannot dive, and no one ventures to affront the genius loci, the mamba or crocodile. I found consolation in the thought that the Expedition had passed without accident through the most dangerous part of the journey. In 18 days, from the 27th of June, to the 14th of July, I had accomplished, despite sickness and all manner of difficulties, a march of 118 indirect statute miles, and had entered K'hutu, the safe rendezvous of foreign merchants.

Resuming our march on the 15th July, we entered the "Doab,"[5] on the western bank of the Mgeta, where a thick and tangled jungle, with luxuriant and putrescent vegetation, is backed by low, grassy grounds, frequently inundated. Presently, however, the dense thicket opened out into a fine park country, peculiarly rich in game, where the calabash and the

---

5. This useful word, which means the land embraced by the bifurcation of two streams, has no English equivalent. "Doab," "Dhun" (Dhoon), "Nullah," and "Ghaut," might be naturalised with advantage in our mother tongue.

giant trees of the seaboard gave way to mimosas, gums, and stunted thorns. Large gnus, whom the porters regard with a wholesome awe, declaring that they are capable of charging a caravan, pranced about, pawing the ground, and shaking their formidable manes; hartebeest and other antelopes clustered together on the plain, or travelled in herds to slake their thirst at the river. The homely cry of the partridge resounded from the brake, and the guinea-fowls looked like large bluebells upon the trees. Small land-crabs took refuge in the pits and holes, which made the path a cause of frequent accidents; whilst ants of various kinds, crossing the road in close columns, attacked man and beast ferociously, causing the caravan to break into a halting, trotting hobble, ludicrous to behold. Whilst crossing a sandy Fiumara, Abdullah, a Baloch, lodged by accident four ounces of lead, the contents of my second elephant-gun, in the head of an ass. After a march of six hours we entered Kiruru, a small, ragged, and muddy village of Wak'hutu, deep in a plantation of holcus, whose tall, stiff canes nearly swept me from the saddle. The weather was a succession of raw mist, rain in torrents, and fiery sunbursts; the land appeared rotten, and the jungle smelt of death. At Kiruru I found a cottage, and enjoyed for the first time an atmosphere of sweet warm smoke. My companion remained in the reeking, miry tent, where he partially laid the foundation of the fever which threatened his life in the mountains of Usagara.

Despite the danger of hyaenas, leopards, and crocodiles to an ass-caravan, we were delayed by the torrents of rain and the depth of the mud for two days at Kiruru. According to the people, the district derives its name "palm leaves," from a thirsty traveller, who, not knowing that water was near, chewed the leaves of the hyphaena-palm till he died. One of the Baloch proposed a "Hammam," – a primitive form of the "lamp bath," practised in most parts of Central Asia, – as a cure for fever: he placed me upon one of the dwarf stools used by the people, and under the many abas or hair-cloaks with which I was invested he introduced a bit of pottery containing live coal and a little frankincense. At Kiruru I engaged six porters to assist our jaded animals as far as the next station. The headman was civil, but the people sold their grain with difficulty.

On the 18th July we resumed our march over a tract which caused sinking of the heart in men who expected a long journey under similar circumstances. Near Kiruru the thick grass and the humid vegetation, dripping till midday with dewy rendered the black earth greasy and slippery. the road became worse as we advanced over deep thick mire interlaced with tree-roots through a dense jungle and forest, chiefly of the distorted hyphaena-palm, in places varied by the Mparamusi and the gigantic Msukulio, over barrens of low mimosa, and dreary savannahs cut by steep nullahs. In three places we crossed bogs from 100 yards to a mile in length, and admitting a man up to the knee; the porters plunged through them like laden animals, and I was obliged to be held upon the ass. This "Yegea Mud," caused by want of water-shed after rain, is sometimes neck-deep; it never dries except when the moisture has been evaporated by sun and wind during the middle of the Kaskazi or N.E. monsoon. The only redeeming feature in the view was a foreground of lovely hill, the highlands of Dut'humi, plum-coloured in the distance and at times gilt by a sudden outburst of sunshine. Towards the end of the march, I forged ahead of the caravan, and passing through numerous villages, surrounded by holcus-fields, arrived at a settlement tenanted by Sayf bin Salim, an Arab merchant, who afterwards proved to be a notorious "mauvais sujet." A Harisi from Birkah in Oman, he was a tall thin-featured venerable-looking man, whose old age had been hurried on by his constancy to pombe-beer. A long residence in Unyamwezi had enabled him to incur the hostility of his fellow-merchants, especially one Salim bin Said el Sawwafi, who, with other Arabs, persuaded Mpagamo, an African chief, to seize upon Sayf, and after tying him up in full view of the plundering and burning of his store-house, to drive him out of the country. Retreating to Dut'humi, he had again collected a small stock in trade, especially of slaves, whom he chained and treated so severely that all men predicted for him an evil end. "Msopora," as he was waggishly nicknamed by the Wanyamwezi, instantly began to backbite Said bin Salim, whom he pronounced utterly unfit to manage our affairs; I silenced him by falling asleep upon a cartel placed under the cool eaves of a hut. Presently staggered in my companion almost too ill to speak; over-fatigue had prostrated his strength. By slow degrees, and hardly able to walk, appeared the Arab, the Baloch, the slaves and the asses, each and every having been bogged in turn. On this occasion Wazira had acted guide, and used to "bog-trotting," he had preferred the short cut to the cleaner road that rounds the swamps.

At Dut'humi we were detained nearly a week; the malaria had brought on attacks of marsh fever, which in my case lasted about 20 days; the paroxysms were mild compared with the Indian or the Sindhian type, yet, favoured by the atonic state of the constitution, they thoroughly prostrated me. I had during the fever-fit, and often for hours afterwards, a queer conviction of divided identity, never ceasing to be two persons that generally thwarted and opposed each other; the sleepless nights brought with them horrid visions, animals of grisliest form, hag-like women and men with heads protruding from their breasts. My companion suffered even more severely, he had a fainting-fit which strongly resembled a sun-stroke, and which seemed permanently to affect his brain. Said bin Salim was the convalescent of the party; the two Goanese yielded themselves wholly to maladies, brought on mainly by hard eating, and had they not been forced to rise, they would probably never have risen again. Our sufferings were increased by other causes than climate. The riding asses having been given up for loads, we were compelled, when premonitory symptoms suggested rest, to walk, sometimes for many miles in a single heat, through sun and rain, through mud and miasmatic putridities. Even ass-riding caused over-fatigue. It by no means deserves in these lands the reputation of an anile exercise, as it does in Europe. Maitre Aliboron in Africa is stubborn, vicious and guilty of the four mortal sins of the equine race, he shies and stumbles, he rears and runs away: my companion has been thrown as often as twice in two hours. The animals are addicted to fidgetting, plunging and pirouetting when mounted, they hog and buck till they burst their frail girths, they seem to prefer holes and hollows, they rush about pig-like when high winds blow, and they bolt under tree-shade when the sun shines hot. They must be led, or, ever preferring the worst ground, they disdain to follow the path, and when difficulties arise the slave will surely drop the halter, and get out of harm's way. If a pace exceeding two miles an hour be required, a second man must follow and flog each of these perfect slugs during the whole march. The roundness of their flanks, the shortness of their backs, and their want of shoulder, combine to make the meagre Arab packsaddle unsafe for anything but a baboon or a boy, whilst the straightness and the rigidity of their goat-like pasterns render the pace a wearisome, tripping hobble. We had, it is true, Zanzibari riding asses, but the delicate animals soon chafed and presently died; we were then reduced to the Koroma or half-reclaimed beast of Wanyamwezi. The laden asses gave us even more trouble. The slaves would not attend to the girthing and the balancing of parcels – the great secret of donkey-loading – consequently the burdens were thrown at every mud or broken ground: the unwilling Baloch only grumbled, sat down and stared, leaving their Jemadars with Said bin Salim and ourselves to reload. My companion and I brought up the rear by alternate days, and sometimes we did not arrive before the afternoon at the camping ground. The ropes and cords intended to secure the herd were regularly stolen, that I might be forced to buy others: the animals were never pounded for the night, and during our illness none of the party took the trouble to number them. Thus several beasts were lost, and the grounding of the Expedition appeared imminent and permanent. The result was a sensation of wretchedness, hard to describe; every morning dawned upon me with a fresh load of cares and troubles, and every evening reminded me as it closed in, that another and a miserable morrow was to dawn. But "in despair," as the Arabs say, "are many hopes;" though sorrow endured for the night – and many were "white" with anxiety – we never relinquished the determination to risk everything, ourselves included, rather than to return unsuccessful.

Dut'humi, one of the most fertile districts in K'hutu, is a plain of black earth and sand, choked with vegetation where not corrected by the axe. It is watered by the perennial stream of the same name, which, rising in the islands, adds its quotum to the waters of the Mgazi, and eventually to the Mgeta and the Kingani Rivers. In such places artificial irrigation is common, the element being distributed over the fields by hollow ridges. The mountains of Dut'humi form the northern boundary of the plain. They appear to rise abruptly, but they throw off southerly lower eminences, which diminish in elevation till confounded with the almost horizontal surface of the champaign; the jagged broken crests and peaks argue a primitive formation. Their lay is to the N.N.W.; after four days' journey, according to the guides, they inosculate with the main chain of the Usagara Mountains, and they are probably the southern buttress of Gnu, or Nauru, the hill region westward of Saadani. This chain is said to send forth the Kingani River, which, gushing from a cave or fissure in the eastern, is swollen to a large perennial stream by feeders from the southern slopes, whilst the Mgeta flows from the western face of the water-parting, and circles the southern base. The cold temperature of these cloud-capped and rainy crags, which never expose their outlines except in the clearest weather, affects the plains; by day bleak north-east and north-west gusts pour down upon the sun-parched Dut'humi, and at night the thermometer will sink to 70°, and even to 65° F. Water is supposed to freeze upon the highlands, yet they are not unhealthy; sheep, goats, and poultry abound; betel-pepper grows there, according to the Arabs, and, as in the lowlands, holcus and sesamum, manioc and sweet-potatoes (*Convolvulus batata*), cucumbers, the turai (*Luffa acutangula*), and beans, plantains, and sugarcane, are plentiful. The thick jungle at the base of the hills shelters the elephant, the rhinoceros in considerable numbers, the gnu, and the koodoo, which, however, can rarely be found when the grass is high; a variety of the ngole – a small Dendraspis – haunts the patriarchs of the forest, and the chirrup of the mongoose, which the people enjoy, as Europeans do the monotonous note of the cricket, is heard in the brakes at eventide. This part of the country, about six hours' march northward from Dut'humi, is called the Inland Magogoni; and it is traversed by the "Mdimu" nullah, which falls into the Mgeta River. The fertile valleys in the lower and southern folds are inhabited by the Wakumbaku (?),[6] and by the Wasuop'hanga tribes; the higher elevations, which apparently range from 3000 to 4000 feet, by the Waruguru. They are compelled to fortify themselves against the cold and the villanous races around them. The plague of the land is now one Kisabengo, a Mzegura of low origin, who, after conquering Ukami, a district extending from the eastern flank of the Dut'humi hills seawards, from its Moslem diwan, Ngozi, alias Kingaru, has raised himself to the rank of a Shene Khambi, or principal headman. Aided by the kidnapping Moslem coast clans of Whinde, a small coast town opposite the island of Zanzibar, and his fellow tribemen of Uzegura, he has transferred by his frequent commandos almost all the people of Ukami, chiefly Wasuop'hanga and Waruguru, to the slave-market of Zanzibar, and, thus compelled to push his depredations further west, he has laid waste

---

6.   This unsatisfactory figure of print will often occur in these pages. Ignorance, error, and causeless falsehood, together with the grossest exaggeration, deter the traveller from committing himself to any assertion which he has not proved to his own satisfaction.

the lands even beyond the Mukondokwa river-valley. The hill tribes, however, still receive strangers hospitably into their villages. They have a place visited even by distant Wazaramo pilgrims. It is described as a cave where a P'hepo or the disembodied spirit of a man, in fact a ghost, produces a terrible subterraneous sound, called by the people Kurero or Bokero; it arises probably from the flow of water underground. In a pool in the cave women bathe for the blessing of issue, and men sacrifice sheep and goats to obtain fruitful seasons and success in war. These hill-races speak peculiar dialects, which, according to the guides, are closely connected with Kik'hutu.

Despite the bad name of Dut'humi as regards climate, Arabs sometimes reside there for some months for the purpose of purchasing slaves cheaply and to repair their broken fortunes for a fresh trip to the interior. This keeps up a perpetual feud amongst the chiefs of the country, and scarcely a month passes without fields being laid waste, villages burnt down, and the unhappy cultivators being carried off to be sold.

At Dut'humi a little expedition was sent against Manda, a petty chief, who, despite the presence of the Sayyid's troops, had plundered a village and had kidnapped five of the subjects of Mgota, his weaker neighbour. I had the satisfaction of restoring the stolen wretches to their hearths and homes, and two decrepid old women that had been rescued from slavery thanked me with tears of joy.

This easy good deed done, I was able, though with swimming head and trembling hands, to prepare accounts and a brief report of proceedings for the Royal Geographical Society. These, together with other papers, especially an urgent request for medical comforts and drugs, especially quinine and narcotics, addressed to Lieut.-Colonel Hamerton, or, in case of accidents, to M. Cochet, Consul de France, were entrusted to Jemadar Yaruk, whom, moreover, I took the liberty of recommending to the prince for the then vacant command of the Bagamoyo garrison. The escort from Kaole, reduced in number by three desertions, was dismissed. All the volunteers had been clamouring to return, and I could no longer afford to keep them. Besides the two supplies of cloth, wire, and beads, which preceded, and which were left to follow us, I had been provided by Ladha Damha with a stock of white and blue cottons, some handsome articles of dress, 20,000 strings of white and black, pink, blue, and green, red and brown porcelain-beads, needles, and other articles of hardware, to defray transit-charges through Uzarama. This provision, valued at 295 dollars, should have carried us to the end of the third month; it lasted about three weeks. Said bin Salim, to whom it had been entrusted, had been generous, through fear, to every half-naked barbarian that chose to stretch forth the hand of beggary; moreover, whilst too ill to superintend disbursements, he had allowed his "children," aided by the Baloch and the "sons of Ramji," to "loot" whatever they could seize and secrete. Ladha Damha, unable to complete our carriage, had hit upon the notable device of converting eighteen pieces of American domestics into saddle-cloths for the asses: the stuff was used at halts as bedding by the Baloch and others; and, – a proof that much had fallen into wrong hands, – the thirteen men composing our permanent guard, increased the number of their laden asses from two to five; moreover, for many weeks afterwards, the "sons of Ramji" could afford to expend four to five cloths upon a goat. On the 21st July the escort from Kaole departed with a general discharge of matchlocks. Their disappearance was hailed as a blessing; they had pestered me for rations, and had begged for asses till midnight. They were the refuse of their service; they thought of, they dreamed of, nothing but food; they would do no work; they were continually attempting violence upon the timid Wak'hutu, and they seemed resolved to make the name of Baloch equally hateful and contemptible.

I had been careful to bring from Zanzibar four hammocks, which, slung to poles, formed the conveyance, called by the

Indians "manchil;" by the Portuguese "manchila;" and in West Africa "tipoia." Sayf bin Salim agreed for the sum of ten dollars to hire his slaves as porters for ourselves and our outfit. On the 24th July, feeling strong enough to advance, we passed out of the cultivation of Dut'humi. Crossing a steep and muddy bed, knee-deep even in the dry season, we entered fields under the outlying hillocks of the highlands. These low cones, like similar formations in India, are not inhabited; they are even more malarious than the plains, the surface is rocky, and the woodage, not ceasing as in higher elevations, extends from base to summit. Beyond the cultivation the route plunges into a jungle, where the European traveller realises every preconceived idea of Africa's aspect, at once hideous and grotesque. The general appearance is a mingling of bush and forest, which, contracting the horizon to a few yards, is equally monotonous to the eye and palling to the imagination. The black greasy ground, veiled with thick shrubbery, supports in the more open spaces screens of tiger and spear-grass, twelve and thirteen feet high, with every blade a finger's breadth; and the towering trees are often clothed from root to twig with huge epiphytes, forming heavy columns of densest verdure, and clustering upon the tops in the semblance of enormous bird's nests. The foot-paths, in places "dead," – as the natives say, – with encroaching bush, are crossed by llianas, creepers and climbers, thick as coir-cables, some connecting the trees in a curved line, others stretched straight down the trunks, others winding in all directions around their supports, frequently crossing one another like network and stunting the growth of even the vivacious calabash, by coils like rope tightly encircling its neck. The earth, ever rain-drenched, emits the odour of sulphuretted hydrogen, and in some parts the traveller might fancy a corpse to be hidden behind every bush. To this sad picture of miasma the firmament is a fitting frame: a wild sky, whose heavy purple nimbi, chased by raffales and chilling gusts, dissolve in large-dropped showers; or a dull, dark grey expanse, which lies like a pall over the world. In the finer weather the atmosphere is pale and sickly; its mists and vapours seem to concentrate the rays of the oppressive "rain-sun." The sensation experienced at once explains the apathy and indolence, the physical debility, and the mental prostration, that are the gifts of climates which moist heat and damp cold render equally unsalubrious and uncomfortable. That no feature of miasma might be wanting to complete the picture, filthy heaps of the rudest hovels, built in holes in the jungle, sheltered their few miserable inhabitants, whose frames are lean with constant intoxication, and whose limbs, distorted by ulcerous sores, attest the hostility of Nature to mankind. Such a revolting scene is East Africa from central K'hutu to the base of the Usagara Mountains.

Running through this fetid flat the path passed on the left sundry shallow salt-pits which, according to the Arabs, are wet during the dry and dry during the wet season. Presently after breaking through another fence of holcus, whose cane was stiffer than the rattans of an Indian jungle, we entered, and found lodgings in Bakera, a pretty little hamlet ringed with papaws and plantains, upon which the doves disported themselves. Here, on our return in 1859, a thick growth of grass waved over the ground-marks of hearth and roof-tree. The African has a superstitious horror of stone walls; he is still a semi-nomade, from the effects of the Wandertrieb, or man's vagabond instinct, uncurbed by the habits of civilisation. Though vestiges of large and stable habitations have been discovered in the barbarous Eastern Horn, in these days, between the parallels of Harar and the ruined Portuguese towns near the Zambezi Rivers, inner Africa ignores a town of masonry. In our theoretical maps, the circlets used by cartographers to denote cities serve only to mislead; their names prove them to be Saltanats – lordships, districts or provinces.

Resuming our course on the next day through hollows and rice-swamps, where almost every ass fell or cast its load, we came after a long tramp to the nearest outposts of the Zungomero district; here were several caravans with pitched tents, piles of ivory and crowds of porters. The gang of thirty-six Wanyamwezi, who had preceded us, having located themselves at a distant hamlet, we resumed our march, and presently were met by a number of our men headed by their guard, the two "sons of Ramji." Ensued a general sword and spear play, each man with howls and cheers brandished his blade or vibrated his missile, rushing about in all directions, and dealing death amongst ideal foes with such action as may often be observed in poultry-yards when the hens indulge in a little merry pugnacity. The march had occupied us four weeks, about double the usual time, and the porters had naturally began to suspect accidents from the Wazaramo.

Zungomero, the head of the great river-valley, is a plain of black earth and sand, prodigiously fertile. It is enclosed on all sides except the eastern, or the line of drainage; northwards rise the peaks of Dut'humi; westwards lie the little Wigo hills and the other spurs of Usagara, uncultivated and uninhabited, though the country is populous up to their feet; and southwards are detached cones of similar formation, steep, rocky, and densely wooded. The sea-breeze is here strong, but beyond its influence the atmosphere is sultry and oppressive; owing to maritime influences the kosi, or southwest wind, sometimes continues till the end of July. The normal day, which varies little throughout the year, begins with the light milky mist which forms the cloud-ring; by degrees nimbi and cumuli come up from the east, investing the heights of Dut'humi, and, when showers are imminent, a heavy line of stratus bisects the highlands and overlies the surface of the plain. At the epochs of the lunar change rain falls once or twice during the day and night, and, when the clouds burst, a fiery sun sucks up poison from the earth's putridity. The early nights are oppressive, and towards the dawn condensation causes a copious deposit of heavy dew, which even the people of the country dread. A prolonged halt causes general sickness amongst the porters and slaves of a caravan. The humidity of the atmosphere corrodes everything with which it comes in contact; the springs of powder-flasks exposed to the damp snap like toasted quills; clothes feel limp and damp; paper, becoming soft and soppy by the loss of glazing, acts as a blotter; boots, books, and botanical collections are blackened; metals are ever rusty; the best percussion caps, though labelled waterproof, will not detonate unless carefully stowed away in waxed cloth and tin boxes; gunpowder, if not kept from the air, refuses to ignite; and wood becomes covered with mildew. We had an abundance of common German phosphor-matches, and the best English wax lucifers; both, however, became equally unserviceable, the heads shrank and sprang off at the least touch, and the boxes frequently became a mere mass of paste. To future travellers I should recommend the "good old plan;" a bit of phosphorus in a little phial half full of olive oil, which serves for light as well as ignition. When accompanied by matchlock-men, however, there is no difficulty about fire; their pouches always contain a steel and flint, and a store of cotton, or of the wild Bombex, dipped in saltpetre or gunpowder solution.

Yet Zungomero is the great Bandari or centre of traffic in the eastern, as are Unyanyembe and Ujiji in the middle and the western regions. Lying upon the main trunk-road, it must be traversed by the up and down-caravans, and, during the travelling season, between June and April, large bodies of some thousand men pass through it every week. Kilwa formerly sent caravans to it, and the Wanyamwezi porters have frequently made that port by the "Mwera road." The Arab merchants usually pitch tents, preferring them to the leaky native huts, full of hens and pigeons, rats and mice, snakes and lizards, crickets and cockroaches, gnats and flies, and spiders of hideous appearance, where the inmates are often routed by swarms of bees, and are ever in imminent danger of fires. The armed slaves accompanying the caravan seize the best huts, which they either monopolise or share with the hapless inmates, and the porters stow themselves away under the projecting eaves of the habitations. The main attraction of the place is the plenty of provisions. Grain is so abundant that the inhabitants exist almost entirely upon the intoxicating pombe, or holcus-beer, – a practice readily imitated by their visitors. Bhang and the datura plant, growing wild, add to the attractions of the spot. The Bhang is a fine large species of the Cannabis Indica, the bang of Persia, the bhang of India, and the benj of Arabia, the fasukh of northern, and the dakha of southern Africa. In the low lands of East Africa it grows before every cottage door. As in hot climates generally, the fibre degenerates, and the plant is only valued for its narcotic properties. The Arabs smoke the sun-dried leaf with, and the Africans without tobacco, in huge waterpipes, whose bowls contain a quarter of a pound. Both ignore the more luxurious preparations, momiya and hashish, ganja and sebzi, charas and maajun. Like the "jangli" or jungle (wild)-bhang of Sindh, affected by kalandars, fakirs, and other holy beggars, this variety, contracting the muscle of the throat, produces a violent whooping-cough, ending in a kind of scream, after a few long puffs, when the smoke is inhaled; and if one man sets the example the others are sure to follow. These grotesque sounds are probably not wholly natural; even the boys may be heard practising them; they appear to be a fashion of "renowning it"; in fact, an announcement to the public that the fast youths are smoking bhang. The Datura stramonium, called by the Arabs and by the Wasawahili "muranha," grows in the well-watered plains; it bears a large whitish flower and a thorn-apple, like that of India. The heathen, as well as their visitors, dry the leaves, the flowers, and the rind of the rootlet, which is considered the strongest preparation, and smoke them in a common bowl or in a water-pipe. This is held to be a sovereign remedy against zik el nafas (asthma) and influenza; it diminishes the cough by loosening the phlegm. The Washenzi never make that horrible use of the plant known to the Indian dhaturiya, or datura-poisoners: many accidents, however, occur from ignorance of its violent narcotism. Meat is scarce: the only cattle are those driven down by the Wanyamwezi to the coast; milk, butter, and ghee are consequently unprocurable. A sheep or a goat will not cost less than a shukkah, or four cubits of domestics, here worth twenty-five cents. The same will purchase only two fowls; and eggs and fruit – chiefly papaws and plantains, cocos and limes – are at fancy prices. For the shukkah eight rations of unhusked holcus, four measures of rice – which must here be laid in by those travelling up-country – and five cakes of tobacco, equal to about three pounds, are generally procurable. Thus the daily expenditure of a large caravan ranges from one dollar to one dollar fifty cents' worth of cloth in the Zanzibar market. The value, however, fluctuates greatly, and the people will shirk selling even at any price.

The same attractions which draw caravans to Zungomero render it the great rendezvous of an army of touters, who, whilst watching for the arrival of the ivory traders, amuse themselves with plundering the country. The plague has now spread like a flight of locusts over the land. The Wak'hutu, a timid race, who, unlike the Wazaramo, have no sultan to gather round, are being gradually ousted from their ancient seats. In a large village there will seldom be more than three or four families, who occupy the most miserable hovels, all the best having been seized by the touters or pulled down for firewood. These men – slaves, escaped criminals, and freemen of broken fortunes, flying from misery, punishment, or death on the coast – are armed with muskets and sabres, bows and spears, daggers and knobsticks. They carry ammunition, and thus are too strong for the country people. When rough language and threats fail, the levelled barrel at once establishes the right to a man's house and property, to his wife and children. If money runs short, a village is fired by night, and the people are sold off to the first caravan. In some parts the pattering of musketry is incessant, as it ever was in the turbulent states of Independent India. It is rarely necessary to have recourse to violence, the Wak'hutu, believing their tyrants to be emissaries, as they represent themselves, from His Highness the Sultan, and the chief nobles of Zanzibar, offer none but the most passive resistance, hiding their families and herds in the bush. Thus it happens that towards the end of the year nothing but a little grain can be purchased in a land of marvellous fertility.

As has been mentioned, these malpractices are severely reprobated by His Highness the Sultan, and when the evil passes a certain point remedial measures are taken. A Banyan, for instance, is sent to the coast with warnings to the Diwans concerned. But what care they for his empty words, when they know that he has probably equipped a similar party of black buccaneers himself? and what hope can there be of reform when there is not an honest man in the country to carry it out? Thus the Government of Zanzibar is rendered powerless; – improvement can be expected only from the hand of Time. The Wak'hutu, indeed, often threaten a deputation to entreat the Arab Sultan for protection in the shape of a garrison of Baloch. This measure has been retarded for sound reasons: no man dares to leave his house for fear of finding it a ruin on his return; moreover, he would certainly be shot if the touters guessed his intention, and, even if he escaped this danger, he would probably be sold, on the way to the coast, by his truculent neighbours the Wazaramo. Finally, if they succeeded in their wishes, would not a Baloch garrison act the part of the man who, in the fable, was called in to assist the horse against the stag? The Arabs, who know the temper of these mercenaries, are too wise ever to sanction such a "dragonnade."

The reader will readily perceive that he is upon the slave-path, so different from travel amongst the free and independent tribes of Southern Africa. The traffic practically annihilates every better feeling of human nature. Yet, though the state of the Wak'hutu appears pitiable, the traveller cannot practise pity: he is ever in the dilemma of maltreating or being maltreated. Were he to deal civilly and liberally with this people he would starve: it is vain to offer a price for even the necessaries of life; it would certainly be refused because more is wanted, and so on beyond the bounds of possibility. Thus, if the touter did not seize a house, he would never be allowed to take shelter in it from the storm; if he did not enforce a "corvee," he must labour beyond his strength with his own hands; and if he did not fire a village and sell the villagers, he might die of hunger in the midst of plenty. Such in this province are the action and reaction of the evil.

Chapter 4

ON THE GEOGRAPHY AND ETHNOLOGY OF THE FIRST REGION

Before bidding adieu to the Maritime Region, it will be expedient to enter into a few details concerning its geography and ethnology.[7]

The first or maritime region extends from the shores of the Indian Ocean in E. long. 39° to the mountain-chain forming the land of Usagara in E. long. 37° 28'; its breadth is therefore 92 geographical miles, measured in rectilinear distance, and its mean length, bounded by the waters of the Kingani and the Rufji rivers, may be assumed at 110. The average rise is under 4 feet per mile. It is divided into two basins; that of the Kingani easterly, and westward that of the Mgeta stream with its many tributaries; the former, which is the principal, is called the land of Uzaramo; the latter, which is of the second order, contains the provinces of K'hutu, by the Arabs pronounced Kutu, and Uziraha, a minor district. The natives of the country divide it into the three lowlands of Tunda, Dut'humi, and Zungomero.

The present road runs with few and unimportant deviations along the whole length of the fluviatile valleys of the Kingani and the Mgeta. Native caravans if lightly laden generally accomplish the march in a fortnight, one halt included. On both sides of this line, whose greatest height above the

---

7.   Those who consider the subject worthy of further consideration are referred, for an ampler account of it, to the Journal of the R. Geographical Society, vol. xxix. of 1860.

sea-level was found by B. P. therm, to be 330 feet, rises the rolling ground, which is the general character of the country. Its undulations present no eminences worthy of notice; near the sea they are short and steep, further inland they roll in longer waves, and everywhere they are covered with abundant and luxuriant vegetation, the result of decomposition upon the richest soil. In parts there is an appearance of park land; bushless and scattered forests, with grass rising almost to the lower branches of the smaller thorns; here and there clumps and patches of impassable shrubbery cluster round knots and knolls of majestic and thickly foliaged trees. The narrow footpaths connecting the villages often plunge into dark and dense tunnels formed by overarching branch and bough, which delay the file of laden porters; the mud lingering long after a fall of rain in these low grounds fills them with a chilly clammy atmosphere. Merchants traverse such spots with trembling: in these, the proper places for ambuscade, a few determined men easily plunder a caravan by opposing it in front or by an attack in rear. The ways are often intersected by deep nullahs and water-courses, dry during the hot season, but unfordable when rain falls. In the many clearings, tobacco, maize, holcus, sesamum, and groundnuts, manioc, beans, pulse, and sweet potatoes flourish; the pine-apple is a weed, and a few cocos and mangoes, papaws, jack-fruit, plantains, and limes are scattered over the districts near the sea. Rice grows abundantly in the lower levels. The villages are hidden deep in the bush or grass: the crowing of the cocks heard all along the road, except in the greater stretches of wilderness, proves them to be numerous; they are, however, small and thinly populated. The versant, as usual in maritime E. Africa, trends towards the Indian Ocean. Water abounds even at a distance from the rivers; it springs from the soil in diminutive runnels and lies in "shimo" or pits, varying from surface-depth to 10 feet. The monsoon-rains, which are heavy, commence in March, about a month earlier than in Zanzibar, and the duration is similar. The climate of the higher lands is somewhat superior to that of the valley, but it is still hot and oppressive. The formation, after passing from the corallines, the limestones, the calcareous tufts, and the rude gravelly conglomerates of the coast, is purely primitive and sandstone: erratic blocks of fine black hornblende and hornblendic rock, used by the people as whetstones and grinding-slabs, abound in the river-beds, which also supply the clay used for pottery. The subsoil is near the sea a stiff blue loam, in the interior ruddy quartzose gravel; the soil is a rich brown or black humus, here and there coated with, or varied by, clean white sand, and in some parts are seams of reddish loam. Fresh-water shells are scattered over the surface, and land-crabs burrow in the looser earths where stone seldom appears. Black cattle are unknown in the maritime region, but poultry, sheep, and goats are plentiful: near the jungle they are protected from the leopards or ounces by large wooden huts, like cages, raised on piles for cleanliness.

As a rule, the fluviatile valleys resemble in most points the physical features of the coast and island of Zanzibar: the general aspect of the country, however u the expression of its climate – undergoes some modifications. Near the sea, the basin is a broad winding line, traversed by the serpentine river, whose bed is now too deep for change. About the middle expanse stony ridges and rocky hills crop out from the rolling ground, and the head of the valley is a low continuous plain. In many places, especially near the estuary, river-terraces, like road embankments, here converging, there diverging, indicate by lines and strews of water-worn pebbles and sea-shells the secular uprise of the country and the declension of the stream to its present level. These raised seabeaches at a distance appear crowned with dwarf rounded cones which, overgrown with lofty trees, are favourite sites for settlements. In the lower lands the jungle and the cultivation are of the rankest and most gigantic description, the effect of a damp, hot region, where atmospheric pressure is excessive. The grass, especially that produced by the black soils in the swamps and marshes, rises to the height of 12-13 feet, and serves to conceal runaway slaves and malefactors: the stalks vary in thickness from a goose-quill to a man's finger. The larger growths, which are so closely planted that they conceal the soil, cannot be traversed without paths, and even where these exist the traveller must fight his way through a dense screen, receiving from time to time a severe blow when the reeds recoil, or a painful thrust from some broken and inclined stump. Even the horny sole of the sandal-less African cannot tread these places without being cut or staked, and everywhere a ride through these grass-avenues whilst still dripping with the cold exhalations of night, with the sun beating fiercely upon the upper part of the body, is a severe infliction to any man not in perfect health. The beds of streams and nullahs are sometimes veiled by the growth of the banks. These crops spring up with the rains, and are burned down by hunters, or more frequently by accident, after about a month of dry weather; in the interim fires are dangerous: the custom is to beat down the blaze with leafy boughs. Such is the variety of species that in some parts of the river-valleys each day introduces the traveller to a grass before unseen. Where the inundations lie long, the trees are rare, and those that exist are slightly raised by mounds above the ground to escape the destructive effects of protracted submergence: in these places the decomposed vegetation exhales a fetid odour. Where the waters soon subside there are clumps of tall shrubbery and seams of forest rising on extensive meadows of grassy land, which give it the semblance of a suite of natural parks or pleasure-grounds, and the effect is not diminished by the frequent herds of gnu and antelope prancing and pacing over their pastures.

The climate is hot and oppressive, and the daily sea-breeze, which extends to the head of the Mgeta valley, is lost in the lower levels. About Zungomero rain is constant, except for a single fortnight in the month of January; it seems to the stranger as if the crops must infallibly decay, but they do not.

At most times the sun, even at its greatest northern declination, shines through a veil of mist with a sickly blaze and a blistering heat, and the overcharge of electricity is evidenced by frequent and violent thunder-storms. In the western parts cold and cutting breezes descend from the rugged crags of Dut'humi.

The principal diseases of the valley are severe ulcerations and fevers, generally of a tertian type. The "Mkunguru" begins with coldness in the toes and finger-tips; a frigid shiver seems to creep up the legs, followed by pains in the shoulders, severe frontal headache, hot eyes, and a prostration and irritability of mind and body. This preliminary lasts for one to three hours, when nausea ushers in the hot stage: the head burns, the action of the heart becomes violent, thirst rages, and a painful weight presses upon the eyeballs: it is often accompanied by a violent cough and irritation. Strange visions, as in delirium, appear to the patient, and the excitement of the brain is proved by unusual loquacity. When the fit passes off with copious perspiration the head is often affected, the ears buzz, and the limbs are weak. If the patient attempts to rise suddenly, he feels a dizziness, produced apparently by a gush of bile along the liver duct: want of appetite, sleeplessness and despondency, and a low fever, evidenced by hot pulses, throbbing temples, and feet painfully swollen, with eruptions of various kinds, and ulcerated mouth, usher in the cure. This fever yields easily to mild remedies, but it is capable of lasting three weeks.

A multitude of roads, whose point of departure is the coast, form a triangle and converge at the "Makutaniro," or junction-place, in Central Uzaramo. The route whose several stations have been described is one of the main lines running from Kaole and Bagamoyo, in a general southwest direction, till it falls into the great trunk road which leads directly west from Mbuamaji. It is divided into thirteen caravan stages, but a well-girt walker will accomplish the distance in a week.

No apology is offered for the lengthiness of the ethnographical descriptions contained in the following pages. The ethnology of Africa is indeed its most interesting, if not its only interesting feature. Everything connected with the habits and customs, the moral and religious, the social and commercial state of these new races, is worthy of diligent observation, careful description, and minute illustration. There is indeed little in the physical features of this portion of the great peninsula to excite the attention of the reader beyond the satisfaction that ever accompanies the victory of truth over fable, and a certain importance which in these "travelling times," – when man appears rapidly rising to the rank of a migratory animal, – must attach to discovery. The subject, indeed, mostly banishes ornament. Lying under the same parallels with a climate whose thermical variations know no extremes, the succession of alluvial valley, ghaut, table-land, and shelving plain is necessarily monotonous, the soil is the same, the productions are similar, and the rocks and trees resemble one another. Eastern and central inter-tropical Africa also lacks antiquarian and historic interest, it has few traditions, no annals, and no ruins, the hoary remnants of past splendour so dear to the traveller and to the reader of travels. It contains not a single useful or ornamental work, a canal or a dam is, and has ever been, beyond the narrow bounds of its civilisation. It wants even the scenes of barbaric pomp and savage grandeur with which the student of occidental Africa is familiar. But its ethnography has novelties: it exposes strange manners and customs, its Fetichism is in itself a wonder, its commerce deserves attention, and its social state is full of mournful interest. The fastidiousness of the age, however, forbidding ampler details, even under the veil of the "learned languages," cripples the physiologist, and robs the subject of its principal peculiarities. I have often regretted that if Greek and dog-Latin be no longer a sufficient disguise for the facts of natural history, human and bestial, the learned have not favoured us with a system of symbols which might do away with the grossness of words.

The present tenants of the First Region are the Wazaramo, the Wak'hutu, and their great sub-tribe, the Waziraha; these form the staple of population, – the Wadoe and the Wazegura being minor and immigrant tribes.

The Wazaramo are no exception to the rule of barbarian maritime races: they have, like the Somal, the Gallas, the Wangindo, the Wamakua, and the Cape Kafirs, come into contact with a civilisation sufficiently powerful to corrupt without subjugating them; and though cultivators of the ground, they are more dreaded by caravans than any tribe from the coast to the Lake Region. They are bounded eastward by the thin line of Moslems in the maritime regions, westward by the Wak'hutu, northward by the Kingani River, and on the south by the tribes of the Rufiji. The Wazaramo, or, as they often pronounce their own name, Wazalamo, claim connection with the semi-nomade Wakamba, who have, within the last few years, migrated to the north-west of Mombasah. Their dialect, however, proves them to be congeners of the Wak'hutu, and distinct from the Wakamba. As in East Africa generally, it is impossible to form the remotest idea of the number of families, or of the total of population. The Wazaramo number many sub-tribes, the principal of which are the Wakamba and the Wap'hangara.

These negroids are able-bodied men, tall and straight, compared with the Coast-clans, but they are inferior in development to most of the inner tribes. The complexion, as usual, varies greatly. The chiefs are often coal-black, and but few are of light colour. This arises from the country being a slave-importer rather than exporter; and here, as among the Arabs, black skins are greatly preferred. The Mzaramo never circumcises, except when becoming a "Mhaji," or Moslem convert; nor does this tribe generally tattoo, though some adorn the face with three long cicatrized cuts, like the Mashali of Mecca, extending down each cheek from the ear-lobes to the corners of the mouth. Their distinctive mark is the peculiarity of dressing their hair. The thick wool is plastered over with a cap-like coating of ochreish and micaceous clay, brought from the hills, and mixed to the consistency of honey with the oil of the sesamum or the castor-bean. The pomatum, before drying, is pulled out with the fingers to the ends of many little twists, which circle the head horizontally, and the mass is separated into a single or a double line of knobs, the upper being above, and the lower below, the ears, both look stiff and matted, as if affected with a bad plica polonica. The contrast between these garlands of small red dilberries and the glossy black skin is, however, effective. The clay, when dry, is washed out with great trouble by means of warm water – soap has yet to be invented – and by persevering combing with the fingers. Women wear the hair-thatch like men; there are, however, several styles. It is usually parted in the centre, from the crinal front-line to the nape of the neck, and allowed to grow in a single or double dense thatch, ridging the head breadthwise from ear to ear: this is coloured or not coloured, according to the wearer's taste. Some of the Wazaramo, again, train lumps of their wool to rise above the region of cautiousness, and very exactly simulate bears' ears. The face is usually lozenge-shaped, the eyes are somewhat oblique, the nose is flat and patulated, the lips tumid and everted, the jaw prognathous, and the beard, except in a few individuals, is scanty. The sebaceous odour of the skin amongst all these races is overpowering: emitted with the greatest effect during and after excitement either of mind or body, it connects the negroid with the negro and separates him from the Somal, the Galla, and the Malagash. The expression of countenance is wild and staring, the features are coarse and harsh, the gait is loose and lounging; the Arab strut and the Indian swagger are unknown in East Africa. The Wazaramo tribe is rich in albinos; three were seen by the Expedition in the course of a single day. They much resemble Europeans of the leucous complexion; the face is quite bald; the skin is rough, and easily wrinkles in long lines, marked by a deeper pink; the hair is short, sharp-curling, and coloured like a silk-worm's cocoon, and the lips are red. The eyes have grey pupils and rosy "whites:" they appear very sensitive to light, and are puckered up so as to distort the countenance. The features are unusually plain, and the stature appears to range below the average. The people who have no prejudice against them, call these leuccethiops Wazungu, "white men."

The Wazaramo tribe is wealthy enough to dress well: almost every man can afford a shukkah or loin-cloth of unbleached cotton, which he stains a dirty yellow, like the Indian gerua, with a clay dug in the subsoil. Their ornaments are extensive girdles and bead necklaces of various colours, white disks, made from the base of a sea-shell, and worn single on the forehead or in pairs at the neck. A massy ring of brass or zinc encircles the wrist. The decoration peculiar to the tribe, and common to both sexes, is the mgoweko, a tight collar or cravat, 1 to 1.50 inches broad, of red and yellow, white and black beads, with cross-bars of different colours at short intervals. Men never appear in public without an ostentatious display of arms. The usual weapons, when they cannot procure muskets, are spears, bows, and arrows, the latter poisoned, and sime, or long knives like the Somali daggers, made by themselves with imported iron. The chiefs are generally seen in handsome attire; embroidered Surat caps bound with a tight snowy turban of a true African shape, which contrasts well with black skins and the short double peaked beards below. The body-garment is a loin-cloth of showy Indian cotton or Arab check; some prefer the long shirt and the kizbao or waistcoat affected by the slaves at Zanzibar. The women are well dressed as the men, a circumstance rare in East Africa. Many of them have the tibia bowed in front by bearing heavy water-pots at too early an age; when not burdened they have a curious mincing gate, they never veil their faces, and they show no shame in the presence of strangers. The child is carried in a cloth at the back.

The habitations of the Wazaramo are far superior in shape and size to those of K'hutu, and, indeed, to any on this side of Unyamwezi. Their buildings generally resemble the humbler sort of English cow-house, or an Anglo-Indian bungalow. In poorer houses the outer walls are of holcus canes, rudely puddled; the better description are built of long and broad sheets of Myombo and Mkora bark, propped against strong uprights inside, and bound horizontally by split bamboos tied outside with fibrous cord. The heavy pent-shaped roof often provided with a double thatch of grass and reeds, projects eaves, which are high enough to admit a man without stooping; these are supported by a long cross bar resting on perpendiculars, tree-trunks, barked and smoothed, forked above, and firmly planted in the ground. Along the outer marginal length of this verandah lies a border of large logs polished by long sittings. The interior is dark and windowless, and party-walls of stiff grass-cane divide it into several compartments. The list of furniture comprises a dwarf cartel about 4 feet long by 16 inches broad, upon which even the married couple manages to make itself comfortable; a stool cut out of a single block, a huge wooden mortar, mtungi or black earthen pots, gourds, ladles of cocoa-nut, cast-off clothes, whetstones, weapons, nets, and in some places creels for fishing. Grain is ground upon an inclined slab of fine-grained granite or syenite, sometimes loose, at other times fixed in the ground with a mud plaster; the classical Eastern handmill is unknown in this part of Africa. The inner roof and its rafters, shining with a greasy soot, in wet weather admit drenching lines of leakage, and the only artifice applied to the flooring is the tread of the proprietors. The door is a close hurdle of parallel holcus-straw bound to five or six cross-bars with strips of bark. In a village there will be from four to twelve "bungalows;" the rest are the normal haycock and beehive hut of Africa. Where enemies are numerous the settlements are palisaded; each has, moreover, but a single entrance, which is approached by a narrow alley of strong stockade, and is guarded by a thick planking that fits into a doorway large enough to admit cattle.

The Wazaramo are an ill-conditioned, noisy, boisterous violent, and impracticable race. A few years ago they were the principal obstacle to Arab and other travellers entering into East Africa. But the seizure of Kaole and other settlements by the late Sayyid of Zanzibar has now given strangers a footing in the land. After tasting the sweets of gain, they have somewhat relented; but quarrels between them and the caravans are still frequent. The P'hazi, or chief of the district, demands a certain amount of cloth for free passage from all merchants on their way to the interior; from those returning he takes cattle, jembe, or iron hoes: shokah or hatchets, in fact, whatever he can obtain. If not contented, his clansmen lie in ambush and discharge a few poisoned arrows at the trespassers: they never have attempted, like the Wagogo, to annihilate a caravan; in fact, the loss of one of their number causes a general panic. They have hitherto successfully resisted the little armies of touters that have almost desolated K'hutu, and they are frequently in hostilities with the coast settlements. The young men sometimes set out on secret plundering expeditions to Bagamoyo and Mbuamaji, and enter the houses at night by mining under the walls. The burghers attempt to defeat them by burying stones and large logs as a foundation, but in vain: their superior dexterity has originated a superstitious notion that they possess a peculiar "medicine," a magic spell called "Ugumba," which throws the household into a deep trance. When a thief is caught in *flagrante delicto*, his head soon adorns a tall pole at the entrance of the settlement: it is not uncommon to see half a dozen bloody or bleached fragments of humanity collected in a single spot. When disposed to be friendly the Wazaramo will act as porters to Arabs, but if a man die his load is at once confiscated by his relatives, who, however, insist upon receiving his bloodmoney, as if he had been slain in battle. Their behaviour to caravans in their own country depends upon the strangers' strength; many trading bodies therefore unite into one before beginning the transit, and even then they are never without fear.

The Wazaramo chiefs are powerful only when their wealth or personal qualities win the respect of their unruly republican subjects. There are no less than five orders in this hereditary master-class. The P'hazi is the headman of the village, and the Mwene Goha is his principal councillor; under these are three ranks of elders, the Kinyongoni, the Chuma and the Kawambwa. The headman, unless exceptionally influential, must divide amongst his "ministry" the blackmail extorted from travellers. The P'hazi usually fills a small village with his wives and families; he has also large estates, and he personally superintends the labour of his slave-gangs. He cannot sell his subjects except for two offences – Ugoni or adultery, and Uchawe or black magic. The latter crime is usually punished by the stake; in some parts of the country the roadside shows at every few miles a heap or two of ashes with a few calcined and blackened human bones mixed with bits of half-consumed charcoal, telling the tragedy that has been enacted there. The prospect cannot be contemplated without horror; here and there, close to the larger circles where the father and mother have been burnt, a smaller heap shows that some wretched child has shared their terrible fate, lest growing up he should follow in his parents' path. The power of conviction is wholly in the hands of the Mganga or medicine-man, who administers an ordeal called Baga or Kyapo by boiling water. If the hand after being dipped show any sign of lesion, the offence is proven, and the sentence is instantly carried into execution.

Instinctively conscious of their moral wants, the Washenzi throughout this portion of East Africa have organised certain customs which have grown to laws. The first is the Sare or brother oath. Like the "manred" of Scotland, the "munh bola bhai" of India, and similar fraternal institutions amongst most of the ancient tribes of barbarians in whom sociability is a passion, it tends to reconcile separate interests between man and man, to modify the feuds and discords of savage society, and, principally, to strengthen those that need an alliance. In fact, it is a contrivance for choosing relations instead of allowing Nature to force them upon man, and the flimsiness of the tie between brothers born in polygamy has doubtless tended to perpetuate it. The ceremony, which is confined to adults of the male sex, is differently performed in the different tribes. Amongst the Wazaramo, the Wazegura, and the Wasagara, the two "brothers" sit on a hide face to face, with legs outstretched to the front and overlapping one another; their bows and arrows are placed across their thighs, whilst a third person, waving a sword over their heads, vociferates curses against any one that may "break the brotherhood." A sheep is then slaughtered, and its flesh, or more often its heart, is brought roasted to the pair, who, having made with a dagger incisions in each other's breasts close to the pit of the stomach, eat a piece of meat smeared with the blood. Among the Wanyamwezi and the Wajiji the cut is made below the left ribs or above the knee; each man receives in a leaf his brother's blood, which, mixed with oil or butter, he rubs into his own wound. An exchange of small presents generally concludes the rite. It is a strong tie, as all men believe that death or slavery would follow its infraction. The Arabs, to whom the tasting of blood is unlawful, usually perform it by proxy. The slave "Fundi," or fattori, of the caravans become brothers, even with the Washenzi, whenever they expect an opportunity of utilising the relationship.

The second custom is more peculiar. The East African dares not appropriate an article found upon the road, especially if he suspect that it belongs to a fellow tribe-man. He believes that a "Kigambo," an unexpected calamity, slavery or death, would follow the breach of this custom. At Zungomero a watch, belonging to the Expedition, was picked up by the country people in the jungle, and was punctually returned, well wrapped round with grass and leaves. But subsequent experience makes the traveller regret that the superstition is not of a somewhat more catholic and comprehensive character.

The religion of the East African will be treated of in a future page. The Wazaramo like their congeners, are as little troubled with ceremony as with belief. In things spiritual as in things temporal they listen to but one voice, that of "Ada," or custom. The most offensive scoffer or sceptic in Europe is not regarded with more abomination than the man who in these lands would attempt to touch a jot or tittle of Ada.

There are no ceremonies on birth-occasions and no purification of women amongst these people. In the case of abortion or of a still-born child they say, "he hath returned," that is to say, to home in earth. When the mother perishes in childbirth, the parents claim a certain sum from "the man that killed their daughter." Neither on the continent nor at Zanzibar do they bind with cloth the head of the new-born babe. Twins, here called Wapacha, and by the Arabs of Zanzibar, Shukfil are usually sold or exposed in the jungle as amongst the Ibos of West Africa. If the child die, an animal is killed for a general feast, and in some tribes the mother does a kind of penance. Seated outside the village, she is smeared with fat and flour, and exposed to the derision of people who surround her, hooting and mocking with offensive jests and gestures. To guard against this calamity, the Wazaramo and other tribes are in the habit of vowing that the babe shall not be shaved till manhood, and the mother wears a number of talismans, bits of wood tied with a thong of snake's skin, round her neck, and beads of different shapes round her head. When carrying her offspring, which she rarely leaves alone, she bears in her hand what is technically called a kirangozi, a "guide" or "guardian," in the form of two sticks a few inches in length, bound with bands of particoloured beads. This article, made up by the Mganga or medicine man, is placed at night under the child's head, and is carried about till it has passed the first stage of life. The kirangozi is intended to guard the treasure against the malevolent spirits of the dead; that almost universal superstition, the Evil Eye, though an article of faith amongst the Arabs, the Wasawahili, and the Wamrima, is unknown to the inner heathen.

A name is given to the child without other celebration than a debauch with pombe: this will sometimes occur at the birth of a male, when he is wanted. The East Africans, having few national prejudices, are fond of calling their children after Arabs and other strangers: they will even pay a sheep for the loan of a merchant's name. There must be many hundred Sayyid Saids and Sayyid Majids now in the country; and as during the eighteen months' peregrination of the East African Expedition every child born on and near the great trunk-line was called Muzungu – the "white" – the Englishman has also left his mark in the land. The period of ablactation, as in South Africa, is prolonged to the second or third year: may this account, in part, for the healthiness of the young and the almost total absence of debility and deformity? Indeed, the nearest approach to the latter is the unsightly protrusion of the umbilical region, sometimes to the extent of several inches, owing to ignorance of proper treatment; but, though conspicuous in childhood, it disappears after puberty. Women retain the power of suckling their children to a late age, even when they appear withered grandames. Until the child can walk without danger, it is carried by the mother, not on the hip, as in Asia, but on the bare back for warmth, a sheet or skin being passed over it and fastened at the parent's breast. Even in infancy it clings like a young simiad, and the peculiar formation of the African race renders the position easier by providing a kind of seat upon which it subsides; the only part of the body exposed to view is the little coconut head, with the small, round, beady black eyes in a state of everlasting stare. Finally, the "kigogo," or child who cuts the two upper incisors before the lower, is either put to death, or is given away or sold to the slave-merchant, under the impression that it will bring disease, calamity, and death into the household. The

Wasawahili and the Zanzibar Arabs have the same impressions, the former kill the child; the latter, after a Khitmah or perlection of the Koran, make it swear, by nodding its head if unable to articulate, that it will not injure those about it. Even in Europe, it may be remembered, the old prejudice against children born with teeth is not wholly forgotten.

Amongst the Wazaramo there is no limitation to the number of wives, except the expense of wedding and the difficulty of supporting a large establishment. Divorce is signified by presenting to the wife a piece of holcus-cane: if a sensible woman she at once leaves the house, and, if not, she is forced to leave. There is no more romance in the affair even before marriage than in buying a goat. The marriageable youth sends a friend to propose to the father: if the latter consents, his first step is, not to consult his daughter – such a proceeding would be deemed the act of a madman- but to secure for himself as many cloths as possible, from six to twelve, or even more, besides a preliminary present which goes by the name of kiremba (kilemba), his "turban." This, however, is a kind of settlement which is demanded back if the wife die without issue; but if she bear children, it is preserved for them by their grand-parents. After the father the mother puts in her claim in behalf of the daughter; she requires a kondavi, or broad parti-coloured band of beads worn round the waist and next the skin; her mukajya or loin-cloth, and her wereko, or sheet in which the child is borne upon the back. In the interior the settlement is made in live-stock, varying from a few goats to a dozen cows. This weighty point duly determined, the husband leads his wife to his own home, an event celebrated by drumming, dancing, and extensive drunkenness. The children born in wedlock belong to the father.

When a man or a woman is at the point of death, the friends assemble, and the softer sex sometimes sings, howls, and weeps: the departing is allowed to depart life upon the kitanda, or cartel. There is, however, little demonstrative sorrow amongst these people, and, having the utmost dread of disembodied spirits, all are anxious to get rid of the corpse and its appertainings. The Wazaramo, more civilised than their neighbours, bury their dead stretched out and in the dress worn during life: their graves have already been described.

The "industry" of Usaramo will occupy but few sentences. Before the great rains of the year set in the land must be weeded, and scratches must be made with a hoe for the reception of seed. The wet season ushers in the period for copal digging: the proceeds are either sold to travelling traders, or are carried down to the coast in makanda – mat-sacks – of light weight, and are sold to the Banyans. Bargaining and huckstering, cheapening and chaffering, are ever the African's highest intellectual enjoyments, and he does not fail to stretch them to their utmost limits. After the autumnal rains during the Azyab, or the north-east monsoon, the grass is fired, when the men seizing their bows, arrows, and spears, indiscriminately slaughter beast and bird – an operation which, yearly repeated, accounts in part for the scarcity of animal life so remarkable in this animal's paradise. When all trades fail, the Mzaramo repairs to the coast, where, despite his bad name, he usually finds employment as a labourer.

Next in order to the maritime Wazaramo are the Wak'hutu, to whom many of the observations upon the subject of their more powerful neighbours equally apply. Their territory extends from the Mgeta River to the mountains of Usagara, and in breadth from the Dut'humi Highlands to the Rufiji River.

The Wak'hutu are physically and, apparently, mentally a race inferior to the Wazaramo; they are very dark, and bear other marks of a degradation effected by pernicious climatory conditions. They have no peculiar tattoo, although individuals raise complicated patterns in small cicatrices upon their breasts. The popular head-dress is the clay-coating of the Wazaramo, of somewhat modified dimensions; and some of them, who are possibly derived from the Wahiao and other southern clans, have a practice – exceptional in these latitudes – of chipping their incisors to sharp points, which imitate well enough the armature of the reptilia. Their eyes are bleared and red with perpetual intoxication, and they seem to have no amusements but dancing and singing through half the night. None but the wealthier can afford to wear cloth; the substitute is a kilt of the calabash fibre, attached by a cord of the same material to the waist. In women it often narrows to a span, and would be inadequate to the purposes of decency were it not assisted by an underclothing of softened goatskin; this and a square of leather upon the bosom, which, however, is often omitted, compose the dress of the multitude. The ornaments are like those of the Wazaramo, but by no means so numerous. The Wak'hutu live poorly, and, having no ghee, are contented with the oil of the sesamum and the castor-bean with their holcus porridge. The rivers supply them with the usual mud-fish; at times they kill game. Their sheep, goats, and poultry they reserve for barter on the coast; and, though bees swarm throughout the land, and even enter the villages, they will not take the trouble to make hives.

As on the Mrima, the proportion of chiefs to subjects seems to increase in the inverse ratio of what is required. Every district in K'hutu has its P'hazi or headman, with his minister the Mwene Goha, and inferior chiefs, the Chandume, the Muwinge, and the Mbara These men live chiefly upon the produce of their fields, which they sell to caravans; they are too abject and timid to insist upon the blackmail which has caused so many skirmishes in Uzaramo; and the only use that they make of their power is to tyrannise over their villages, and occasionally to organise a little kidnapping. With the aid of slavery and black magic they render their subjects' lives as precarious as they well can: no one, especially in old age, is safe from being burnt at a day's notice. They are civil to strangers, but wholly unable to mediate between them and the tribe. The Wak'hutu have been used as porters; but they have proved so treacherous, and so determined to desert, that no man will trust them in a land where prepayment is the first condition of an agreement. Property amongst them is insecure: a man has always a vested right in his sister's children; and when he dies his brothers and relations carefully plunder his widow and orphans.

The dirty, slovenly villages of the Wak'hutu are an index of the character of the people. Unlike the comfortable cottages of the coast, and the roomy abodes of the Wazaramo, the settlements of the Wak'hutu are composed of a few straggling hovels of the humblest description-with doors little higher than an English pigsty, and eaves so low that a man cannot enter them except on all fours. In shape they differ, some being simple cones, others like European haystacks, and others like our old straw beehives. The common hut is a circle from 12 to 25 feet in diameter; those belonging to the chiefs are sometimes of considerable size, and the first part of the erection is a cylindrical framework composed of tall stakes, or the rough trunks of young trees, interwoven with parallel and concentric rings of flexible twigs and withies, which are coated inside and outside with puddle of red or grey clay. In some a second circle of wall is built round the inner cylinder, thus forming one house within the other. The roof, subsequently added, is of sticks and wattles, and the weight rests chiefly upon a central tree. It has eaves-like projections, forming a narrow verandah, edged with horizontal bars which rest upon forked uprights. Over the sticks interwoven with the frame, thick grass or palm-fronds are thrown, and the whole is covered with a coat of thatch tied on with strips of tree bark. During the first few minutes of heavy rain, this roofing, shrunk by the parching suns, admits water enough to patch the interior with mud. The furniture of the cottages is like that of the Wazaramo; and the few square feet which compose the area are divided by screens of wattle into dark pigeon-holes, used as stores, kitchen, and sleeping-rooms. A thick field of high grass is allowed to grow in the neighbour-hood of each village, to baffle pursuers in case of need; and some cottages are provided with double doorways for easier flight. In the middle of the settlement there is usually a tall tree, under which the men lounge upon cots scarcely large enough for an English child; and where the slaves, wrangling and laughing, husk their holcus in huge wooden mortars. These villages can scarcely be called permanent: even the death of a chief causes them to be abandoned, and in a few months long grass waves over the circlets of charred stakes and straw.

The only sub-tribe of the Wak'hutu which deserves notice is the Waziraha, who inhabit the low grounds below the Mabruki Pass, in the first parallel of the Usagara Mountains. They are remarkable only for having beards somewhat better developed than in the other Eastern races: in sickly appearance they resemble their congeners.

Remain for consideration the Wadoe and the Wazegura. The proper habitat of the Wadoe is between the Watondwe or the tribes of Saadani, on the littoral, and the Wak'hwere, near K'hutu, on the west; their northern frontier is the land of the Wazegura, and their southern the Gama and the Kingani Rivers. Their country, irrigated by the waters of the Gama, is plentiful in grain, though wanting in cattle; they export to Zanzibar sorghum and maize, with a little of the chakazi or unripe copal.

The Wadoe once formed a powerful tribe, and were the terror of their neighbours. Their force was first broken by the Wakamba, who, however, so weakened themselves, that they were compelled to emigrate in mass from the country, and have now fixed themselves in a region about 14 marches to the north-west of Mombasah, which appears to have been anciently called that of the Meremongao. During this struggle the Wadoe either began or, what is more likely, renewed a practice which has made their name terrible even in African cars. Fearing defeat from the Wakamba, they proceeded, in presence of the foe, to roast and devour slices from the bodies of the fallen. The manoeuvre was successful; the Wakamba could dare to die, but they could not face the idea of becoming food. Presently, when the Wazegura had armed themselves with muskets, and the people of Whinde had organised their large plundering excursions, the Wadoe lost all power. About ten years ago Juma Mfumbi, the late Diwan of Saadani, exacted tribute from them, and after his death his sons succeeded to it. In 1857, broken by a famine of long continuance, many Wadoe fled to the south of the Kingani River, and obtained from the Wazaramo lands near Sagesera and Dege la Mhora.

The Wadoe differ greatly in colour and in form. Some are tall, well-made, and light-complexioned Negroids, others are almost black. Their distinctive mark – in women as well as men – is a pair of long cuts down both cheeks, from the temple to the jaw; they also frequently chip away the two inner sides of the upper central incisors, leaving a small chevron-shaped hole. This however is practised almost throughout the country. They are wild in appearance, and dress in softened skins, stained yellow with the bark and flowers(?) of the mimosa. Their arms are a large hide-shield, spears, bows, and arrows, shokah or the little battle-axe, the sime-knife, and the rungu or knobstick. They are said still to drink out of human skulls, which are not polished or prepared in any way for the purpose. The principal chief is termed Mweme: his privy councillors are called Makunga(?), and the elders M'ana Mirao(?). The great headmen are buried almost naked, but retaining their bead ornaments, sitting in a shallow pit, so that the forefinger can project above the ground. With each man are interred alive a male and a female slave, the former holding a mundu or billhook wherewith to cut fuel for his lord in the cold death-world, and the latter, who is seated upon a little stool, supports his head in her lap. This custom has been abolished by some of the tribes: according to the Arabs, a dog is now buried in lieu of the slaves. The subdivisions of the Wadoe are numerous and unimportant.

The Wazegura, who do not inhabit this line of road, require some allusion, in consequence of the conspicuous part which they have played in the evil drama of African life. They occupy the lands south of the Pangani River to the Cape of Utondwe, and they extend westward as far as the hills of Nauru. Originally a peaceful tribe, they have been rendered terrible by the possession of fire-arms; and their chiefs have now collected large stores of gunpowder, used only to kidnap and capture the weaker wretches within their reach. They thus supply the market of Zanzibar with slaves, and this practice is not of yesterday. About twenty years ago the Wazegura serfs upon the island, who had been cheaply bought during a famine for a few measures of grain, rose against their Arab masters, retired into the jungle, and, reinforced by malefactors and malcontents, began a servile war, which raged with the greatest fury for six months, when the governor, Ahmed bin Sayf, maternal uncle to His Highness the late Sayyid Said, brought in a body of mercenaries from Hazramaut, and broke the force of this Jacquerie by setting a price upon their heads, and by giving the captives as prizes to the captors. The exploits of Kisabengo, the Mzegura, have already been alluded to. The Arab merchants of Unyanyembe declare that the road will never be safe until that person's head adorns a pole: they speak with bitterness of heart, for he exacts an unconscionable "blackmail."

The Wazegura are in point of polity an exception to the rule of East Africa: instead of owning hereditary sultans, they obey the loudest tongue, the most open hand, and the sharpest spear. This tends practically to cause a perpetual blood-feud, and to raise up a number of petty chiefs, who, aspiring to higher positions, must distinguish themselves by bloodshed, and must acquire wealth in weapons, especially fire-arms, the great title to superiority, by slave-dealing. The only occasion when they combine is an opportunity of successful attack upon some unguarded neighbour. Briefly, the Wazegura have become an irreclaimable race, and such they will remain until compelled to make a livelihood by honest industry.

Chapter 5

HALT AT ZUNGOMERO,
AND FORMATION OF THE CARAVAN

I halted to collect carriage and to await the arrival of the twenty-two promised porters for about a fortnight at that hot-bed of pestilence, Zungomero, where we nearly found "wet graves." Our only lodging was under the closed eaves of a hut built African-fashion, one abode within the other. The roof was a sieve, the walls were systems of chinks, and the floor was a sheet of mud. Outside the rain poured pertinaciously, as if K'hutu had been situated in the "black north" of Hibernia; the periodical S. and S.W. winds were raw and chilling, the gigantic vegetation was sopped to decay, and the tangled bank of the Mgeta River, lying within pistol-shot of our hovels, added its quotum of miasma. The hardships of a march in inclement weather had taken effect upon the Baloch guard: expecting everything to be done for them they endured seven days of wet and wind before they could find energy to build a shed, and they became almost mutinous because left to make shelter for themselves. They stole the poultry of the villagers like gipsies, they quarrelled violently with the slaves, they foully abused their temporal superior, Said bin Salim, and three of the thirteen were accused of grossly insulting the women of the Wak'hutu. The latter charge, after due investigation, was "not proven:" we had resolved, in case of its being brought home, severely to flog the culprits or to turn them out of camp.

On the 27th July, Sayf bin Salim returned to Dut'humi with his gang of thirty slaves, who also had distinguished themselves by laying violent hands on sheep, goats, and hens. Their patroon had offered to carry our baggage half-way over the mountains to Ugogo, for a sum of sixty dollars; thinking his conditions exorbitant, I stipulated for conveyance the whole way. He refused, declaring that he was about to organise another journey up-country. I doubted his assertion, as he was known to have audaciously defrauded Musa Mzuri, an Indian merchant, who had entrusted him with a large venture of ivory at Kazeh: yet he spoke truth; nearly a year afterwards we met him on his march to the "Sea of Ujiji." During his visit he had begged for drugs, tea, coffee, sugar, spices, everything, but the stores were already far wasted by the improvidence of the Goanese, who seemed to think that they were living in the vicinity of a bazar. To punish me for not engaging his gang, he caused the desertion of nine porters hired at Dut'humi, by declaring that I was bearing them into slavery. As they carried off, in addition to half their pay, sundry sundries and Muinyi Wazird's sword, I sent three slave-musketeers to recover the stolen goods per force if necessary. With respect to the cloth, Sayf bin Salim wrote back to say that as I could well afford the loss of a few "domestics," he would not compel the fugitives to restore it: at the same time that he did himself the honour to return the sword, which I might want. This man proved himself the sole "base exception" to the hospitality and the courteousness of the Omani Arabs. I forwarded an official complaint to H. M. the Sayyid Majid, but the arm of Zanzibar has not yet reached K'hutu.

At Zungomero five fresh porters were engaged, making up the whole party to a total of 132 souls. They were drafted into the men of Muinyi Wazira, whose open indulgence in stingo had made his society at meals distasteful to Moslem sticklers for propriety. He was an able interpreter, speaking five African dialects, which is not, however, in these lands a remarkable feat, and when sober, he did at first the work of three men. But linguists are a dangerous race, as the annals of old India prove: – I doubt a bilingual Eastern man, and if he can speak three languages I do not doubt him at all. Moreover, true to his semi-servile breed – his dam was a Mzaramo slave, and his sire a half-caste Wawa-hill – he began well and he finished badly. His deep undying fondness for pombe or holcus beer, kept him in alternate states of maudlin apathy or of violent pugnacity. He had incurred heavy debts upon the coast. After his arrival at Unyamwezi, letters were sent urging upon the Arabs his instant arrest, but fortunately for him the bailiff and the jailor are not, as the venerable saying declares the schoolmaster to be, abroad. Muinyi Wazira, however, did not sight the Sea of Ujiji in my service, and his five messmates, who each received 15 dollars' worth of cloth for the journey thither and back, were not more fortunate.

Before marching from Zungomero into the mountains I will order, for the reader's inspection, a muster of the party, and enlist his sympathies in behalf of the unhappy being who had to lead it.

Said bin Salim may pass on: he has been described in Blackwood (February, 1858) and he scarcely deserves a second notice. He is followed by his four slaves, including the boy Faraj, who will presently desert, and without including his acting wife, the lady Halimah. That young person's pug-dog countenance and bulky charms seem to engross every thought not appropriated to himself. One day, however, my ears detect the loud voice of wail proceeding from the lady Halimah, accompanying methinks the vigorous performance of a stick; the peccadillo was – but I eschew scandal and request the lady to advance.

My companion's gun carrier, Seedy Mubarak Bombay, a negro from Ushio, has twice been sketched in Black-wood (March, 1858 and September, 1859), he also requires no further celebrity. My henchman, Muinyi Mabruki, had been selected by his fellow-tribeman Bombay at Zanzibar; he was the slave of an Arab Shaykh, who willingly let him for the sum of 5 dollars per mensem. Mabruki is the type of the bull-headed negro, low-browed, pig-eyed, pug-nosed, and provided by nature with that breadth and power, that massiveness and muscularity of jaw, which characterise the most voracious carnivors. He is at once the ugliest and the vainest of the party: his attention to his toilette knows no limit. His temper is execrable, ever in extremes, now wild with spirits, then dogged, depressed, and surly, then fierce and violent. He is the most unhandy of men, he spoils everything entrusted to him, and presently he will be forbidden to engage in any pursuit beyond ass-leading and tent-pitching. These worthies commenced well. They excited our admiration by braving noon-day suns, and by snoring heavily through the rawest night with nothing to warm them but a few smouldering embers. In an evil hour compassion-touched, I threw over their shoulders a pair of English blankets, which in the shortest time completely demoralised them. They learned to lie a-bed o' mornings, and when called up their shrugged shoulders and shrinking forms were wrapped tightly round, lest the breath of dawn should visit them too roughly. Idleness marked them for her own: messmates and sworn brothers; they made at the halt huts out of hail, lest they should be called to do work. As a rule, however, Englishmen have the art of spoiling Eastern servants: we begin with the utmost stretch of exertion, and we expect this high pressure system to last. Of course the men's energies are soon exhausted, their indolence and apathy contrast with their former activity; we conceive dislikes to them, and we end by dismissing them. This, however, was not the case with Bombay and Mabruki. They returned with us to Zanzibar, and we parted *á l'aimable*, especially with the former, who, after a somewhat protracted fit of the "blue devils," became once more, what he before had been, a rara avis in the lands, an active servant and an honest man.

Regard for the Indian perusers of these pages, who know by experience how "banal" a character is the half-caste oriental Portuguese, prevents my offering anything but a sketch of Valentine A. and Gaetano B. I had hired them at Bombay for Co.'s rs. 20 per mensem, besides board and lodging. Scions of that half Pariah race which yearly issues from Goa, Daman and Diu to gather rupees as "cook boys," dry-nurses, and "buttrels," in wealthy British India, the hybrids had their faults: a pride of caste, and a contempt for Turks and heathen, heretics and infidels, which often brought them to grief; a fondness for acting triton amongst the minnows; a certain disregard for the seventh commandment, in the matter of cloth and clothes, medicines and provisions; a constitutional repugnance to "Signior Sooth;" a wastefulness of other men's goods, and a peculiar tenacity of their own; a deficiency of bodily strength and constitutional vigour; a voracity which induced indigestion once a day; and, finally, a habit of frequent phlebotomy which, deferred, made them sick. They had also their merits. Valentine was a good specimen of the neat-handed and ready-witted Indian: in the shortest time he learned to talk Kisawahili sufficiently for his own purposes, and to read a chronometer and thermometer sufficiently for ours: he had, however, one blemish, an addiction to "fudging," which rendered the severest overseeing necessary. A "Davy do a' things," he was as clever at sewing a coat as at cooking a curry. Gaetano had a curious kind of tenderness when acting nurse, and, wonderful to relate, an utter disregard for danger: he would return alone through a night-march of jungle to fetch his forgotten keys, and would throw himself into an excited mob of natives with a fearlessness which, contrasted with his weakly body, never failed to turn their wrath into merriment. He suffered severely from the secondaries of fever, which, in his case, as in his master's, assumed a cerebral form. At Msene he was seized with fits resembling epilepsy; and as he seemed every month to become more addle-headed and scatterbrained, more dirty and untidy, more wasteful and forgetful, more loath to work without compulsion, and more prone to start and feed the fire with ghee when it. was the scarcest of luxuries, I could not but attribute many of his delinquencies to disease.

The Baloch are now to appear. My little party were servants of His Highness the Sayyid Majid of Zanzibar, who had detached them as an escort upon the usual "deputation-allowance" of ten dollars per mensem. They had received the command of their master to accompany me wherever I might please to march, and they had been rendered responsible to him for the safety of my person and property. As has been mentioned, Lieut.-Col. Hamerton had advanced to them before departure a small sum for outfit, and had promised them, on condition of good conduct, an ample reward on the part of H. M.'s Government after return to Zanzibar. These men were armed with the usual matchlock, the Cutch sabre,- one or two had Damascus blades, – the Indian hide-targe, decorated with its usual tinsel, the long khanjar or dagger, extra matches, flints and steels, and toshdan, or ammunition pouches, sensibly distributed about their persons.

The Jemadar Mallok led from Zanzibar seven warriors of fame, yclept severally, Mohammed, Shahdad, Ismail, Belok, Abdullah, Darwaysh, and the Seedy Jelai; at Kaole he persuaded to follow his fortunes, Khuda-bakhsh, Musa, Gul Mohammed, Riza, and Hudul a tailor boy.

The Jemadar Mallok is a monocular, and the Sanscrit proverb declares:

"Rare a Kana (one-eyed man) is a good man and sound,
Rare a ladye gay will be faithful found."

Mallok is no exception to this rule of the "Kana." He is a man with fine Italian features, somewhat disfigured by the small-pox: but his one eye never looks you "in the face," and there is an expression about the mouth which forbids implicit trust in his honesty. He proclaims himself to be somewhat fonder of fighting than of feeding, yet suspicious circumstances led me to believe that he was one of those whom the Arabs describe as "first at the banquet and last at the brawl." He began with a display of zeal and activity which died young; he lapsed, through grumbling and discontent, into open insubordination as we progressed westward, or from home; he became submissive and somewhat servile as we returned to the coast, and when he took leave of me he shed a flood of crocodile's tears.

Mohammed is the Rish Safid, or greybeard of the caravan, and without a greybeard no eastern caravan considers itself *en regle*. Of these indispensable veterans I had two specimens; but of what use they were, except to teach hot youth the cold caution of eld, I never could divine, – *vieux soldat, vielle bete*. In the civilised regiment age is not venerable in the private, as every grey hair is a proof that he has not merited or has forfeited promotion; so in the East, where there is a paucity of competitors in the race of fortune, the Rish Safid of humble fortune may be safely set down as a fool or a foolish knave, and though his escort is sought, he generally proves himself to be no better than he should have been.

Mohammed's body is apparently hard as a rock, his mind is soft as putty, and his comrades, disappointed in their hopes of finding brains behind those wrinkles, derisively compare him to a rotten walnut, and say before his face, "What! grey hairs and no wits?" He has invested the fifteen dollars advanced to him as outfit by Lieut.-Col. Hamerton, in a slave-boy, whom presently he will exchange for a slave-girl, despite all the inuendoes of his friends, He was at first a manner of peace-maker, but soon my refusal to enlist and pay his slave as a hired porter acted like Ithuriel's spear. This veteran of fractious temper and miserly habits ended, in a question of stinted rations, by drawing his sabre upon and cutting at his Jemadar; an offence which I was compelled to visit with a bastinado, inflicted out of the sight of man by the hand of Khudabakhsh.

Shahdad is the Chelebi of the party, the fast young man. He is decidedly not handsome. A figure short and *trapu*, a retrussed nose, small pigs' eyes, a beard like a blackberry bush, and a crop of hair which, projecting its wiry waves in a deep long curtain from beneath a diminutive scarlet fez, makes his head appear top-heavy. Yet he does sad havoc amongst female hearts by means of his zeze or guitar, half a gourd with an arm to which is attached a single string, and by his lively accompaniment is a squeaking falsetto, which is here as fascinating and emollient to the sex as ever was the organ of Rubini in Europe. During a lengthened sojourn at Bombay he has enlarged his mind by the acquisition of the Hindostani tongue and of Indian trickery. He is almost the only Eastern whom I remember that abused the poor letter H like a thoroughbred Londoner. His familiarity with Anglo-Europeans, and his experience touching the facility of gulling them, has induced in him a certain proclivity for peculation, grumbling, and mutiny. His brother – or rather cousin, for in these lands all fellow-tribesmen are brethren

"Ismail" is a confirmed invalid, a man with a "broken mouth," deeply sunken cheeks, and emaciated frame, who, though earnestly solicited to return eastwards, will persist in accompanying the party till he falls a victim to a chronic malady in Unyamwezi.

Belok is our snob; a youth of servile origin, with coarse features, wide mouth, everted lips, and a pert, or rather an impudent expression of countenance, which, acting as index to his troublesome character, at once prejudices the physiognomist against him. Belok's comrades have reason to quote the Arab saw, "Defend me from the beggar become wealthy, and from the slave become a freeman!" He has invested his advance of salary in a youth; and the latter serves and works for the rest of the mess, who must patiently and passively endure the insolence of the master for fear of losing the offices of the man. After the fashion of a certain sort of fools, he applies the whole of his modicum of wit to mischief-making, and he succeeds admirably where better men, whose thoughts attempt a wider range, would fail. By his exertions the Baloch became, in point of social intercourse, not unlike the passengers of a ship bound on a long voyage: after the first month the society divides itself into two separate and adverse cliques; after the second it breaks up into little knots; and after the third it is a chequer-work of pairs and solitaires. Arrived at the "Pond of Ugogo," I was compelled to address an official letter to Zanzibar, requesting the recal of Belok and his coadjutor in mischief, Khudabakhsh.

Abdullah is the type of the respectable, in fact, of the good young man. It is really pathetic to hear him recount, with accents broken by emotion, the "tale full of waters of the eye," – the parting of an only son, who was led away to an African grave, from the aged widow his mamma; to listen to her excellent advice, and to his no less excellent resolves. He is capable of calling his bride elect, were such article a subject ever to be mentioned amongst Moslems, "his choicest blessing." With an edifying mingling of piety and discipline, he never neglects the opportunity of standing in prayer behind the Jemadar Mallok, whose elevation to a superior grade – *honneur oblige!* – has compelled him to rub up a superficial acquaintance with the forms of devotion. Virtue in the abstract I revere; in the concrete I sometimes suspect. The good young man soon justified this suspicion by repeatedly applying to Said bin Salim for beads, in my name, which he converted to his own purposes.

Of Darwaysh little need be said. He is a youth about twenty-two years old, with a bulging brow, a pair of ferret-eyes, a "peaky" nose, a thin chin; in fact, with a face the quintessence of curiosity. He is the "brother" – that is to say, the spy – of the Jemadar, and his principal peculiarity is a repugnance to obeying an order because it is an order. With this individual I had at first many a passage of words. Presently prostrated in body and mind by severe disease, he obtained relief from European drugs; and from that time until the end of the journey, he conducted himself with a certain stiffness and decorum which contrasted pleasantly enough with the exceeding "bounce" of his earlier career.

The Seedy Jelai calls himself a Baloch, though palpably the veriest descendant of Ham. He resents with asperity the name of "Nigger," or "Nig" – Jupiter Tonans has heard of the offensive dissyllable, which was a household word before the days of the Indian mutiny, but has he heard of the more offensive monosyllable which was forced upon the abbreviating Anglo-Saxon by the fatal necessity of requiring to repeat the word so frequently? Jelai clothes his long lank legs – cucumber-shinned and bony-kneed – in calico tights, which display the full deformity of those members; and taking a pride in the length of his mustachios, which distinguishes him from his African-born brethren, he twists them *en croc* like a hidalgo in the days of Gil Bias. The Seedy, judging from analogy, ought to be brave, but he is not. On the occasion of alarm in the mountains of Usagara, he privily proposed to his comrades to "bolt" and leave us. Moreover, on the "Sea of Ujiji," where he was chosen as an escort, he ignobly deserted me.

Khudabakhsh was formed by nature to be the best man of the party; he has transformed himself into the worst. A man of broad and stalwart frame, with stern countenance, and a quietness of demeanour which usually argues sang-froid and persistency, his presence is in all points soldier-like and prepossessing. But his temper is unmanageable: he enters into a quarrel when certain of discomfiture; he is utterly reckless, – on one occasion he amused himself by blowing a charge of gunpowder into the calves of African warriors who were dancing in front of him; – and lastly, his innate propensity for backbiting, intrigue, and opposition to all authority, render him a dangerous member of the Expedition. He herds with Belok, whose tastes lie in the same line: he is the head and front of all mischief, and presently his presence will become insupportable.

Musa, a tall, gaunt, and dark-brown old man, is the assistant Rish Safid, or greybeard; in fact, the complement of "Greybeard Mohammed." After a residence of twenty years at Mombasah, he has clean forgotten Persian; he speaks only a debased Mekrani dialect, and the Kisawahili, which, as usual with his tribe, he prefers. An old soldier, he compensates for want of youth and vigour by artfulness; an old traveller – nothing better distinguishes in these lands the veteran of the road from the griffin or greenhorn, than the careful and systematic consideration of his comforts – he carries the lightest matchlock, he starts in the cool of the morning, he presses forward to secure the best quarters, and throughout he thinks only of himself. His character has a want of wrath, which, despite his white hairs, causes him to be little regarded. Greybeard Mohammed is considered a fool; Greybeard Musa, an old woman. Yet he troubles himself little about the opinions of his fellows, he looks well after his morning and evening meals, his ghee, his pipe, and his sleeping mat; and knowing that he will last out all the novices, with enviable philosophy he casts ambition to the winds.

Gul Mohammed is the most civilised man of the party. He has straight and handsome features, of the old Grecian type, a reddish-brown skin – the skin by excellence – and a Central-Asian beard of largest dimensions. His mind is as civilised as his body; he is an adept after the fashion of his tribe, in divinity especially, in medicine and natural history; and when landing at Marka, he actually took the trouble to visit, for curiosity, the Juba River. Unfortunately, "Gul Mohammed" is a mixture of Baloch mountaineer-blood with the Sindhian of the plain, and the cross is, throughout the East, renowned for representing the worst points of both progenitors. Gul Mohammed is brave and treacherous, fair-spoken and detractive, honourable and dishonest, good-tempered and bad-hearted.

Of the Baloch remain Riza, and Hudul, the tailor-boy: the former is a kind of Darwaysh, utterly insignificant, but by no means so disagreeable as his fellows: the only marking corporeal peculiarity of the latter is a deficiency of skin; his mouth appears ever open, and his teeth resemble those of an old rabbit. His mental organisation has its petite pointe, its little twist; he is under the constant delusion that those who speak in unknown tongues are employed specially in abusing him. His first complaint was against the Goanese: as he could not understand a word of their language, it was dismissed with some derision; he then charged me to his comrades with his normal grievance, and in due time he felt aggrieved by my companion.

A proper regard to precedence induces me now to marshal the "sons of Ramji," who acted as interpreters, guides, and war-men. They were armed with the old "Tower-musket," which, loaded with nearly an ounce of powder, they never allowed to quit the hand; and with those antiquated German cavalry sabres which find their way over all the East: their accoutrements were small leathern boxes, strapped to the waist, and huge cow-horns, for ammunition. The most part called themselves Muinyi (master), the title of an African freeman, because they had been received in pawn by the Banyan Ramji from their parents or uncles, who had forgotten to redeem the pledge, and they still claimed the honour of noble birth. Of these there were eight men under their Mtu Mku, or chief man, Kidogo – Anglice, Mr. Little. Kidogo had preceded the Expedition, escorting the detachment of thirty-six Wanyamwezi porters to Zungomero, and he possessed great influence over his brother slaves, who all seemed to admire and to be proud of him. He was by no means a common man. "Natione magis quam ratione barbarus;" he had a fixed and obstinate determination: amongst these puerile, futile African souls he was exceptional as "a sage Sciote or a green horse." His point of honour consisted in the resolve that his words should be held as Median laws, and he had, as the Africans say, a "large head," namely, abundant self-esteem, that blessed quality which makes man independent of his fellows. Muinyi Kidogo is a short, thin, coal-black person, with a something arguing gentle blood in his tribe, the Wadoe Cannibals; he has a peaked beard, a bulging brow, close thin lips, a peculiar wall-eyed roll of glance, and a look fixed, when unobserved, with a manner of fascination which men felt. His attitude is always humble and deprecatory, he drops his chin upon the collar of reflection, he rarely speaks, save in dulcet tones, low, plaintive, and modulated; yet agreeing in every conceivable particular, he never fails to introduce a most pertinacious "but," which brings him back precisely to his own starting-point. The vehemence of his manner, and the violence of his temper, win for him the fears of the porters; having a wife and children in Unyamwezi, he knows well the languages, the manners, and the customs of the people; he never hesitates, when necessary, to enforce his mild commands by a merciless application of the staff, or to air his blade and to fly at the recusant like a wild cat. In such moods, he is always seized by his friends, and led forcibly away, as if dangerous. To insure some regularity on the road, I ordered him to meet Said bin Salim and Muinyi Wazira every evening at my tent, for a "Mashauri," or palaver, about the next day's march and halt. The measure was rendered futile by Kidogo, who soon contrived so to browbeat the others, that they would not venture an opinion in his presence. As a chief, he would have been in the right position; as a slave, he was falsely placed, because determined not to obey. He lost no time in demanding that he and his brethren should be considered Askari, soldiers, whose sole duty it was to carry a gun; and he took the first opportunity of declaring that his men should not be under the direction of the Jemadar. Having received for answer that we could not all be Sultans, he retired with a "Ngema" – a "very well," accompanied by a glance that boded little good. From that hour the "sons of Ramji" went wrong. Before, servilely civil, they waxed insolent; they learned their power – without them I must have returned to the coast – and they presumed upon it. They assumed the "swashing and martial outside" of valiant men: they disdained to be "mechanical;" they swore not to carry burdens; they objected to loading and leading the asses; they would not bring up articles left behind in the camp or on the road; they claimed the sole right of buying provisions; they arrogated to themselves supreme command over the porters; and they pilfered from the loads whenever they wanted the luxuries of meat and beer; they drank deep; and on more than one occasion they endangered the caravan by their cavalier proceedings with the fair sex. It was "water-painting" to complain; they had one short reply to all objections, namely, the threat of desertion. Preferring anything to risking the success of the Expedition, I was reduced to the bitter alternative of long-suffering, but it was with the hope of a revanche at some future time. The suffering was perhaps not wholly patient. Orientals advise the traveller "to keep his manliness in his pocket for braving it and ruffling at home." Such, however, is not exactly the principle or the practice of an Englishman, who recognises a primary duty of commanding respect for himself, for his successors, and for the noble name of his nation. On the return of the Expedition, Kidogo proved himself a "serviceable villain," but an extortionate; anything committed to him was, as the Arabs say, in "ape's custody," and the only remedy was to remove him from all power over the outfit.

Under the great Kidogo were the Muinyi Mboni, Buyuni, Hayja, and Jako; these four took precedence as being the sons of Diwans, whilst the commonalty was represented by the Muinyi Shehe, Mbaruko, Wulaydi, and Khamisi.

The donkey-men, five in number, had been hired at the rate of thirty dollars per head for the whole time of exploration. Their names were Musangesi, Sangora, Nasibu, Hasani, and Saramalla. Of their natures little need be said, except that they were a trifle less manageable than the "sons of Ramji:" perfect models of servile humanity, obstinate as asses and vicious as mules, gluttonous and lazy, noisy and overbearing, insolent and quarrelsome as slaves.

Lowest in rank, and little above the asses even in their own estimation, are the thirty-six Wanyamwezi Pagazi, or porters, who formed the transport-corps. Concerning these men and their burdens, a few words of explanation will be necessary.

In collecting a caravan the first step is to "make," as the people say, a "Khambi," or kraal. The Mtongi, or proprietor of the goods, announces, by pitching his tent in the open, and by planting his flag, that he is ready to travel; this is done because amongst the Wanyamwezi a porter who persuades others to enlist does it under pain of prosecution and fine-paying if a death or an accident ensue. Petty chiefs, however, and their kinsmen will bring with them in hope of promotion a number of recruits, sometimes all the male adults of a village, who then recognise them as headmen. The next step is to choose a Kirangozi or guide. Guides are not a peculiar class; any individual of influence and local knowledge who has travelled the road before is eligible to the post. The Kirangozi must pay his followers to acknowledge his supremacy, and his Mganga or medicine-man for providing him with charms and prophylactics. On the march he precedes his porters, and any one who breaks this rule is liable to a fine. He often undergoes abuse for losing the way, for marching too far or not far enough, for not halting at the proper place, and for not setting out at the right time. In return he enjoys the empty circumstance of command, and the solid advantage of better food and a present, which, however, is optional, at the end of the journey: he carries a lighter load, and his emoluments frequently enable him to be attended by a slave. The only way of breaking the perverse and headstrong herd into a semblance of discipline, is to support the Kirangozi at all conjunctures, and to make him, if possible, dole out the daily rations and portion the occasional presents of meat.

At the preliminary Khambi the Mtongi superintends the distribution of each Muzigo or load. The Pagazi or porters are mostly lads, lank and light, with the lean and clean legs of leopards. Sometimes, however, a herculean form is found with the bullet-head, the broad bull-like neck, the deep wide chest, and the large strong extremities that characterise the

Hammal of Stamboul. There is usually a sprinkling of grey-beards, who might be expected, as the proverb is, to be "leaning against the wall." Amongst these races, however, the older men, who have learned to husband their strength, fare better than their juniors, and the Africans, like the Arabs, object to a party which does not contain veterans in beard, age, and experience. In portioning the loads there is always much trouble: each individual has his favourite fancy, and must choose, or, at any rate, must consent to his burden. To load porters properly is a work of skill. They will accept at the hand of a man who knows their nature a weight which, if proposed by a stranger, would be rejected with grunts of disgust. They hate the inconvenience of boxes, unless light enough to be carried at both ends of a "Banghi"-pole by one man, or heavy enough to be slung between two porters. The burden must never be under a fair standard, especially when of that description that it decreases by expenditure towards the end of the journey; a lightly-laden man not only becomes lazy, he also makes his fellows discontented. The nature of the load, however, causes an inequality of weight. Cloth is tightly rolled up in the form of a huge bolster, five feet long by eighteen to twenty-four inches in diameter, protected against wear and weather by Makanda or coarse matting of brab-leaf, and corded over. This bundle is fastened, for the purpose of preserving its shape and for convenience of stacking, in a cradle of three or more flexible branches, cut from a small tree below the place of junction, barked and trimmed, laid along the length of the load, and confined at the open end by a lashing of fibre-rope. Besides his weapons and marching kit, a man will carry a pack of two Frasilah or seventy pounds, and this perhaps is the maximum. Beads are placed in long, narrow bags of domestics, matted, corded, and cradled in sticks like cloth; being a less elastic load, they are more difficult to carry, and therefore seldom exceed fifty pounds. Brass, and other wires, are carried in daur, khata, or circles, lashed to both ends of a pole, which is generally the large midrib of a palm-frond, with a fork cut in its depth at one extremity to form a base for the load when stacked, and provided at the point of junction with a Kitambara or pad of grass, rag, or leather. Wire is the lightest, as ivory is the heaviest, of loads.

The African porter will carry only the smallest burdens upon his head, and the custom is mostly confined to women and children. The merchants of course carry nothing but themselves, except in extreme cases; but when the sudden sickness or the evasion of a porter endangers the safety of his load, they shoulder it without hesitation. The chief proprietor usually follows his caravan, accompanied by some of his partners and armed slaves, to prevent the straggling which may lead to heavy loss; he therefore often endures the heat and tedium of the road longer than the rest of his party.

The loads of the Pagazi, it has appeared, are composed of beads, cloth, and wire, which in this land of "round trade" or barter, supply the wants of a circulating medium, and they severally represent copper, silver, and gold. For a detailed notice, the reader is referred to the appendix; in this place a few general remarks will suffice to set before him the somewhat complicated use of the articles.

Of beads there are about 400 varieties, some of which have each three or four different names. The cheapest, which form the staple of commerce, are the Hafizi, Khanyera or Ushanga Waupe, a round white porcelain, the price of which averages at Zanzibar 1 dollar per 5 or 6 lbs. avoirdupois. The most expensive are the Samsam or Samesame, also called Joho (scarlet cloth), Kimara-p'hamba (food-finishers), because a man will part with his dinner to obtain them, and Kifunjya-mji (town-breakers), because the women will ruin themselves and their husbands for them: these are the small coral-bead, scarlet enamelled upon a white ground, they are of fifteen different sizes, and the value at Zanzibar is from 13 to 16 dollars per 35 lbs. Beads are purchased from the Banyan monopolisers unstrung, and are afterwards mounted by the merchant upon T'hembe, or threads of palm-fibre; much depends for success in sale upon the regularity and the attractiveness of the line. The principal divisions are the bitil and the khete, which may represent the farthing and the penny. The former is a single length from the tip of the index to the wrist; the latter, which comprises four of the former, is a double length round the thumb to the elbow-bone, or what is much the same, twice the circumference of the throat. Ten khete compose the fundo or knot, which is used in the larger purchases, and of these from two to three were daily expended in our small expenses by the Goanese servants, whilst the usual compensation for rations to an African is a single khete. The utmost economy should be exercised in beads: apparently exhaustless a large store goes but a little way, and a man's load rarely outlasts a month. It is difficult to divine what becomes of these ornaments: for centuries ton after ton has been imported into the country, they are by no means perishable substances, and the people carry, like the Indians, their wealth upon their persons. Yet not a third of the population was observed to wear any considerable quantity; possibly the excessive demand in the lands outlying direct intercourse with the coast, tends to disperse them throughout the vast terra incognita of the central African basin.

The African preserves the instincts of infancy in the higher races. He astonished the enlightened De Gama some centuries ago by rejecting with disdain jewels, gold, and silver, whilst he caught greedily at beads and other baubles, as a child snatches at a new plaything. To the present day he is the same. There is something painfully ludicrous in the expression of countenance, the intense and all-absorbing admiration, and the greedy wistfulness with which he contemplates the rubbish. Yet he uses it as a toy: after sacrificing perhaps his goat or his grain to become the happy possessor of a khete, he will hang it round his neck for a few days, and then, child-like, weary of the acquisition, he will do his best to exchange it for another. In all bargains beads must be thrown in, especially where women are concerned: their sisters of civilisation would reproach themselves with an unconscious lapse into the "nil ad-mirari" doctrines so hateful to the muscular system of the age, and with a cold indifference to the charms of diamonds and pearls, could they but witness the effect of a string of scarlet porcelains upon the high-born dames in Central Africa.

The cloths imported into East Africa are of three kinds, Merkani, Kaniki, and "cloths with names."

"Merkani," in which we detect the African corruption of American, is the article "domestics" – unbleached shirting and sheeting from the mills near Salem. Kaniki, is the common Indian indigo dyed cotton. "Cloths with names," as they are called by the Africans, are Arab and Indian checks, and coloured goods, of cotton or silk mixed with cotton. Of these the most common is the Barsati, a dark blue cotton cloth with a broad red stripe, which representing the dollar in the interior is useful as presents to chiefs. Of double value is the Dabwani, made at Maskat, a small blue and white check, with a quarter breadth of red stripe, crossed with white and yellow: this showy article is invariably demanded by the more powerful Sultans for themselves and their wives, whilst they divide the Merkani and Kaniki, which composes their Honga – "blackmail" or dash – amongst their followers.

The people of East Africa, when first visited by the Arabs, were satisfied with the coarsest and flimsiest Kaniki imported by the Banyans from Cutch. When American merchants settled at Zanzibar, Kaniki yielded before the advance of "Merkani," which now supplies the markets from Abyssinia to the Mozambique. But the wild men are fast losing their predilection for a stuff which is neither comfortable nor durable, and in many regions the tribes satisfied with goat-skins and tree barks, prefer to invest their capital in the more attractive beads and wire. It would evidently be advantageous if England or her colonies could manufacture an article better suited to the wants of the country than that now in general use; but as long as the Indian short-stapled cotton must be used, there is little probability of her competing with the produce of the New World.

In Eastern Africa cotton cloth is used only for wear. The popular article is a piece of varying breadth but always of four cubits, or six feet, in length: the braca of Portuguese Africa, it is called by the Arabs, shukkah, by the Wasawahili, unguo, and in the far interior upande or lupande. It is used as a loin-wrapper, and is probably the first costume of Eastern Africa and of Arabia. The plate borrowed from Montfaucon's edition of the "Topographia Christiana," by Dr. Vincent (Part I. Appendix to the Periplus) shows the Shukkah, to be the general dress of Ethiopians, as it was of the Egyptians, and the spear their weapon. The use of the Shukkah during the Meccan pilgrimage, when the devotees cast off such innovations as coats and breeches for the national garb of their ancestors, proves its antiquity throughout the regions eastward of the Red Sea. On the African coast the Shukkah Merkani is worth about 0.25 dollars = ls. 1/2d., in the interior it rises to the equivalent of a dollar (4s. 2d.) and even higher. The Kaniki is but little cheaper than the Merkani, when purchased upon the sea-board; its increase of value in the interior, however, is by no means in proportion to its prime cost, and by some tribes it is wholly rejected. A double length of Shukkah, or twelve feet, the article worn by women who can afford it, is called a Doti, and corresponds with the Tobe of Abyssinia and of the Somali country. The whole piece of Merkani, which contains from seven to eleven Doti, is termed a Jurah or Gorah.

After beads and piece-goods, the principal imports into Eastern Africa, especially on the northern lines and in the western portion of the great central route, are Masango or brass wires of large sizes, Nos. 4 and 5. They are purchased at Zanzibar, when cheap, at 12, and when dear at 16, dollars per Frasilah of 35 lbs. When imported up-country the Frasilah is divided into three or four large coils, called by the Arabs "daur," and by the Africans "khata:" the object is convenience of attachment to the porters' banghy-poles. Arrived at Unyanyembe they are converted by artisans into the kitindi, or coil-bracelet, a peculiarly African decoration. It is a system of concentric circles extending from the wrist to the elbow; at both extremities it is made to bulge out for grace and for allowing the joints to play; and the elasticity of the wire keeps it in its place. It weighs nearly 3 lbs., yet – "vanity knows no sore" – the women of some tribes will wear four of these bulky decorations upon their arms and legs. It is mostly a feminine ornament. In the Lake Regions, however, men assume the full-sized armlet, and in the mountains of Usagara their wrists, arms, and ankles are often decorated with half and quarter lengths, which being without terminal bulges, appear to compress the limbs painfully. At Unyanyembe the value of a kitindi varies from two to four shukkah; at Ujiji, where the ornament is in demand it rises to four or five.

The remainder of the live stock forming the personnel of the caravan is composed of asses. At Zanzibar I had bought five riding animals to mount the chiefs of the party, including Said bin Salim and the Goanese. The price varied from fifteen to forty dollars. Of the twenty-nine asses used for carriage, only twenty remained when the muster was made at Zungomero, and the rapid thinning of their numbers by loss, death and accident began to suggest uncomfortable ideas.

The following "Equipment of the Expedition," sent by me to Mr. Francis Galton, the South African traveller, and bearing date, "Camp Zungomero in Khutu, Sunday, 2nd August, 1857," is here republished: it will assist the reader in picturing to himself the mass of material which I am about to drag over the mountains.

Provisions, &c – 1 dozen brandy (to be followed by 4 dozen more); 1 box cigars; 5 boxes tea (each 6 lbs.); a little coffee; 2 bottles curry stuff, besides ginger, rock and common salt, red and black pepper, one bottle each, pickles, soap, and spices; 20 lbs. pressed vegetables; 1 bottle vinegar; 2 bottles oil; 20 lbs. sugar (honey is procurable in the country).

Arms and Ammunition, including 2 smooth bores, 3 rifles, a Colt's carbine, and 3 revolvers, spare fittings, &c., and 3 swords. Each gun has its leather bag with three compartments, for powder-flask, ball, caps, patches, &c. 100 lbs. gunpowder (in 2 safety copper magazines and others); 60 lbs. shot; 380 lbs. lead bullets, cast of hardened material at the Arsenal, Bombay, placed in boxes 40 lbs. each for convenience of carriage, also to serve as specimen boxes, and screwed down to prevent pilfering; 20,000 copper caps; wadding.

The Baloch are armed with matchlocks, shields, swords, daggers and knives. They have for ammunition – - 40 lbs. gunpowder (4 kegs); 1000 lead bullets; 1000 flints for slaves' muskets, and are to be followed by about an equal quantity of ammunition.

Camp Furniture. – 1 sepoy's rowtie; 1 small (gable-shaped) tent of two sails joined, to cover and shelter property in this land of perpetual rains; 1 table and chair; 1 tin Crimean canteen, with knives and forks, kettle, cooking-pots, &c.; bedding, painted tarpaulin cover, 2 large cotton pillows for stuffing birds, 1 air pillow, 2 waterproof blankets (most useful), 1 Maltese blanket (remarkably good), and 2 other blankets; 1 cork bed, with 2 pillows, 3 blankets, and mosquito net. The Goanese have thick cotton padded mattresses, pillows, and blankets, and all the servants have some kind of bedding. 3 solid leather portmanteaus for clothes arid books; 1 box, like an Indian petarah, for books; 1 patent leather bag for books, washing materials, diaries, drawing-books, &c.; 1 small couriers' bag, for instruments, &c.; 5 canvas bags for kit generally; 3 mats, used as carpets.

Instruments. – 1 lever watch; 2 chronometers; 2 prismatic compasses, slings, and stands; 1 ship's azimuth compass; 2 pocket compasses; 1 pocket thermometer; 1 portable sun-dial; 1 rain gauge; 1 evaporating dish; 2 sextants and boxes, with canvas bags to be slung over porters' shoulders; 2 artificial horizons (with a little extra mercury, to be followed by more);

1 pocket lens; 1 mountain barometer lent by Bombay Geographical Society (very delicate); 3 thermometers; 1 measuring tape (100 ft.); 1 sounding lead; 2 boiling thermometers; 1 box of mathematical instruments; 1 glass; 1 telescope; 2 ft. rule with brass slide; 1 pocket pedometer by Dixie; 1 parallel ruler.

Stationery. – Foolscap paper; 1 ream common paper; 6 blank books; 3 Letts' diaries; 2 dozen pencils; 6 pieces caoutchouc; 6 metallic note books; 3 memorandum ditto; 1 box wafers and sealing wax; 2 field books; steel pens; quill ditto; ink powder which makes up well without acid; 3 bottles ink; 1 bottle native ink; 2 sets meteorological tables, blank; 4 tin cylinders for papers (very bad, everything rusts in them); Nautical Almanacs for 1857 and 1858; charts, Mr. Cooley's maps; "Mombas mission map"; skeleton maps; table of stars; account book; portfolio; wooden and tin cylinders for pens, &c.

Tools. – 1 large turnscrew; 1 hand saw; 1 hammer; 20 lbs. nails; 1 hand vice; 1 hone; 9 hatchets (as a rule every porter carries an axe); 2 files; 9 Jembe or native hoe; 9 Mas'ha or native dibbles; 1 cold chisel; 1 heavy hammer; 1 pair pincers. To be followed by 1 bench vice; 1 hand ditto; 12 gimlets of sizes; 1 18-inch stone grinder, with spindle and handle; 6 splitting axes; 12 augers of sizes; 2 sets centre-bits, with stock; 12 chisels; 4 mortise chisels; 2 sets drills; 24 saw files; 6 files of sorts; 4 gouges of sizes; 50 lbs. iron nails; 2 planes, with 2 spare irons; 3 hand saws; screws. These things were expected to be useful at the lakes, where carpenters are in demand.

Clothing, Bedding, and Shoes. – Shirts, flannel and cotton; turbans and thick felt caps for the head. (N.B. not looking forward to so long a journey, we left Zanzibar without a new outfit; consequently we were in tatters before the end, and in a climate where flannel fights half the battle of life against death, my companion was compelled to invest himself in overalls of American domestics, and I was forced to cut up blankets into coats and wrappers. The Goanese also had laden themselves with rags which would have been refused by a Jew; they required to be re-clothed in Kaniki, or blue cotton. African travel is no favourable opportunity for wearing out old clothes; the thorny jungles, and the practice of packing up clothes wet render a double outfit necessary for long journeys. The second should be carried packed up in tin – flannel-shirts, trousers and stocks, at least six of each, – not to be opened till required.

The best bedding in this country would be a small horse-hair mattress with two blankets, one thick the other thin, and mosquito curtains that would pack into the pillow. A simple carpet-bag without leathern or other adjuncts, should contain the travelling clothes, and all the bedding should roll up into a single bundle, covered with a piece of waterproof canvass, and tightly bound with stout straps.

As regards shoes, the best would be ammunition boots for walking and jack boots for riding. They must be of light colour, and at least one size too large in England; they should be carefully protected from external air which is ruinous to leather, and they must be greased from time to time, – with fat not with oil – otherwise they will soon become so hard and dry, that it is impossible to draw them on unless treated after the Indian plan, viz. dipped in hot water and stretched with a stuffing of straw.

Books and Drawing Materials. – Norie; Bowdich; Thompson's 'Lunar Tables;' Gordon's 'Time Tables;' Galton's 'Art of Travel;' Buist's 'Manual of Observation;' Jackson's 'What to Observe;' Jackson's 'Military Surveying;' 'Admiralty Manual;' Cuvier's 'Animal Life;' Prichard's 'History of Man;' Keith's 'Trigonometry;' Krapf's 'Kisuaheli Grammar;' Krapf's 'Kinika Testament;' Amharic Grammar (Isenberg's); Belcher's 'Mast Head Angles;' Cooley's 'Geography of N'yassi;' and other miscellaneous works; 1 paint-box complete, soft water colours; 1 small ditto, with Chinese ink, sepia and Prussian blue; 2 drawing books; 1 large drawing book; I camera lucida.

Portable domestic Medicine Chest. – Vilely made. Some medicines for natives in packages. Application was made to Zanzibar for more quinine, some morphia, Warburg's drops, citric acid, and chiretta root.

Miscellaneous. – 10 pieces scarlet broad-cloth for presents (3 expended); 3 knives for servants; 4 umbrellas; 1 hank salmon gut; 1 dozen twisted gut; 1 lb. bees' wax; courier's box with brass clasps to carry sundries on the road; 2 dozen penknives; 2000 fishing hooks; 42 bundles fishingline; 2 lanterns (policeman's bull's eye and common horn); 2 iron ladles for casting lead; 1 housewife, with buttons, needles, thread, silk, pins, &c.; needles (sailor's) and palms; 2 pair scissors; 2 razors; 1 hone; 2 pipes; 1 tobacco pouch; 1 cigar case; 7 canisters of snuff; 1 filter; 1 pocket filter; 1 looking-glass; 1 small tin dressing-case, with soap, nail-brush and tooth-brush (very useful); brushes and combs; 1 union jack; arsenical paste for specimens; 10 steels and flints.

Life at Zungomero I have said was the acme of discomfort. The weather was, as usual at the base of the mountains, execrable; pelting showers descended in a succession, interrupted only by an occasional burst of fiery sunshine which extracted steam from the thick covert of grass, bush, and tree. The party dispersing throughout the surrounding villages, in which it was said about 1000 travellers were delayed by the inundations, drank beer, smoked bhang, quarrelled amongst themselves, and by their insolence and violence caused continual complaints on the part of the villagers. Both the Goanese being prostrated with mild modifications of "yellow jack," I was obliged to admit them into the hut, which was already sufficiently populated with pigeons, rats, and flies by day, and with mosquitos, bugs, and fleas, by night. At length weary of waiting the arrival of the twenty-two promised porters, we prepared our papers, which I committed to the confidential slave of a coast Diwan, here dwelling as caravan-touter, for his uncle Ukwere of Kaolc. His name was somewhat peculiar, Chomwi la Mtu Mku Wambele, or the "Headman Great Man of Precedence;" – these little Jugurthas have all the titles of emperors, with the actual power of country squires; – he never allowed himself to appear in public sober, and to judge from the list of stations with which he obliged me – of eighteen not one was correct – I hesitated to entrust his slave with reports and specimens. But the Headman Great Man of Precedence did as he promised to do, and as his charge arrived safely, I here make to him the "amende honorable."

Chapter 6

WE CROSS THE EAST AFRICAN GHAUTS

On the 7th August, 1857, the Expedition left Zungomero. We were martyred by miasma; my companion and I were so feeble, that we could scarcely sit our asses, and weakness had almost deprived us of the sense of hearing. It was a day of severe toil. We loaded with difficulty, for the slaves and porters did not assemble till past 8 A.M., and instead of applying for their loads to Said bin Salim, every man ran off with the lightest burden or the easiest ass.

From Central Zungomero to the nearest ascent of the Usagara Mountains is a march of five hours. The route, emerging from the cultivated districts, leaves to the right the Wigo Hills, so called, probably, from the fishing weirs in the stagnant waters below, and in the Mgeta River, which flows through the plain. On the left, and distant four or five miles, is a straggling line of low cones: at the foot of one, somewhat larger than its neighbours, rises the thermal spring known to the people as the Maji ya W'heta, the Geyser, jetting-water, or *fontaine qui bouille.* Its position is a gentle slope between the hill-base and a dwarf Savannah which is surrounded by high walls of jungly forest, and the watershed is from south to north. The hot water boils and bubbles out of a white sand, here and there stained and encrusted with oxide of iron. Upon the surface lie caked and scaly sheets of calcareous tufa, expressed by the spring, and around it are erratic boulders blackened probably by the thermal fumes. the earth is dark, sometimes sandy, and sprinkled over with fragments of quartzite and sandstone; in other places a screen of brab-tree backs a bold expanse of ground, treacherous, boggy, and unstable as water. The area is about 200 feet in diameter, and the centre of ebullition is unapproachable, owing to the heat and the instability of the soil. According to the guides, it is subject to occasional eruptions, when the water bursts out with violence, and fragments of lime are flung high in the air. Animals are said to refuse it, and tales are told of wild beasts having been bogged in the seething mire.

With the Mgeta thrown on the left hand, we passed by a path almost invisible, through dense grass and trees, and presently we entered the luxuriant cultivation surrounding the westernmost villages of K'hutu. As the land beyond this point, for three long marches, lies barren, the slaves and porters had comfortably housed themselves. The prospect of another night in the plains made me desperate; I dislodged them, and persuaded them to advance once more. The settlements were of the most miserable description; many were composed of a few sticks lashed together at the top, and loosely covered with a few armfuls of holcus-cane. Here we sighted the cocoa-tree for the last time. The rats were busy in the fields, and the plundered peasants were digging them out for food. At almost every corner of the deeply-pitted path stood a mtego, or trap for small birds, a cage of rush or split bamboo planted in the ground near some corn, where a boy lies waiting till the prey nibbles at the bait, and then creeping up, bars with his hand the little doorway left in one of the sides. Beyond the villages the path forded six times the sandy bed of the Mgeta, whose steep and slippery banks supported dense screens of shrub and grass. Beyond the sixth passage, the road falls into the gravelly river-shoals, with the stream flowing in the other half of the course, under well-wooded masses of primitive hill. After again thrice fording the cold and muddy water, which even in the dry season is here ankle, there foot-deep, the road passed some clearings where porcupines and the African red squirrel, a sturdy little animal, with a long thick fur of dark brown, shot with green on the back, and a bright red waistcoat, muzzle, and points, were observed. About noon we diverged a few yards from the Mgeta, and ascended the incline of the first gradient in Usagara, rising about 300 feet from the plain below. This, the frontier of the second region, or ghauts, and the debris encumbering the lowest escarpment, is called Mzizi Mdogo, or the "Little Tamarind," to distinguish it from the "Great Tamarind" station which lies beyond. There was no vestige of building upon the spot – no sight nor sound of man – the blood-feud and the infernal slave-trade had made a howling desert of the land. We found, however, a tattered kraal erected by the last passing caravan, and, spent with fatigue, we threw ourselves on the short grass to rest. The porters and the asses did not appear till the evening, when it became apparent that two of the latter had been lost by their drivers, Hayja and Khamisi, sons of Ramji, who preferred sitting in the shade, and chatting with passing caravans, to the sore task of doing their duty. The animals were recovered on the morrow, by sundry parties sent in search. During the fordings of the Mgeta, however, they had not been unpacked; our salt and sugar, therefore, had melted away; soap, cigars, mustard, and arsenical paste, were in pulp; the tea was spoiled, the compressed vegetables presently became musty, and the gunpowder in a fire-proof copper magazine was caked like stale bread.

There was a wondrous change of climate at Mzizi Mdogo, strength and health returned as if by magic; even the Goanese shook off the obstinate bilious remit-tents of Zungomero. Truly delicious was the escape from the nebulous skies, the fog-driving gusts, the pelting rain, the clammy mists veiling a gross growth of fetor, the damp raw cold, rising as it were from the earth, and the alternations of fiery and oppressive heat; in fact, from the cruel climate of the river-valley, to the pure sweet mountain-air, alternately soft and balmy, cool and reviving, and to the aspect of clear blue skies, which lent their tints to highland ridges well wooded with various greens. Dull mangrove, dismal jungle, and monotonous grass, were supplanted by tall solitary trees, amongst which the lofty tamarind rose conspicuously graceful, and a card-table-like swamp, cut by a network of streams, nullahs, and stagnant pools, gave way to dry healthy slopes, with short steep pitches, and gently shelving hills. The beams of the large sun of the equator – and nowhere have I seen the rulers of night and day so large – danced gaily upon blocks and pebbles of red, yellow, and dazzling snowy quartz, and the bright sea-breeze waved the summits of the trees, from which depended graceful llianas, and wood-apples large as melons, whilst creepers, like vine tendrils, rising from large bulbs of brown-grey wood, clung closely to their stalwart trunks. Monkeys played at hide-and-seek, chattering behind the bolls, as the iguana, with its painted scale-armour, issued forth to bask upon the sunny bank; white-breasted ravens cawed when disturbed from their perching-places; doves cooed on the well-clothed boughs, and hawks soared high in the transparent sky. The field-cricket chirped like the Italian cigala in the shady bush, and everywhere, from air, from earth, from the hill slopes above, and from the marshes below, the hum, the buzz, and the loud continuous voice of insect life, through the length of the day, spoke out its natural joy. Our gipsy encampment lay

> *"By shallow rivers, to whose falls*
> *Melodious birds sing madrigals."*

By night, the soothing murmurs of the stream at the hill's base rose mingled with the faint rustling of the breeze, which at times broken by the scream of the night-heron, the bellow of the bull-frog in his swampy home, the cynhyaena's whimper, and the fox's whining bark, sounded through the silence most musical, most melancholy. Instead of the cold night rain, and the soughing of the blast, the view disclosed a peaceful scene, the moonbeams lying like sheets of snow upon the ruddy highlands, and the stars hanging like lamps of gold from the dome of infinite blue. I never wearied with contemplating the scene, for, contrasting with the splendours around me, still stretched in sight the Slough of Despond, unhappy Zungomero, lead-coloured above, mud-coloured below, wind-swept, fog-veiled, and deluged by clouds that dared not approach these Delectable Mountains.

During a day's halt at this sanitarium fresh diversions agitated the party. The Baloch, weary of worrying one another, began to try their 'prentice hands upon the sons of Ramji, and these fortified by the sturdy attitude of Muinyi Kidogo, manfully resolved to hold their own. The asses fought throughout the livelong night, and, contrary to the custom of their genus, strayed from one another by day. And as,

"When sorrows come, they come not single spies,
But in battalions,"

Said bin Salim, who hated and was hated by the Baloch, on account of their divided interests, began to hate and to be hated by the sons of Ramji. His four children, the most ignoble of their ignoble race, were to him as the apples of his eyes. He had entered their names as public porters, yet, with characteristic egotism and self-tenderness, he was resolved that they should work for none but their master, and that even in this their labour should as much as possible fall upon the shoulders of others. His tent was always the first pitched and his fire the first built; his slaves were rewarded with such luxuries as ghee, honey, and turmeric, when no one in camp, ourselves included, could procure them. When all wanted clothes he clad his children out of the outfit as if it had been his own, and, till strong remonstrances were made, large necklaces of beads decked their sooty necks. On the return-march he preferred to pay hire for three porters rather than to allow the fat lazy knaves to carry a bed or a few gourds. They became of course insolent and unmanageable – more than once they gave trouble by pointing their muskets at the Baloch and the porters, and they would draw their knives and stab at a man who refused to give up his firewood or his hearth-stones, without incurring a word of blame from their master. Encouraged by impunity they robbed us impudently; curry-stuff was soon exhausted, the salt-bottles showed great gaps, and cigar-ends were occasionally seen upon the road-side. The Goanese accused the slaves, and the slaves the Goanese; probably both parties for once spoke the truth.

Said bin Salim's silly favouritism naturally aroused the haughty Kidogo's bile; the sons of Ramji, consequently, worked less than before. The two worthies, Arab and African, never, however, quarrelled, no harsh word passed between them; with smiles upon their faces, and a bitter hate at heart, they confined themselves to all manner of backbiting and talebearing. Said bin Salim sternly declared to me that he would never rest satisfied until Kidogo's sword was broken and his back was scarified at the flagstaff of Zanzibar; but I guessed that this "wrathful mouse and most magnanimous dove" would, long before his journey's end, have forgotten all his vengeance. Kidogo asserted that the Muarabu or Arab was a green-horn, and frequently suggested the propriety of "planting" him. At last this continual harping upon the same chord became so offensive, that B'ana Saidi was forbidden to pronounce the name of Muinyi Kidogo, and Muinyi Kidogo was ordered never to utter the words B'ana Saidi before the exasperated leader of the Expedition, who could not, like these squabblers, complain, resent, forget and forgive, in the short space of a single hour.

We left Mzizi Mdogo on the 9th August, much cheered by the well-omened appearance of a bird with red bill, white breast, and long tail-feathers. The path ran over a succession of short steep hills with a rufous-brown soil, dotted with blocks and stones, thinly veiled with grass, and already displaying signs of aridity in the growth of aloetic and thorny plants, the Cactus and the larger Aselepias, the Euphorbia or Spurgewort, and the stunted Mimosa. The Calabash, however, still rose a stately tree, and there was a sprinkling of the fine Tamarinds which have lent their name to the district. The Tamarind, called by the Arabs of Zanzibar "Subar," extends from the coast to the Lake Regions: with its lofty stem, its feathery leaflets, and its branches spreading dark cool shade, it is a beautiful feature in African landscape. The acidulated fruit is doubtless a palliative and a corrective to bilious affections. The people of the country merely peel and press it into bark baskets, consequently it soon becomes viscid, and is spoiled by mildew; they ignore the art of extracting from it an intoxicating liquor. The Arabs, who use it extensively in cooking, steam, sun-dry, and knead it, with a little salt and oil to prevent the effects of damp, into balls: thus prepared and preserved from the air, it will keep for years.

On the way we were saddened by the sight of the clean-picked skeletons, and here and there the swollen corpses, of porters who had perished in this place of starvation. A single large body which had lost fifty of its number by small-pox, had passed us but yesterday on the road, and the sight of their deceased comrades recalled to our minds terrible spectacles; men staggering on blinded by disease, and mothers carrying on their backs infants as loathsome objects as themselves. The wretches would not leave the path, every step in their state of failing strength was precious; he who once fell would never rise again; no village would admit death into its precincts, no relation nor friend would return for them, and they would lie till their agony was ended by the raven and vulture, the Fisi and the fox. Near every Khambi or Kraal I remarked detached tents which, according to the guides, were set apart for those seized with the fell disease. Under these circumstances, as might be expected, several of our party caught the infection; they lagged behind and probably threw themselves into some jungle, for the path when revisited showed no signs of them.

We spent 4 hrs. 30' in weary marching, occasionally halting to reload the asses that threw their packs. Near the Mgeta

River, which was again forded six times, the vegetation became tall and thick, grasses obstructed the path, and in the dense jungle on the banks of the stream, the Cowhage (*Dolichos prurlens,*) and stiff reeds known as the "wild sugar-cane," annoyed the half-naked porters. Thus bounded and approached by muddy and slippery, or by steep and stony inclines, the stream shrank to a mountain torrent, in places hardly fifty feet broad; the flow was swift, the waters were dyed by the soil a ruddy brown, and the bed was sandy and sometimes rocky with boulders of primitive formation, streaked with lines of snow-white quartz. Near the end of the marsh we ascended a short steep staircase of rock and root, with a dwarf precipice overhanging the river on the right, which was dangerous for the laden beasts as they crawled like beetles up the path. At 3 P.M. we arrived at a kraal called Cha K'henge – of the iguana, from the number of these animals found near the stream. It was a delightful spot, equal to Mzizi Mdogo in purity of air, and commanding a fair prospect of the now distant Dut'humi Highlands.

The next day was a forced halt at Cha K'henge. Of two asses that had been left behind one was recovered, the other was abandoned to its fate. The animals purchased at Zanzibar were falling off visibly in condition. Accustomed to a kind of grass which nowhere grows upon these sunburnt hills, they had regular feeds of holcus, but that, as Said bin Salim expressed himself, was only coffee to them. The Wanyamwezi asses, however, managed to pick a sustenance from the rushes and from the half-burned stubbles, when fortunate enough to find any. Sickness again declared itself. Shahdad the Baloch bellowed like a bull with fever pains, Gaetano complained that he was suffering tortures generally, two of the Wanyamwezi were incapacitated by the symptoms preliminary to small-pox from carrying their packs, and a third was prostrated by ague. We started, however, on the next day for a long march which concluded, the passage of the "Tamarind Hills." Crossing a country broken by dry nullahs, or rather ditches, we traversed a seam of forest with a deep woody ravine on the right, and twice unpacked and reloaded the asses, who lay down instead of breasting the difficulties: a muddy swamp full of water-courses, and the high earth-banks of the Rufuta a Fiumara, here dry during the hot season. Thence, winding along a hill-flank, to avoid a bend in the bed, the path plunged into the sole of the Rufuta. This main-drain of the lower gradients carries off, according to the guides, the waters of the high ground around it into the Mgeta. The bed, which varies from three to sixteen feet in breadth, serpentines abruptly through the hills: its surface is either deep sand or clay, sopped with water, which near the head becomes a thin fillet, ankle-deep, now sweet, then salt: the mud is tinged in places with a solution of iron, showing, when stagnant, prismatic and iridescent tints. Where narrowest, the tall grasses of the banks meet across the gut, which, after a few yards of short, sharp winding, opens out again. The walls are in some parts earth, in others blocks of gray syenite, which here and there encumber the bed: on the right, near the end of the stage, the hills above seem to overhang the Fuimara in almost perpendicular masses of sandstone, from whose chinks spring the gnarled roots of tall trees corded with creepers, overgrown with parasites; and hung with fruits like footballs, dangling from twines sometimes thirty feet long. The lower banks, where not choked with rush, are overgrown with the brightest verdure, and with the feathery bamboo rising and falling before the wind. The corpses of porters were even more numerous than on the yester: our Muslems passed them with averted faces and with the low "la haul!" of disgust, and a decrepid old Mnyamwezi porter gazed at them and wept for himself. About 2 P.M., turning abruptly from the bed, we crawled up a short stony steep strewed with our asses and their loads; and reaching the summit of a dwarf cone near the foot of the "Goma Pass," we found the usual outlying huts for porters dying of small-pox, and an old kraal, which we made comfortable for the night. In the extensive prospect around, the little beehive villages of the Wakaguru and the Wakwivi, sub-tribes of the Wasagara, peeped from afar out of the forest nooks on the distant hill-folds. The people are rich in flocks and grain, but a sad experience has taught them to shun inter-course with all strangers, Arabs and Wasawahili, Wamrima and Wanyamwezi. In happier days the road was lined with large villages, of which now not a trace remains.

A Boiling Point Thermometer by Cox, the gift of Lieut.-Colonel Hamerton, and left with him by Captain, now Admiral Smyth, F. R. G. S., who had used it in measuring the Andes, had been accidentally broken by my companion at Cha K'henge. Arrived at Rufuta, I found that a second B. P. by Newman, and a Bath-Thermometer by the same maker, had been torn so violently from their box that even the well-soldered handles were wrenched off. But a few days after-wards our third B. P. was rendered useless by the carelessness of Gaetano. Thus, of the only three really accurate hypsomet-rical instruments which we possessed, – the Barometer had come to grief, and no aneroid had been sent from Bombay – not one was spared to reach the Lake. We saved, however, two Bath-Thermometers marked Newman, and Johnson and Co., Bombay, which did good service, and one of which was afterwards corrected by being boiled at sea-level. I may here observe that on such journeys, where triangulation is impossi-ble, and where the delicate aneroid and the Mountain Barom-eter can scarcely be carried without accident, the thermometer is at present the traveller's stand-by. It abounds, however, in elements of error. The elasticity of the glass, especially in a new instrument, causes the mercury to subside below the graduated scale. The difference of level in a covered "shav-ing-pot" and in an open pan exposed to the wind, will some-times amount to $1°$ F. = 500 feet: they therefore are in error who declare that any vessel suffices for the purpose of boil-ing. Finally, in all but the best instruments the air is not thor-oughly expelled from the tube: indeed some writers, Dr. Buist, for instance, actually advise the error.

Another ass was left at Rufuta unable to stand, and anxiously eyeing its stomach, whereby the Baloch conjectured that it was dying of a poisonous grass. Having to ascend on the 12th August the Goma Pass of the Rufuta, or the Eastern Range, I had arranged with Kidogo and the Kirangozi, or guide, that the porters should proceed with their packs, and after topping the hill, should return, for a consideration, to assist the asses. None, however, reappearing, when the sun had risen a spear's length we set out, hugging the hill-flanks, with deep ravines yawning on the right. Presently after passing through a clear forest of tall scattered trees, between whose trunks were visible on both sides in perspective, far below, long rolling tracts of well-wooded land broken by ravines and cut by water-courses, we arrived at the foot of a steep hill. The ascent was a kind of ramp, composed of earth-steps, clods bound by strong tenacious roots, and thickly strewn with blocks of schiste, micacious grit, and a sandstone showing the presence of iron. The summit of this "kloof" was ascertained to rise 2,235 feet above sea-level. It led to an easy descent along the flank of a hill commanding on the left hand, below a precipitous foreground, a fine bird's-eye view of scattered cone and wavy ridge rising and falling in a long roll, and on a scale decreasing till they settled into a line of hazy-blue horizon, which had all the effect of a circumambient ocean. We reached the remains of a kraal on the summit of a dwarf hill called Mfu'uni, from the abundance of the Mfu'u tree, which bears an edible apple externally like the smallest "crab," but containing a stone of inordinate proportions: below the encamping ground the Pagazi found a runnel of pure water, which derived its name from the station. In former times Mfu'uni was a populous settlement; the kidnapping parties from the coast, and especially the filibusters of Whinde, have restored it to the fox and the cynhyaena, its "old inhabitants." I spent a sleepless night in watching each star as it sank and set in its turn, piercing with a last twinkle the thin silhouette of tall trees that fringed the hilly rim of the horizon, and in admiring the hardness of the bullheaded Mabruki, as he lay half-roasted by the fire and half-frozen by the cold southern gale.

Rations had been issued at K'hutu to all hands for three days, the time in which they expected to make the principal provisioning-place, "Muhama." They had consumed, as usual, their stores with the utmost possible quickness; it was our fifth days and Muhama was still a long march distant. On the 13th August, therefore, in that hot haste which promises cold speed, we loaded at dawn, and ascended the last step of the pass by an easy path. The summit was thickly wooded; the hills were crowned with trees; the ravines were a mass of tangled verdure; and from the Dub (*Cynodon dactylon*, a nutritive and favourite food for cattle in India) and other grasses arose a sickening odour of decay. A Scotch mist, thick and raw, hung over the hill-tops, and about 10 P.M. a fiery outburst of sunshine told severely upon hungry and fewer-stricken men. From the level table-summit of the range the route descended rapidly at first, but presently stretching out into gentle slopes, totally unlike the abrupt eastern or seaward face of the mountains: I counted twelve distinct rises and fifteen falls, separated by tree-clad lines of half-dried nullahs, which were choked with ill-savoured weeds. We halted every quarter of an hour to raise and reload the asses; when on the ground, they were invariably abandoned by the donkey-men. My companion's bedding was found near the path, where it had been left by its porter, a slave given at Zungomero to Muinyi Wazira by his drunken brother. The fellow had been sworn by his mganga, or medicine-man, not to desert, and he had respected his oath for the long length of a week. A dispute with another man, however, had irritated him: he quietly threw his burden, and ran down the nearest steep, probably to fall into the hands of the Wakwivi. As the rain-catching peaks were left behind, the slopes of dry soil began to show sunburnt herbage and tufty grass. Signs of lions appeared numerous, and the cactaceous and aloetic plants that live on arid soil again met the eye. About noon we forded the little Zonhwe River, a stream of sweet water here flowing westward, in a bed of mire and grass, under high banks bearing a dense bush. Two hours afterwards I suddenly came upon the advance-guard, halted, and the asses unloaded, in a dry water-course, called in the map, from our misadventure, "Overshot Nullah." A caravan of Wanyarnwezi had misdirected them, Muinyi Wazira had in vain warned them of their error, he was over-ruled by Kidogo, and the Baloch had insisted upon camping at the first place where they expected to find a spring. Like all soft men, they were most impatient of thirst, and nothing caused so much grumbling and discontent as the cry of "Maji mb'hali!" (water is far!) That night, therefore, after a long march of fifteen miles, they again slept supperless.

On the 14th of August we loaded early, and through spit-ting rains from the south-east hills we marched back for two hours from the Overshot Nullah to Zonhwe, the small and newly-built settlement which we had missed on the preceding day. Several of the porters had disappeared during the night. Men were sent in all directions for provisions, which came in, however, slowly and scantily; and the noise made by the slaves – they were pulling down Said bin Salim's hut, which had accidentally caught fire – frightened away the country-people. We were, therefore, detained in this unwholesome spot for two days.

Zonhwe was the turning-point of the Expedition's diffi-culties. Another ass had died, reducing the number to twenty-three, and the Baloch, at first contented with two, doubled their requirements, and on the 14th August took a fifth, besides placing all their powder upon our hard-worked ani-mals. I therefore proposed to the Jemadar that the cloth, the beads, and the other similar luggage of his men, should be packed, sealed up, and inserted into the porters' loads, of which several had shrunk to half-weight. He probably thought the suggestion a ruse on my part to discover the means by which their property had almost trebled its quantity; his men, moreover, had become thoroughly weary of a journey where provisions were not always obtainable, and they had persuaded themselves that Lieut.-Col. Hamerton's decease had left me without support from the government of Zanzibar. After a priming with opium, the monocular returned and reported that his men refused to open their baggage, declaring their property to be "on their own heads." Whilst I was explaining the object of the measure, the escort appeared in mass, and, with noise sufficient for a general action, ostentatiously strewed their old clothes upon the ground, declaring that at Zanzibar they were honourable men, and boasting that the Baloch were entrusted with lacs of dollars by the Sayyid Said. Again I offered reasons, which, as is the wont of the world in such cases, served only to make them more hopelessly unreasonable. The Jemadar accused me of starving the party. I told him not to eat abominations, upon which, clapping hand to hilt, he theatrically forbade me to repeat the words. Being prostrated at the time by fever, I could only show him how little dangerous he was by using the same phrase half a dozen times. He then turned fiercely upon the timid Said bin Salim, and having safely vented the excess of his wrath, he departed to hold a colloquy with his men.

The debate was purposely conducted in so loud a tone that every word reached my ears. Khudabakhsh, from first to last my evil genius and the mainspring of all mischief, threatened to take "that man's life," at the risk of chains for the remainder of his days. Another opined, that "in all Nazarenes there is no good." All complained that they had no "hishmat" (respect!), no food, and, above everything, no meat.

Presently Said bin Salim was deputed by them to state that for the future they would require one sheep per diem — men who, when at Zanzibar, saw flesh probably once a year on the Eed. This being inadmissible, they demanded three cloths daily instead of one. I would willingly have given them two, as long as provisions continued scarce and dear, but the shade of concession made them raise the number to four.

They declared that in case of refusal they would sleep at the village, and on the next day would return to Zanzibar. Receiving a contemptuous answer, they marched away in a body, noisily declaring that they were going to make instant preparation for departure.

Such a proceeding on the part of several of these mercenaries was inexcusable. They had been treated with kindness, and even indulgence. They had hitherto never complained, simply because they had no cause for complaint. One man, Ismail, who suffered from dysentery, had been regularly supplied with food cooked by the Goanese; and even while we dragged along our fevered frames on foot, he was allowed to ride an ass. Yet the recreant never attempted a word of dissuasion, and deserted with the rest.

After the disappearance of the Baloch, the Sons of Ramji were summoned. I had privily ascertained from Said bin Salim the opinions of these men concerning their leader: they said but little evil, complaining principally of the Englishman's "heat," and that he was not wholly ruled by their rascalities, whereas the Baloch in their private confabs never failed to indulge in the choicest of Oriental Billingsgate. The slaves, when they heard the state of the case, cheerfully promised to stand by us, but on the same evening, assembled by Kidogo, they agreed to follow the example of the escort on the first justifiable occasion. I did not learn this till some days afterwards, and even if I had been told it on the spot, it would have mattered little. My companion and I had made up our minds, in case of the escort and the slaves deserting, to bury our baggage, and to trust ourselves in the hands of the Wanyamwezi porters. The storm, however, – a *brutum fulmen* – blew over with only noise.

A march was ordered for the next day – the 17th August. As the asses were being loaded, appeared the one-eyed Jemadar, with Greybeard Musa and Darwaysh, looking more crestfallen and foolish than they had ever looked before. They took my hand with a polite violence, begged suppliantly for a paper of dismissal to "cover their shame," and declared that, so far from deserting me, I was deserting them. As this required no reply, I mounted and rode on.

The path fell easily westwards down a long grassy and jungly incline, cut by several water-courses. About noon, I lay down half-fainting in the sandy bed of the Muhama Nullah – the "Palmetto," or "Fan-palm;" and retaining Wazira and Mabruki, I urged the caravan forwards, that my companion might send me back a hammock from the halting-place. Suddenly appeared the whole body of deserters shouldering – as porters and asses had been taken from them – their luggage, which outwardly consisted of cloth, dirty rags, green skins, old earthen pots, and greasy gourds and calabashes. They led me to a part of the nullah where stagnant water was found, and showing abundant penitence, they ever and anon attempted excuses, which were reserved for consideration. At 3 P.M., no hammock appearing, I remounted, and pursued a path over rolling ground, with masses of dwarf-hill flanking a low bottom, which renewed the scenery of the "Slough of Despond" – Zungomero. Again the land, matted with putrid grass, displayed the calabash and the hyphaena, the papaw and the palmetto; the holcus and maize were of luxuriant dimensions, and deep rat-holes, enlarged by the boy-hunters, broke the grassy path. I found two little villages, inhabitated by Wangindo and Mandandu immigrants from the vicinity of Kilwa. Then appeared on a hill-side the Kraal in which the caravan had halted; the party had lost the road, and had been dispersed by a swarm of wild bees, an accident even more frequent in East Africa than in India.

Next morning the Baloch were harangued; they professed themselves profoundly penitent, and attributing their unsoldier-like conduct to opium, and to the Wiswas, the temptations of Sathanas, they promised to reform. The promise was kept till we reached Ugogi. They were, however, always an encumbrance; they did no good beyond creating an impression, and "making the careless Æthiopians afraid." I saw them, it is true, in their worst colours. They held themselves to be servants of their prince, and as no Eastern man can or will serve two masters, they forfeited all claim to their sole good quality – manageability. As men, they had no stamina; after a few severe marches they murmured that

"Famine, despair, thirst, cold, and heat,
Had done their work on them by turns."

Their constitutions, sapped by long residence at Zanzibar, were subject to many ailments, and in sickness they were softer than Indian Pariahs. Under the slightest attack of fever, they threw themselves moaning upon the ground; they were soon deterred by the sun from bringing up the rear, and by night they would not keep watch or ward even when in actual danger of robbery. Notwithstanding their affectation of military carriage their bravery was more than problematical; they were disciplined only by their fears. As men at arms, one and all deserved to wear the wooden spoon: I saw the whole garrison of Kaole firing for an hour, without effect, at a shell, stuck on a stick, distant about a dozen paces: our party expended thirty pounds of gunpowder without bagging a pair of antelope, and it was impossible to trust them with ammunition; when unable to sell it, they wasted it upon small birds. Ever claiming for themselves "hishmat," or respect, they forgot their own proverb that "courtesy hath two heads;" they complained that they were not seated half the day in our tents, and the being "told to depart," when their terribly long visits rendered the measure necessary, was a standing grievance. Like the lower races of Orientals, they were ever attempting to intrude, to thrust themselves forwards, to take an ell when an inch was offered; they considered all but themselves fools, ready to be imposed upon by the flimsiest lie, by the shallowest artifices. Gratitude they ignored; with them a favour granted was but an earnest of favours to come, and one refusal obliterated the trace of a hundred largesses. Their objects in life seemed to be eating, and buying slaves; their pleasures, drinking and intrigue. Insatiable beggars were they; noisy, boisterous, foul-mouthed knaves, swearers "with voices like cannons;" rude and forward in manner, low and abusive in language, so slanderous that for want of other subjects they would calumniate one another, and requiring a periodical check to their presumption. I might have spent the whole of my day in superintending the food of these thirteen "great eaters and little runners." Repeatedly warned, both by myself and by my companion, that their insubordination would prevent our recommending them for recompense at the end of the journey, they could not check repeated ebullitions of temper. Before arrival at the coast they seemed to have made up their minds that they had not fulfilled the conditions of reward. After my departure from Zanzibar, however, they persuaded Lieut.-Col. Hamerton's successor to report officially to the Government of Bombay "the claims of these men, the hardships they endured, and the fidelity and perseverance they showed!"

At Muhama I halted three days, a delay which generally occurred before long desert marches for which provisions are required. On the first, Kidogo would bring about sixty pounds of grain; on the second, he would disperse his men throughout the villages, and procure the 300 pounds required for five marches; and on the third, he would cause it to be husked and pounded, so as to be ready for the morrow. Three up-caravans, containing a total of about 150 men, suffering severely from small-pox, here passed us. One was commanded by Khalfan bin Muallim Salim and his brother Id, coast Arabs, whom we afterwards met at two places. He told me several deliberate falsehoods about the twenty-two porters that were to follow us, for instance, that he had left them, halted by disease, at Kidunda, in the maritime region, under the command of one Abdullah bin Jumah, and thus he led me to expect them at a time when they had not even been engaged. He and his men also spread reports in Ugogo and other places where the people are peculiarly suspicious concerning the magical and malignant powers of the "whites;" in fact, he showed all the bad spirit of his bastard blood. At Muhama, the furthest point westward to which the vuli or autumnal rains extend, the climate was still that of the Rufuta Range, foggy, misty mornings, white rags of cloudbank from the table-cloths outspread upon the heights, clear days, with hot suns and chilling south winds, and raw dewy nights. I again suffered from fever; the attack, after lasting seven days, disappeared, leaving, however, hepatic complications, which having lasted uninterruptedly ten months, either wore themselves out, or yielded to the action of acids, narcotics, and stimulants tardily forwarded from Zanzibar. Here also over-fatigue, in a fruitless shooting-excursion, combined with the mephitic air of stagnant, weedy waters, caused a return of my companion's fever.

Two other Wanyamwezi porters were laid up with smallpox. One ass died of fatigue, whilst a second torn by a hyaena, and a third too weak to walk, were left, together with the animal that had been stung by bees, in charge of Mpambe, headman of the Wangindo. Being now reduced to the number of nineteen beasts, I submitted to Said bin Salim the advisability of leaving behind wire and ammunition, either cached in the jungle, as is the custom of these lands, or entrusted to the headman. The Arab approved; Kidogo, however, dissented. I took the opinion of the latter, he was positive that the effects once abandoned would never be recovered, and that the headman, who appeared a kind of cunning idiot, was not to be trusted. Some months afterwards I commissioned an Arab merchant, who was marching towards the coast, to recover the asses left in the charge of Mpambe; the latter refused to give them up, thus proving the soundness of Kidogo's judgment.

Having collected with difficulty – the land was sun-cracked, and the harvest-store had been concealed by the people – some supplies, but scarcely sufficient for the long desert tract, we began, on the 21st of August, to cross the longitudinal plain that gently shelving westward separates the Rufuta from the second, or Mukondokwa Range. The plain was enclosed on all sides by low lines of distant hill, and cut by deep nullahs, which gave more than the usual amount of trouble. The tall Palmyra (*Borassus Flabelliformis*), whose majestic bulging column renders it so difficult to climb, was a novel feature in the scenery. This tree, the Mvumo of East Africa, and the Deleb-palm of the Upper Nile, is scattered through the interior, extending to the far south. On this line it is more common in Western Unyamwezi, where, and where only, an intoxicating toddy is drawn from the cut frond, than elsewhere. The country abounded in game, but we were both too weak to work – my companion, indeed, was compelled to lag behind – and the Baloch, to whom the guns were lent, returned empty-handed. Sign of the Mbogo (*Bos Caffer*) here appeared; it is general in East Africa, especially upon the river plains where water abounds. These wild cattle are fine animals, somewhat larger than the common-sized English bullock, with uniform dun skins, never parti-coloured like the tame herds, and with thick black-brown horns, from twelve to thirteen inches broad at the base, diverging outwards, and incurved at the points, which in large specimens are distant about three feet from each other; they are separated by a narrow channel, and this in age becomes a solid mass of bone. The Mbogo is as dull of comprehension as it is fierce and powerful; affecting particular spots, it will often afford several chances of a successful shot to the Fundi – Shikari, or Chasseur – of a caravan: the Africans kill it with arrows. The flesh, though considered heating and bilious, is eaten, and the hide is preferred for thongs and reins to that of the tame animal.

The approach to the kraal was denoted by a dead level of dry, caked, and cracked mud, showing the subsidence of an extensive inundation. We passed a large camping-ground, affected by down-caravans, on the near side of the Makata, a long river-like "tank," whose lay is E. by N. The oozy banks of this water, which is said to flow after rains into the Mukondokwa River, are fringed with liliaceous and other large aquatic plants; the water, though dark, is potable. After fording the tank, which was then breast-deep, we found on the further side the kraal used by porters of up-caravans, who sensibly avoid commencing the day with hard labour, and who fear that a sudden fall of rain might compel them to intempestive halts. In such places, throughout the country, there are two distinct khambi, one on each side of the obstacle, whether this be a river, a pass, or a populous clearing; in the latter case, caravans unload at the farther end of the cultivation, prepared to escape from a fray into the jungle, without running the gauntlet of the villages. That evening I tried to reduce the ever-increasing baggage of the sons of Ramji, who added to the heaps piled upon the wretched asses, now burdened with rations for several days, their drums and sleeping-hides, and their cocks and hens, whilst they left the beds and the cooking-utensils of the Goanese upon the ground. They informed me that if our animals could not carry their property, they could not drive our animals. The reply was significant. With some exertion of the "rascally virtue" – Prudence – I retired.

The night was disturbed only by mosquitoes. These piping pests, however, are less troublesome in this part of East Africa than might be expected from the nature and the position of the country, and the bite has little venom compared with those of the Mozambique, or even of Western India. The common culex is a large variety, of brownish or dun colour; its favourite breeding-places are the backwaters on the banks of rivers, and the margins of muddy pools, and upon the creeks of the maritime regions, and the Central Lakes.

Pursuing our march on the next day, I witnessed a curious contrast in this strange African nature, which is ever in extremes, and where extremes ever meet, where grace and beauty are seldom seen without a sudden change to a hideous grotesqueness. A splendid view charmed me in the morning.

Above lay a sky of purest azure, flaked with fleecy opal-tinted vapours floating high in the empyrean, and catching the first roseate smiles of the unrisen sun. Long lines, one bluer than the other, broken by castellated crags and towers of most picturesque form, girdled the far horizon; the nearer heights were of a purplish-brown, and snowy mists hung like glaciers about their folds. The plain was a park in autumn, burnt tawny by the sun, patched with a darker hue where the people were firing the grass- a party was at work merrily, as if preparing for an English harvest-home – to start the animals, to promote the growth of a young crop, and, such is the popular belief, to attract rain. Calabashes, Palmyras, Tamarinds, and clumps of evergreen trees were scattered over the scene, each stretching its lordly arms over subject circlets of deep dew-fed verdure. Here the dove cooed loudly, and the guinea-fowl rang its wild cry, whilst the peewit chattered in the open stubble, and a little martin, the prettiest of its kind, contrasted by its nimble dartings along the ground with the condor wheeling slowly through the upper air. The most graceful of animals, the zebra and the antelope, browsed in the distance: now they stood to gaze upon the long line of porters, then, after leisurely pacing, with retrospective glances, in an opposite direction, they halted motionless for a moment, faced about once more to satiate curiosity, and lastly, terrified by their own fancy, they bounded in ricochets over the plain.

About noon the fair scene vanished as if by enchantment. We suddenly turned northwards into a tangled mass of tall fetid reeds, rank jungle and forest, with its decaying trunks encroaching upon the hole-pierced goat-track that zigzaged towards the Myombo River. This perennial stream rises, according to the guides, in an elevation opposite to the highlands of Dut'humi. It is about fifty feet broad at the ford, breast-deep, and the swift brown waters swirl under a canopy of the trees whose name it bears. The "Myombo" is a fine specimen of African timber, apparently unknown to the people of Zanzibar, but extending almost from the coast to the

Lake Regions. The flower is greenish, with the overpowering smell of the Indian jasmines; the fruit is a large pod, containing ten or twelve long hard acorns, of a brown-black colour, set in cups which resemble red sealing-wax. The coarse bark is used for building huts and kraals, the inner fibre for "bast" and ropes, and the wood makes what Easterns call a hot fire, lasting long, and burning well out. After the fiery sun and the dry atmosphere of the plains, the sudden effect of the dank and clammy chill, the result of exceeding evaporation, under the impervious shades that line the river banks, was overpowering. In such places one feels as if poisoned by miasma; a shudder runs through the frame; and a cold perspiration, like the prelude for a fainting-fit, breaks from the brow. Unloading the asses, and fording the stream, we ascended the left bank, and occupied a kraal, with fires still smoking, on its summit. Though another porter was left behind with small-pox, I had little difficulty with the luggage on this march: the more I worked the men, the harder they worked. Besides, they seldom fell sick on the road, though often prostrated when halting, a phenomenon which my companion explained by their hard eating and little exercise when stationary, and which Said bin Salim more mercifully attributed to the fatigue and exposure of the journey taking effect when the excitement had passed away.

At dawn on the 23rd of August we resumed our journey, and in 4hrs 30' concluded the transit of the lateral plain, which separates the Rufuta from the Mukondokwa Range. The path wound over a wintry land, green with vegetation only in the vicinity of water. After struggling through a forest of canes, we heard a ngoma, or large drum, which astonished us, as we had not expected to find a village. Presently, falling into a network of paths, we lost our way. After long wandering we came upon a tobacco-field which the Baloch and the sons of Ramji had finished stripping, and conducted by some Wanyamwezi who had delayed returning to guide us, in order to indulge their love for drumming and plundering, we arrived at the debris of a once flourishing village of Wasagara, called Mbumi from its headman. A pitiable scene here presented itself. The huts were torn and half-burnt, and the ground was strewed with nets and drums, pestles and mortars, cots and fragments of rude furniture; and though no traces of blood were observed, it was evident that a Commando had lately taken place there. Said bin Salim opined this ruin to be the work of Khalfan bin Salim, the youth who had preceded us from Muhama; ever suspicious, he saw in it a plan adopted by the coast-Arab in order to raise against us the people of the mountains. Kidogo, observing that the damage was at least ten days' old, more acutely attributed it to the Moslem kidnappers of Whinde, who, aided by the terrible Kisabengo, the robber-chief of Ukami, near K'hutu, harry the country with four or five hundred guns. Two of the wretched villagers were seen lurking in the jungle, not daring to revisit the wreck of their homes. Here again the Demon of Slavery will reign over a solitude of his own creation. Can it be that, by some inexplicable law, where Nature has done her best for the happiness of mankind, man, doomed to misery, must work out his own unhappiness? That night was spent at the deserted village by our men in drumming, singing, and gleaning all that Khalfan's gang had left; they were, moreover, kept awake by fear lest they might be surprised by the remnants of the villagers.

Late in the morning of the 24th of August, after losing another ass, torn by a cynhyaena, we followed the path that leads from Mbumi along the right bank of the Mukondokwa River to its ford. The marescent vegetation, and the tall, stiff, and thick-stalked grass, dripped with dew, which struck cold as a freezing-mixture. The path was slippery with mud, and man and beast were rendered wild by the cruel stings of a small red ant and a huge black pismire. The former cross the road in dense masses like the close columns of an army. They are large-headed, showing probably that they are the defenders of the republic, and that they perform the duties of soldiers in their excursions. Though they cannot spring, they show great quickness in fastening themselves to the foot or ankle as it brushes over them. The pismire, known to the people as the "chungu-fundo," or "siyafu" from the Arabic "siyaf," is a horse-ant, about an inch in length, whose bulldog-like head and powerful mandibles enable it to destroy rats and mice, lizards and snakes. It loves damp places upon the banks of rivers and stagnant waters; it burrows but never raises hills, and it appears scattered for miles over the paths. Like the other species, it knows neither fear nor sense of fatigue; it rushes to annihilation without hesitating, and it cannot be expelled from a hut except by fire or boiling water. Its bite, which is the preamble to its meal, burns like a pinch with a red-hot needle; and when it sets to work, twisting itself round and "accroupi" in its eagerness for food, it may be pulled in two without relaxing its hold. The favourite food of this pismire is the termite: its mortal enemy is a large ginger-coloured ant, called from its painful wound "maji m'oto," or "hot-water." In this foul jungle our men also suffered severely from the tzetze. This fly, the torment of Cape travellers, was limited, by Dr. Livingstone, to the regions south of the Zam-bezi river. A specimen, brought home by me and submitted to Mr. Adam White, of the British Museum, was pronounced by him to be a true Glossina morsitans, and Mr. Petherick has fixed its limits about eight degrees north of the equator. On the line followed by the Expedition, the tzetze was found extending from Usagara westward as far as the Central Lakes; its usual habitat is the jungle-strip which encloses each patch of cultivated ground, and in the latter it is rarely seen. It has more persistency of purpose even than the Egyptian fly, and when beaten off it will return half a dozen times to the charge; it cannot be killed except by a smart blow, and its long sharp proboscis draws blood even through a canvas hammock. It is not feared by the naked traveller; the sting is as painful as that of an English horsefly, and leaves a lasting trace, but this hard-skinned people expect no evil consequences from it. In the vicinity of Kilwa it was heard of under the name of "kipanga," the "little sword." It is difficult to conceive the purpose for which this plague was placed in a land so eminently fitted for breeding cattle and for agriculture, which without animals cannot be greatly extended, except as an exercise for human ingenuity to remove. Possibly at some future day, when the country becomes valuable, the tzetze may be exterminated by the introduction of some insectivorous bird, which will be the greatest benefactor that Central Africa ever knew.

After about an hour's march, the narrow tunnel in the jungle – it was so close that only one ass could be led up and unloaded at a time – debouched upon the Mukondokwa ford. The view was not unpleasing. The swift brown stream was broadened by a branch-islet in its upper bed to nearly a hundred yards, and its margins were fringed with rushes backed by a screen of dense verdure and tall trees which occupied the narrow space between the water and the hills. The descent and the landing-place were equally bad. Slipping down the steep miry bank the porters sank into the river breast-deep, causing not a little damage to their loads: the ford now wetted the waist then the knee, and the landing-place was a kind of hippopotamus-run of thick slushy mud, floored with roots and branches, snags and sawyers, and backed by a quagmire rendered passable only by its matwork of tough grass-canes laid by their own weight. Having crossed over on our men's backs, we ascended a little rise and lay down somewhat in the condition of travelling Manes fresh from the transit of the Styx. I ordered back Kidogo with a gang of porters to assist Said bin Salim who was bringing up the rear: he promised to go but he went the wrong way – forwards. Resuming our march along the river's left or northern bank, we wound along the shoulders and the bases of hills, sometimes ascending the spurs of stony and jungly eminences, where the paths were unusually rough and precipitous, at other times descending into the stagnant lagoons, the reedy and rushy swamps, and the deep bogs which margin the stream. After a total of six hours we reached a kraal situated upon the sloping ground at the foot of the northern walls which limit the grassy river basin: through this the Mukondokwa flows in a dark turbid stream now narrowed to about forty feet. The district of "Kadetamare" was formerly a provisioning station where even cattle were purchase-able, a rare exception to the rule in the smaller settlements of Usagara. I at once sent men to collect rations, none, however, were procurable: meeting a small party that were bringing grain from Rumuma, they learned that there was a famine in the land.

At Kadetamare the only pedometer, a patent watch-shaped instrument, broke down, probably from the effects of the climate. Whilst carried by my companion it gave a steady exaggerative rate, but being set to the usual military pace of 30 inches, when transferred to the person of "Seedy Bombay" and others, it became worse than useless, sometimes showing 25 for 13 miles. I would suggest to future explorers in these regions, as the best and the most lasting means of measuring distances, two of the small wheelbarrow perambulators – it is vain to put trust in a single instrument – which can each be rolled on by one man. And when these are spoilt or stolen, timing with the watch, and a correct estimate of the walking rate combined with compass-bearings, the mean of the oscillations being taken when on the march, would give a "dead-reckoning," which checked by latitudes, as often as the cloudy skies permit, and by a few longitudes at crucial stations, would afford materials for a map approximating as nearly to correctness as could be desired in a country where a "handful of miles" little matters. The other instruments, though carefully protected from the air, fared not better than the pedometer: with three pocket-chronometers and a valuable lever-watch, we were at last reduced to final time by a sixpenny sun-dial. Before the first fortnight after our second landing in Africa had elapsed, all these instruments, notwithstanding the time and trouble devoted to them by my companion, at Zanzibar, failed in their ratings and became useless for chronometric longitudes. Two of them (Ed. Baker, London, No. 863, and Barraud, London, No.$^2/_{537}$), stopped without apparent reason. A third, a first-rate article (Parkinson and Frodsham, No. 2955), issued to me from the Royal Observatory Greenwich, at the kind suggestion of Capt. Belcher, of the Admiralty, had its glass broken and its second-hand lost by the blunderer Gaetano: we remedied that evil by counting the ticks without other trouble than that caused by the odd number, – 5 to 2 seconds. This instrument also summarily struck work on the 9th November, 1858, the day before we intended to have "made a night of it" at Jiwe la Mkoa. This may serve as a warning for future travellers to avoid instruments so delicate that a jolt will disorder them – the hair-spring of the lever watch was broken by my companion in jumping out of a canoe – and which no one but a professional can attempt to repair. A box chronometer carried in a "pet-arah" by a pole swung between two men so as to preserve its horizontality, might outlast the pocket-instruments, yet we read in Capt. Owens celebrated survey of the African coasts, that out of nine not one kept rate without fluctuations. The best plan would be to purchase half-a-dozen sound second-hand watches, carefully inspected and cleaned, and to use one at a time; if gold-mounted, they would form acceptable presents to the Arabs, and ultimately would prove economical by obviating the necessity of parting with more valuable articles.

The break-down of the last chronometer disheartened us for a time. Presently when our brains, addled by sun and sickness, had recovered tone by a return to the Usagara sanitarium, we remembered a rough and ready succedaneum for instruments. I need scarcely tell the reader that, unhappily for travellers, the only means of ascertaining the longitude of a place is by finding the difference between the local and Greenwich times, and that this difference of time with certain corrections is converted into distance of space. We split a 4 oz. rifle-ball, inserted into it a string measuring 39 inches from the point of suspension to the centre of the weight, and fixed it by hammering the halves together. The loose end of the cord was attached to a three-edged file as a pivot, and this was lashed firmly to the branch of a tree sheltered as much as possible from the wind. Local time was ascertained with a sextant by taking the altitude of a star or a planet; Greenwich time by a distance between the star or planet and the moon, and the vibrations of our rude pendulum did all that a watch could do, by registering the seconds that elapsed between the several observations.

I am somewhat presuming upon the subject, but perhaps it may here be better to chronicle the accidents which happened to the rest of our instruments. We had two Schmalcalder's compasses (H. Barron & Co., 26, Oxenden Street), which, when the paste-board faces had been acclimatized and no longer curled up against their glasses, did good service; one of them was trodden upon by my companion, the other by a sailor during a cruise on the lake. We returned with a single instrument, the gift of my old friend Lieut.-General Monteith; it had surveyed Persia, and outlasting two long excursions into Eastern Africa, it still outlives and probably will outlive many of the showy articles now supplied by the trade. Finally, a ship's compass, mounted in gimbals for boat-work and indented for upon the Engineer's Stores, Bombay, soon became lumber, its oscillations were too sluggish to be useful.

We left Kadetamare on the 25th August, to ascend the fluviatile valley of the Mukondokwa. According to the guides this stream is the upper course of the Kingani River, with which it anastomoses in Uzaramo (?) It cuts its way through the chain to which it gives a name, by a transversal valley perpendicular to the lay, and so conveniently disposed that the mountains seem rather to be made for their drain than the drain for its mountains. The fluviatile valley is apparently girt on all sides by high peaks, with homesteads smoking and cattle grazing on all sides. Crippled by the night-cold that rose from the river-bed, and then wet through with the dew that dripped from the tall grass, we traversed, within ear-shot of the frightened villagers who hailed one another from the heights, some fields of grain and tobacco that had been lately reaped. After an hour and a half of marching we arrived at the second ford of the Mukondokwa. Receiving less drainage than in the lower bed, the stream was narrower and only knee-deep; the landing-place of sloppy mud caused, however, many accidents to the asses, and on inspecting our stores a few days afterwards we found them all soft and mildewed. The reader will wonder that on these occasions we did not personally inspect the proceedings of our careless followers. The fact is we were physically and morally incapacitated for any exertion beyond balancing ourselves upon the donkeys; at Kadetamare I had laid in another stock of fever, and my companion had not recovered from his second severe attack. After fording the Mukondokwa we followed the right bank through cultivation, grass, and trees, up a gradually broaden-ing valley peculiarly rich in field-rats. the path then crossing sundry swamps and nullahs, hill-spurs and "neat's tongues," equally rough thorny and precipitous, presently fell into a river-reach where pools of water, breast deep, and hedged in by impassable jungle and long runs of slushy mire festering in a furious sun, severely tried the porters and asses. Thence the road wound under the high hills to the South, whose flanks were smoking with extensive conflagrations, whilst on the opposite or left bank of the river, the opening valley displayed a forest of palms and tall trees. About 2 P.M. I reached the ground, a hutless circle of thorns, called by our people Muinyi: the rear-guard, however, did not straggle in before 6 P.M., and the exhaustion of the asses – seventeen now remained – rendered a day's halt necessary.

During the last two marches the Baloch had been, they declared, without grain; the sons of Ramji and the porters, more provident, had reserved a small store. moreover they managed to procure a sheep from the next station. On the morrow a party, headed by Muinyi Wazira, set out to forage among the mountain settlements, bearing no arms in token of peace. About noon they returned, and reported that at the sight of strangers the people had taken to flight, after informing the party that they were in the habit of putting to death all Murungwana or freemen found trespassing off the road; however, that on this occasion the lives of the strangers should be spared. But Ambari, a slave belonging to Said bin Salim, presently tattled the true tale. The gallant foragers had not dared to enter the village; when the war-cry flew from hamlet to hamlet, and all the Wasagara, even the women and children, seized their spears and stood to arms, they at once threw themselves into the jungle and descended the hill with such unseemly haste that most of them bore the wounds of thorns and stones. Two of Baloch, Riza and Belok, lit their matches and set out proudly to provide themselves by their prowess; they were derided by Kidogo: "Verily, O my brethren! ye go forth to meet men and not women!" and after a hundred yards' walk they took second thoughts and returned. The Mukondokwa Mountains, once a garden, have become a field for fray and foray; cruelty and violence have brutalised the souls of the inhabitants, and they have learned, as several atrocities committed since our passage through the country prove, to wreak their vengeance upon all weaker than themselves.

On the 27th August we resumed our way under fresh difficulties. The last march had cost us another ass. Muhinna, a donkey-driver, complaining of fever, had been mounted by Kidogo without my permission, and had summarily departed, thus depriving us of the services of a second, whilst all were in a state of weakness which compelled them to walk at their slowest pace. On the other hand, the men of the caravan, hungry and suffering from raw south-east wind and the chilly cold, the result not of low temperature but of humidity and extensive evaporation, were for pushing forward as fast as possible. The path was painful, winding along the shoulders of stony and bushy hills, with rough re-entering angles, and sometimes dipping down into the valley of the Mukondokwa, which, hard on the right, spread out in swamps, nearly two miles broad, temporary where they depended upon rain, and permanent where their low levels admitted of free infiltration. On the steep eminences to the left of the path rose tall and thick the thorny aloetic and cactaceous growth of arid Somaliland; the other side was a miniature of the marine lagoons, the creeks, and the bayous of green Zanzibar. After three hours of hard marching, the labour came to its crisis, where the path, breaking off at a right angle from the river, wound up an insecure ladder of loose earth and stones, which caused several porters and one ass to lose their footing, and to roll with their loads through the thorny bushes of the steep slope, near the off side, into the bed of rushes below. Then leaving the river-valley on the right, we fell into a Fiumara of deep loose sand, about a hundred yards broad, and occupying the centre of a widening table-land. The view now changed, and the "wady" afforded pleasant glimpses of scenery. Its broad, smooth and glistening bed, dinted by the footprints of cattle, was bounded by low perpendicular banks of stilt red clay, margined by mighty masses of brilliant green tamarinds, calabashes, and sycomores, which stood sharply out against the yellow stubbles beyond them. The Mkuyu or sycomore in Eastern Africa is a magnificent tree; the bole, composed of a pillared mass, averages from eight to ten feet in height, and the huge branches, thatched with thick cool foliage, extend laterally, overshadowing a circle whose perimeter, when the sun is vertical, sometimes attains five hundred feet. The fruit, though eaten by travellers, is a poor berry, all rind and seeds, with a slender title to the name of fig. There are apparently two varieties of this tree, resembling each other in general appearance, but differing in details. The Mtamba has a large, heavy, and fleshy leaf; its fruit is not smooth like that of the Mkuyu, but knobbed with green excrescences, and the bole is loftier than the common sycomore's trunk. The roots of the older trees, rising above the earth, draw up a quantity of mould which, when the wood is decayed or destroyed, forms the dwarf mounds that in many parts encumber the surface of the country. Traces of extensive cultivation – fields of bajri or panicum, the staple cereal which here supplants the normal African holcus, or Kafir corn, and plantations of luxuriant maize, of beans, of the vetch known as the voiandzeia subterranea, of tobacco, and other plants – showed that this district is beyond the reach of the coast-kidnappers. From the rising ground on the left hand we heard the loud tattoo of the drum. The Baloch, choosing to be alarmed, fired several shots, much to the annoyance of the irascible Kidogo, who had laid down as a law that waste of powder in this region was more likely to invite than to prevent an attack. As we ascended the Fiumara it narrowed rapidly, and its head was encumbered with heaps of boulders from which sprang a runnel of the sweetest water. The camping-ground was upon the left bank of the bed. The guide called it Ndabi, probably from a small gnarled tree here abundant, bearing a fruit like a pale red currant, which tastes like sweetened gum dissolved in dirty water. I lost no time in sending for provisions, which were scarce and dear. Bombay failed in procuring a sheep, though the Baloch, by paying six cloths, were more fortunate. One of Kidogo's principles of action, in which he was abetted by Said bin Salim, was to prevent our buying provisions, however necessary, at high prices, fearing lest the tariff thus established might become an "ada," a precedent or custom for future travellers, himself and others. We were, therefore, fain to content ourselves and our servants with a little bajri and two eggs.

After a day's halt at Ndabi we resumed the journey on the 29th August. The path crossed a high and stony hill-shoulder, where the bleak raw air caused one of the porters to lie down torpid like a frozen man. It then stretched over gradually rising and falling ground to a dense bush of cactaceae and milk-bush, aloetic plants and thorns, based upon a surface of brick-dust-red. Beyond this point lay another plateau of wavy surface, producing dwarfed and wind-wrung calabashes, and showing grain-fields carefully and laboriously ridged with the hoe. Flocks and herds now appeared in all directions. The ground was in some places rust-coloured, in others dazzlingly white with a detritus of granite; mica glittered like silver-filings in the sun, and a fine silky grass waved in the wind, bleached clean of colour by the glowing rays. This plateau ended in a descent with rapid slopes, over falls and steps of rock and boulder into the basin of the Rumuma River. It is a southern influent, or a bifurcation of the Mukondokwa, and it drains the hills to the south-west of the Rumuma district, whereas the main stream, arising in the highlands of the Wahumba or Wanmsai, carries off the waters of the lands on the west. Losing our way, we came upon this mountain-torrent, which swirls through blocks and boulders under stiff banks of red earth densely grown with brush and reeds; and to find the kraal we were obliged to travel up the bed-side, through well-hoed fields irrigated by raised water-courses. The khambi was badly situated in the dwarf hollow between the river and the hills, and having lately been tenanted, as the smoking embers showed, it was uncleanly in the extreme. It was heart-breaking to see the asses that day. I left them to Said bin Salim, who, with many others, did not appear till eventide.

Rumuma is a favourite resting-place with caravans, on account of the comparative abundance of its supplies. I halted here two whole days, to rest and feed the starving porters, and to repair the sacks, the packsaddles, and the other appointments of the asses. Here, for the first time, the country people descended in crowds from the hills, bringing fowls, hauling along small but beautifully formed goats, lank sheep, and fine bullocks – the latter worth twelve cloths – and carrying on their heads basket-platters full of the Voandzeia, bajri, beans, and the Arachis Hypogoea. The latter is called by the Arabs Sumbul el Sibal, or "Monkey's Spikenard;" on the coast, Njugu ya Nyassa; in Unyam-wezi, Karanga or K'haranga, and further west, Mayowwa or Mwanza. It is the Bhuiphali, or "earth-fruit" of India, and the Bik'han of Maharatta land, where it is used by cheap confectioners in the place of almonds, whose taste it simulates. Our older Cape travellers term it the pig-nut. The plant extends itself along the surface of the ground, and puts forth its fruit at intervals below. It is sown before the rains, and ripens after six months, – in the interior about June. The Arabs fry it with cream that has been slightly salted, and employ it in a variety of rich dishes; it affords them also a favourite oil. The Africans use it princi-pally on journeys. The price greatly varies according to the abundance of the article; when moderate, about two pounds may be purchased for a "khete" of coral beads.

The Wasagara of Rumuma are short, black, beardless men. They wear their hair combed off the forehead, and twisted into a fringe of little pig-tails, which extend to the nape of the neck. Few boast of cloth, the general body con-tenting themselves with a goatskin flap somewhat like a cob-bler's apron tied over one shoulder, as we sling a game-bag. Their ornaments are zinc and brass earrings in rolls, which distend the ear-lobe, bangles, or armlets of similar metal, and iron chains with oblong links as anklets. Their arms are bows and arrows, assegais with long lanceated heads, and bull-hide shields, three feet long by one broad, painted black and red in perpendicular stripes. I was visited by their Sultan Njasa, a small grizzled old man, with eyes reddened by liquor, a wide mouth, a very thin beard, a sooty skin, and long straggling hair, "a la malcontent." He was attired in an antiquated Bar-sati, or blue and red Indian cotton, tucked in at the waist, with another thrown over his shoulders, and his neck was decked with many strings of beads. He insisted upon making "sare" or brotherhood with Said bin Salim, who being forbidden by his law to taste blood, made the unconscientious Muinyi Wazira his proxy. The two brothers being seated on the ground opposite each other, with legs well to the fore, one man held over their heads a drawn sword, whilst another addressed to them alternately a little sermon, denouncing death or slavery as the penalty for proving false to the vow. Then each brother licked a little of the other's blood, taken with the finger from a knife-cut above the heart, or rather where the heart is popularly supposed to be. The Sultan then presented to the Muinyi, in memoriam, a neat iron chain-anklet, and the Muinyi presented to the Sultan a little of our cloth.

The climate of Rumuma was new to me, after the incessant rains of the maritime valley, and the fogs and mists of the Rufuta Range. It was, however, in extremes. At night the thermometer, under the influence of dewy gusts, sank in the tent to 48° F., a killing temperature in these latitudes to half-naked and houseless men. During the day the mercury ranged between 80° and 90° F.; the sun was fiery, whilst a furious south wind coursed through skies purer and bluer than I had ever seen in Greece or Italy. At times, according to the people, the hill-tops are veiled, especially in the mornings and evenings, with thick nimbus, vapours, and spitting clouds, which sometimes extend to the plain, and discharge heavy showers that invariably cause sickness. Here my companion once more suffered from an attack of "liver," brought on, he supposed, from over-devotion to a fat bullock's hump. Two of the Wanyamwezi porters were seized with preliminary symptoms of small-pox, euphuistically termed by Said bin Salim "shurua," or chicken-pox. Several of the slaves, including the charming Halimah, were laid up; the worst of all, however, was Valentine, who complained of an unceasing racking headache, whilst his puffed cheeks and dull-yellow skin gave him the look of one newly deceased. At length, divining his complaint, he was cupped by a Mnyamwezi porter, and he recovered after the operation strength and appetite.

The 2nd of September saw us en route to Marenga Mk'hali, or the "brackish water." Fording the Rumuma above the spot where it receives the thin supplies of the Marenga Mk'hali, we marched over stony hills and thorny bushes, dotted with calabash and mimosa, the castor-shrub and the wild egg-plant, and gradually rising, we passed into scattered fields of holcus and bajri, pulse and beans. Here, for the first time, bee-hives, called by the coast-people Mazinga, or cannons, from their shape, hollowed cylindrical logs, closed with grass and puddle at both ends, and provided with an oval opening in the centre, were seen hanging to the branches of the foliaged trees. Cucumbers, water-melons, and pumpkins grew apparently without cultivation. The water-melon, called by the Arabs Johh, and by the Wasawahili Tikiti, flourishes throughout the interior, where it is a favourite with the people. It is sown before the rainy season, gathered after six months, and placed to ripen upon the flat roofs of the villages. Like the produce of Kafir-land, it is hard, insipid, fleshy, and full of seeds, having nothing but the name in common with the delicious fruit of Egypt and Afghanistan. The Junsal, or Boga, the pumpkin, is, if possible, worse than the water-melon. Its red meat, simply boiled, is nauseously sweet; it is, however, considered wholesome, and the people enjoy the seeds toasted, pounded, and mixed with the "Mboga," or wild vegetables, with which a veritable African can, in these regions, keep soul and body together for six months. About 10 A.M., I found Khalfan's caravan halted in a large kraal amongst the villages, on the eastern hill above the "brackish water." They were loading for the march, and my men looked wistfully at the comfortable huts; but their halt had been occasioned by small-pox, I therefore hurried forwards across the streamlet to a windswept summit of an opposite hill. The place was far from pleasant, the gusts were furious; by night the thermometer showed 54° F., by day there was but scanty shelter from the fiery sun, and the "Marenga Mk'hali," which afforded the only supplies of water, was at a considerable distance. Moreover our umbrellas and bedding suffered severely from a destructive host of white ants, that here became troublesome for the first time. The "Chunga Mehwa" or termite, abounds throughout the sweet red clay soils, and cool damp places, avoiding heat, sand, and stone, and it acts like a clearer and scavenger; without it, indeed, some parts of the country would be impassable, and it is endowed with extraordinary powers of destruction. A hard clay-bench has been drilled and pierced like a sieve by these insects in a single night, and bundles of reeds placed under bedding, have in a few hours been converted into a mass of mud; straps were consumed, cloths and umbrellas were reduced to rags, and the mats used for covering the servants' sleeping-gear were, in the shortest possible time, so tattered as to be unserviceable. Man revenges himself upon the white ant, and satisfies his craving for animal food, which in these regions becomes a principle of action, – a passion, – by boiling the largest and fattest kind, and eating it as a relish with his insipid ugali, or porridge. The termite appears to be a mass of live water. Even in the driest places it finds no difficulty in making a clay-paste for the mud-galleries, like hollow tree-twigs, with which it disguises its approach to its prey. The phenomenon has been explained by the conjecture that it combines by vital force the atmospheric oxygen with the hydrogen evolved by its food. When arrived at the adult state, the little peoples rise ready-winged, like thin curls of pipe-smoke, generally about even-tide, from the ground. After a flight of a few yards, the fine membranes, which apparently serve to disperse the insects into colonies, drop off. In East Africa there is also a semi-transparent brown ant, resembling the termite in form, but differing in habits, and even exceeding it in destructiveness. It does not, like its congener, run galleries up to the point of attack. Each individual works for itself in the open air, tears the prey with its strong mandibles, and carries it away to its hole. The cellular hills of the termites in this country rarely rise to the height of three feet, whereas in Somaliland they become dwarf towers, forming a conspicuous feature in the view.

No watch was kept by the Baloch at Marenga Mk'hali, though we were then in the vicinity of the bandit Wahumba.

On the next day we were harangued by Kidogo, who proceeded to expound the principles that must guide us through the unsafe regions ahead. The caravan must no longer straggle on in its usual disorder, the van must stop short when separated from the main body, and the rear must advance at the double when summoned by the sound of the Barghumi, or the koodoo-horn, which acts as bugle in Eastern Africa. I thought, at the time, that Kidogo might as well address his admonitions to the wind, and I thought rightly.

The route lay through the lateral plain which separates the Mukondokwa or second, from the Rubeho or third parallel range of the Usagara Mountains. At Marenga Mk'hali, situated as it is under the lee of the two eastern walls, upon which the humid N.E. and S.E. trade-winds impinge, the eye no longer falls, as before, upon a sheet of monotonous green, and the nose is not offended by the death-like exhalations of a pestilent vegetation. The dew diminishes, the morning-cloud is rare upon the hill-top, and the stratus is not often seen in the valley; rain, moreover, seldom falls heavily, except during its single appointed season. The climate is said to be salubrious, and the medium elevation of the land, 2500 feet, raises it high above the fatal fever-level, without attaining the altitudes where dysentery and pleurisy afflict the inhabitants. For many miles beyond Marenga, Mk'hali water is rarely found. Caravans, therefore, resort to what is technically called a "Tirikeza," or afternoon march. In the Kisawahili, or coast-language, "ku Tirikeza," or "Tilikeza," and in Kinyamwezi, "ku Witekezea," is the infinitive of a neuter verb signifying "to march after noon-day"; by the Arabs it is corrupted into a substantive. Similarly the verb ku honga, to pay "dash", tribute, passage-money, or blackmail, becomes in the mouths of the stranger, ku honga, or Honga. The tirikeza is one of the severest inflictions that African travelling knows. At 11 A.M. everything is thrown into confusion, although two or three hours must elapse before departure; loads are bound up, kitchen-batteries are washed and packed, tents are thrown, and stools are carried off by fidgeting porters and excited slaves. Having drunk for the last time, and filled their gourds for the night, the wayfarers set out when the midday ends. The sun is far more severely felt after the sudden change from shade, than during the morning marches, when its increase of heat is slow and gradual. They trudge under the fireball in the firmament, over ground seething with glow and reek, through an air which seems to parch the eyeballs, and they endure this affliction till their shadows lengthen out upon the ground. The tirikeza is almost invariably a lengthy stage, as the porters wish to abridge the next morning's march, which leads to water. It is often bright moonlight before they arrive at the ground, with faces torn by the thorns projecting across the jungly path, with feet lacerated by stone and stub, and occasionally a leg lamed by stumbling into deep and narrow holes, the work of field-rats and of various insects.

We left Marenga Mk'hali at 1 P.M., on the 3rd September, and in order to impressionise a large and well-armed band of the country people that had gathered to stare at, to criticise, and to deride us, we indulged in a little harmless sword-play, with a vast show of ferocity and readiness for fight. The road lay over several rough, steep, and bushy ridges, where the wretched asses, rushing away to take advantage of a yard of shade, caused constant delays. The Wanyamwezi animals having a great persistency of character, could scarcely be dislodged; and when they were, they threw their loads in pure spite. After topping a little "col" or pass, we came in sight of an extensive basin, bounded by distant blue hills, to which the porters pointed with a certain awe, declaring them to be the haunts of the fierce Wahumba. A descent of the western flank led us to a space partially cleared by burning, when the cry arose that men were lurking about. We then plunged into a thick bush of thorny trees, based upon a red clayey soil caked into the semblance of a rock. Contrary to expectation, when crossing a deep nullah trending northwards, we found a little rusty, ochreish water, in one of the cups and holes that dented the sandstone of the soles. Thence the path, gradually descending, fell into a coarse scrub, varied with small open savannahs, and broken, like the rest of the road, by deep, narrow watercourses, which carry off the waters of the southern hills to the northern lowlands. About 6 P.M., we came upon a cleared space in a thick thorn-jungle, where we established ourselves for the night. The near whine of the hyaena, and the alarm of the asses, made sleep a difficulty. The impatience and selfishness of thirst showed strongly in the Baloch. Belok had five large gourds full of water, perhaps three gallons, yet he would not part with a palmful to the sick Ismail. That day I was compelled to dismiss my usual ass-leader Shahdad, the zeze-player and fracturer of female hearts, who preferring the conversation of his fellows, dragged the animal through thorns and alongside of trees so artistically, that my nether garments were soon in strips. I substituted for him Musa the Greybeard, who, after a few days, begged, with bitter tears, to be excused. It was his habit to hurry on towards the kraal and shade, and the slow hobble of the ass detained him a whole hour in sore discomfort. The task was then committed to the tailor-youth Hudul, who lost no time in declaring that I had abused him – that he was a Baloch – that he was not an asinego. Then I tried Abdullah, – the good young man. I dismissed him because every day brought with it a fresh demand for cloth or beads, gourds or sandals, for a "chit" to the Balyuz – the Consul, or a general good character as regards honesty, virtue, and the et ceteras. Finally the ass was entrusted to the bull-headed slave Mabruki, who thinking of nothing but chat with his "'brother," Seedy Bombay, and having that curious mania for command which seems part of every servile nature, hurried my monture so recklessly, that earth-cracks and rat-holes caused us twain many a severe fall. My companion had entrusted himself to Bombay, who, though he did nothing well rarely did anything very badly.

The 4th September began with an hour's toil through the dense bush, to a rapid descent over red soil and rocks, which necessitated frequent dismounting, – no pleasant exercise after a sleepless night. Below, lay a wide basin of rolling ground, surrounded in front by a rim of hills. It was one of the many views which "catching the reflex of heaven," and losing by indistinctness the harshness of defined outline and the deformity of individual feature, assume, viewed from afar, a peculiar picturesqueness. Traces of extensive cultivation, flocks and herds, were descried in the lower levels, which were a network of sandy nullahs; and upon the rises, the regular and irregular square or oblong habitations, called "Tembe," were seen for the first time. Early September is, in this region, the depth of winter. Under the burning, glaring sun, the grass becomes white as the ground; the fields, stubbles stiff as harrows, are stained only by the shadow of passing clouds; the trees, except upon the nullah-banks, are gaunt and bare, the animals are walking skeletons, and nothing seems to flourish but flies and white ants, caltrops and grapple-plants. After crossing deep water-cuts trending N.E. and N.N.E., we descended a sharp incline and a rough ladder of boulders, and found a dirty and confined kraal, on the side of a rocky khad[8] or ravine, which drains off the surplus moisture of the westerly crags and highlands, and which affords sweet springs, that cover the soil as far as they extend with a nutritious and succulent grass. As this was to be a halting-place, a more than usually violent rush was made by the Baloch, the sons of Ramji, and the porters, to secure the best quarters. The Jemadar remaining behind with three of the Wanyamwezi, who were unable to walk, did not arrive till after noon, and my companion, suffering from a paroxysm of bilious fever, came in even later. Valentine was weaker than usual, and Gaetano groaned more frequently, "ang duk'hta" – body

---

8.   The Indian "khad" is the deep rocky drain in hilly countries, thus differing from the popular idea of a "ravine," and from the nullah, which is a formation in more level lands.

pains! To add other troubles, an ass had been lost, and "Khamsin," – No. 50 – my riding-animal, had by breaking a tooth in fighting incapacitated itself for food or drink: its feebleness compelled me to transfer the saddle to the last of the Zanzibar riding-asses, Siringe, – the Quarter-dollar – and Siringe, sadly back-sore, cowering in the hams, and slipping from under me every few minutes, showed present signs of giving in.

The basin of Inenge lies at the foot of the Rubeho or "Windy Pass," the third and westernmost range of the Usagara Mountains. The climate, like that of Rumuma, is ever in extremes – during the day a furnace, and at night a refrigerator – the position is a funnel, which alternately collects the fiery sunbeams and the chilly winds that pour down from the misty highlands. The villagers of the settlements overlooking the ravine, flocked down to barter their animals and grain. Here, for the first time since our departure from the coast, honey, clarified butter, and, greatest boon of all, milk, fresh and sour, were procurable. The man who has been restricted to a diet so unwholesome as holcus and bajri, with an occasional treat of kennel-food, – broth and beans, – will understand that the first unexpected appearance of milk, butter, and honey formed an epoch in our journey.

The halt was celebrated with abundant drumming and droning, which lasted half the night; it served to cheer the spirits of the men, who had talked of nothing the whole day but the danger of being attacked by the Wahumba. On the next morning arrived a caravan of about 400 Wanyamwezi porters marching to the coast, under the command of Isa bin Hijji and three other Arab merchants. An interchange of civilities took place. The Arabs lacking cloth could not feed their slaves and porters, who deserted daily, imperilling a valuable investment in ivory. The Europeans could afford a small contribution of three Gorah or pieces of domestics: they received a present of fine white rice, a few pounds of salt, and a goat, in exchange for a little perfumed snuff and assafoetida, which after a peculiar infusion is applied to wounds, and which, administered internally, is considered a remedy for many complaints. I was allured to buy a few yards of rope, indispensable for packing the animals. The number of our asses being reduced from thirty to fifteen, and the porters from thirty-six to thirty, it was necessary to recruit. The Arabs sold two Wanyamwezi animals for ten dollars each, payable at Zanzibar. One proved valuable as a riding ass, and carried me to the Central Lake, and back to Unyanyembe: the other, though caponized and blind on the off-side, had become by bad treatment so obstinate and so cleverly vicious, that the Baloch called him "Shaytan yek-cham," or the "one-eyed fiend." he carried, besides sundries, four boxes of ammunition, weighing together 160 pounds, and even under these he danced like a deer. Nothing was against him but his character: after a few days he was cast adrift in the wilderness of Mgunda M'khali, because no man dared to load and lead him. Knowing that the Arab merchants upon this line hold it a point of honour to discourage, by refusing a new engagement, the down-porters in their proclivity to desert, and believing that it was a stranger's duty to be even stricter than they are, I gave most stringent orders that any fugitive porter detected in my caravan should be sent back a prisoner to his employers. But the Coast-Arabs and the Wasawahili ignore this commercial chivalry, and shamelessly offer a premium to "levanters:" moreover, in these lands it is hard to make men understand the rapport between sayings and doings. Seven or eight fellows, who secretly left the party, were sent back; one, however, was taken on without my knowledge. Said bin Salim persuaded the merchants to lend us the services of three Wanyamwezi, who for sums varying from eight Shukkah to two cloths, and a coil large enough to make three wire bracelets, undertook to carry packs as far as Unyanyembe. Our Ras Kafilah had increased in Uzaramo his suite by the addition of "Zawada," – the "nice gift," a parting present of the headman Kizaya. She was a woman about thirty, with a black skin shining like a patent-leather boot, a bulging brow, little red eyes, a wide mouth which displayed a few long, strong, scattered teeth, and a figure considerably too bulky for her thin legs, which were unpleasantly straight, like ninepins. Her morale was superior to her physique; she was a patient and hard-working woman, and respectable in the African acceptation of the term. She was at once married off to old Musangesi, one of the donkey-men, whose nose and chin made him a caricature of our dear old friend Punch. After detecting her in a lengthy walk, perhaps not solitary, through the jungle, he was palpably guilty of such cruelty that I felt compelled to decree a dissolution of the marriage. After passing through sundry adventures she returned safely to Zanzibar, where, for aught I know, she may still grace the harem of Said bin Salim. At Inenge another female slave was added to the troop, in the person of the lady Sikujui, "Don't know," a "muller nigris dignissima barris," whose herculean person and virago manner raised her value to six cloths and a large coil of brass wire. The channel of her upper lip had been pierced to admit a disk of bone; her Arab master had attempted to correct the disfigurement by scarification and the use of rock-salt, yet the distended muscles insisted upon projecting sharply from her countenance, like a duck's bill, or the beak of an ornithorhyncus. This truly African ornamentation would have supplied another instance to the ingenious author of "Anthropometamorphosis."[9] "Don't know's" morals were frightful. She was duly espoused – as the forlorn hope of making her an "honest woman" – to Goha, the sturdi-

---

9.   Anthropometamorphosis: Man-transformed: or the Artificial Changeling, historically presented, In the mad and cruel Gallantry, foolish Bravery, Ridiculous Beauty, filthy Finenesse, and loathsome Loveliness of most NATIONS, fashioning and attiring their Bodies from the mould intended by NATURE; with figures of these Transfigurations. To which artificial and affected Deformations are added, all the Native and National Monstrosities that have appeared to disfigure the Humane Fabrick. With a VINDICATION of the Regular Beauty and Honesty of NATURE. With an Appendix of the Pedigree of the ENGLISH GALLANT. Scripsit J. B. Cognomento Chirosophus, M.D. "In nova fert animus, mutatas dicere formas." London: Printed by William Hunt, Anno. Dora. 1653.

est of the Wak'hutu porters; after a week she treated him with a sublime contempt. She gave him first one, then a dozen rivals; she disordered the caravan by her irregularities; she broke every article entrusted to her charge, as the readiest way of lightening her burden, and – "le moindre defaut d'une femme galante est de l'etre" – she deserted so shamelessly that at last Said bin Salim disposed of her, at Unyanyembe, for a few measures of rice, to a travelling trader, who came the next morning to complain of a broken head.

Isa bin Hijji did us various good services. He and his companions kindly waited some days to superintend our preparations for crossing the Rubeho Range. They supplied useful hints for keeping the caravan together at different places infamous for desertion. They gave me valuable information about Ugogo and Ujiji, and they placed at my disposal their house at Unyanyembe. They "wigged" the Kirangozi, or guide, for carelessness in not building a kraal-fence every night, and for not bringing in, as the custom is, wood and water. Kidogo was reproved for allowing his men to load our asses with their luggage, and the Baloch for their continual complaints about food. The latter had long forgotten the promises made at Muhama; they returned at every opportunity to their old tactic, that of obtaining, by all manner of pretexts, as much cloth and beads as possible, ostensibly for provisions, really for trading and buying slaves. At Rumuma they declared that one cloth per diem starved them. Said bin Salim sent them its value, about fifty pounds of beans, and they had abundant rations of beef and mutton, but they could not eat beans. At Inenge they wanted flour, and as the country people sold only grain, they gave themselves up to despair. I sent for the Jemadar and told him, in presence of the merchants, that, as a fitting opportunity had presented itself, I was willing to weed the party, by giving official dismissal to Khudabakhsh and Belok, to the invalid Ismail and his musical "brother" Shahdad. All four, when consulted, declared that they would die rather than blacken their faces by abandoning the "Haji

Abdullah;" that same evening, however, as I afterwards learned, they wrote, by means of the Arabs, a heartrending complaint to their chief Jemadar at Zanzibar, declaring that he had thrown them into the fire (of affliction), and that their blood was upon his hands. My companion prepared official papers and maps for the Secretary of the Royal Geographical Society, and I again indented upon the Consul and the Collector of Customs for drugs, medical comforts, and an extra supply of cloth and beads, to the extent of 400 dollars, for which a cheque upon my agents in Bombay was enclosed. The Arabs took leave of us on the 2nd September. I charged them repeatedly not to spread reports of our illness, and I saw them depart with regret. It had really been a relief to hear once more the voice of civility and sympathy.

The great labour still remained. Trembling with ague, with swimming heads, ears deafened by weakness, and limbs that would hardly support us, we contemplated with a dogged despair the apparently perpendicular path that ignored a zigzag, and the ladders of root and boulder, hemmed in with tangled vegetation, up which we and our starving drooping asses were about to toil. On the 10th September we hardened our hearts, and began to breast the Pass Terrible. My companion was so weak that he required the aid of two or three supporters; I, much less unnerved, managed with one. After rounding in two places wall-like sheets of rock – at their bases green grass and fresh water were standing close to camp, and yet no one had driven the donkeys to feed – and crossing a bushy jungly step, we faced a long steep of loose white soil and rolling stones, up which we could see the Wanyamwezi porters swarming, more like baboons scaling a precipice than human beings, and the asses falling after every few yards. As we moved slowly and painfully forwards, compelled to lie down by cough, thirst, and fatigue, the "sayhah" or war-cry rang loud from hill to hill, and Indian files of archers and spearmen streamed like lines of black ants in all directions down the paths. The predatory Wahumba, awaiting the caravan's departure, had seized the opportunity of driving the cattle and plundering the villages of Inenge. Two passing parties of men, armed to the teeth, gave us this information; whereupon the negro "Jelai" proposed, fear-maddened – *a sauve qui peut* – leaving to their fate his employers, who, bearing the mark of Abel in this land of Cain, were ever held to be the head and front of all offence. Khudabakhsh, the brave of braves, being attacked by a slight fever, lay down, declaring himself unable to proceed, moaned like a bereaved mother, and cried for drink like a sick girl. The rest of the Baloch, headed by the Jemadar, were in the rear; they had levelled their matchlocks at one of the armed parties as it approached them, and, but for the interference of Kidogo, blood would have been shed.

By resting after every few yards, and by clinging to our supporters, we reached, after about six hours, the summit of the Pass Terrible, and there we sat down amongst the aromatic flowers and bright shrubs – the gift of mountain dews – to recover strength and breath. My companion could hardly return an answer; he had advanced mechanically and almost in a state of coma. The view from the summit appeared eminently suggestive, perhaps unusually so, because disclosing a retrospect of severe hardships, now past and gone. Below the foreground of giant fractures, huge rocks, and detached boulders, emerging from a shaggy growth of mountain vegetation, with forest glens and hanging woods, black with shade gathering in the steeper folds, appeared, distant yet near, the tawny basin of Inenge, dotted with large square villages, streaked with lines of tender green, that denoted the watercourses, mottled by the shadows of flying clouds, and patched with black where the grass had been freshly fired. A glowing sun gilded the canopy of dense smoke which curtained the nearer plain, and in the background the hazy atmosphere painted with its azure the broken wall of hill which we had traversed on the previous day.

Somewhat revived by the *tramontana* which rolled like an ice-brook down the Pass, we advanced over an easy step of rolling ground, decked with cactus and the flat-topped mimosa, with green grass and bright shrubs, to a small and dirty khambi, in a hollow flanked by heights, upon which several settlements appeared. At this place, called the "Great Rubeho," in distinction from its western neighbour, I was compelled to halt. My invalid sub. had been seized with a fever-fit that induced a dangerous delirium during two successive nights; he became so violent that it was necessary to remove his weapons, and, to judge from certain symptoms, the attack had a permanent cerebral effect. Death appeared stamped upon his features, yet the Baloch and the sons of Ramji clamoured to advance, declaring that the cold disagreed with them.

On the 12th September the invalid, who, restored by a cool night, at first proposed to advance, and then doubted his ability to do so, was yet hesitating when the drum-signal for departure sounded without my order. The Wanyamwezi porters instantly set out. I sent to recal them, but they replied that it was the custom of their race never to return; a well-sounding principle against which they never offended except to serve their own ends. At length a hammock was rigged up for my companion, and the whole caravan broke ground.

The path ran along the flank of an eminence, and, ascending a second step, as steep but shorter than the Pass Terrible, placed us at the Little Rubeho, or Windy Pass, the summit of the third and westernmost range of the Usagara Mountains, raised 5,700 feet above the sea-level. It is the main water-parting of this ghaut-region. At Inenge the trend is still to the S.E.; beyond Rubeho the direction is S.W. Eventually, however, the drainage of both slope and counter-slope finds its way to the Indian Ocean, the former through the Mukondokwa and the Kingani, the latter through the Raw and the Rufiji Rivers.

A lively scene awaited my arrival at the "Little Rubeho." From a struggling mass of black humanity, which I presently determined to be our porters, proceeded a furious shouting and yelling. Spears and daggers flashed in the sun, and cud-gels played with a threshing movement which promised many a broken head. At the distance of a few yards, with fierce faces and in motionless martial attitudes, the right hand upon the axe-handle stuck in the waist-belt, and the left grasping the bow and two or three polished assegais, stood a few strong fellows, the forlorn hope of the fray. In the midst of the crowd, like Norman Ramsay's troop begirt by French cavalry – to compare small things with great – rose and fell the chubby, thickset forms of Muinyi Wazira and his four Wak'hutu, who, undaunted by numbers, were dealing death to nose and scalp. Charge! Mavi ya Gnombe ("Bois de Vache") charge! On! Mashuzi ("Fish Fry-soup ") on! Bite, Kuffan Kwema ("To die is good") bite, Smite, Na daka Mall ("I want wealth") smite! At length, when

"Blood (t'was from the nose) began to flow,"

a little active interference rescued the five "enfans perdus." The porters had been fighting upon the question whether the men with small-pox should, or should not, be admitted into the kraal, and Muinyi Wazira and his followers, under the influence of potations which prevented their distinguishing friend from foe, had proved themselves, somewhat unneces-sarily heroes. It is usually better to let these quarrels work themselves out; if prematurely cut short, the serpent, wrath, is scotched, not slain. A little "punishment" always cools the blood, and secures peace and quiet for the future. Moreover, the busy peacemaker here often shares the fate of M. Porceaugnac, and earns the reward of those who, according to the proverb, in quarrels interpose, it is vain to investigate, where all is lie, the origin of the squabble. Nothing easier, as the Welsh justice was fond of declaring, than to pronounce judgment after listening to one side of the question; but an impartial hearing of both would strike the inquiring mind with a sense of impotence. Perhaps it is not unadvisable to treat the matter after the fashion adopted by a "police-officer," a certain captain in the X. Y. Z. army, who deemed it his duty to discourage litigiousness and official complaints amongst the quarrelsome Sindhi population of Hyderabad. The story is somewhat out of place; though so being, I will here recount it.

Would enter, for instance, two individuals in an oriental costume considerably damaged; one has a cloth carefully tied round his head, the other has artificially painted his eye and his ear with a few drops of blood from the nose. They express their emotions by a loud drumming of the tom-tom accompanying the high-sounding Cri de Haro – Faryad! Faryad! Faryad! –

"I'll 'Faryad' yer, ye — "

After these, the usual appellatives with which the "native" was in those days, on such occasions received, the plaintiff is thus addressed: –

"Well, you—fellow! your complaint, what is it?" "Oh, Sahib! Oh, cherisher of the poor! this man who is, the same hath broken into my house, and made me eat a beating, and called my ma and sister naughty names, and hath stolen my brass pot, and – "

"Bas! bas! enough!" cries the beak; "tie him" – the defendant – "up, and give him three dozen with thine own hand."

The wrathful plaintiff, as may be imagined, is nothing loath. After being vigorously performed upon by the plaintiff aforesaid, the defendant is cast loose, and is in turn addressed as follows: –

"Well, now, you fellow, what say you?"

"Oh, nay lord and master! Oh, dispenser of justice! what lies hath not this man told? What abominations hath he not devoured? Behold (pointing to his war-paint) the sight! He hath met me in the street; he hath thrown me down; he hath kicked and trampled upon me; he hath – "

"Bas! enough!" again cries the beak; "tie him – the plaintiff – up, and see if you can give *him* a good three dozen."

Again it may be imagined that the three dozen are well applied by the revengeful defendant, and that neither that plaintiff nor that defendant ever troubled that excellent "police-officer" again.

On Rubeho's summit we found a single village of villanous Wasagara; afterwards "made clean" – as the mild Hindu expresses the extermination of his fellow-men – by a caravan in revenge for the murder of a porter. We were delayed on the hill-top a whole day, despite the extreme discomfort of all hands. Water had to be fetched from a runnel that issued from a rusty pool shaded by tilted-up strata of sandstone, at least a mile distant from camp. Rain fell daily, alternating with eruptions of sun; a stream of thick mist rolled down the ravines and hollows, and at night the howling winds made Rubeho their meeting-place. Yet neither would the sons of Ramji carry my companion's hammock, nor would Said bin Salim allow his children to be so burdened; moreover, whatever measures one attempted with the porters, the other did his best to thwart. "Men," say the Persians, "kiss an ass for an object." I attempted with Kidogo that sweet speech which, according to Orientals, is stronger than chains, and administered "goose's oil" in such quantities that I was graciously permitted to make an arrangement for the transport of my companion with the Kirangozi.

On the 14th September, our tempers being sensibly cooled by the weather, we left the hill-top and broke ground upon the counterslope or landward descent of the Usagara Mountains. Following a narrow footpath that wound along the hill-flanks, on red earth growing thick clumps of cactus and feathery mimosa, after forty-five minutes' march we found a kraal in a swampy green gap, bisected by a sluggish rivulet that irrigated scanty fields of grain, gourds, and watermelons, the property of distant villagers. For the first time since many days I had strength enough to muster the porters and to inspect their loads. The outfit, which was expected to last a year, had been half exhausted in three months. I summoned Said bin Salim, and passed on to him my anxiety. Like a veritable Arab, he declared, without the least emotion, that we had enough to reach Unyanyembe, where we certainly should be joined by the escort of twenty-two porters. "But how do you know that?" I inquired. "Allah is all-knowing," replied Said; "but the caravan will come." Such fatalism is infectious. I ceased to think upon the subject.

On the 15th September, after sending forward the luggage, and waiting as agreed upon for the return of the porters to carry my companion, I set out about noon, through hot sunshine tempered by the cool hill: breeze. Emerging from the grassy hollow, the path skirted a well-wooded hill and traversed a small savannah, overgrown with stunted straw and hedged in by a bushy forest. At this point massive trees, here single, there in holts and clumps, foliaged more gloomily than churchyard yews, and studded with delicate pink-flowers, rose from the tawny sunburned expanse around, and defended from the fiery glare braky rings of emerald shrubbery, sharply defined as if by the forester's hand. The savannah extended to the edge of a step which, falling deep and steep, suddenly disclosed to view, below and far beyond the shaggy ribs and the dark ravines and folds of the foreground, the plateau of Ugogo and its Eastern desert. The spectacle was truly impressive. The vault above seemed "an ample aether," raised by its exceeding transparency higher than it is wont to be. Up to the curved rim of the western horizon, lay, burnished by the rays of a burning sun, plains rippled like a yellow sea by the wavy reek of the dancing air, broken towards the north by a few detached cones rising island-like from the surface, and zebra'd with long black lines, where bush and scrub and strip of thorn jungle, supplanted upon the watercourses, trending in mazy network southwards to the Raw River, the scorched grass and withered cane-stubbles, which seemed to be the staple growth of the land. There was nothing of effeminate or luxuriant beauty, nothing of the flush and fulness characterising tropical Nature, in this first aspect of Ugogo. It appeared what it is, stern and wild, – the rough nurse of rugged men, – and perhaps the anticipation of dangers and difficulties ever present to the minds of those preparing to endure the waywardness of its children, contributed not a little to the fascination of the scene. After lingering for a few minutes upon the crest of the step, with feelings which they will understand who after some pleasant months – oases in the grim deserts of Anglo-Indian life – spent among the tree-clad heights, the breezy lakes, and the turfy valleys of the Himalayas and the Neilgherries, sight from their last vantage-ground the jaundiced and fevered plains below, we scrambled down an irregular incline of glaring red clay and dazzling white chalk, plentifully besprinkled with dark-olive silex in its cherty crust. Below the descent was a level space upon a long ridge, where some small villages of Wasagara had surrounded themselves with dwarf fields of holcus, bajri, and maize. A little beyond this spot, called the "Third Rubeho," we found a comfortless kraal on uneven ground, a sloping ledge sinking towards a deep ravine.

At the third Rubeho we were delayed for a day – as is customary before a "Tirikeza" – by the necessity of laying in supplies for a jungle march, and by the quarrels of the men. The Baloch were cross as naughty children, ever their case when cold and hungry: warm and full, they become merry as crickets. The Kirangozi in hot wrath brought his flag to Said bin Salim, and threatened to resign, because he had been preceded on the last stage by two of the Baloch: his complaints of this highly irregular proceeding were with difficulty silenced by force of beads. I remarked, however, a few days afterwards, when travelling through Ugogo, that the Kirangozi, considering himself in danger, applied to me for a vanguard of matchlockmen. The sons of Ramji combined with the porters in refusing to carry my companion, and had Bombay and Mabruki not shown good-will, we might have remained a week in the acme of discomfort. The asses, frightened by wild beasts, broke loose at night, and one was lost.

The atmosphere was ever in excesses of heat and cold: in the morning, a mist so thick that it displayed a fog-rainbow – a segment of an arch, composed of faint prismatic tints – rolled like a torrent down the ravine in front: the sun, at noon, made us cower under the thin canvas, and throughout the twenty-four hours a gale like a "vent de bise," attracted by the heat of the western plains, swept the encamping ground.

Sending forward my invalid companion in his hammock, I brought up the rear: Said bin Salim, who had waxed unusually selfish and surly, furtively left to us the task; he wore only sandals – he could not travel by night. Some of the Baloch wept at the necessity of carrying their gourds and skins.

On the 17th September, about 2 P.M., we resumed the descent of the rugged mountains. The path wound to the N.W. down the stony and bushy crest of a ridge with a deep woody gap on the right hand: presently after alternations of steep and step, and platforms patched with odoriferous plants, it fell into the upper channel of the Mandama or the Dungomaro, the "Devil's Glen." Dungomaro in Kisawahili is the proper name of an evil spirit, not in the European but in the African sense, – some unblessed ghost who has made himself unpopular to the general; – perhaps the term was a facetiousness on the part of the sons of Ramji.

It was a "via mala" down this great surface-drain of the western slopes, over boulders and water-rolled stones reposing upon deep sand, and with branches of thorny trees in places canopying the bed. After a march of five hours, I found the porters bivouacking upon a softer spot, and with difficulty persuaded four of the sons of Ramji to return and to assist the weary stragglers: horns were sounded, and shots were fired to guide the Baloch, who did not, however, arrive before 10 P.M.

On the 18th September, a final march of four hours placed us in the plains of Ugogo. Leaving the place of the last night's bivouac, we pursued the line of the Dungomaro, occasionally quitting it where boulders obstructed progress, and presently we came to its lower bed, where perennial rills, exuding from its earth-walls and trickling down its side, veiled the bottom with a green and shrubby perfumed vegetation. As the plain was neared, the difficulties increased, and the scenery became curious. The Dungomaro appeared a large crevasse in lofty rocks of pink and gray granite, streaked with white quartz, and pudding'd with greenstone and black horneblend; the sole, strewed with a rugged layer of blocks, was side-lined with narrow ledges and terraces of brown humus, supporting dwarf cactus and stunted thorny trees; whilst high above towered stony wooded peaks, closing in the view on all sides. Farther down the bed huge boulders, sunburnt, and stained by the courses of rain torrents, rose, perpendicularly as walls, to the height of one hundred and one hundred and twenty feet, and there the flooring was a sheet or slide of shiny and shelving rock, with broad fissures, and steep drops, and cups, "potholes," baths, and basins, filed and cut by the friction of the gravelly torrents, regularly as if turned with the lathe. Where water lay, deep mud and thick clumps of grass and reed forced the path to run along the ledges at the sides of the base. Gradually, as the angle of inclination became more obtuse, the bed widened out, the tall stone-walls gave way to low earth-banks clad with gum-trees; pits, serving as wells, appeared in the deep loose sand, and the Dungomaro, becoming a broad, smooth Fiumara, swept away verging southwards into the plain. Before noon, I sighted from a sharp turn in the bed our tent pitched under a huge sycomore on a level step that bounded the Fiumara to the right. It was a pretty spot in a barren scene, grassy, and grown with green mimosas, spreading out their feathery heads like parachutes, and shedding upon the ground a filmy shade that fluttered and flickered in the draughty breeze.

The only losses experienced during the scrambling descent, were a gun-case, containing my companion's store of boots, and a chair and table. The latter, being indispensable on a journey where calculations, composition, and sketching were expected, I sent, during the evening halts, a detachment consisting of Muinyi Wazira, the Baloch, Greybeard Musa, and a party of slaves, to bring up the articles, which had been cache'd on the torrent bank. They returned with the horripilatory tale of the dangers lately incurred by the Expedition, which it appeared from them had been dogged by an army of Wasagara, thirsting for blood and furious for booty:-under such circumstances, how could they recover the chair and table? Some months afterwards an up-caravan commanded by a Msawahili found the articles lying where we had left them, and delivered them, for a consideration, to us at Unyanyembe. The party sent from Ugogo doubtless had passed a quiet, pleasant day, dozing in the shade at the nearest well.

Chapter 7

THE GEOGRAPHY AND ETHNOLOGY OF THE SECOND REGION

The second or mountain region extends from the western frontier of K'hutu, at the head of the alluvial valley, in E. long. 37° 28', to the province of Ugogi, the eastern portion of the flat table-land of Ugogo, in E. long. 36° 14'. Its diagonal breadth is 85 geographical and rectilinear miles; and native caravans, if lightly laden, generally traverse it in three weeks, including three or four halts. Its length cannot be estimated. According to the guides, Usagara is a prolongation of the mountains of Nauru, or Gnu, extending southwards, with a gap forming the fluviatile valley of the Raw or Rufiji River, to the line of highlands of which Noes in Ushio is supposed to be the culminating apex: thus the feature would correspond with the Eastern Ghouls of the Indian Peninsula. The general law of the range is north and south; in the region now under consideration, the trend is from north by west to south by east, forming an angle of 10° 12' with the meridian. The Usagara chain is of the first order in East Africa; it is indeed the only important elevation in a direct line from the coast to western Unyamwezi; it would hold, however, but a low grade in the general system of the earth's mountains. The highest point above sea-level, observed by B.P. Theorem., was 5,700 feet; there are, however, peaks which may rise to 6,000 and even to 7,000 feet, thus rivaling the inhabited portion of the Neilgherries. As has appeared, the chain, where crossed, was divided into three parallel ridges by longitudinal plains.

Owing to the lowness of the basal regions at the seaward slope, there is no general prospect of the mountains from the East, where, after bounding the plains of K'hutu on the north, by irregular bulging lines of rolling hill, the first gradient of insignificant height springs suddenly from the plain. Viewed from the west, the counterslope appears a long crescent, with the gibbus to the front, and the cusps vanishing into distance; the summit is in the centre of the half-moon, whose profile is somewhat mural and regular. The flanks are rounded lumpy cones, and their shape denotes an igneous and primary origin, intersected by plains and basins, the fractures of the rocky system. Internally the lay, as in granitic formations generally, is irregular; the ridges, preserving no general direction, appear to cross one another confusedly. The slope and the counterslope are not equally inclined. Here, as usual in chains fringing a peninsula, the seaward declivities are the more abrupt; the landward faces are not only more elongated, but they are also shortened in proportion as the plateau into which they fall is higher than the mountain-plains from which they rise. To enter, therefore, is more toilsome than to return.

From the mingling of lively colours, Usagara is delightful to the eye, after the monotonous tracts of verdure which pall upon the sight at Zanzibar and in the river valleys. The sub-soil, displayed in the deeper cuts and ravines, is either of granite, greenstone, schiste, or a coarse incipient sandstone, brown or green, and outcropping from the ground with strata steeply tilted up. In the higher elevations, the soil varies in depth from a few inches to thirty feet; it is often streaked with long layers of pebbles, apparently water-rolled. The colour is either an ochreish brick-red, sometimes micaceous, and often tinted with oxide of iron; or it is a dull grey, the debris of comminuted felspar, which, like a mixture of all the colours, appears dazzlingly white under the sun's rays. The plains and depressions are of black earth, which after a few showers becomes a grass-grown sheet of mire, and in the dry season a deeply-cracked, stubbly savannah. Where the elevations are veiled from base to summit with a thin forest, the crops of the green-stone and sandstone strata appear through a brown coat of fertile humus, the decay of vegetable matter. A fossil Bulimus was found about 3,000 feet above sea-level, and large Achatinae, locally called Khowa, are scattered over the surface. On the hill-sides, especially in the lower slopes, are strewed and scattered erratic blocks and boulders, and diminutive pieces of white, dingy-red, rusty-pink, and yellow quartz, with large irregularly-shaped fragments and small nodules of calcareous kunkur. Where water lies deep below the surface, the hills and hill-plains are clothed with a thin shrubbery of mimosas and other thorny gums. Throughout Eastern Africa these forests are the only spots in which travelling is enjoyable: great indeed is their contrast with the normal features – bald glaring fields, fetid bush and grass, and monotonous expanses of dull dead herbage, concealing swamps and watercourses, hedged in by vegetation whose only varieties are green, greener, and greenest. In these favoured places the traveller appears surrounded by a thick wood which he never reaches, the trees thinning out as he advances. On clear and sunny days the scenery is strange and imposing. The dark-red earth is prolonged half-way up the tree-trunks by the ascending and descending galleries of the termite: contrasting with this peculiarly African tint, the foliage, mostly confined to the upper branches, is of a tender and lively green, whose open fret-work admits from above the vivid blue or the golden yellow of an unclouded sky. In the basins where water is nearer the surface, and upon the banks of water-courses and rivulets, the sweet and fertile earth produces a rich vegetation, and a gigantic growth of timber, which distinguishes this region from others further west. Usagara is peculiarly the land of jungle-flowers, and fruits, whose characteristic is a pleasant acidity, a provision of nature in climates where antiseptics and correctives to bile are almost necessaries of life. They are abundant, but, being uncultivated, the fleshy parts are undeveloped. In the plains, the air, heavy with the delicious perfume of the jasmine (*Jasminum Abyssinicum*?), with the strong odour of a kind of sage (*Salvia Africana*, or *Abyssinica*?), and with the fragrant exhalations of the mimosa-flowers, which hang like golden balls from the green clad boughs, forms a most enjoyable contrast to the fetid exhalations of the Great Dismal Swamps of the lowlands. The tamarind, everywhere growing wild, is a gigantic tree. The Myombo, the Mfu'u, the Ndabi, and the Mayagea, a spreading tree with a large fleshy red flower, and gourds about eighteen inches long and hanging by slender cords, are of unusual dimensions; the calabash is converted into a hut; and the sycomore, whose favourite habitat is the lower counterslope of Usagara, is capable of shading a regiment. On the steep hill-sides, which here and there display signs of cultivation and clearings of green or sunburnt grass, grow parachuteshaped mimosas, with tall and slender trunks, and crowned by domes of verdure, rising in tiers one above the other, like umbrellas in a crowd.

The plains, basins, and steps, or facets of table-land found at every elevation, are fertilised by a stripe-work of streams, runnels, and burns, which anastomosing in a single channel, flow off into the main drain of the country. Cultivation is found in patches isolated by thick belts of thorny jungle, and the villages are few and rarely visited. As usual in hilly countries, they are built upon high ridges and the slopes of cones, for rapid drainage after rain, a purer air and fewer mosquitoes, and, perhaps, protection from kidnappers. The country people bring down their supplies of grain and pulse for caravans. There is some delay and difficulty on the first day of arrival at a station, and provisions for a party exceeding a hundred men are not to be depended upon after the third or fourth marketing, when the people have exhausted their stores. Fearing the thievish disposition of the Wasagara, who will attempt even to snatch away a cloth from a sleeping man, travellers rarely lodge near the settlements. Kraals of thorn, capacious circles enclosing straw boothies, are found at every march, and, when burned or destroyed by accident, they are rebuilt before the bivouac. The roads, as usual in East Africa, are tracks trodden down by caravans and cattle, and the water-course is ever the favourite Pass. Many of the ascents and descents are so proclivitous that donkeys must be relieved of their loads; and in fording the sluggish streams, where no grass forms a causeway over the soft, viscid mire, the animals sink almost to the knees. The steepest paths are those in the upper regions; in the lower, though the inclines are often severe, they are generally longer, and consequently easier. At the foot of each hill there is either a mud or a water-course dividing it from its neighbour. These obstacles greatly reduce the direct distance of the day's march.

The mountains are well supplied with water, which tastes sweet after the brackish produce of the maritime valley, and good when not rendered soft and slimy by lying long on rushy beds. Upon the middle inclines the burns and runnels of the upper heights form terraces of considerable extent, and of a picturesque aspect. The wide and open sole, filled with the whitest and cleanest sand, and retaining pools of fresh clear water, or shallow wells, is edged by low steep ledges of a dull red clay, lined with glorious patriarchs of the forest, and often in the bed is a thickly wooded branch or shoal-islet, at whose upper extremity heavy driftwood, arrested by the gnarled mimosa-clumps, and the wall of shrubs, attests the violence of the rufous-tinted bore of waves with which a few showers fill the broadest courses. Lower down the channels which convey to the plains the surplus drainage of the mountains are heaps and sheets of granite, with long reaches of rough gravel; their stony walls, overrun with vegetation, tower high on either hand, and the excess of inclination produces after heavy rains torrents like avalanches, which cut their way deep into the lower plains. During the dry season, water is drawn from pits sunk from a few inches to 20 feet in the re-entering angles of the beds. Fed by the percolations of the soil, they unite the purity of springs with the abundance of rain-supplies, – a comfort fully appreciated by down-caravans after the frequent tirikeza, or droughty afternoon-marches in the western regions.

The versant of the mountains varies. In the seaward and the central sections streams flow eastward, and swell the Kingani and other rivers. The southern hills discharge their waters south and south-west through the Maroro River, and various smaller tributaries, into the "Raw," which is the proper name for the upper course of the Rufiji. In the lateral plains between the ridges, and in the hill-girt basins, stagnant pools, which even during the Masika, or rainy season, inundate, but will not flow, repose upon beds of porous black earth, and engendering, by their profuse herbage of reeds and rush-like grass, with the luxuriant crops produced by artificial irrigation, a malarious atmosphere, cause a degradation in the people.

The climate of Usagara is cold and damp. It has two distinct varieties, the upper regions being salubrious, as the lower are unwholesome. In the sub-ranges heavy exhalations are emitted by the decayed vegetation, the nights are raw, the mornings chilly and misty, and the days are bright and hot. In the higher levels, near the sources of the Mukondokwa River, the climate suggests the idea of the Mahabalcshwar and the Neilgherry Hills in Western India. Compared with Uzaramo or Unyamwezi, these mountains are a sanatorium, and should Europeans ever settle in Eastern Africa as merchants or missionaries, here they might reside until acclimatised for the interior. The east wind, a local deflection of the south-east trade, laden with the moisture of the Atlantic and the Indian Oceans, and collecting the evaporation of the valley, impinges upon the seaward slope, where, ascending, and relieved from atmospheric pressure, it is condensed by a colder temperature; hence the frequent precipitations of heavy rain, and the banks and sheets of morning-cloud which veil the tree-clad peaks of the highest gradients. As the sun waxes hot, the atmosphere acquires a greater capacity for carrying water; and the results are a milky mist in the basins, and in the upper hills a wonderful clearness broken only by the thin cirri of the higher atmosphere. After sunset, again, the gradual cooling of the air causes the deposit of a copious dew, which renders the nights peculiarly pleasant to a European. The diurnal sea-breeze, felt in the slope, is unknown in the counterslope of the mountains, where, indeed, the climate is much inferior to that of the central and eastern heights. As in the Sawalik Hills, and the sub-ranges of the Himalayas, the sun is burning hot during the dry season, and in the rains there is either a storm of thunder and lightning, wind and rain, or a stillness deep and depressing, with occasional gusts whose distinct moaning shows the highly electrical state of the atmosphere. The Masika, here commencing in early January, lasts three months, when the normal easterly winds shift to the north and the north-west. The Vuli, confined to the eastern slopes, occurs in August, and, as on the plains, frequent showers fall between the vernal and the autumnal rains.

The people of Usagara suffer in the lower regions from severe ulcerations, from cutaneous disorders, and from other ailments of the plain. Higher up they are healthier, though by no means free from pleurisy, pneumonia, and dysentery. Fever is common; it is more acute in the range of swamps and decomposed herbage, and is milder in the well-ventilated cols and on the hill-sides. The type is rather a violent bilious attack, accompanied by remittent febrile symptoms, than a regular fever. It begins with cold and hot fits, followed by a copious perspiration, and sometimes inducing delirium; it lasts as a quotidian or a tertian from four to seven days; and though the attacks are slight, they are followed by great debility, want of appetite, of sleep, and of energy. This fever is greatly exacerbated by exposure and fatigue, and it seldom fails to leave behind it a legacy of cerebral or visceral disease.

The mountains of Usagara are traversed from east to west by two main lines; the Mukondokwa on the northern and the Kiringawana on the southern line. The former was closed until 1856 by a chronic famine, the result of such a neighbourhood as the Wazegura and the people of Whinde on the east, the Wahumba and the Wamasai northwards, and the Warori on the south-west. In 1858 the mountaineers, after murdering by the vilest treachery a young Arab trader, Salim bin Nasir, of the Bu Saidi, or the royal family of Zanzibar, attempted to plunder a large mixed caravan of Wanyamwezi and Wasawahili, numbering 700 or 800 guns, commanded by a stout fellow, Abdullah bin Nasib, called by the Africans "Kisesa," who carried off the cattle, burned the villages, and laid waste the whole of the Rubeho or western chain.

The clans now tenanting these East African ghauts are the Wasagara, – with their chief sub-tribe the Wakwivi, – and the Wahehe; the latter a small body inhabiting the south-western corner, and extending into the plains below.

The limits of the Wasagara have already been laid down by the names of the plundering tribes that surround them. These mountaineers, though a noisy and riotous race, are not overblessed with courage: they will lurk in the jungle with bows and arrows to surprise a stray porter; but they seem ever to be awaiting an attack – the best receipt for inviting it. In the higher slopes they are fine, tall and sturdy men; in the low lands they appear as degraded as the Wak'hutu. They are a more bearded race than any other upon this line of East Africa, and, probably from extensive intercourse with the Wamrima, most of them understand the language of the coast. The women are remarkable for a splendid development of limb, whilst the bosom is lax and pendent.

The Wasagara display great varieties of complexion, some being almost black, whilst the others are chocolate-coloured. This difference cannot be accounted for by the mere effects of climate – level and temperature. Some shave the head; others wear the Arab's shushah, a kind of skull-cap growth, extending more or less from the poll. Amongst them is seen, for the first time on this line, the classical coiffure of ancient Egypt. The hair, allowed to attain its fullest length, is twisted into a multitude of the thinnest ringlets, each composed of two thin lengths wound together; the wiry stiffness of the curls keeps them distinct and in position. Behind, a curtain of pigtails hangs down to the nape; in front the hair is either combed off the forehead, or it is brought over the brow and trimmed short. No head-dress has a wilder nor a more characteristically African appearance than this, especially when, smeared with a pomatum of micaceous ochre, and decorated with beads, brass balls, and similar ornaments, it waves and rattles with every motion of the head. Young men and warriors adorn their locks with the feathers of vultures, ostriches, and a variety of bright-plumed jays, and some tribes twist each ringlet with a string of reddish fibre. It is seldom combed out, the operation requiring for a head of thick hair the hard work of a whole day; it is not, therefore, surprising that the pediculus swarms through the land. None but the chiefs wear caps. Both sexes distend the ear-lobe; a hole is bored with a needle or a thorn, it is enlarged by inserting bits of cane, wood, or quills, increasing the latter to the number of twenty, and it is kept open by a disk of brass, ivory, wood, or gum, a roll of leaf or a betel-nut; thus deformed it serves for a variety of purposes apparently foreign to the member; it often carries a cane snuff-box, sometimes a goatshorn pierced for a fife, and other small valuables. When empty, especially in old age, it depends in a deformed loop to the shoulders. The peculiar mark of the tribe is a number of confused little cuts between the ears and the eyebrows. Some men, especially in the eastern parts of the mountains, chip the teeth to points.

The dress of the Wasagara is a shukkah or loin-cloth, 6 feet long, passed round the waist in a single fold, – otherwise walking would be difficult – drawn tight behind, and with the fore extremities gathered up, and tucked in over the stomach, where it is sometimes supported by a girdle of cord, leather, or brass wire: it is, in fact, the Arab's "uzar." On journeys it is purposely made short and scanty for convenience of running. The material is sometimes indigo-dyed, at other times unbleached cotton, which the Wasagara stain a dull yellow. Cloth, however, is the clothing of the wealthy. The poor content themselves with the calabash "campestre" or kilt, and with the softened skins of sheep and goats. It is curious that in East Africa, where these articles have from time immemorial been the national dress, and where amongst some tribes hides form the house, that the people have neither invented nor borrowed the principles of rude tanning, even with mimosa-bark, an art so well known to most tribes of barbarians. Immediately after flaying, the stretched skin is pegged, to prevent shrinking, inside upwards, in the sun, and it is not removed till thoroughly cleansed and dried. The many little holes in the margin give it the semblance of ornamentation, and sometimes the hair is scraped off, leaving a fringe two or three inches broad around the edge: the legs and tail of the animal are favourite appendages with "dressy gentlemen." These skins are afterwards softened by trampling, and they are vigorously pounded with clubs: after a few days' wear, dirt and grease have almost done the duty of tanning. The garb is tied over either shoulder by a bit of cord or simply by knotting the corners; it therefore leaves one side of the body bare, and, being loose and ungirt, it is at the mercy of every wind. On journeys it is doffed during rain, and placed between the burden and the shoulder, so that, arrived at the encamping ground, the delicate traveller may have a "dry shirt."

Women of the wealthier classes wear a tobe, or double-length shukkah, tightly drawn under the arms, so as to depress whilst it veils the bosom, and tucked in at either side. Dark stuffs, indigo-dyed and Arab checks, are preferred to plain white for the usual reasons. The dress of the general is a short but decorous jupe of greasy skin, and a similar covering for the bosom, open behind, and extending in front from the neck to the middle of the body: the child is carried in another skin upon the back. The poorest classes of both sexes are indifferently attired in the narrow kilt of bark-fibre, usually made in the maritime countries from the ukhindu or brab tree; in the interior from the calabash. The children wear an apron of thin twine, like the Nubian thong-garments. Where beads abound, the shagele, a small square napkin of these ornaments strung upon thread, is fastened round the waist by a string or a line of beads. There are many fanciful modifications of it: some children wear a screen of tin plates, each the size of a man's finger: most of the very juniors, however, are simply attired in a cord, with or without beads, round the waist.

The ornaments of the Wasagara are the normal beads and wire, and their weight is the test of wealth and respectability. A fillet of blue and white beads is bound round the head, and beads, – more beads, – appear upon the neck, the arms, and the ankles. The kitindi, or coil of thick brass wire, extends from the elbow to the wrist; others wear little chains or thick bangles of copper, brass, or zinc, and those who can afford it twist a few circles of brass wire under the knee. The arms of the men are bows and arrows, the latter unpoisoned, but armed with cruelly-barbed heads, and spines like fish-bones, cut out in the long iron shaft which projects from the wood. Their spears and assegais are made from the old hoes which are brought down by the Wanyamwezi caravans; the ferule is thin, and it is attached to the shaft by a cylinder of leather from a cow's tail, drawn over the iron, and allowed to shrink at its junction with the wood: some assegais have a central swell in the shaft, probably to admit of their being used in striking like the rangu or knobstick. Men seldom leave the house without a billhook of peculiar shape – a narrow sharp blade, ending in a right angle, and fixed in a wooden handle, with a projection rising above the blade. The shield is rarely found on this line of East Africa. In Usagara it is from three to four feet in length by one to two feet in breadth, composed of two parallel belts of hardened skin. The material is pegged out to stretch and dry, carefully cleaned, sometimes doubled, sewn together with a thin thong longitudinally, and stained black down one side, and red down the other. A stout lath is fastened lengthwise as a stiffener to the shield, and a central bulge is made in the hide, enabling the hand to grasp the wood. The favourite materials are the spoils of the elephant, the rhinoceros, and the giraffe; the common shields are of bull's-hide, and the hair is generally left upon the outside as an ornament, with attachments of zebra and cows' tails. It is a flimsy article, little better than a "wisp of fern or a herring-net" against an English "clothyard:" it suffices, however, for defence against the puny cane-arrows of the African archer.

As a rule, each of these villages has its headman, who owns, however, an imperfect allegiance to the Mutwa or district chief, whom thc Arabs call "sultan." The Mgosi is his wazir, or favourite councillor, and the elders or headmen of settlements collectively are Wabaha. Their principal distinction is the right to wear a fez, or a Surat cap, and the kizbao, a sleeveless waistcoat. They derive a certain amount of revenue by trafficking in slaves: consequently many of the Wasagara find their way into the market of Zanzibar. Moreover, the game laws as regards elephants are here strictly in favour of the Sultan. An animal found dead in his district, though wounded in another, becomes his property on condition of his satisfying his officials with small presents of cloth and beads: the flesh is feasted upon by the tribe, and the ivory is sold to travelling traders.

The Wahehe, situated between the Wasagara and Wagogo, partake a little of the appearance of both. They are a plain race, but stout and well grown. Though to appearance hearty and good-humoured, they are determined pilferers: they have more than once attacked caravans, and only the Warori have prevented them from cutting off the road to Ugogo. During the return of the Expedition in 1858 they took occasion to drive off unseen a flock of goats; and at night no man, unless encamped in a strong kraal, was safe from their attempts to snatch his goods. On one occasion, being caught in flagrant delict, they were compelled to restore their plunder, with an equivalent as an indemnity. They are on bad terms with all their neighbours, and they unite under their chief Sultan Bumbumu.

The Wahche enlarge their ears like the Wagogo, they chip the two upper incisors, and they burn beauty-spots in their forearms. Some men extract three or four of the lower incisors: whenever an individual without these teeth is seen in Ugogo he is at once known as a Mhehe. For distinctive mark they make two cicatrised incisions on both cheeks from the zygomata to the angles of the mouth. They dress like the Wagogo, but they have less cloth than skins. The married women usually wear a jupe, in shape recalling the old swallow-tailed coat of Europe, with kitindi, or coil armlets of brass or iron wire on both forearms and above the elbows. Unmarried girls amongst the Wahehe are known by their peculiar attire, a long strip of cloth, like the Indian "languti or T-bandage," but descending to the knees, and attached to waistbelts of large white or yellow porcelain or blue glass beads. Over this is tied a kilt of calabash fibre, a few inches deep. The men wear thick girdles of brass wire, neatly wound round a small cord. Besides the arms described amongst the Wasagara, the Wahehe carry "sime," or double-edged knives, from one to two feet long, broadening out from the haft, and rounded off to a blunt point at the end. The handle is cut into raised rings for security of grip, and, when in sheath, half the blade appears outside its rude leathern scabbard. The Tembe, or villages of the Wahehe, are small, ragged, and low, probably to facilitate escape from attack. They do business in slaves, and have large flocks and herds, which are, however, often thinned by the Warori, whom the Wahehe dare not resist in the field.

Chapter 8

WE SUCCEED IN TRAVERSING UGOGO

Ugogo, the reader may remember, was the ultimate period applied to the prospects of the Exploration by the worthy Mr. Rush Ramji, in conversation with the respectable Ladha Damha, Collector of Customs, Zanzibar.

I halted three days at Ugogi to recruit the party and to lay in rations for four long desert marches. Apparently there was an abundance of provisions, but the people at first declined to part with their grain and cattle even at exorbitant prices, and the Baloch complained of "cleanness of teeth." I was visited by Ngoma Mroma, alias Sultan Makande, a diwan or head-man, from Ugogo, here settled as chief, and well known on the eastern seaboard: he came to offer his good services. But he talked like an idiot, he begged for every article that met his eye: and he wished me – palpably for his own benefit – to follow the most northerly of the three routes leading to Unyam-wezi, upon which there were not less than eight "sultans" described by Kidogo as being "one hungrier than the other." At last, an elephant having been found dead within his limits, he disappeared, much to my relief, for the purpose of enjoying a gorge of elephant-beef.

Ugogi is the half-way district between the coast and Unyanyembe, and it is usually made by up-caravans at the end of the second month. The people of this "no man's land" are a mongrel race: the Wasagara claim the ground, but they have admitted as settlers many Wahehe and Wagogo, the latter for the most part men who have left their country for their country's good. The plains are rich in grain, and the hills in cattle, when not harried, as they had been, a little before our arrival, by the Warori. The inhabitants sometimes offer for sale milk and honey, eggs and ghee, but – only the civilised rogue can improve by adulteration – the milk falls like water off the finger, the honey is in the red stage of fermentation, of the eggs there are few without the rude beginnings of a chicken, and the ghee, from long keeping, is sweet above and bitter below. The country still contains game, kanga, or guinea-fowls, in abundance, the ocelot, a hyrax like the coney of the Somali country, and the beautiful "silver jackal." The elephant and the giraffe are frequently killed on the plains. the giraffe is called by the Arabs Jamal el Wahshl, a translation of the Kisawahili Ngamia ya Muytu, "Camel of the Wild," and throughout the interior Tiga or Twiga. Their sign is often seen in the uncultivated parts of the country; but they wander far, and they are rarely found except by accident; the hides are converted into shields and saddle-bags, the long tufty tails into "chauri," or fly-flappers, and the flesh is a favourite food. At Ugogi, however, game has suffered from the frequent haltings of caravans, and from the carnivorous propensities of the people, who, huntsmen all, leave their prey no chance against their nets and arrows, their pitfalls and their packs of yelping curs.

Ugogi stands 2760 feet above sea level, and its climate, immediately after the raw cold of Usagara, pleases by its elasticity and by its dry healthy warmth. The nights are fresh and dewless, and the rays of a tropical sun are cooled by the gusts and raffales which, regularly as the land and sea-breezes of the coast, sweep down the sinuosities of Dungomaro. As our "gnawing stomachs" testified, the air of Usagara had braced our systems. My companion so far recovered health that he was able to bring home many a brace of fine partridge, and of the fat guinea-fowl that, clustering upon the tall trees, awoke the echoes of the rocks as they called for their young. The Baloch, the sons of Ramji, and the porters began to throw off the effects of the pleurisies and the other complaints, which they attributed to hardship and exposure on the mountaintops. The only obstinate invalids were the two Goanese. Gaetano had another attack of the Mukunguru, or seasoning fever, which, instead of acclimatising his constitution, seemed by ever increasing weakness and depression, to pave the way for a fresh visitation. Valentine, with flowing eyes, pathetically pointed to two indurations in his gastric region, and bewailed his hard fate in thus being torn from the dearly-loved shades of Panjim and Margao, to fatten the inhospitable soil of Central Africa.

Immediately before departure, when almost in despair at the rapid failure of our carriage – the asses were now reduced to nine – I fortunately secured, for the sum of four cloths per man, the services of fifteen Wanyamwezi porters. In all a score, they had left at Ugogi their Mtongi, or employer, in consequence of a quarrel concerning the sex. They dreaded forcible seizure and sale if found without protection travelling homewards through Ugogo; and thus they willingly agreed to carry our goods as far as their own country, Unyanyembe. Truly is travelling like campaigning, – a pennyweight of luck is better than a talent of all the talents! And if marriages, as our fathers used to say, are made in the heavens, the next-door manufactory must be devoted to the fabrication of African explorations. Notwithstanding, however, the large increase of conveyance, every man appeared on the next march more heavily laden than before: – they carried grain for six days, and water for one night.

From Ugogi to the Ziwa or Pond, the eastern limits of Ugogo, are four marches, which, as they do not supply provisions, and as throughout the dry season water is found only in one spot, are generally accomplished in four days. The lesser desert, between Ugogi and Ugogo, is called Marenga M'khali, or the Brackish Water: it must not be confounded with the district of Usagara bearing the same name.

We left Ugogi on the 22nd September, at 3 P.M., instead of at noon. As all the caravan hurried recklessly forward, I brought up the rear accompanied by Said bin Salim, the Jemadar, and several of the sons of Ramji, who insisted upon driving the asses for greater speed at a long trot, which, after lasting a hundred yards, led to an inevitable fall of the load. Before emerging from Ugogi, the road wound over a grassy country, thickly speckled with calabashes. Square Tembe appeared on both sides, and there was no want of flocks and herds. As the villages and fields were left behind, the land became a dense thorny jungle, based upon a sandy red soil. The horizon was bounded on both sides by gradually-thinning lines of lumpy outlying hill, the spurs of the Rubeho Range, that extended, like a scorpion's claws, westward; and the plain, gently falling in the same direction, was broken only by a single hill-shoulder and by some dwarf descents. As we advanced through the shades – a heavy cloud-bank had shut out the crescent moon – our difficulties increased; thorns and spiky twigs threatened the eyes; the rough and rugged road led to many a stumble, and the frequent whine of the cyn-hyaena made the asses wild with fear. None but Bombay came out to meet us; the porters were overpowered by their long march under the fiery sun. About 8 P.M., directed by loud shouts and flaring fires, we reached a kraal, a patch of yellow grass, offering clear room in the thorny thicket. That night was the perfection of a bivouac, cool from the vicinity of the hills, genial from their shelter, and sweet as forest-air in these regions ever is.

On the next day we resumed our labour betimes: for a dreary and thirsty stage lay before us. Toiling through the sunshine of the hot waste I could not but remark the strange painting of the land around. At a distance the plain was bright-yellow with stubble, and brown-black with patches of leafless wintry jungle based upon a brick-dust soil. A closer approach disclosed colours more vivid and distinct. Over the ruddy plain lay scattered untidy heaps of grey granite boulders, surrounded and capped by tufts of bleached white grass. The copse showed all manner of strange hues, calabashes purpled and burnished by sun and rain, thorns of a greenish coppery bronze, dead trees with trunks of ghastly white, and gums (the blue-gum tree of the Cape?) of an unnatural sky-blue, the effect of the yellow outer pellicle being peeled off by the burning rays, whilst almost all were reddened up to a man's height, by the double galleries, ascending and descending, of the white ants. Here too, I began to appreciate the extent of the nuisance, thorns. Some were soft and green, others a finger long, fine, straight and woody – they serve as needles in many parts of the country – one, a "corking pin," bore at its base a filbert-like bulge, another was curved like a cock's spur; the double thorns, placed dos-h-dos, described by travellers in Abyssinia and in the Cape Karroos, were numerous, the "wait-a-bit," a dwarf sharply bent spine with acute point and stout foundation, and a smaller variety, short and deeply crooked, numerous and tenacious as fish-hooks, tore without difficulty the strongest clothing, even our woollen Arab "Abas," and our bed-covers of painted canvas.

Travelling through this broom-jungle and crossing grassy plains, over paths where the slides of elephants' feet upon the last year's muddy clay showed that the land was not always dry, we halted after 11 A.M. for about an hour at the base of a steep incline, apparently an offset from the now distant Rubeho Range. The porters would have nighted at the mouth of a small drain which, too steep for ascent, exposed in its rocky bed occasional sand-patches and deep pools; Kidogo, however, forced them forwards, declaring that if the asses drank of this "brackish water," they would sicken and die. His assertion, suspected of being a "traveller's tale," was subsequently confirmed by the Arabs of Unyanyembe, who declared that the country people never water their flocks and herds below the hill; there may be poisonous vegetation in the few yards between the upper and the lower pools, but no one offered any explanation of the phenomenon.

Ascending with difficulty the eastern face of the step, which presented two ladders of loose stones and fixed boulders of grey syenite, hornblende, and greenstone, with coloured quartzes, micacious schistes, and layers of talcose slate glittering like mother-o'-pearl upon the surface, we found a half-way platform some 150 feet of extreme breadth. Upon its sloping and irregular floor, black-green pools, sadly offensive to more senses than one, spring-fed, and forming the residue of the rain-water which fills the torrent, lay in muddy holes broadly fringed with silky grass. Travellers drink without fear this upper Marenga Mk'haIi, which, despite its name, is rather soft and slimy, than brackish, and sign of wild-beasts – antelope and buffalo, giraffe and rhinoceros – appear upon its brink. It sometimes dries up in the heart of the hot season, and then deaths from thirst occur amongst the porters who, mostly Wanyanwezi, are not wont to practise abstinence in this particular. "Sucking-places" are unknown to them, water-bearing bulbs might here be discovered by the South African traveller; as a rule, however, the East African is so plentifully supplied with the necessary that he does not care to provide for a dry day by unusual means. Ascending another steep incline we encamped upon a small step, the half-way gradient of a higher level.

The 24th Sept. was to be a tirikeza: the Baloch and the sons of Ramji spent the earlier half in blowing away gunpowder at antelope, partridge and parrot, guinea-fowl and floriken, but not a head of game found its way into camp. The men were hot, tired and testy, those who had wives beat them, those who had not "let off the steam" by quarreling with one another. Said bin Salim, sick and surly, had words concerning a water-gourd with the brave Khudabakhsh, and the monocular Jemadar, who made a point of overloading his porters, bitterly complained because they would not serve him. At 2 P.M. we climbed up the last ladder of the rough and stony incline, which placed us a few hundred feet above the eastern half of the Lesser Desert. We took a pleasant leave of the last of the rises; on this line of road, between Marenga Mk'hali and Western Unyam-wezi, the land, though rolling, has no steep ascents nor descents.

From the summit of the Marenga Mk'hali step we travelled till sunset – the orb of day glaring like a fireball in our faces, – through dense thorny jungle and over grassy plains of black, cracked earth, in places covered with pebbles and showing extensive traces of shallow inundations during the rains; in the lower lands huge blocks of weathered granite stood out abruptly from the surface, and on both sides, but higher on the right hand, rose blue cones, some single, others in pairs like "brothers." The caravan once rested in a thorny coppice, based upon rich red and yellow clay whence it was hurriedly dislodged by a swarm of wild bees. As the sun sank below the horizon the porters called a halt on a calabash-grown plain, near a block of stony hill veiled with cactus and mimosa, below whose northern base ran a tree-lined Nullah where, they declared, from the presence of antelope and other game, that water might be found by digging. Vainly Kidogo urged them forwards declaring that they would fail to reach the Ziwa or Pond in a single march; they preferred "crowing" and scooping up sand till midnight to advancing a few miles, and some gourdsfull of dirty liquid rewarded their industry.

On the morning of the 26th of September, I learned that we had sustained an apparently irreparable loss. When the caravan was dispersed by bees, a porter took the opportunity of deserting. This man, who represented himself as desirous of rejoining at Unyamyembe, his patron Abdullah bin Musa, the son of the well-known Indian merchant, had been engaged for four cloths by Said bin Salim at Ugogi. The Arab with his usual after-wit found out, when the mishap was announced, that he had from the first doubted and disliked the man so much that he had paid down only half the hire. Yet to the new porter had been committed the most valuable of our packages, a portmanteau containing the Nautical Ahnanac for 1858, the surveying books, and most of our paper, pens and ink. Said bin Salim, however, was hardly to be blamed, his continual quarrels with the Baloch and the sons of Ramji absorbed all his thoughts. Although the men were unanimous in declaring that the box never could be recovered, I sent back Bombay Mabruki and the slave Ambari with particular directions to search the place where we had been attacked by bees; it was within three miles, but, as the road was deemed dangerous, the three worthies preferred passing a few quiet hours in some snug neighbouring spot.

At 1.30 P.M. much saddened by the disaster, we resumed our road and after stretching over a monotonous grassy plain variegated with dry thorny jungle, we arrived about sunset at a waterless kraal where we determined to pass the night. Our supplies of liquid ran low, the Wanyamwezi porters, who carried our pots and gourds, had drained them on the way, and without drink an afternoon-march in this droughthy land destroys all appetite for supper. Some of the porters presently set out to fill their gourds with the waters of the Ziwa, thence distant but a few miles; they returned after a four hours' absence with supplies which restored comfort and good humour to the camp.

Before settling for the night Kidogo stood up, and to loud cries of "Maneno! maneno!" – words! words! – equivalent to our parliamentary hear! hear! delivered himself of the following speech: –

"Listen, O ye whites! and ye children of Sayyidi Majidi! and ye sons of Ramji! hearken to my words, O ye offspring of the night! The journey entereth Ugogo – Ugogo (the orator threw out his arm westward). Beware, and again beware (he made violent gesticulations). You don't know the Wagogo, they are —s and —s! (he stamped.) Speak not to those Washenzi pagans; enter not into their houses (he pointed grimly to the ground). Have no dealings with them, show no cloth, wire, nor beads (speaking with increasing excitement). Eat not with them, drink not with them, and make not love to their women (here the speech became a scream). Kirangozi of the

Wanyamwezi, restrain your sons! Suffer them not to stray into the villages, to buy salt out of camp, to rob provisions, to debauch with beer, or to sit by the wells!" And thus, for nearly half an hour, now violently, then composedly, he poured forth the words of wisdom, till the hubbub and chatter of voices which at first had been silenced by surprise, brought his eloquence to an end.

We left the jungle-kraal early on the 26th September, and after hurrying through thick bush we debouched upon an open stubbly plain, with herds of gracefully bounding antelopes and giraffes, who stood for a moment with long outstretched necks to gaze, and presently broke away at a rapid, striding, camel's-trot, their heads shaking as if they would jerk off, their limbs loose, and their joints apparently dislocated. About 9 P.M. we sighted the much-talked of Ziwa. The Arabs, fond of "showing a green garden," had described to me at Inenge a piece of water fit to float a man-of-war. But Kidogo, when consulted, had replied simply with the Kisawahili proverb, "Khabari ya mb'hali;" i.e., "news from afar;" —*a beau mentir qui vient de loin.* I was not therefore surprised to find a shallow pool, which in India would barely merit the name of tank.

The Ziwa, which lies 3,100 feet above the sea, occupies the lowest western level of Marenga Mk'hali, and is the deepest of the many inundated grounds lying to its north, northeast, and north-west. The extent greatly varies: in September, 1857, it was a slaty sheet of water, with granite projections on one side, and about 300 yards in diameter; the centre only could not be forded. The bottom and the banks were of retentive clay: a clear ring, whence the waters had subsided, margined the pool, and beyond it lay a thick thorny jungle. In early December, 1858, nothing remained but a surface of dry, crumbling, and deeply-cracked mud, and, according to travellers, it had long, in consequence of the scanty rains, been in that. state. Caravans always encamp at the Ziwa when they find water there. The country around is full of large game, especially elephants, giraffes, and zebras, who come to drink at night; a few widgeon are seen breasting the little waves; "kata" (sand-grouse), of peculiarly large size and dark plumage, flock there with loud cries; and at eventide the pool is visited by guinea-fowl, floriken, curlews, peewits, wild pigeons, doves, and hosts of small birds. When the Ziwa is desiccated, travellers usually encamp in a thick bush, near a scanty clearing, about one mile to the north-west, where a few scattered villages of Wagogo have found dirty white water, hard and bad, in pits varying from twenty to thirty feet in depth. Here, as elsewhere in eastern Africa, the only trough is a small ring sunk in the retentive clayey soil, and surrounded by a little raised dam of mud and loose stones. A demand is always made for according permission to draw water – a venerable custom, dating from the days of Moses. "Ye shall buy meat of them (the Edomites) for money, that ye may eat; and ye shall also buy water of them for money, that ye may drink." – Deut. ii. 6. Yet as thirsty, like hungry men, are not to be trifled with, fatal collisions have resulted from this inhospitable practice. Some years ago a large caravan of Wanyamwezi was annihilated in consequence of a quarrel about water, and lately several deaths occurred in a caravan led by an Arab merchant, Sallum bin Hamid, because the wells were visited before the rate of payment was settled. In several places we were followed upon the march lest a gourd might be furtively filled. To prevent exhaustion the people throw euphorbia, asclepias, and solanaceous plants into the well after a certain hour, and when not wanted it is bushed over, to keep off animals, and to check evaporation.

At the Ziwa the regular system of kuhonga, or blackmail, so much dreaded by travellers, begins in force. Up to this point all the chiefs are contented with little presents; but in Ugogo tribute is taken by force, if necessary. None can evade payment; the porters, fearing lest the road be cut off to them in future, would refuse to travel unless each chief is satisfied; and when a quarrel arises they throw down their packs and run away. Ugogo, since the closing of the northern line through the Wahumba and the Wamasai tribes, and the devastation of the southern regions by the Warori, is the only open line, and the sultans have presumed upon their power of stopping the way. There is no regular tariff of taxes: the sum is fixed by the traveller's dignity and outfit, which, by means of his slaves, are as well known to every sultan as to himself. Properly speaking, the exaction should be confined to the up-caravans; from those returning a head or two of cattle, a few hoes, or some similar trifle, are considered ample. Such, however, was not the experience of the Expedition. When first travelling through the country the "Wazungu" were sometimes mulcted to the extent of fifty cloths by a single chief, and the Arabs congratulated them upon having escaped so easily. On their downward march they pleaded against a second demand as exorbitant as the first, adducing the custom of caravans, who are seldom mulcted in more than two cows or a pair of jembe, or iron hoes; the chiefs, however, replied that as they never expected to see white faces again, it was their painful duty to make the most from them.

The kuhonga, however, is not unjust. In these regions it forms the customs-dues of the government: the sultan receives it nominally, but he must distribute the greater part amongst his family and councillors, his elders and attendants. It takes the place of the fees expected by the Balderabba of the Abyssinians, the Mogasa of the Gallas, the Abban of the Somal, and the Ghafir and Rafik amongst the Bedouin Arabs, which are virtually assertions of supremacy upon their own ground. These people have not the idea which seems prevalent in the south, namely, that any man has a right to tread God's earth gratis as long as he does not interfere with property. If any hesitation about the kuhonga be made, the first question put to the objector will be, "Is this your ground or my ground?" The practice, which is sanctioned by the customs of civilised nations, is, however, vitiated in East Africa by the slave-trade: it becomes the means of intrusion and extortion, of insolence and violence. The Wagogo are an importing people, and they see with envy long strings of what they covet passing through their territory from the interior to the coast. They are strong enough to plunder any caravan; but violence they know would injure them by cutting off communication with the markets for their ivory. Thus they have settled into a silent compromise, and their nice sense of self-interest prevents any transgression beyond the bounds of reason. The sultans receive their kuhonga, and the subjects entice away slaves from every caravan, but the enormous interest upon capital laid out in the trade still leaves a balance in favour of the merchants. The Arabs, however, declaring that the evil is on the increase, propose many remedies – such as large armed caravans, sent by their government, and heavy dues to be exacted from those Wagogo who may visit the coast. But they are wise enough to murmur without taking steps which would inevitably exacerbate the evil. Should it pass a certain point, a new road will be opened, or the old road will be reopened, to restore the balance of interests.

At the Ziwa we had many troubles. One Marema, the sultan of a new settlement situated a few hundred yards to the north-west visited us on the day of our arrival and reproving us for "sitting in the jungle," pointed out the way to his village. On our replying that we were about to traverse Ugogo by another route, he demanded his Ada or customs, which being newly-imposed were at once refused by Kidogo. The sultan, a small man, a "mere thief," – as a poor noble is graphically described in these lands, – threatened violence, whereupon the asses were brought in from grazing and were ostentatiously loaded before his eyes: when he changed his tone from threats to beggary. Kidogo relenting gave him two cloths with a few strings of beads, preferring this slender disbursement to the chance of a flight of arrows during the night. His good judgment was evidenced by the speedy appearance of the country-people, who brought with them bullocks, sheep, goats and poultry, water-melons and pumpkins, honey, butter-milk, whey and curdled-milk, an abundance of holcus and calabash-flour. The latter is made from the hard dry pulp surrounding the bean-like seed contained in the ripe gourd: the taste is a not unpleasant agro-dolce, and the people declare it to be strengthening food, especially for children; they convert it into porridge and rude cakes.

This abundance of provaunt caused a halt of four days at the Ziwa, and it was spent in disputes between the great Said and the greater Kidogo. The ostensible "bone of contention," was cloth advanced by the former to the porters – who claimed as their perquisitc a bullock before entering Ugogo – without consulting the hard-headed slave, who wounded in his tenderest place of pride, had influence enough to halt the caravan. The real cause of the dispute was kept from my ears till some months afterwards, but secrets in this land are as the Arabs say, "Like musk, murder, and Basrah-garlic," they must out, and Bombay, who could never help blurting forth the tacenda with the dicenda, at last accidentally unveiled the mystery. Said had deferred taking overcharge of the outfit from Kidogo till our arrival at the Ziwa, and the latter felt aggrieved by the sudden yet tardy demand, which deprived him of the dignity and the profits of stewardship. Sickness became rife in camp, the effect of the cold night-winds and the burning suns, and as usual when men are uncomfortable violent quarrels ensued. Again the officious Wazira, shook the torch of discord by ordering Khamisi, an exceedingly drunken and debauched son of Ramji, to carry certain bundles which usually graced the shoulders of Goha, one of the Wak'hutu porters. When words were exhausted Khamisi drew his blade upon Goha and was tackled by Wazira, whilst Goha brought the muzzle of my elephant-gun to bear upon Khamisi and was instantly collared by Bombay. Being thus "in chancery" both heroes waxed so "exceedingly brave – particular," that I was compelled to cool their noble bile with a long pole. At length it became necessary to make Kidogo raise his veto against the advance of the caravan. He did not appear before me till summoned half-a-dozen times: when he at last vouchsafed so to do I dragged rather than led him to the mat, where sat in surly pride Said bin Salim, with the monocular Jemadar, and I ordered the trio to quench with the waters of explanation the fire of anger. After an apparently satisfactory arrangement Kidogo started up and disappeared in the huts of his men; it presently proved that he had so done for the purpose of proposing to his party, who were now the sole interpreters, that to Said bin Salim, an ignoramus in such matters, should be committed the weighty task of settling the amount of our blackmail and presents with the greedy chiefs of Ugogo. Had the mischievous project been carried into execution, we should have been sufferers to some extent: lack of unanimity however caused the measure to be thrown out. A march was fixed for the next day, when the bullock, on this occasion the scape-grace, broke its tether and plunged into the bush: it was followed by the Baloch and the porters, whose puny arrows, when they alighted upon the beast's stern, only goaded it forwards, and at least threescore matchlock balls were discharged before one bullet found its billet in the fugitive. The camp of course then demanded another holiday to eat beef.

The reader must not imagine that I am making a "great cry," about a little matter. Four days are not easily spent when snowed-up in a country inn, and that is a feeble comparison for the halt in East Africa, where outfit is leaking away, the valuable travelling-time is perhaps drawing to a closer health is palpably failing, and nothing but black faces made blacker still by ill-humour and loud squabbles, meet the eye and ear. Insignificant things they afterwards appear viewed through the medium of memory, these petty annoyances of travel; yet at the moment they are severely felt, and they must be resented accordingly. The African traveller's fitness for the task of exploration depends more upon his faculty of chafing under delays and kicking against the pricks, than upon his power of displaying the patience of a Griselda or a Job.

On the 30th September, the last day of our detention at the Jiwa, appeared a large caravan headed by Said bin Mohammed of Mbuamaji, with Khalfan bin Khamis, and several other Coast-Arabs. They brought news from the sea-board, and, – wondrous good fortune! – the portmanteau containing books which the porter, profiting by the confusion caused by the swarm of bees, had deposited in the long grass, at the place where I had directed the slaves to seek it. Some difficulty was at first made about restitution: the Arab law of "lakit," or things trove, being variable, complicated, and altogether opposed to our ideas. However, two cloths were given to the man who had charge of it, and the Jemadar and Said bin Salim were sent to recover it by any or all means. The merchants were not offended. They consented to sell for the sum of thirty-five dollars a strong and serviceable but an old and obstinate African ass, which after carrying my companion for many a mile, at last broke its heart when toiling up the steeps from whose summit the fair waters of the Central Lake were first sighted. Moreover, they proposed that for safety and economy the two caravans should travel together under a single flag, and thus combine to form a total of 190 men. These Coast-Arabs travelled in comfort. The brother of Said Mohammed had married the daughter of Fundikira, Sultan of Unyanyembe, and thus the family had a double home, on the coast and in the interior. All the chiefs of the caravan carried with them wives and female slaves, negroid beauties, tall, bulky and "plenty of them," attired in tulip-hues, cochineal and gamboge, who walked the whole way, and who when we passed them displayed an exotic modesty by drawing their head-cloths over cheeks which we were little ambitious to profane. They had a multitude of Fundi, or managing men, and male slaves, who bore their personal bag and baggage, scrip and scrippage, drugs and comforts, stores and provisions, and who were always early at the ground to pitch, to surround with a "pai," or dwarf drain, and to bush for privacy, with green boughs, their neat and light ridge-tents of American domestics. Their bedding was as heavy as ours and even their poultry travelled in wicker cages. This caravan was useful to us in dealing with the Wagogo: it always managed, however, to precede us on the march, and to monopolise the best kraals. The Baloch and the sons of Ramji, when asked on these occasions why they did not build a palisade, would reply theatrically, "Our hearts are our fortification!" – methought a sorry defence.

By Kidogo's suggestion I had preferred the middle line through the hundred miles of dreaded Ugogo: it was the beaten path, and infested only by four Sultans, namely: 1. Myandozi of Kifukuru. 2. Magomba of Kanyenye. 3. Maguru-Mafupiof K'hok'ho; and 4. Ki-baya of Mdaburu. On the 1st October, 1857, we left the Ziwa late in the morning, and after passing through the savannahs and the brown jungles of the lower levels, where giraffe again appeared, the path crested a wave of ground and debouched upon the table-land of Ugogo. The aspect was peculiar and unprepossessing. Behind still towered in sight the Delectable Mountains of Usagara, mist-crowned and robed in the lightest azure, with streaks of a deep plum-colour, fronting the hot low land of Marenga Mk'hali, whose tawny face was wrinkled with lines of dark jungle. On the north was a tabular range of rough and rugged hill, above which rose three distant cones pointed out as the haunts of the robber Wahumba: at its base was a deep depression, a tract of brown brush patched with yellow grass, inhabited only by the elephant, and broken by small outlying hillocks. Southwards scattered eminences of tree-crowned rock rose a few yards from the plain which extended to the front, a clearing of deep red or white soil, decayed vegetation based upon rocky or sandy ground, here and there thinly veiled with brown brush and golden stubbles: its length, about four miles, was studded with square villages, and with the stately but grotesque calabash. This giant is to the vegetable what the elephant is to the animal world: – the Persians call it the "practice-work of nature" – its disproportionate conical bole rests upon huge legs exposed to view by the washing away of the soil, and displays excrescences which in pious India would merit a coat of vermilion. From the neck extend gigantic gnarled arms, each one a tree, whose thinnest twig is thick as a man's finger, and their weight causes them to droop earthwards, giving to the outline the shape of a huge dome. In many parts the unloveliness of its general appearance is varied by the wrinkles and puckerings which, forming by granulation upon the oblongs where the bark has been removed for fibre, give the base the appearance of being chamfered and fluted; and often a small family of trunks, four or five in number, springs from the same root. At that season all were leafless; at other times they are densely foliaged, and contrasting with their large timber and with their coarse fleshy leaf, they are adorned with the delicatest flowers of a pure virgin-white, which, opening at early dawn, fade and fall before eventide. The babe-tree issues from the ground about one foot in diameter: in Ugogo, however, all those observed were of middle age. The young are probably grubbed up to prevent their encumbering the ground, and when decayed enough to be easily felled, they are converted into firewood. By the side of these dry and leafless masses of dull dead hue, here and there a mimosa or a thorn was beginning to bear the buds of promise green as emeralds. The sun burned like the breath of a bonfire, a painful glare – the reflection of the terrible crystal above, – arose from the hot earth; warm Siroccos raised clouds of dust, and in front the horizon was so distant, that, as the Arabs expressed themselves, "a man might be seen three marches off."

We were received with the drumming and the ringing of bells attached to the ivories, with the yells and frantic shouts of two caravans halted at Kifukuru: one was that of Said Mohammed, who awaited our escort, the other a return "Safari," composed of about 1,000 Wanyamwezi porters, headed by four slaves of Salim bin Rashid, an Arab merchant settled at Unyanyembe. The country people also flocked to stare at the phenomenon; they showed that excitement which some few years ago might have been witnessed in more polished regions when a "horrible murder" roused every soul from Tweed banks to Land's End; when, to gratify a morbid destructiveness, artists sketched, literati described, tourists visited, and curio-hunters met to bid for the rope and the murderer's whiskers. Yet I judged favour-ably of the Wagogo by their curiosity, which stood out in strong relief against the apathy and the uncommunicativeness of the races lately visited. Such inquisitiveness is amongst barbarians generally a proof of improvability, – of power to progress. One man who had visited Zanzibar could actually speak a few words of Hindostani, and in Ugogo, and there only, I was questioned by the chiefs concerning Uzungu "White-land," the mysterious end of the world in which beads are found under ground, and where the women weave such cottons. From the day of our entering to that of our leaving the country, every settlement turned out its swarm of gazers, men and women, boys and girls, some of whom would follow us for miles with explosions of Hi! – i! – i! screams of laughter and cries of excitement, at a long high trot, – most ungraceful of motion! – and with a scantiness of toilette which displayed truly unseemly spectacles. The matrons, especially the aged matrons, realised Madame Pernelle's description of an unpleasant female –

"Un peu trop forte en gueule et fort impertinente;

and of their sex the old men were ever the most pertinacious and intrusive, the most surly and quarrelsome. Vainly the escort attempted to arrest the course of this moving multitude of semi-nude barbarity. I afterwards learned that the two half-caste Arabs who had passed us at Muhama, Khalfan and Id, the sons of Muallim Salim of Zanzibar, had, whilst preceding us, spread through Ugogo malevolent reports concerning the Wazungu. They had one eye each and four arms; they were full of "knowledge," which in these lands means magic; they caused rain to fall in advance and left droughts in their rear;

they cooked water melons and threw away the seeds, thereby generating small-pox; they heated and hardened milk, thus breeding a murrain amongst cattle; and their wire, cloth, and beads caused a variety of misfortunes; they were kings of the sea, and therefore white-skinned and straight-haired – a standing mystery to these curly-pated people – as are all men who live in salt water; and next year they would return and seize the country. Suspicion of our intentions touching "territorial aggrandisement" was a fixed idea: everywhere the value attached by barbarians to their homes is in inverse ratio to the real worth of the article. Hence mountaineers are proverbially patriotic. Thus the lean Bedouins of Arabia and the lank Somal, though they own that they are starving, never sight a stranger without suspecting that he is spying out the wealth of the land. "What will happen to us?" asked the Wagogo; "we never yet saw this manner of man!" But the tribe cannot now forfeit intercourse with the coast: they annoyed us to the utmost, they made the use of their wells a daily source of trouble, they charged us double prices, and when they brought us provisions for sale, they insisted upon receiving the price of even the rejected articles; yet they did not proceed to open outrage. Our timid Arab, the Baloch, the sons of Ramji, and the porters humoured them in every whim. Kidogo would not allow observations to be taken with a bright sextant in presence of the mobility. He declined to clear the space before the tent, as the excited starers, some of whom had come from considerable distances, were apt under disappointment to wax violent; and though he once or twice closed the tent-flaps, he would not remove the lines of men, women, and children, who stretched themselves for the greater convenience of peeping and peering, lengthways upon the ground. Whenever a Mnyamwezi porter interfered, he was arrogantly told to begone, and he slunk away, praying us to remember that these men are "Wagogo." Caravan after caravan had thus taught them to become bullies, whereas a little manliness would soon have reduced them to their proper level. They are neither brave nor well-armed, and their prestige rests solely upon their feat in destroying about one generation ago a caravan of Wanyamwezi – an event embalmed in a hundred songs and traditions. They seemed to take a fancy to the Baloch, who received from the fair sex many a little souvenir in the shape of a kid or a watermelon. Whenever the Goanese Valentine was sent to a village he was politely and hospitably welcomed, and seated upon a three-legged stool by the headman; and generally the people agreed in finding fault with their principal Sultans, declaring that they unwisely made the country hateful to "Wakonongo," or travellers. Fortunately for the Expedition several scions of the race saw the light safely during our transit of Ugogo: had an accident occurred to a few babies or calves, our return through the country would have been difficult and dangerous. All received the name of "Muzungu," and thus there must now be a small colony of black "white men" in this part of the African interior.

At Kifukuru I was delayed a day whilst settling the blackmail of its Sultan Miyandozi. Said bin Salim, the Jemadar, and Kidogo called upon him in the morning and were received in the gateway of a neat "Tembe," the great man disdaining to appear on so trivial an occasion. This Sultan is the least powerful of the four; he is plundered by the Warori tribes living to the south-west, and by his western neighbour, Magomba; his subjects are poorly clad, and are little ornamented compared with those occupying the central regions, where they have the power to detain travellers and to charge them exorbitantly for grain and water. Yet Miyandozi demanded four white and six blue shukkahs; besides which I was compelled to purchase for him from the sons of Ramji, who of course charged treble its value, a "Sohari" or handsome silk and cotton loin-cloth. In return he sent – it appeared to be in irony – one kayla, or four small measures of grain. The slaves of Salim bin Rashid obliged me with a few pounds of rice, for which I gave them a return in gunpowder, and they undertook to convey to Zanzibar a package of reports, indents, and letters, which was punctually delivered. An ugly accident had nearly happened that night; the Wanyamwezi porters managed to fire the grass round a calabash tree, against which they had stretched their loads, and a powder-magazine – fortunately fire-proof – was blackened and charred by the flames. A traveller cannot be too careful about his ammunition in these lands. I have seen a slave smoking a water pipe, tied for convenience of carriage to a leaky keg of powder; and another in the caravan of Salim bin Sayf of Dut'humi, resting the muzzle of his musket against a barrel of ammunition, fired it to try its strength, and blew himself up with several of his comrades.

On the 3rd October we quitted Kifukuru in the afternoon, and having marched nearly six hours we encamped in one of the strips of waterless brown jungles which throughout Ugogo divide the cultivated districts from one another, and occupy about half the superficies of the land. The low grounds, inundated during the rains, were deeply cracked, and my weak ass, led by the purblind Shahdad, fell with violence upon my knee, leaving a mixture of pain and numbness which lasted for some months. On the next day we resumed our journey betimes through a thick rugged jungle and over a rolling grassy plain, which extended to the frontier of Kanyenye, where Sultan Magomba rules. The 5th October saw us in the centre of Kanyenye, a clearing about ten miles in diameter. The surface is a red tamped clayey soil, dotted with small villages, huge calabashes, and stunted mimosas; water is found in wells or rather pits sunk from ten to twelve feet in the lower lands, or in the sandy beds of the several Fiumaras. Flocks and herds abound, and the country is as cultivated and populous as the saline nitrous earth, and the scarceness of the potable element, which often tarnishes silver like sulphur-fumes, permits.

At Kanyenye I was delayed four days to settle blackmail with Magomba, the most powerful of the Wagogo chiefs. He was on this, as on a subsequent occasion, engaged in settling a cause arising from Uchawi or Black Magic; yet all agree that in Ugogo, where, to quote the "Royal Martyr's" words,

"Plunder and murder are the kingdom's laws,"

there is perhaps less of wizardhood and witchcraft, and consequently less of its normal consequences, fiscs and massacres, than in any other region between the Atlantic and the Indian Ocean. "Arrow-heads" employed every art of wild diplomacy to relieve me of as much cloth as possible. I received, when encamped at the Ziwa, a polite message declaring his desire to see white men; but – "the favour of the winds produces dust" – I was obliged to acknowledge the compliment with two cottons. On arrival at his head-quarters I was waited upon by an oily cabinet of Wazirs and elders, who would not depart without their "respects" – four cottons. The next demand was made by his favourite wife, a peculiarly hideous old princess with more wrinkles than hairs, with no hair black and no tooth white, and attended by ladies in waiting as unprepossessing as herself: she was not to be dismissed without a fee of six cottons. At last, accompanied by a mob of courtiers, who crowded in like an African House of Commons, appeared in person the magnifico. He was the only Sultan that ever entered my tent in Ugogo – pride and a propensity for strong drink prevented other visits. He was much too great a man to call upon the Arab merchants, but in our case curiosity had mastered state considerations. Magomba was a black and wrinkled elder, drivelling and decrepid, with a half-bald head from whose back and sides depended a few straggling corkscrews of iron gray: he wore a coat of castor-oil and a "Barsati" loin-cloth, which grease and use had changed from blue to black. A few bead strings decorated his neck, large flexible anklets of brass wire adorned his legs, solid brass rings, single and in coils, which had distended his earlobes almost to splitting, were tied by a string over his cranium, and his horny soles were defended by single-soled sandals, old, dirty, and tattered. He chewed his quid and he expectorated without mercy; he asked many a silly question, yet he had ever an eye to the main chance. He demanded and received five "cloths with names," which I was again compelled to purchase at an exorbitant price from the Baloch and slaves, one coil of brass wire, four blue cottons, and ten "domestics;" the total amounted to fifty shukkahs, here worth at least fifty dollars, and exhausting nearly two-thirds of a porter's load. His return present was the leanest of calves; when it was driven into camp with much parade, his son, who had long been looking out for a fit opportunity, put in a claim for three cottons.

Magomba before our departure exacted from Kidogo an oath that his Wazungu would not smite the land with drought or with fatal disease, declaring that all we had was in his hands. He boasted, and with truth, of his generosity. It was indeed my firm conviction from first to last, that in case of attack or surprise I had not a soul except my companion to stand by me: all those who accompanied us could, and consequently would, have saved their lives; – we must have perished. We should have been as safe with six as with sixty guns; but I would by no means apply to these regions Mr. Galton's opinion, "that the last fatal expedition of Mungo Park is full of warning to travellers who propose exploring with a large body of men." For though sixty guns do not suffice to prevent attack in Ugogo, 600 stout fellows armed with the "hot-mouthed weapon" might march through the length and breadth of Central Africa.

During our four days' detention at Kanyenye, I was compelled to waste string after string of beads in persuading the people to water the porters and asses. Yet their style of proceeding proved that it was greed of gain, not scarcity of the element, which was uppermost in their minds; they would agree to supply us with an unlimited quantity, and then would suddenly gather round the well and push away the Wanyamwezi, bidding them go and fetch more beads. All the caravan took the opportunity of loading itself with salt. Whilst the halt lasted, my companion brought in a fine-flavoured pallah and other antelopes, with floriken, guinea-fowl, and partridge. Neither he nor I, however, had strength enough, nor had we time, to attack the herds of elephants that roam over the valley whose deep purple line separates the table-land of Ugogo from the blue hills of the Wahumba to the north. And here, perhaps, a few words concerning the prospects of sportsmen in this part of Africa, may save future travellers from the mistake into which I fell. I expected great things, and returned without realising a single hope. This portion of the peninsula is a remarkable contrast to the line traversed by Dr. Livingstone, where the animals standing within bow-shot were so numerous and fearless, that the burden of provisions was often unnecessary. In the more populous parts game has melted away before the woodman's axe and the hunters' arrows: even where large tracks of jungle abound with water and forage, the note of a bird rarely strikes the ear, and during a long day's march not a single large animal will be seen from the beaten track. It is true that in some places, there is

> *"— enough*
> *Of beastes that be chaseable."*

The park lands of Dut'humi, the jungles and forests of Ugogi and Mgunda Mk'hali, the barrens of Usukuma, and the tangled thickets of Ujiji, are full of noble game, – lions and leopards, elephants and rhinoceroses, wild cattle, giraffes, gnus, zebras, quaggas, and ostriches. But these are dangerous regions where the sportsman often cannot linger for a day. Setting aside the minor considerations of miasma and malaria, – the real or fancied perils of the place, and the want of food, or the difficulty of procuring water, would infallibly cause the porters to desert. Here are no Cape-waggons, at once house, store, and transport; no "Ships of the Desert," never known to run away; in fact there is no vehicle but man, and he is so impatient and headstrong, so suspicious and timorous, that he must be humoured in every whim. As sportsmen know, it is difficult to combine surveying operations and collection of specimens with a pursuit which requires all a man's time; in these countries, moreover, no merely hunting-expedition would pay, owing to the extraordinary expense of provisions and carriage. Thus Venator will be reduced to use his "shooting-iron" on halting days, and at the several periods of his journey, and his only consolation will be the prospect of wreaking vengeance upon the hippopotamus and the crocodile of the coast, if his return there be entered in the book of Time. Finally, East Africa wants the vast variety of animals, especially the beautiful antelopes, which enrich the lists of the Cape Fauna. The tale of those observed in short: the horns of the oryx were seen, the hartebeest and steinbok, the saltiana and the pallah, – the latter affording excellent venison, – were shot. The country generally produces the "Suiya," a little antelope with reddish coat and diminutive horns, about the size of an English hare, the swangura, or sungula, an animal somewhat larger than the saltiana, and of which, according to the people, the hind only has horns; and at K'hutu my companion saw a double-horned antelope which he thought resembled the "Choukasinga," (*Tetraceros Quadricornis*) of Nepaul. The species of birds, also, are scarcely more numerous than the beasts; the feathered tribe is characterised by sombreness of plumage, and their song is noisy but not harmonious, unpleasant, perhaps because strange, to the European ear.

On the 8th October appeared at Kanyenye a large down. caravan headed by Abdullah bin Nasib, a Msawahili of Zanzibar, whose African name is Kisesa. This good man began with the usual token of hospitality, the gift of a goat, and some measures of the fine Unyanyembe rice, of which return-parties carry an ample store: he called upon me at once with several companions, – one of them surprised me not a little by an English "good morning," – and he kindly volunteered to halt a day whilst we wrote reports and letters, life-certificates, and duplicate-in-dents upon Zanzibar for extra supplies of drugs and medical comforts, cloth and beads. The asses were now reduced to five, and as Magomba refused to part with any of his few animals, at any price, – on the coast I had been assured that asses were as numerous as dogs in Ugogo – Abdullah gave me one of his riding-animals, and would take nothing for it except a little medicine, and a paper acknowledging his civility. Several of the slaves and porters had been persuaded by the Wagogo to desert, and Abdullah busied himself to recover them. One man, who had suddenly deposited his pack upon the path and had disappeared in the jungle during the noonday halt, was pointed out by a woman to Kidogo, and was found lurking in a neighbouring village, where the people refused to give him up. Abdullah sent for Magomba's four chief "ministers," and persuaded them to render active aid: they seized the fellow, took from him his wire and his nine cloths, appropriated four, and left me five wherewith to engage another porter. The deserter was of course dismissed, but the severity of the treatment did not prevent three desertions on the next day.

The 10th October ushered in an ugly march. Emerging betimes from the glaring white and red plains of Kanyenye, dotted with fields, villages, and calabashes, we unloaded in a thin jungle of mimosa and grass-bunches, near sundry pools, then almost dried up, but still surrounded by a straggling growth of chamaerops and verdurous thorns. The bush gave every opportunity to the porters, who had dispersed in the halt, to desert with impunity. In our hurried morning tramp, want of carriage had caused considerable confusion, and at 2 P.M., when again the word "load" was given for a tirikeza, everything seemed to go wrong. Said bin Salim and the Jemadar hurried forwards, leaving me to manage the departure with Kidogo, who, whilst my companion lay under a calabash almost unable to move, substituted for his strong Mnyamwezi ass a wretched animal unable to bear the lightest load. The Baloch Belok was asked to carry our only gourd full of water;

he pleaded sickness as an excuse. And, when the rear of the caravan was about to march, Kidogo, who alone knew the way, hastened on so fast that he left us to wander through a labyrinth of elephants' tracks, hedged in by thorns and brambly trees, which did considerable damage to clothes and cutis.

Having at length found the way, we advanced over a broad, open, and grassy plain, striped with southwards-trending sandy water-courses of easy ascent and descent, and lined with a green aromatic vegetation, in which the tall palm suggested a resemblance to the valley-plains of the Usagara Mountains. As night fell upon us like a pall, we entered the broken red ground that limits the flat westwards, and, ascending a dark ridge of broken, stony, ground, and a dense thornbush, we found ourselves upon a higher level. The asses stumbled, the men grumbled, and the want of water severely tried the general temper.

From this cold jungle – the thermometer showed a minimum of 54° F. – we emerged at dawn on the 11th October, and after three hours' driving through a dense bush of various thorns, with calabashes reddened by the intense heat, and tripping upon the narrow broken path that ran over rolling ground, we found the porters halted at some pits full of sweet clear water. Here the caravan preserved a remarkable dead silence. I inquired the cause. The Coast-Arabs who accompanied us were trying an experiment, which, had it failed, would have caused trouble, expense, and waste of time; they were attempting to pass without blackmail the little clearing of Usek'he, which lay to the south of the desert-road, and they knew that its Sultan, Ganza Mikono, usually posted a party upon the low masses of bristling hill hard by, to prevent caravans evading his dues. As no provisions were procurable in the jungle, it was judged better to proceed, and the sun was in the zenith before we reached the district of K'hok'ho. We halted under a spreading tree, near the head-quarter village of its villanous Sultan, in an open plain of millet and panicum-stubbles. Presently Kidogo, disliking the appearance of things

– the men, rushing with yells of excitement from their villages, were forming a dense ring around us; the even more unmanageable old women stared like sages femmes, and already a Mnyamwezi porter had been beaten at the well – stirred us up and led the way to an open jungle about a mile distant. There we were safe; no assailant would place himself upon the plain, the Coast-Arabs were close at hand, and in the bush we should have been more than a match for the Wagogo.

The Baloch, fatigued by the tedious marches of the last two days, had surlily refused their escort to our luggage, as well as to ourselves. When the camp was pitched, I ordered a goat to be killed; and, serving out rations to the sons of Ramji and the porters, I gave them none, a cruel punishment to men whose souls centered in their ingesta. The earlier part of the evening was spent by them in enumerating their grievances – they were careful to speak in four dialects, so that all around might understand them, in discussing their plans of desertion, and in silencing the contradiction of their commander, the monocular Jemadar, who, having forsworn opium, now headed the party in opposition to the mutineers. They complained that they were faint for want of meat – the fellows were driving a bullock and half a dozen goats, which they had purchased with cloth, certainly not their own. I had, they grumbled, given them no ghee or honey, consequently they were obliged to "eat dry" – they knew this to be false, as they had received both at Kanyenye. We had made them march ten "Cos" in our eagerness to obtain milk – they were the first to propose reaching a place where provisions were procurable. The unmanageables, Khudabakhsh, Shahdad, and Belok, proposed an immediate departure, but a small majority carried the day in favour of desertion next morning. Kidogo and the sons of Ramji ridiculed, as was their wont, the silly boasters with, "Of a truth, brethren! the coast is far off, and ye are hungry men!" On the ensuing day, when a night's reflection had cooled down their noble bile, they swallowed their words like buttered parsnips. I heard no more of their plans, and in their demeanour they became cringing as before.

The transit of the K'hok'ho clearing, which is also called the Nyika, or wilderness, is considered the nucleus of travellers' troubles in Ugogo. The difficulty is caused by its Sultan, M'ana Miaha, popularly known as Maguru Mafupi, or Shortshanks. This petty tyrant, the most powerful, however, of the Wagogo chiefs, is a toothache to strangers, who complain that he cannot even plunder *à l'aimable*. He was described to me as a short elderly man, nearly bald, chocolate-coloured, and remarkable for the duck-like conformation which gave origin to his nickname. His dress was an Arab check round his loins, and another thrown over his shoulders. He becomes man, idiot, and beast with clockwork-regularity every day; when not disguised in liquor he is surly and unreasonable, and when made merry by his cups he refuses to do business. He is in the habit of detaining Wanyamwezi caravans to hoe his fields, and he often applies them to a corvee of five or six days during the spring-time, before he will consent to receive his blackmail.

We were delayed five days at K'hok'ho to lay in provisions for four marches, and by the usual African pretexts, various and peculiar. On the afternoon of arrival it would have been held indecent haste to trouble His Highness. On the first morning His Highness's spouse was unwell, and during the day he was "sitting upon Pombe," in other words, drinking beer. On the second he received, somewhat scurvily, a deputation headed by Said bin Salim, the Coast-Arab merchants, and the Jemadar. Two Wazagira, or chief-councillors, did the palaver, which was conducted, for dignity, outside the royal hovel. He declared that the two caravans must compound separately, and that in my case he would be satisfied with nothing under six porters' loads. As about one-twelfth of his demand was offered to him, he dismissed them with ignominy, affirming that he held me equal to the Sayyid of Zanzibar, and accordingly that he should demand half the outfit.

The third day was spent by the Coast-Arabs in haggling with the courtiers before His Highness, who maintained a solemn silence, certainly the easiest plan; and the present was paraded, as is customary on such occasions, in separate heaps, each intended for a particular person, but Her Highness, justly offended by the flimsiness of a bit of chintz, seized a huge wooden ladle and hooted and hunted the offenders out of doors. After high words the Arabs returned, and informed me that things were looking desperate. I promised assistance in case of violence being offered to them, – a civility which they acknowledged by sending a shoulder of beef. The fourth day was one of dignified idleness. We received a message that the court was again sitting upon Pombe, and we too well understood that His Highness, with his spouse and cabinet, were drunk as drunk could be. On the morning of the fifth day, a similar delaying process was attempted; but as the testy Kidogo, who had taken the place of the tame Said, declared that the morrow should see us march in the afternoon, the present was accepted, and the two or three musket shots usual on such occasions sounded the joyful tidings that we were at liberty to proceed. The unconscionable extortioner had received one coil of brass wire, four "cloths with names," eight domestics, eight blue cottons, and thirty strings of coral beads. Not contented with this, he demanded two Arab checks, and these failing, a double quantity of beads, and another domestic. I compromised the affair with six feet of crimson broadcloth, an article which I had not produced, as the Coast-Arabs, who owned none, declared that such an offering would cause difficulties in their case. But as they charged me double and treble prices for the expensive cloths which the Sultan required, and which, as they had been omitted in our outfit, it was necessary to purchase from them, I at length thought myself justified in economising by the only means in my power. The fiery-tempered Coast-Arabs left K'hok'ho with rage in their hearts and curses under their tongues. These men usually think outside their heads, but they know that in Ugogo the merest pretext – the loosing a hot word, touching a woman, offending a boy, or taking in vain the name of the Sultan – infallibly leads to being mulcted in cloth.

I was delighted to escape from the foul strip of crowded jungle in which we had halted. A down-caravan of Wanyamwezi had added its quotum of discomfort to the place. Throughout the fiery day we were stung by the Tzetze, and annoyed by swarms of bees and pertinacious gadflies. On one occasion an army of large poisonous siyafu, or black pismire, drove us out of the tent by the wounds which it inflicted between the fingers and on other tender parts of the body, before a kettle of boiling water persuaded them to abandon us. These ant-fiends made the thin-skinned asses mad with torture. The nights were cold and raw, and when we awoke in the morning we found some valuable article rendered unserviceable by the termites. K'hok'ho was an ill-omened spot. There my ass "Seringe," sole sur-voice of the riding animals brought from Zanzibar, was so torn by a hyena that I was compelled to leave it behind. I was afterwards informed that it had soon died of its wounds. The next mishap was the desertion of the fifteen Wanyamwezi porters who had been hired and paid at Ugogi. These men had slept in the same kraal with the somnolent sons of Ramji, and had stealthily disappeared during the night. As usual, though they carried off their own, they had left our loads behind, that they might reach their homes with greater speed. They would choose a jungle road, to avoid the danger of slavery, and living the while upon roots and edible grasses, would traverse the desert separating them from their country in three or four days. This desertion of fifteen men first suggested to me that my weary efforts and wearing anxiety about carriage were to a certain extent self-inflictions. Expecting to see half the outfit left upon the ground, I was surprised by the readiness with which it disappeared. The men seemed to behave best whenever things were palpably at the worst; besides which, as easily as the baggage of 50 porters was distributed amongst 100, so easily were the loads of 100 men placed upon the shoulders of 50. Indeed, the original Wanyamwezi gang, who claimed by right extra pay for carrying extra weight, though fiercely opposed to lifting up an empty gourd gratis, were ever docile when a heavier pack brought with it an increase of cloth and beads.

However, the march on the 17th October had its trifling hardships. My companion rode forward on the ass lately given to us by Abdullah bin Nasib, whilst I, remaining behind and finding that no carriage could be procured for two bags of clothes and shoes, placed them upon my animal the Mnyamwezi bought at Inenge, inasmuch as it appeared somewhat stronger than the half-dozen wretched brutes that flung themselves upon the ground apparently too fagged to move. I had, however, overrated its powers: it soon became evident that I must walk, or that the valuable cargo must be left behind. Trembling with weakness, I set out to traverse the length of the Mdaburu Jungle. The memory of that march is not pleasant: the burning sun and the fiery reflected heat arising from the parched ground – here a rough, thorny, and waterless jungle, where the jasmine flowered and the frankincense was used for fuel; there a grassy plain of black and sun-cracked earth – compelled me to lie down every half-hour. The watergourds were soon drained by my attendant Baloch; and the sons of Ramji, who, after reaching the resting-place, had returned with ample stores for their comrades, hid their vessels on my approach. Sarmalla, a donkey-driver, the model of a surly negro, whose crumpled brow, tightened eyes and thick lips which shot-out on the least occasion of excitement, showed what was going on within his head, openly refused me the use of his gourd, and – thirst is even less to be trifled with than hunger – found ample reason to repent himself of the proceeding. Near the end of the jungle I came upon a party of the Baloch, who, having seized upon a porter belonging to a large caravan of Wanyamwezi that had passed us on that march, were persuading him, half by promises and half by threats, to carry their sleeping mats and their empty gourds. The strict and positive orders as regards enticing away deserters which I had issued at Inenge, were looked upon by them, in their all engrossing egotism, as a mere string of empty words. I could do nothing beyond threatening to report their conduct to their master, and dismissing the man, who obviously stood in fear of death, with his tobacco and hoes duly counted back to him. Towards the end of that long march I saw with pleasure the kindly face of Seedy Bombay, who was returning to me in hot haste, leading an ass, and carrying a few scones and hard-boiled eggs. Mounting, I resumed my way, and presently arrived at the confines of Mdaburu, where, under a huge calabash, stood our tent, amidst a kraal of grass boothies, surrounded by a heaped-up ridge of thorns.

Mdaburu is the first important district in the land of Uyanzi, which, beginning from Western K'hok'ho, extends as far as Tura, the eastern frontier of Unyamwezi-land. It is a fertile depression of brick-red earth, bisected by a broad, deep, and sandy Fiumara, which, trending southwards, supplies from five pits water in plenty even during the driest season. It is belted on all sides by a dense jungle, over whose dark brown line appeared the summits of low blue cones, and beyond them long streaks of azure ridge, beautified by distance into the semblance of a sea. We were delayed two days at this, the fourth and westernmost district of Ugogo. It was necessary to lay in a week's provision for the party – ever a tedious task in these regions, but more especially in the dead of winter – moreover, the Sultan Kibuya expected the settlement of his blackmail. From this man we experienced less than the usual incivility: by birth a Mkimbu foreigner, and fearing at that time wars and rumours of wars on the part of his villanous neighbour, Maguru Mafupi, he contented himself with a present which may be estimated at nineteen cloths, whereas the others had murmured at forty and fifty. However, he abated nothing of his country's pretentious pride. A black, elderly man, dressed in a grimy cloth, without other ornament but a broad ivory bracelet covering several inches of his right wrist, he at first refused to receive the deputation because his "ministers" were absent; and during the discourse about the amount of blackmail, he sat preserving an apathetic silence, outside his dirty lodging in the huge kraal which forms his capital. The demand concluded with a fine silk-cotton cloth, on the part of his wife; and when "ma femme" appears on such occasions in these regions, as in others further west, it is a sure sign that the stranger is to be taken in. As usual with the East African chiefs, Kibuya was anxious to detain me, not only in order that his people might profitably dispose of their surplus stores, but also because the presence of so many guns would go far to modify the plans of his enemies. His attempts at delay, however, were skilfully out-manoeuvred by Said bin Salim, who broke through all difficulties with the hardihood of fear. The little man's vain terrors made him put the ragged kraal which surrounded us into a condition of defence, and every night he might be seen stalking like a troubled spirit amongst the forms of sleeping men.

At Mdaburu I hired two porters from the caravan that accompanied us; and Said bin Salim began somewhat tardily to take the usual precautions against desertion. He was ordered, before the disappearance of the porters that levanted at K'hok'ho, to pack their hire in our loads, and every evening to chain up the luggage heaped in front of our tent. The accident caused by his neglect rendered him now quasi-obedient. Moreover, two or three Baloch were told off to pre-cede the line, and as many to bring up the rear. The porters, as I have said, hold it a point of honour not to steal their packs; but if allowed to straggle forwards, or to loiter behind, they will readily attempt the recovery of their goods by opening their burdens, which they afterwards abandon upon the road. The Coast-Arabs, in return for some small shot, which is here highly prized, assisted me by carrying some surplus luggage. Amongst other articles, two kegs of gunpowder were committed to them: both were punctually returned at Unyanyembe, where gunpowder sells at two cloths, or half a Frasilah (17.5 lbs.) of ivory per lb; but the bungs had been stove in, and a quarter of the contents had evaporated. The evening of the second day's halt closed on us before the rations for the caravan were collected, and seventeen shukkah, with about a hundred strings of beads, barely produced a sufficiency of grain.

From the Red Vale of Mdaburu three main lines traverse the desert between Ugogo and Unyamwezi. The northernmost, called Njia T'humbi, leads in a west-north-westerly direction to Usukuma. Upon this track are two sultans and several villages. The central "Ka-rangasa," or "Mdaburu," is that which will be described in the following pages. The southernmost, termed Uyanzi, sets out from K'hok'ho, and passes through the settlements known by the name of Jiwe la Singa. It is avoided by the porters, dreading to incur the wrath of Sultan Kibuya, who would resent their omitting to visit his settlement, M'daburu.

These three routes pass through the heart of the great desert and elephant-ground "Mgunda Mk'hali" – explained by the Arabs to mean in Kinyarawezi, the Fiery "Shamba" or Field. Like Marenga Mk'hali, it is a desert, because it contains no running water nor wells, except after rain. The name is still infamous, but its ill-fame rests rather upon tradition than actuality; in fact, its dimensions are rapidly shrinking before the torch and axe. About fifteen years ago it contained twelve long stages, and several tirikeza; now it is spanned in eight marches. The wildest part is the first half from Mdaburu to Jiwe la Mkoa, and even here, it is reported, villages of Wakimbu are rising rapidly on the north and south of the road. The traveller, though invariably threatened with drought and the death of cattle, will undergo little hardship beyond the fatigue of the first three forced marches through the "Fiery Field;" in fact, he will be agreeably surprised by its contrast with the desert of Marenga Mk'hali.

From east to west the diagonal breadth of Mgunda Mk'hali is 140 miles. The general aspect is a dull uniform bush, emerald-coloured during the rains, and in the heats a network of dry and broom-like twigs. Except upon the banks of nullahs – "rivers" that are not rivers – the trees, as in Ugogo, wanting nutriment, never afford timber, and even the calabash appears stunted. The trackless waste of scrub, called the "bush" in Southern Africa, is found in places alternating with thin gum-forest; the change may be accounted for by the different depths of water below the level of the ground. It is a hardy vegetation of mimosas and gums mixed with evergreen succulent plants, cactaceae, aloes, and euphorbias: the grass, sometimes tufty, at other times equally spread, is hard and stiff; when green it feeds cattle, and when dry it is burned in places by passing caravans to promote the growth of another crop.

The groundwork of Mgunda Mk'hali is a detritus of yellowish quartz, in places white with powdered felspar, and, where vegetation decays, brown-black with humus. Water-worn pebbles are sprinkled over the earth, and the vicinity of Fiumaras abounds in a coarse and modern sandstone-conglomerate. Upon the rolling surface, and towering high above the tallest trees, are based the huge granitic and syenitic outcrops before alluded to. The contrast between the masses and the dwarf rises which support them at once attracts the eye. Here and there the long waves that diversify the land appear in the far distance like blue lines bounding the nearer superficies of brown or green. Throughout this rolling table-land the watershed is to the south. In rare places the rains stagnate in shallow pools, which become systems of mud-cakes during the drought. At this season water is often unprocurable in the Fiumaras, causing unaccustomed hardships to caravans, and death to those beasts which, like the elephant and the buffalo, cannot long exist without drinking.

On the 20th October we began the transit of the "Fiery Field," whose long broad line of brown jungle, painted blue by the intervening air, had, since leaving K'hok'ho, formed our western horizon. The waste here appeared in its most horrid phase. The narrow goat-path serpentined in and out of a growth of poisonous thorny jungle, with thin, hard grass-straw, growing on a glaring white and rolling ground; the view was limited by bush and brake, as in the alluvial valleys of the maritime region, and in weary sameness the spectacle surpassed everything that we had endured in Marenga Mk'hali. We halted through the heat of the day at some water-pits in a broken course; and resuming our tedious march early in the afternoon, we arrived about sunset at the bed of a shallow nullah, where the pure element was found in sand-holes about five feet deep.

On the 2nd day we reached the large Mabunguru Fiumara, a deep and tortuous gash of fine yellow quartzoze sand and sunburnt blocks of syenite: at times it must form an impassable torrent, even at this season of severe drought it afforded long pools of infiltrated rainwater, green with weeds and abounding with shell-fish, and with the usual description of Silurus. In the earlier morning the path passed through a forest already beautified by the sprouting of tender green leaves and by the blooming of flowers, amongst which was a large and strongly perfumed species of jasmine, whilst young grass sprouted from the fire-blackened remnants of the last year's crop. Far upon the southern horizon rose distant hills and lines, blue, as if composed of solidified air, and mocking us by their mirage-likeness to the ocean. Nearer, the ground was diversified by those curious evidences of igneous action, which extend westward through eastern Unyamwezi, and northwards to the shores of the Nyanza Lake. These outcrops of gray granite and syenite are principally of two different shapes, the hog's back and the turret. The former usually appears as a low lumpy dome of various dimensions; here a few feet long, there extending a mile and a half in diameter: the outer coat scales off under the action of the atmosphere, and in places it is worn away by a network of paths. The turret is a more picturesque and changing feature. Tall rounded blocks and conical or cylindrical boulders, here single, there in piles or ridges, some straight and stiff as giant ninepins, others split as if an alley or a gateway passed between them, rise abruptly and perpendicularly almost without foundation-ary elevation, cleaving the mould of a dead plain, or – like gypseous formations, in which the highest boulders are planted upon the lowest and broadest bases – they bristle upon a wave of dwarfish rocky hill. One when struck was observed to give forth a metallic clink, and not a few, bal-anced upon points, reminded me of· the tradition-bearing rocking stones. At a distance in the forest, the larger masses might be mistaken for Cyclopean walls, towers, steeples, minarets, loggans, dwelling houses, and ruined castles. They are often overgrown with a soft grass, which decaying, forms with the degradation of the granite a thin cap of soil; their summits are crowned with tufty cactus, a stomatiferous plant which imbibes nourishment from the oxygen of the air; whilst huge creepers, imitating trees, project gnarled trunks from the deeper crevices in their flanks. Seen through the forest these rocks are an effective feature in the landscape, especially when the sunbeams fall warm and bright upon their rounded summits and their smooth sides, here clothed with a mildew-like lichen of the tenderest leek-green, there yellowed like Italian marbles by the burning rays, and there streaked with a shining black as if glazed by the rain, which, collecting in cupfuls upon the steps and slopes, at times overflows, cours-ing in mimic cataracts down the heights.

That march was a severe trial; we had started at dawn, we did not, however, arrive at the Mabunguru Fiumara before noon, and our people straggled in about evening-tide. All our bullet-moulds, and three boxes of ammunition, were lost. Said bin Salim, the Jemadar, and three other men had fol-lowed in the rear, driving on the "One-Eyed Fiend," which, after many a prank, lay down upon the ground, and positively declined to move. The escort, disliking the sun, abandoned it at once to its fate, and want of provisions, and the inordinate length of the marches, rendered a halt or a return for the valuable load – four boxes of ammunition – out of the question. An article once abandoned in these deserts is rarely if ever recovered; the caravan-porters will not halt, and a small party dares not return to recover it.

The 22nd October saw us at Jiwe la Mkoa, the half-way-house of Mgunda Mk'hali. The track, crossing the rough Mabunguru Fiumara, passed over rolling ground through a thorny jungle that gradually thinned out into a forest; about 8 A.M. a halt was called at a water in the wilderness. My companion being no longer able to advance on foot, an ass was unloaded, and its burden of ammunition was divided, for facility of porterage, amongst the sons of Ramji. After noon we resumed our march, and the Kirangozi, derided by the rival guide of the Coast-Arabs' caravan, and urged forward by Kidogo, who was burning to see his wife and children in Unyamwezi, determined to "put himself at the head of himself." The jungle seemed interminable. The shadows of the hills lengthened out upon the plains, the sun sank in the glory of purple, crimson, and gold, and the crescent-moon rained a flood of silvery light upon the topmost twig-work of the trees; we passed a dwarf clearing, where lodging and perhaps provisions were to be obtained, and we sped by water near the road where the frogs were chanting their vesper-hymn; still far, – far ahead we heard the horns and the faint march-cries of the porters. At length, towards the end of the march, we wound round a fantastic mass of cactus-clad boulders, and crossing a low ridge we found at its base a single Tembe or square village of emigrant Wakimbu, who refused to admit us. The little basin beyond it displayed, by "black jacks" and felled tree-trunks, evidences of modern industry, and it extended to the Jiwe or Rock, which gives its name to the clearing. We were cheered by the sight of the red fires glaring in the Kraal, but my companion's ass, probably frightened by some wild beast to us invisible, reared high in the air, bucked like a deer, broke his frail Arab girths, and threw his invalid rider heavily upon the hard earth. Arrived at the Kraal, I found every boothy occupied by the porters, who refused shelter until dragged out like slaughtered sheep. Said bin Salim's awning was as usual snugly pitched; ours still lay on the ground. The little Arab's "duty to himself" appeared to attain a higher limit every stage; once comfortably housed, he never thought of offering cover to another, and his children knew him too well even to volunteer such a service to any one but himself. On a late occasion, when our tent had not appeared, Said bin Salim, to whom a message had been sent, refused to lend us one half of the awning committed to him, a piece of canvas cut out to serve as a tent and lug-sail. Bombay then distinguished himself by the memorable words, – "If you are not ashamed of your master, be ashamed of his servant!" which had the effect of bringing the awning and of making Said bin Salim testily refuse the half returned to him.

Jiwe la Mkoa, or the Round Rock, is the largest of the many hogs'-backs of grey syenite that stud this waste. It measures about two miles in extreme diameter, and the dome rises with a gentle slope to the height of 200 or 300 feet above the dead level of the plain. Tolerable water is found in pits upon a swamp at its southern base, and well covered Mtego or elephant traps, deep grave-like excavations, like the Indian "Ogi," prove dangerous to travellers; in one of these the Jemadar disappeared suddenly, as if by magic. The smooth and rounded surface of the rock displays deep hoof-shaped holes, which in a Moslem land would at once be recognised as the Asr, or the footprints of those holy quadrupeds, Duldul or Zu'l Jenah. In places the Jiwe, overgrown with scattered tufts of white grass, and based upon a dusty surface blackened by torrent rains, forcibly suggested to the Baloch the idea of an elderly negro's purbald poll.

We encamped close to the Jiwe, and in so doing we did wrong: however pleasant may be the shadow of a tall rock in a thirsty land by day, way-wise travellers avoid the vicinity of stones which, by diminished radiation, retain their heat throughout the night. All caravans passing through this clearing clamour to be supplied with provisions; our porters, who, having received rations for eight days, which they consumed in four, were no exceptions to the rule. As the single little village of Jiwe la Mkoa could afford but one goatskin of grain and a few fowls, the cattle not being for sale, and no calves having been born to the herds, the porters proposed to send a party with cloth and beads to collect provaunt from the neighbouring settlements. But the notable Khalfan bin Khamis, the most energetic of the Coast-Arabs in whose company we were travelling, would brook no delay: he had issued as usual three days' rations for a long week's march, and thus by driving his porters beyond their speed, he practised a style of economy usually categorised by us at home as "penny-wise and pound-foolish." His marching was conducted upon the same principle; determining to save time, he pushed on till his men began to flag, presently broke down, and finally deserted.

At Jiwe la Mkoa the neck of the desert is broken: the western portion of Mgunda Mk'hali has already thinned out. On the 23rd October, despite the long march of the preceding day, Khalfan proposed a Tirikeza, declaring that the heavy nimbus from the west, accompanied by a pleasant cold, portended rain, and that this rain, like the "Choti Barsat" of India, announces the approach of the great Masika, or vernal wet season. Yielding to his reasons, we crossed the "Round Rock," and passing through an open forest of tall trees, with here and there an undulating break, now yellow with quartz, then black with humus, we reached, after about three hours, another clearing like Jiwe la Mkoa, which owes its origin to the requirements of commerce. "Kirurumo" boasted of several newly built Tembe of Wakimbu, who supplied caravans at an exorbitant rate. The blackness of the ground, and the vivid green of vegetation, evidenced the proximity of water. The potable element was found in pits, sunk in a narrow nullah running northwards across the clearing; it was muddy and abundant. On the next day the road led through a thin forest of thorns and gums, which, bare of bush and underwood, afforded a broad path and pleasant, easy travelling. Sign of elephant and rhinoceros, giraffe and antelope, crossed the path, and as usual in such places, the asses were tormented by the Tzetze. After travelling four hours and thirty minutes, we reached a new settlement upon the western frontier of Uganzi, called "Jiweni," "near the stones," from the heaps of block and boulder scattered round pits of good water, sunk about three feet in the ground. The Mongo Nullah, a deep surface-drain, bisects this clearing, which is palpably modern. Many of the trees are barked previous to felling, and others have fallen prostrate, apparently from the depredations of the white ant. On the 25th, after another desert march of 2 hrs. 20' through a flat country, where the forest was somewhat deformed by bush and brake, which in places narrowed the path to a mere goat-track, we arrived at the third quarter of Mgunda Mk'hali. "Mgongo T'hembo," or the Elephant's Back, derives its name from a long narrow ridge of chocolate-coloured syenite, outcropping from the low forest lands around it; the crest of the chain is composed of loose rocks and large detached boulders. Like the other inhabited portions of Mgunda Mk'hali, it is a recent clearing; numerous "black-jacks," felled trees, and pollarded stumps still cumber the fields. The "Elephant's Back" is, however, more extensive and better cultivated than any of its neighbours, – Mdaburu alone excepted, – and water being abundant and near the surface, it supports an increasing population of mixed Wakimbu and Wataturu, who dwell in large substantial Tembe, and live by selling their surplus holcus, maize, and fowls to travellers. They do not, like the Wakimbu of Jiwe la Mkoa, refuse entrance to their villages, but they receive the stranger with the usual niggard guest-rites of the slave-path, and African-like, they think only of what is to be gained by hospitality. Here I halted for a day to recruit and to lay in rations. The length of the stages had told upon the men; Bombay had stumped himself, several of the sons of Ramji, and two of Said bin Salim's children were unable to walk; the asses, throwing themselves upon the ground, required to be raised with the stick, and all preferred rest even to food. Mboni, one of the sons of Ramji, carried off a slave girl from the camp of the Coast-Arabs; her proprietor came armed to recover her, swords were drawn, a prodigious clash and clatter of tongue arose, friends interfered, and blades were sheathed. Khalfan bin Khamis, losing all patience at this delay, bade us adieu, promising to announce our approach at Unyanyembe; about a week afterwards, however, we found him in most melancholy plight, halted half-way, because his over-worked porters had taken "French leave."

We resumed our march on the 27th October, and after a slow and painful progress for seven hours over a rolling country, whose soil was now yellow with argile, then white with felspar, then black-brown with humus, through thorny bush, and forest here opening out, there densely closing in, we arrived at the "Tura Nullah," thc deepest of the many surface drains winding tortuously to the S.W. The trees lining the margin were of the noblest dimensions; the tall thick grass that hedged them in showed signs of extensive conflagration, and water was found in shallow pools and in deep pits beneath the banks, on the side to which the stream, which must be furious during the rainy season, swings. When halted in a clear place in the jungle, we were passed by a down caravan of Wanyamwezi; our porters shouted and rushed up to greet their friends, the men raised their right hands about a dozen times, and then clapped palm to palm, and the women indulged in "vigelegele," the African "lulliloo," which rang like breech-loaders in our ears.

On the next day we set out betimes through the forest, which, as usual when nearing populous settlements, spread out, and which began at this season to show a preponderance of green over brown. Presently we reached a large expanse of yellow stover where the van had halted, in order that the caravan might make its first appearance with dignity. Ensued a clearing, studded with large stockaded villages, peering over tall hedges of dark green milk-bush, fields of maize and millet, manioc, gourds, and water-melons, and showing numerous flocks and herds, clustering around the shallow pits. The people swarmed from their abodes, young and old hustling one another for a better stare; the man forsook his loom and the girl her hoe, and for the remainder of the march we were escorted by a tail of screaming boys and shouting adults; the males almost nude, the women, bare to the waist and clothed only knee-deep in kilts, accompanied us, puffing pipes the while, with wallets of withered or flabby flesh flapping the air, striking their hoes with stones, crying "Beads! beads!" and ejaculating their wonder in strident explosions of "Hi! hi! – Hui! ih!" and "Ha! – a! – a!" It was a spectacle to make an anchorite of a man, – it was at once ludicrous and disgusting.

At length the Kirangozi fluttered his red flag in the wind, and the drums, horns, and larynxes of his followers began the fearful uproar which introduces a caravan to the admiring "natives." Leading the way, our guide, much to my surprise, – I knew not then that such was the immemorial custom of Unyamwezi, – entered uninvited and sans ceremony the nearest large village; the long string of porters flocked in with bag and baggage, and we followed their example. The guests at once dispersed themselves through the several courts and compounds into which the interior hollow was divided, and lodged themselves with as much regard for self and disregard for their grumbling hosts as possible. We were placed under a wall-less roof, bounded on one side by the bars of the village palisade, and the mob of starers that relieved one another from morning till night made me feel like the denizen of a menagerie.

Chapter 9

THE GEOGRAPHY AND ETHNOGRAPHY OF UGOGO, – THE THIRD REGION

The third division of the country visited is a flat tableland extending from the Ugogi "Dhun," or valley, at the western base of the Wasagara Mountains, in E. long. 36° 14', to Tura, the eastern district of Unyamwezi, in E. long. 33° 57'; occupying a diagonal breadth of 155 geographical rectilinear miles. The length from north to south is not so easily estimated. The Wahumba and the Wataturu in the former, and the Wahehe and Warori in the latter direction, are migratory tribes that spurn a civilised frontier; according to the Arabs, however, the Wagogo extend three long marches on an average to the north and four or five southwards. This, assuming the march at 15 miles, would give a total of 120. The average of the heights observed is 3,650 feet, with a gradual rise westwards to Jiwe la Mkoa, which attains an altitude of 4,200 feet (?).

The third region, situated to leeward of a range whose height compels the south-east trades to part with their load of vapours, and distant from the succession of inland seas, which, stationed near the centre of the African continent, act as reservoirs to restore the balance of humidity, is an arid, sterile land, a counterpart, in many places, of the Kalahari and the Karroo, or South African desert-plains. The general aspect is a glaring yellow flat, darkened by long growths of acrid, saline, and succulent plants, thorny bush, and stunted trees, and the colouring is monotonous in the extreme. It is sprinkled with isolated dwarf cones bristling with rocks and boulders, from whose interstices springs a thin forest of gums, thorns, and mimosas. The power of igneous agency is displayed in protruding masses of granitic formation, which rise from the dead level with little foundationary elevation; and the masses of sandstone, superincumbent upon the primitive base in other parts of the country, here disappear. On the north rises the long tabular range of the Wahumba Hills, separated by a line of lower ground from the plateau. Southwards, a plain, imperceptibly shelving, trends towards the Raw River. There are no rivers in Ugogo: the periodical rains are carried off by large nullahs, whose clay banks are split and cut during the season of potent heat into polygonal figures like piles of columnar basalt. On the sparkling nitrous salinas and the dull-yellow or dun-coloured plains the mirage faintly resembles the effects of refraction in desert Arabia. The roads are mere foot-tracks worn through the fields and bushes. The kraals are small dirty circles enclosing a calabash or other tree, against which goods are stacked. The boothies are made of dried canes and stubble, surrounded by a most efficient chevaux de frise of thorn-boughs. At the end of the dry season they are burnt down by inevitable accident. The want of wood prevents their being made solidly, and for the same reason "bois de vache" is the usual fuel of the country.

The formation of the subsoil is mostly sandstone bearing a ruddy sand. The surface is in rare places a brown vegetable humus, extending but a few inches in depth, or more generally a hard yellow-reddish ferruginous clay covered with quartz nodules of many colours, and lumps of carbonate of lime, or white and siliceous sand, rather resembling a well-metalled road or an "untidy expanse of gravel-walk" than the rich moulds which belong to the fertile African belt. In many parts are conical anthills of pale red earth; in others ironstone crops out of the plain; and everywhere fine and coarse grits abound. The land is in parts condemned to perpetual drought, and nowhere is water either good or plentiful. It is found in the serpentine beds of nullahs, and after rain in ziwa, vleys, tanks, pools, or ponds, filled by a gentle gravitation, and retained by a strong clay, in deep pits excavated by the people, or in shallow holes "crowed" in the ground. The supplies of this necessary divide the country into three great districts. On the east is Marenga Mk'hali, a thick bush, where a few villages, avoided by travellers, are scattered north and south of the road. The heart of the region is Ugogo, the most populous and the best cultivated country, divided into a number of small and carefully cultivated clearings by tracts of dense bush and timber-less woods, a wall of verdure during the rains, and in the hot season a system of thorns and broomwork which serves merely to impede a free circulation of the air. These seams of waste land appear strange in a country populated of old; the Arabs, however, declare that the land is more thinly inhabited than it used to be. Mgunda Mk'hali, the western division, is a thin forest and a heap of brakey jungle. The few hills are thickly clothed with vegetation, probably because they retain more moisture than the plains.

The climate of Ugogo is markedly arid. During the transit of the Expedition in September and October, the best water-colours faded and hardened in their pans; India-rubber, especially the prepared article in squares, became viscid, like half-dried birdlime; "Macintosh" was sticking plaister, and the best vulcanized elastic-bands tore like brown paper. During almost the whole year a violent east wind sweeps from the mountains. There are great changes in the temperature, whilst the weather apparently remains the same, and alternate currents of hot and cold air were observed. In the long summer the climate much resembles that of Sindh; there are the same fiery suns playing upon the naked surface with a painful dazzle, cool crisp nights, and clouds of dust. The succulent vegetation is shrivelled up and carbonised by heat, and the crackling covering of clayey earth and thin sand, whose particles are unbound by dew or rain, rises in lofty whirling columns like water-spouts when the north wind from the

Wahumba Hills meets the gusts of Usagara, which are soon heated to a furnace-breath by the glowing surface. These "p'hepo" or "devils" scour the plain with the rapidity of horsemen, and, charged with coarse grain and small pebbles, strike with the violence of heavy hail. The siccity and repercussion of heat produce an atmosphere of peculiar brilliancy in Ugogo: the milky haze of the coast-climate is here unknown. The sowing season, at which time also trees begin to bud and birds to breed, is about the period of the sun's greatest southern declination, and the diminution of temperature displays in these regions the effects of the tepid winds and the warm vernal showers of the European continent. There is no Vuli, and thus the climate is unrefreshed by the copious tropical rains. About the middle of November the country is visited by a few preliminary showers, accompanied by a violent tramontana, and the vital principle which appears extinct starts once more into sudden and excessive activity. Towards the end of December the Masika, or rainy season, commences with the wind shifting from the east to the north and north-east, blowing steadily from the high grounds eastward and westward of the Nyanza Lake, which have been saturated by heavy falls beginning in September. The "winter" seldom exceeds the third month, and the downfall is desultory and uncertain, causing frequent droughts and famine. For this reason the land is much inferior in fertility to the other regions, and the cotton and tobacco, which flourish from the coast to the Tanganyika Lake, are deficient in Ugogo, whilst rice is supplanted by the rugged sorghum and maize.

Arab and other travellers unaccustomed to the country at first suffer from the climate, which must not, however, be condemned. They complain of the tourbillons, the swarms of flies, and the violent changes from burning heat to piercing cold, which is always experienced in that region when the thermometer sinks below 60° – 55° F. Their thin tents, pitched under a ragged calabash, cannot mitigate the ardour of an unclouded sun; the salt-bitter water, whose nitrous and saline deposits sometimes tarnish a silver ring like the fumes of sulphur, affects their health; whilst the appetite, stimulated by a purer atmosphere and the coolness of the night air, is kept within due bounds only by deficiency in the means of satisfying it. Those who have seen Africa further west, are profuse in their praises of the climate on their return-march from the interior. The mukunguru, or seasoning fever, however, rarely fails to attack strangers. It is, like that of the second region, a violent bilious attack, whose consequences are sleeplessness, debility, and severe headaches: the hot fit compared with the algid stage is unusually long and rigorous. In some districts the parexia is rarely followed by the relieving perspiration; and when natural diaphoresis appears, it by no means denotes the termination of the paroxysm. Other diseases are rare, and the terrible ulcerations of K'hutu and Eastern Usagara are almost unknown in Ugogo. There is little doubt that the land, if it afforded good shelter, purified water, and regular diet, would be eminently wholesome.

In the uninviting landscape a tufty, straggling grass, like living hay, often raised on little mounds, with bald places between, thinly strewed with bits of quartz and sandstone, replaces the tall luxuriant herbage of the maritime plain, and the arboraceous and frutescent produce of the mountains. The dryness of the climate, and the poverty of the soil, are displayed in the larger vegetation. The only tree of considerable growth is the calabash, and it is scattered over the country widely apart. A variety of frankincense overspreads the ground; the bark is a deep burnished bronze, whitened above with an incrustation, probably nitrous, that resembles hoarfrost; and the long woody twigs are bleached by the falling off of the outer integuments. The mukl or bdellium tree rises like a dwarf calabash from a low copse. The Arabs declare this produce of Ugogo (*Balsamodendron Africanum?*), to be of good quality. Rubbed upon a stone and mixed with water it is applied with a pledget of cotton to sluggish and purulent sores; and women use it for fumigation. The Africans ignore its qualities, and the Baloch, though well acquainted with the bdellium, gugal, or guggur, in their own country, did not observe it in Ugogo. The succulent plants, cactus, aloe, and euphorbia, will not burn; the air within them expands with heat, and the juices gushing out extinguish the flame. Amongst various salsolsae, or saltworts, the shrub called by the Arabs arak, the Capparis Sodata of Sindh and Arabia, with its currant-like bunches of fruit, is conspicuous for its evergreen verdure; the ragged and stunted mtungulu rains its apples upon the ground; and the mbembu, in places sheltered from the sun, bears a kind of medlar which is eagerly sought by the hungry traveller. The euphorbiae here rise to the height of 35 or 40 feet, and the hard woody stem throws out a mass of naked arms, in the shape of a huge cap, impervious to the midday sun.

Wild animals abound through these jungles, and the spoor lasts long upon the crisp gravelly soil. In some districts they visit by night the raised clay water-troughs of the cultivators. The elephant prefers the thick jungle, where he can wallow in the pools and feed delicately upon succulent roots and fruits, bark, and leaves. The rhinoceros loves the dark clumps of trees, which guard him from the noonday sun, and whence he can sally out all unexpected upon the assailant. The mbogo, or Bos Caffer, driven from his favourite spots, low grassy plains bordering on streams, wanders, like the giraffe, through the thinner forests. As in Unyamwezi, the roar of the lion strikes the ear by night, and the cry of the ostrich by day. The lion upon this line of Eastern Africa is often heard, but rarely seen; on only two occasions its footprints appeared upon the road. The king of beasts, according to the Arabs, is of moderate stature: it seldom attains its maximum of strength, stature, and courage, except in plain countries where game abounds, as in the lands north of the Cape, or in hills and mountains, where cattle can be lifted at discretion, as in Northern Africa. In Unyamwezi its spoils, which are yellow, like those of the Arab lion, with a long mane, said to hang over the eyes, and with a whitish tinge under the jaws, become the property of the Sultan. The animal is more common in the high lands of Karagwah than in the low countries; it has, however, attacked the mbogo, or wild bull, and has destroyed cattle within sight of the Arabs at Kazeh in Unyanyembe. The lion is rarely a man-eater; this peculiarity, according to some writers, being confined to old beasts, whose worn teeth are unfit for fight.

The "polygamous bird" was first observed on the Ugogo plateau; it extends through Unyamwezi and Usukuma to Ujiji. The eggs are sold, sometimes fresh, but more generally stale. Emptied and dried, they form the principal circulating-medium between the Arab merchants and the coffee-growing races near the Nyanza Lake, who cut them up and grind them into ornamental disks and crescents. The young birds are caught, but are rarely tamed. In Usukuma the bright and glossy feathers of the old male are much esteemed for adorning the hair; yet, curious to say, the bird is seldom hunted. Moreover, these East Africans have never attempted to export the feathers, which, when white and uninjured, are sold, even by the Somal, for 8 dollars per lb. The birds are at once wild and stupid, timid and headstrong: their lengthened strides and backward glances announce terror at the sight of man, and it is impossible to stalk them in the open grounds, which they prefer. The leopard and the cynhyaena, the koodoo and the different species of antelope, are more frequently killed in these deserts than in any other part of the line. Hog of reddish colour, and hares with rufous fur, are sometimes started by caravans. The hyrax of the Somali country basks upon the rocks and boulders, and the carapace of a small land-turtle, called khasa, fastened to a branch, serves as a road-sign. The k'hwalu, a small green parrot, with yellow shoulders, the upupa or hoopoe, a great variety of fly-catchers, larks with jet-black heads and yellow bodies, small bustards, hornbills, nightjars, muscicapae, green pigeons, sparrow-hawks, and small doves, are seen in every jungle. Near the settlements the white-necked raven and the common chil of India (*Falco cheela*), attest the presence of man, as the monkey does the proximity of water. The nest of the loxia swings to and fro in the fierce simoom; the black Bataleur eagle of Somaliland, a splendid bird, towering shily in the air, with his light under-plume gleaming like a silver plate, and large vultures (condors?) flocking from afar, denote the position of a dead or dying animal.

Until late years the Wagogo, being more numerous than they are now, deterred travellers from traversing their country: in those early days the road to Unyam-wezi, running along the left or northern bank of the Raw, through the Warori tribe, struck off near Usanga and Usenga. It is related, when the first caravan, led by Jumah Mfumbi, the late Diwan of Saadani, entered Ugogo, that the people, penetrated with admiration of his corpulence, after many experiments to find out whether it was real or not, determined that he was and must be the Deity. Moreover, after coming to this satisfactory conclusion, they resolved that, being the Deity, he could improve their country by heavy rains; and when he protested against both these resolutions, they proposed to put him to death. A succession of opportune showers, however, released him. By degrees the ever-increasing insolence and violence of the Warori drove travellers to this northern line, and the Wagogo learned to see strangers without displaying this Lybian mania for sacrificing them.

Three main roads, leading from Western Usagara westward, cross the Desert of Marenga Mk'hali. The most northern is called Ya Nyika – of the wilderness – a misnomer, if the assertion of the guides be correct that it is well watered, and peopled by the subjects of eight sultans. The central line, described in the preceding pages, is called, from its middle station, Marenga Mk'hali: it is invariably preferred when water is scarce. The southern road is termed Nya Ngaha, a continuation of the Kiringwana route, previously alluded to: it has provisions, but the people cause much trouble.

The superiority of climate, and probably the absence of that luxuriant vegetation which distinguishes the eastern region, have proved favourable to the physical development of the races living in and about Ugogo. The Wagogo, and their northern neighbours the Wahumba, are at once distinguishable from the wretched population of the alluvial valleys, and of the mountains of Usagara; though living in lower altitudes, they are a fairer race – and therefore show better blood – than the Wanyamwezi. These two tribes, whose distinctness is established by difference of dialect, will be described in order.

The Wagogo extend from the landward base of Usagara in direct distance to Mdaburu a five days' march: on the north they are bounded by the Wataturu, on the south by the Wabena tribes; the breadth of their country is computed at about eight stages. In the north, however, they are mingled with the Wahumba, in the south-east with the Wahehe, and in the south with the Warori.

The Wagogo display the variety of complexion usually seen amongst slave-purchasing races: many of them are fair as Abyssinians; some are black as negroes. In the eastern and northern settlements they are a fine, stout, and light-complexioned race. Their main peculiarity is the smallness of the cranium compared with the broad circumference of the face at and below the zygomata: seen from behind the appearance is that of a small half-bowl fitted upon one of considerably larger bias; and this, with the widely-extended ears, gives a remarkable expression to the face. Nowhere in Eastern Africa is the lobe so distended. Pieces of cane an inch or two in length, and nearly double the girth of a man's finger, are so disposed that they appear like handles to the owner's head. The distinctive mark of the tribe is the absence of the two lower incisors; but they are more generally recognised by the unnatural enlargement of their ears – in Eastern Africa the "aures perforatae" are the signs, not of slavery, but of freedom. There is no regular tattoo, though some of the women have two parallel lines running from below the bosom down the abdomen, and the men often extract only a single lower incisor. The hair is sometimes shaved clean, at others grown in mop-shape – more generally it is dressed in a mass of tresses, as amongst the Egyptians, and the skin, as well as the large bunch of corkscrews, freely stained with ochre and micaceous earths, drips with ghee, the pride of rank and beauty. The Wagogo are not an uncomely race: some of the younger women might even lay claim to prettiness. The upper part of the face is often fine, but the lips are ever thick, and the mouth coarse; similarly the body is well formed to the haunches, but the lean calf is placed peculiarly high up the leg. The expression of the countenance, even in the women, is wild and angry; and the round eyes are often reddened and bleared by drink. The voice is strong, strident, and commanding.

Their superiority of clothing gives the Wagogo, when compared with the Wasagara or the Wanyamwezi, an aspect of civilisation; a skin garment is here as rare as a cotton farther west. Even the children are generally clad. The attire of the men is usually some Arab check or dyed Indian cotton: many also wear sandals of single hide. Married women are clothed in "cloths with names," when wealthy, and in domestics when poor. The dress of the maidens under puberty is the languti of Hindostan, a kind of T-bandage, with the front ends depending to the knees; it is supported by a single or double string of the large blue glass-beads called Sungomaji. A piece of coarse cotton cloth two yards long, and a few inches broad, is fastened to the girdle behind, and passing under the fork, is drawn tightly through the waistbelt in front; from the zone the lappet hangs mid-down to the shins, and when the wearer is in rapid motion it has a most peculiar appearance. The ornaments of both sexes are kitindi, and bracelets and anklets of thick iron and brass-wires, necklaces of brass chains, disks and armlets of fine ivory, the principal source of their wealth, and bands of hide-strip with long hair, bound round the wrists, above the elbows, and below the knees: they value only the highest priced beads, coral and pink porcelains. As usual the males appear armed. Some import from Unyamwezi and the westward regions the long double-edged knife called sime, a "serviceable dudgeon" used in combat or in peaceful avocations, like the snick-an-snee of the ancient Dutch. Shields are unknown. The bow is long: the handle and the horns are often adorned with plates of tin and zinc, and the string is whipped round the extremities for strength. The spear resembles that used by the Wanyamwezi in the elephant-hunt: it is about four feet long, and the head is connected with a stout wooden handle by an iron neck measuring half the length of the weapon. In eastern Ugogo, where the Masai are near, the Wagogo have adopted their huge shovel-headed spears and daggers, like those of the Somal. It is the fashion for men to appear in public with the peculiar bill-hook used in Usagara; and in the fields the women work with the large hoe of Unyamwezi.

The villages of the Wagogo are square Tembe, low and mean-looking for want of timber. The outer walls are thin poles, planted in the ground and puddled with mud. The huts, partitioned off like ships' bunks, are exceedingly dirty, being shared by the domestic animals, dogs, and goats. They are scantily furnished with a small stool, a cot of cow's hide stretched to a small framework, a mortar for grain, and sundry gourds and bark corn-bins. About sunset all the population retires, and the doors are carefully barricaded for fear of the plundering Wahumba. At night it is dangerous to approach the villages.

The language of Ugogo is harsher than the dialects spoken by their eastern and western neighbours. In the eastern parts the people understand the Masai tongue. Many can converse fluently in the Kisawahili, or coast-tongue. The people, however, despise all strangers except the Warori and the Wahumba, and distinguish the Wanyamwezi by the name of Wakonongo, which they also apply to travellers in general.

Within the memory of man one Kafuke, of Unyamwezi, a great merchant, and a Mtongi or caravan leader, when traversing Ugogo with some thousands of followers, became involved in a quarrel about paying for water. After fifteen days of skirmishing, the leader was slain and the party was dispersed. The effect on both tribes has lasted to the present day. After the death of Kafuke no rain fell for some years – a phenomenon attributed by the Wagogo to his powers of magic; and the land was almost depopulated. The Wanyamwezi, on the other hand, have never from that time crossed the country without fear and trembling. In the many wars between the two tribes the Wagogo have generally proved themselves the better men. This superiority has induced a brawling and bullying manner. They call themselves Wana Wadege, or sons of birds – that is to say, semper parati. The Wanyamwezi studiously avoid offending them; and the porters will obey the command of a boy rather than risk an encounter. "He is a Mgogo," said before the Bobadil's face, makes him feel himself forty times a man; yet he will fly in terror before one of the Warori or the Wahumba.

The strength of the Wagogo lies in their comparative numbers. As the people seldom travel to the coast, their scattered villages are full of fighting men. Moreover, Uchawi or black magic here numbers few believers, consequently those drones of the social hive, the Waganga, or medicine-men, are not numerous. The Wagogo seldom sell their children and relations, yet there is no order against the practice. They barter for slaves their salt and ivory, the principal produce of the country. No caravan ever passes through the country without investing capital in the salt-bitter substance which is gathered in flakes efflorescing from the dried mud upon the surface of the Mbuga, or swampy hollows; the best and the cheapest is found in the district of Kanyenye. It is washed to clear it of dirt, boiled till it crystallises, spread upon clean and smoothed ground, and moulded with the hands into rude cones about half a foot in length, which are bought at the rate of 7 – 10 for a Shukkah, and are sold at a high premium after a few days' march. Ugogo supplies western Usagara and the eastern regions of Unyamwezi with this article. It is, however, far inferior to the produce of the Rusugi pits, in Uvinza, which, on account of its "sweetness," finds its way throughout the centre of Africa. Elephants are numerous in the country: every forest is filled with deep traps, and during droughthy seasons many are found dead in the jungle. The country is divided into districts; the tusks become the property of the Sultan within whose boundaries the animal falls, and the meat is divided amongst his subjects. Ivory is given in barter for slaves: this practice assures to caravans a hold upon the people, who, having an active commerce with the coast, cannot afford to be shut out from it. The Wagogo are so greedy of serviles that every gang leaves among them some of its live stock – the principal want of the listless and indolent cultivator. The wild captives bought in the interior, wayworn and fond of change, are persuaded by a word to desert; they take the first opportunity of slipping away from their masters, generally stealing a weapon and a little cloth or rations for immediate use. Their new masters send them off the road lest they should be recognised and claimed: after a time a large hoe is placed in their hands, and the fools feel, when too late, that they have exchanged an easy for a hard life. The Wagogo sell their fellow tribe-men only when convicted of magic; though sometimes parents, when in distress, part with their children. The same is the case amongst their northern neighbours, the Wamasai, the Wahumba, and the Wakwafi, who, however, are rarely in the market, and who, when there, though remarkable for strength and intelligence, are little prized, in consequence of their obstinate and untameable characters; many of them would rather die under the stick than level themselves with women by using a hoe.

The Wagogo are celebrated as thieves who will, like the Wahehe, rob even during the day. They are importunate beggars, who specify their long list of wants without stint or shame; their principal demand is tobacco, which does not grow in the land; and they resemble the Somal, who never sight a stranger without stretching out the hand for "Bori." The men are idle and debauched, spending their days in unbroken crapulence and drunkenness, whilst the girls and women hoe the fields, and the boys tend the flocks and herds. They mix honey with their pombe, or beer, and each man provides entertainment for his neighbours in turn. After midday it would be difficult throughout the country to find a chief without the thick voice, fiery eyes, and moldered manners, which prove that he is either drinking or drunk.

The Arabs declaim against the Wagogo as a "curst," ill-conditioned and boisterous, a violent and extortionate race. They have certainly no idea of manners: they flock into a stranger's tent, squat before him, staring till their curiosity is satisfied, and unmercifully quizzing his peculiarities. Upon the road a mob of both sexes will press and follow a caravan for miles. The women, carrying their babes in leopard-skins bound behind the back, and with unveiled bosoms, stand or run, fiercely shouting with the excitement of delight, and the girls laugh and deride the stranger as impudently as boys would in more modest lands. Yet, as has been said, this curiosity argues to a certain extent improvability; the most degraded tribes are too apathetic to be roused by strange sights. Moreover, the Wagogo are not deficient in rude hospitality. A stranger is always greeted with the "Yambo" salutation. He is not driven from their doors, as amongst the Wazaramo and Wasagara; and he is readily taken into brotherhood. The host places the stool for his guests, seating himself on the ground: he prepares a meal of milk and porridge, and on parting presents, if he can afford it, a goat or a cow. The African "Fundi" or "Fattori" of caravans are rarely sober in Ugogo. The women are well disposed towards strangers of fair complexion, apparently with the permission of their husbands. According to the Arabs, the husband of the daughter is also de jure the lover of her mother.

The Sultan amongst the Wagogo is called Mtemi, a high title. He exercises great authority, and is held in such esteem by his people, that a stranger daring to possess the same name would be liable to chastisement. The ministers, who are generally brothers or blood-relations, are known as Wazagira (in the singular Mzagira), and the councillors, who are the elders and the honourables of the tribe, take the Kinyamwezi title "Wanyapara."

The necessaries of life are dear in Ugogo. The people will rarely barter their sheep, goats, and cows for plain white or blue cottons, and even in exchange for milk they demand coral, pink, or blue glass beads. A moderate sized caravan will expend from six to ten shuk-kah per diem. The Wanyamwezi travelling-parties live by their old iron hoes, for which grain is returned by the people, who hold the metal in request.

The Wahumba, by some called Wahumpa, is one of the terrible pastoral nations "beyond the rivers of Æthiopia." To judge from their dialect they are, like the Wakwafi, a tribe or a subtribe of the great Masai race, who speak a language partly South-African and partly Semitico-African, like that of the Somal. The habitat of the Wahumba extends from the north of Usagara to the eastern shores of the Nyanza or Ukerewe Lake; it has been remarked that a branch of the Mukondokwa River rises in their mountains. The blue highlands occupied by this pastoral race, clearly visible, on the right hand, to the traveller passing from Ugogo westwards, show where the ancient route from Pangani-town used to fall into the main trunk-road of Unyamwezi. Having but little ivory, they are seldom visited by travellers: their country, however, was explored some years ago by an Arab merchant, Hamid bin Salim, for the purpose of buying asses. He set out from Turn, in eastern Unyamwezi, and, traversing the country of the wild Wataturu, arrived on the eighth day at the frontier district I'ramba, where there is a river which separates the tribes. He was received with civility; but none have since followed his example.

The Wahumba are a fair and comely race, with the appearance of mountaineers, long-legged, and lightly made. They have repeatedly ravaged the lands of Usagara and Ugogo: in the latter country, near Usek'he, there are several settlements of this people, who have exchanged the hide-tent for the hut, and the skin for the cotton-cloth. They stain their garments with ochreish earth, and their women are distinguished by wearing Kitindi of full and half-size above and below the elbows. The ear lobes are pierced and distended by both sexes, as amongst the Wagogo. In their own land they are purely pastoral; they grow no grain, despise vegetable food, and subsist entirely upon meat or milk according to the season. Their habitations are hemispheres of boughs lashed together and roofed with a cow's hide; it is the primitive dwelling-place, and the legs of the occupant protrude beyond the shelter. Their arms, which are ever hung up close at hand, are broad-headed spears of soft iron, long "Sine," or double-edged daggers, with ribbed wooden handles fastened to the blade by a strip of cow's tail shrunk on, and "Rungu," or wooden knob-kerries, with double bulges that weight the weapon as it whirls through the air. They ignore and apparently despise the bow and arrows, but in battle they carry the Pavoise, or large hide-shield, affected by the Kafirs of the Cape. The Arabs, when in force, do not fear their attacks.

The Wahumba, like their congeners the Wakwafi bandage the infant's leg from ankle to knee, and the ligature is not removed till the child can stand upright. Its object is to prevent the development of the calf, which, according to their physiology, diminishes the speed and endurance of the runner. The specimens of Wahumba seen in different parts of Ugogo showed the soleus and gastroenemeius muscles remarkably shrunken, and the projection of the leg rising close below the knee.

Chapter 10

WE ENTER UNYAMWEZI, THE FAR-FAMED LAND OF THE MOON

The district of Tura, though now held, like Jiwe la Mkoa and Mgongo T'hembo, by Wakimbu, is considered the eastern frontier of Unyamwezi proper, which claims superiority over the minor neighbouring tribes. Some, however, extend the "land of the moon" eastward as far as Jiwe la Mkoa, and the porters when entering the "Fiery Field," declare that they are setting foot upon their own ground. The word "Tura," pronounced by the Wanyamwezi "Tula" or "Itula," means "put down!" (scil. your pack): as the traveller, whether from the east or from the west, will inevitably be delayed for some days at this border settlement. Tula is situated in S. lat. 5° 2' and E. long. 33° 57', and the country rises 4,000 feet above sea level. After the gloomy and monotonous brown jungles and thorn ibrests of Mgunda Mk'hali, whose sinuous line of thick jungle still girds the northern horizon, the fair champaign, bounded on either hand by low rolling and rounded hills of primary formation, with a succession of villages and many a field of holcus and sesamum, maize, millet, and other cereals, of manioc and gourds, water melons and various pulses, delights the sight, and appears to the African traveller a Land of Promise.

The pertinacious Kidogo pressed me to advance, declaring the Wakimbu of Tura to be a dangerous race: they appeared however a timid and ignoble people, dripping with castor and sesamum oil, and scantily attired in shreds of unclean cotton or greasy goat-skins. At Tura the last of the thirty asses bought at Zanzibar paid the debt of nature, leaving us, besides the one belonging to the Jemadar, but three African animals purchased on the road. A few extra porters were therefore engaged. Our people, after the discomforts of the bivouac, found the unsavoury village a perfect paradise; they began somewhat prematurely to beg for Bakhshish, and Muinyi Wazira requested dismissal on the plea that a slave sent by him on a trading-expedition into the interior had, by dying, endangered the safety of the venture. On the morning of the 30th October Kidogo led us over the plain through cultivation and villages to another large settlement on the western outskirt of the Tura district. As I disappointed him in his hopes of a Tirikeza, he passed the night in another Tembe, which was occupied by the caravans of Coast-Arabs and their slave girls, to one of whom, said Scan. Mag., he had lost his heart, and he punished me by halting through the next day. As we neared the end of the journey the sons of Ramji became more restive under their light loads; their dignity was hurt by shouldering a pack, and day after day, till I felt weary of life, they left their burdens upon the ground. However, on the 1st November, they so far recovered temper that the caravan was able to cross the thin jungle, based upon a glaring white soil, which divides the Tura from the Rubuga District. After a march of 6 hrs. and 30', we halted on the banks of the Kwale or "Partridge" Nullah, where, though late in the season, we found several long pools of water. The porters collected edible bivalves and caught a quantity of mud-fish by the "rough and ready" African process, a waist-cloth tied to a pair of sticks, and used by two men as a drag-net. At Rubuga, which we reached in 5 hrs. and 45', marching over a plain of black earth, thinly garnished with grass and thorn-trees, and then through clearings overgrown with stubble, I was visited by an Arab merchant, Abdullah bin Jumah, who, with a flying-caravan, had left Konduchi on the coast 2 months and 20 days after our departure. According to him his caravan had lately marched thirty miles in the twenty-four hours: it was the greatest distance accomplished in these regions; but the Arabs are fond of exaggeration, the party was small and composed of lightly laden men, and moreover it required two days' rest after so unusual an exertion. This merchant unwittingly explained a something which had puzzled me; whenever an advance beyond Unyanyembe had been made the theme of conversation, Said bin Salim's countenance fell, and he dropped dark hints touching patience and the power of Allah to make things easy. Abdullah rendered the expression intelligible by asking me if I considered the caravan strong enough to dare the dangers of the road – which he grossly exaggerated – between Unyamwezi-Land and Ujiji. I replied that I did, and that even if I did not, such bugbears should not cause delay; Ab-dullah smiled, but was too polite to tell me that he did not believe me.

A "doux marcher" of 2 hrs. 40' on the 3rd November, led us to the western limit of the Rubuga District. During the usual morning-halt under a clump of shady milk-bush, I was addressed by Maura or Maula, the Sultan of a large neighbouring village of Wanyamwezi: being a civilised man and a coast-traveller, he could not allow the caravan of the "Wazungu" to pass his quarters without presenting to him a bullock, and extracting from him a little cloth. Like most chiefs in the "Land of the Moon," he was a large-limbed, gaunt, angular, tall old man, with a black oily skin, seamed with wrinkles; and long wiry pigtails thickened with grease, melted butter, and castor-oil, depending from the sides of his purbald head. His dress – an old Barsati round the loins, and a grimy Subai loosely thrown over the shoulders – was redolent of boiled frankincense; his ankles were concealed by a foot-depth of brass and copper "Sambo," thin wires twisted round a little bundle of elephant's, buffalo's, or zebra's hair; and he wore single-soled sandals, decorated with four disks of white shell, about the size of a crown-piece, bound to the thongs that passed between the toes and girt the heel. He recognised the Baloch, greeted all kindly, led the way to his village, ordered lodgings to be cleared and cleaned, caused the cartels or bedsteads, – the first seen by us for many months, – to be vacated, and left us to look for a bullock. At the village door I had remarked a rude attempt at fashioning a block of wood into what was palpably intended for a form human and feminine; the Moslems of course pronounced it to be an idol, but the people declared that they paid no respect to it. They said the same concerning the crosses and the serpent-like ornaments of white ashes – in this land lime is unknown – with which the brown walls of their houses were decorated.

We made bonne chere at Rubuga, which is celebrated for its milk and meat, ghee and honey. On the wayside were numerous hives, the Mazinga or "cannons," before described; here however they were raised out of the reach of the ants, white and black, upon a pair of short forked supports, instead of being suspended from the branches of a tall tree. My companion brought from a neighbouring swamp a fine Egyptian, or ruddy goose, and a brace of crane-like water-fowl: these the Wanyamwezi porters, expecting beef, disdained, because rejected by the Baloch, yet at Inenge they had picked the carcase of a way-spent ass. Presently we were presented by the Sultan with one of the fattest of his fine bulls; it was indeed

"A grazier's without and a butcher's within;"

withal, so violent and unmanageable that no man could approach, much less secure it: it rushed about the village like a wild buffalo, scattering the people, who all fled except the Sultan, till it was stopped dead in a most determined charge, with a couple of rifle-bullets, by my companion. In return, Maula received a crimson cloth and two domestics, after which he begged for everything, including percussion caps, for which he had no gun. He appeared most anxious to detain the caravan, and in the evening his carefully concealed reasons leaked out – he wanted me to cure his son of fever, and to "put the colophon" upon a neighbouring hostile chief. At 8

P.M., I was aroused by my gun-carrier, Mabruki, who handed to me my Ferrara, and by the Baloch Riza, who reported that the palisade was surrounded by a host of raging blacks. I went out into the village, where the guard was running about in a state of excitement which robbed them of their wits, and I saw a long dark line of men sitting silently and peaceably, though armed for fight, outside the strong stockade. Having caused our cloth to be safely housed, and given orders to be awakened if work began, I returned to the hut, determined to take leave of Sultan Maura and his quarrels on the next day.

The porters were all gorged with beef, and three were "stale-drunk" with the consequences of pombe; yet so anxious were they rendered by the gathering clouds, and the spitting showers to reach their homes before the setting in of the "sowing rains," that my task was now rather to restrain than to stimulate their ardour: the moon was resplendent, and had I wished it, they would have set out at midnight. On the 4th November we passed through another jungle-patch, to a village in the fertile slopes of Ukona, where the Cannabis and the Datura, with its large fetid flowers, disputed the ground with brinjalls and castor-plants, holcus and panicum: tobacco grew luxuriantly, and cotton-plots, carefully hedged round against the cattle, afforded material for the loom, which now appeared in every village.

On the next day, we passed out of the fertile slopes of Ukona, and traversed an open wavy country, streaked with a thin forest of Mimosa, the Mtogwe or wood-apple, and a large quadrangular cactus. Beyond this point, a tract of swampy low level led to the third district of Eastern Unyamwezi, called Kigwa, or Mkigwa. We found quarters in a Tembe which was half-burned and partly pulled down, to be re-erected.

The 6th November saw us betimes in the ill-omened Forest, that divided us from the Unyanyembe district; it is a thin growth of gum-trees, mimosas, and bauhinias, with tiers, earth-waves, and long rolling lines of tawny-yellow hill —

mantled with umbrella-shaped trees, and sometimes capped with blocks and boulders – extending to a considerable distance on both sides. The Sultan of Kigwa, one Manwa, has taken an active part in the many robberies and murders which have rendered this forest a place of terror, and the Arabs have hitherto confined themselves to threats, though a single merchant complains that his slave-caravans have at different times lost fifty loads of cloth. Manwa is aided and counselled by Mansur, a Coast-Arab, who, horsewhipped out of the society of his countrymen at Kazeh, for drunken and disorderly conduct, has become a notorious traitor. Here also Msimbira, a Sultan of the Wasukuma, or Northern Wanyamwezi, who has an old and burning hatred against the Arabs, sends his plundering parties. On the 6th November the Baloch set out at 1 A.M., we followed at 2.15 A.M.: they had been prevented from obtaining beads on false pretences, consequently they showed temper, and determined to deny their escort. Their beards were now in my hand, they could neither desert nor refuse to proceed, but they desired to do me a harm, and they did it. During the transit of the forest, an old porter having imprudently lagged behind, was clubbed and cruelly bruised by three black Mohawks, who relieved him of his load, a leathern portmanteau, containing clothes, umbrellas, books, ink, journals, and botanical collections. I afterwards heard that the highwaymen had divided their spoils in the forest, and that separating into two parties, they had taken the route homewards. On the way, however, they were seized by a plundering expedition sent by Kitambi, the Sultan of Uyuwwi, a district half a day's march N.E. from Kazeh. The delict was flagrant; the head of one robber at once decorated the main entrance of Kitambi's village, but the other two escaped Jeddart-justice with their share of the plunder to his mortal enemy Msimbira. A present of a scarlet waistcoat and four domestics recovered our clothes from Kitambi; but Msimbira, threatening all the penalties of sorcery, abused, plundered, and expelled Masud ibn Musallam el Wardi, an old Arab merchant, sent to him from Unyanyembe for the purpose of recovering the books, journals, and collections. The perpetual risk of loss discourages the traveller in these lands; he never knows at what moment papers which have cost him months of toil may be scattered to the winds. As regards collections, future explorers are advised to abandon the hope of making them on the march upwards, reserving their labour for the more leisurely return. The precautions with which I prefaced our down-march may not be useless as suggestions. My field and sketch-books were entrusted to an Arab merchant, who preceded me to Zanzibar; they ran no other danger except from the carelesness of the Consul who, unfortunately for me, succeeded Lieut.-Col. Hamerton. My companion's maps, papers, and instruments, were committed to a heavy "petarah," a deal-box with pent-lid and hide-bound as a defence against rain, to be carried "Mziga-ziga," as the phrase is – suspended on a pole between the two porters least likely to desert. I loaded one of the sons of Ramji with an enamelled leathern bag, converted from a dressing-case into a protection for writing and sketching materials; and a shooting-bag, hung during the march over the shoulders of Nasiri, a Coast-Arab youth engaged as ass-leader at Unyanyembe, contained my vocabularies, ephemeris, and drawing-books.

Considering the conduct of the escort, I congratulated myself upon having passed through the Kigwa forest without other accident. Two or three days after our arrival at Kazeh several loads of beads were plundered from a caravan belonging to Abdullah bin Salih. Shortly afterwards Msimbira sent a large foraging party with a view to cutting off the road: they allowed themselves to be surprised during sleep by Mpagamo's men, who slew twenty-five of their number and dispersed the rest. This accident, however, did not cure their propensity for pillage; on our return-march, when halted at a village west of the Kigwa forest, a body of slaves passed us in hot haste and sore tribulation: they had that day been relieved by bandits of all their packs.

Passing from the Kigwa forest and entering the rice-lands of the Unyanyembe district we found quarters a vile cow-house – in a large dirty village called Hanga. The aspect of the land became prepossessing: the route lay along a valley bisected by a little rivulet of sweet water, whose course was marked by a vivid leek-green line; the slopes were bright with golden stubble upon a surface of well-hoed field, while to the north and south ran low and broken cones of granite blocks and slabs, here naked, there clothed from base to brow with dwarf parasol-shaped trees, and cactaceae of gigantic size.

From this foul village I was urged by Kidogo to conclude by a tirikeza the last stage that separated the caravan from Kazeh in Unyanyembe, the place which he and all around him had apparently fixed as the final bourne of the exploration. But the firmament seemed on fire, the porters were fagged, and we felt feverish, briefly, an afternoon's march was not judged advisable. To temper, however, the wind of refusal, I served out to each of the sons of Ramji five rounds of powder for blowing away on entering the Arab head-quarters. All of course had that private store which the Arabs call "El Akibah" – the ending; it is generally stolen from the master and concealed for emergencies with cunning care. They had declared their horns to be empty, and said Kidogo, "Every pedlar fires guns here – shall a great man creep into his Tembe without a soul knowing it?"

On the 7th November, 1857, – the 134th day from the date of our leaving the coast – after marching at least 600 miles, we prepared to enter Kazeh, the principal Bandari of Eastern Unyamwezi, and the capital village of the Omani merchants. We left Hanga at dawn. The Baloch were clothed in that one fine suit without which the Eastern man rarely travels: after a few displays the dress will be repacked, and finally disposed of in barter for slaves. About 8 A.M, we halted for stragglers at a little village, and when the line of porters becoming compact began to wriggle, snake-like, its long length over the plain, with floating flags, booming horns, muskets ringing like saluting mortars, and an uproar of voice which nearly drowned the other noises, we made a truly splendid and majestic first appearance. The road was lined with people who attempted to vie with us in volume and variety of sound: all had donned their best attire, and with such luxury my eyes had been long unfamiliar. Advancing I saw several Arabs standing by the wayside, they gave the Moslem salutation and courteously accompanied me for some distance. Amongst them were the principal merchants, Snay bin Amir, Said bin Majid, a young and handsome Omani of noble tribe, Muhinna bin Sulayman, who, despite elephantiasis, marched every year into Central Africa, and Said bin Ali el Hinawi, whose short, spare, but well-knit frame, pale face, small features, snowy beard, and bald head, surmounted by a red fez, made him the type of an Arab old man.

I had directed Said bin Salim to march the caravan to the Tembe kindly placed at my disposal by Isa bin Hijji, and the Arabs met at Inenge. The Kirangozi and the porters, however, led us on by mistake (?) to the house of "Musa Mzuri" – handsome Moses – an Indian merchant settled at Unyanyembe for whom I bore an introductory letter, graciously given by H. H. the Sayyid Majid of Zanzibar. As Musa was then absent on a trading-journey to Karagwah, his agent, Snay bin Amir, a Harisi Arab, came forward to perform the guest-rites, and led me to the vacant house of Abayd bin Sulayman who had lately returned to Zanzibar.

After allowing me, as is the custom, a day to rest and to dismiss the porters, who at once separated to their homes, all the Arab merchants, then about a dozen, made the first ceremonious call, and to them was officially submitted the circular addressed by the Prince of Zanzibar to his subjects resident in the African interior. Contrary to the predictions of others, nothing could be more encouraging than the reception experienced from the Omani Arabs; striking, indeed, was the contrast between the open-handed hospitality and the hearty good-will of this truly noble race, and the niggardness of the savage and selfish African – it was heart of flesh after heart of stone. A goat and a load of the fine white rice grown in the country were the normal prelude to a visit and to offers of service which proved something more than a mere vox et proeterea nihil. Whatever I alluded to, onions, plantains, limes, vegetables, tamarind-cakes, coffee from Karagwah, and similar articles, only to be found amongst the Arabs, were sent at once, and the very name of payment would have been an insult. Shay bin Amir, determining to surpass all others in generosity, sent two goats to us and two bullocks to the Baloch and the sons of Ramji: sixteen years before, he had begun life a confectioner at Maskat, and now he had risen to be one of the wealthiest ivory and slave-dealers in Eastern Africa. As his health forbade him to travel he had become a general agent at Kazeh, where he had built a village containing his store-houses and his depots of cloth and beads, slaves and ivory. I have to acknowledge many an obligation to him. Having received a "wa-kalat-namah," or "power of attorney" he enlisted porters for the caravan to Ujiji. He warehoused my goods, he disposed of my extra stores, and, finally, he superintended my preparations for the down-march. During two long halts at Kazeh he never failed, except through sickness, to pass the evening with me, and from his instructive and varied conversation was derived not little of the information contained in the following pages. He had travelled three times between Unyam-wezi and the coast, besides navigating the great Lake Tanganyika and visiting the northern kingdoms of Karagwah and Uganda. He first entered the country about fifteen years ago, when the line of traffic ended at Usanga and Usenga, and he was as familiar with the languages, the religion, the manners, and the ethnology of the African, as with those of his natal Oman. He was a middle-aged man with somewhat of the Quixotic appearance, high-featured, sharp and sunken-eyed, almost beardless, light-coloured, tall, gaunt, and large-limbed. He had read much, and, like an oriental, for improvement, not only for amusement: he had a wonderful memory, fine perceptions and passing power of language. Finally, he was the stuff of which friends are made; brave as all his race, prudent withal, ready to perish for the "Pundo-nor," and, – such is not often the case in the East, – he was as honest as he was honourable.

Before proceeding with the thread of my narrative, the reader is requested to bear with the following few lines upon the subject of Unyanyembe.

Unyanyembe, the central and principal province of Unyamwezi, is, like Zungomero in Khutu, the great Bandari or meeting-place of merchants, and the point of departure for caravans which thence radiate into the interior of Central Intertropical Africa. Here the Arab merchant from Zanzibar meets his compatriot returning from the Tanganyika Lake and from Uruwwa. Northwards well-travelled lines diverge to the Nyanza Lake, and the powerful kingdoms of Karagwah, Uganda, and Unyoro; from the south Urori and Ubena, Usanga and Usenga, send their ivory and slaves; and from the southwest the Rukwa Water, K'hokoro, Ufipa, and Marungu must barter their valuables for cottons, wires, and beads. The central position and the comparative safety of Unyanyembe have made it the head-quarters of the Omani or pure Arabs, who, in many cases, settle here for years, remaining in charge of their depots, whilst their factors and slaves travel about the country and collect the items of traffic. At Unyanyembe the merchants expect some delay. The porters, whether hired upon the coast or at the Tanganyika Lake, here disperse, and a fresh gang must be collected – no easy task when the sowing season draws nigh.

Unyanyembe, which rises about 3480 feet above sea-level, and lies 356 miles in rectilinear distance from the eastern coast of Africa, resembles in its physical features the lands about Tura. The plain or basin of Ihara, or Kwihara, a word synonymous with the "Bondei" or low-land of the coast, is bounded on the north and south by low, rolling hills, which converge towards the west, where, with the characteristically irregular lay of primitive formations, they are crossed almost at right angles by the Mfuto chain. The position has been imprudently chosen by the Arabs; the land suffers from alternate drought and floods, which render the climate markedly malarious. The soil is aluminous in the low levels – a fertile plain of brown earth, with a subsoil of sand and sandstone, from eight to twelve feet below the surface; the water is often impregnated with iron, and the higher grounds are uninhabited tracts covered with bulky granite-boulders, bushy trees, and thorny shrubs.

Contrary to what might be expected this "Bandari-district" contains villages and hamlets, but nothing that can properly be termed a town. The Mtemi or Sultan Fundikira, the most powerful of the Wanyamwezi chiefs, inhabits a Tembe, or square settlement, called "Ititenya," on the western slope of the southern hills. A little colony of Arab merchants has four large houses at a neighbouring place, "Mawiti." In the centre of the plain lies "Kazeh," another scattered collection of six large hollow oblongs, with central courts, garden-plots, store-rooms, and outhouses for the slaves. Around these nuclei cluster native villages – masses of Wanyamwezi hovels, which bear the names of their founders.

This part of Unyanyembe was first colonised about 1852, when the Arabs who had been settled nearly ten years at Kigandu of P'huge, a district of Usukuma, one long day's march north of Kazeh, were induced by Mpagamo, to aid them against Msimbira, a rival chief, who defeated and drove them from their former seats. The details of this event were supplied by an actor in the scenes; they well illustrate the futility of the people. The Arabs, after five or six days of skirmishing, were upon the point of carrying the boma or palisade of Msimbira, their enemy, when suddenly at night their slaves, tired of eating beef and raw groundnuts, secretly deserted to a man. The masters awaking in the morning found themselves alone, and made up their minds for annihilation. Fortunately for them, the enemy, suspecting an ambuscade, remained behind their walls, and allowed the merchants to retire without an attempt to cut them off. Their employer, Mpagamo, then professed himself unable to defend them; when, deeming themselves insecure, they abandoned his territory. Snay bin Amir and Musa Mzuri, the Indian, settled at Kazeh, then a desert, built houses, sunk wells, and converted it into a populous place.

It is difficult to average the present number of Arab merchants at Unyanyembe who, like the British in India, visit but do not colonise; they rarely, however, exceed twenty-five in number; and during the travelling season, or when a campaign is necessary, they are sometimes reduced to three or four; they are too strong to yield without fighting, and are not strong enough to fight with success. Whenever the people have mustered courage to try a fall with the strangers, they have been encouraged to try again. Hitherto the merchants have been on friendly terms with Fundikira, the chief. Their position, however, though partly held by force of prestige, is precarious. They are all Arabs from Oman, with one solitary exception, Musa Mzuri, an Indian Kojah, who is perhaps in these days the earliest explorer of Unyamwezi. In July, 1858, an Arab merchant, Silim bin Masud, returning from Kazeh to his home at Msene, with a slave-porter carrying a load of cloth, was, though well armed and feared as a good shot, attacked at a water in a strip of jungle westward of Mfuto, and speared in the back by five men, who were afterwards proved to be subjects of the Sultan Kasanyare, a Mvinza. The Arabs organised a small expedition to revenge the murder, marched out with 200 or 300 slave-musketeers, devoured all the grain and poultry in the country, and returned to their homes without striking a blow, because each merchant-militant wished his fellows to guarantee his goods or his life for the usual diyat, or blood-money, 800 dollars. This impunity of crime will probably lead to other outrages.

The Arabs live comfortably, and even splendidly, at. Unyanyembe. The houses, though single-storied, are large, substantial, and capable of defence. Their gardens are extensive and well planted; they receive regular supplies of merchandise, comforts, and luxuries from the coast; they are surrounded by troops of concubines and slaves, whom they train to divers crafts and callings; rich men have riding-asses from Zanzibar, and even the poorest keep flocks and herds. At Unyanyembe, as at Msene, and sometimes at Ujiji, there are itinerant fundi, or slave-artisans – blacksmiths, tinkers, masons, carpenters, tailors, potters, and rope-makers, – who come up from the coast with Arab caravans. These men demand exorbitant wages. A broken matchlock can be repaired, and even bullets cast; good cord is purchaseable; and for tinning a set of seventeen pots and plates five shukkah merkani are charged. A pair of Arab stirrups are made up for one shukkah besides the material, and chains for animals at about double the price. Fetters and padlocks, however, are usually imported by caravans. Pack-saddles are brought from Zanzibar: in caravans a man may sometimes be found to make them. There is, moreover, generally a pauper Arab who for cloth will make up a ridge-tent; and as most civilised Orientals can use a needle, professional tailors are little required. Provisions are cheap and plentiful; the profits are large; and the Arab, when wealthy, is disposed to be hospitable and convivial. Many of the more prosperous merchants support their brethren who have been ruined by the chances and accidents of trade. When a stranger appears amongst them, he receives the "hishmat l'il gharlb," or the guest-welcome, in the shape of a goat and a load of white rice; he is provided with lodgings, and is introduced by the host to the rest of the society at a general banquet. The Arabs' great deficiency is the want of some man to take the lead. About fifteen years ago Abdullah bin Salim, a merchant from Zanzibar, with his body of 200 armed slaves, kept the whole community in subjection: since his death, in 1852, the society has suffered from all the effects of disunion where union is most required. The Arab, however, is even in Africa a Pantisocrat, and his familiarity with

the inferior races around him leads to the proverbial consequences.

The houses of the Arabs are Moslem modifications of the
African Tembe, somewhat superior in strength and finish.
The deep and shady outside-verandah, supported by stout
uprights, shelters a broad bench of raised earthwork, where
men sit to enjoy the morning cool and the evening serenity,
and where they pray, converse, and transact their various avocations. A portcullis-like door, composed of two massive
planks, with chains thick as a ship's cable – a precaution rendered necessary by the presence of wild slaves – leads into
the barzah, or vestibule. The only furniture is a pair of clay
benches extending along the right and left sides, with pillow-
shaped terminations of the same material; over these, when
visitors are expected, rush mats and rugs are spread. From
this barzah a passage, built at the angle proper to baffle the
stranger's curiosity, leads into the interior, a hollow square or
oblong, with the several rooms opening upon a courtyard,
which, when not built round, is completely closed by a
"liwan" – a fence of small tree-trunks or reeds. The apart-
ments have neither outward doors nor windows: small bull's-
eyes admit the air, and act as loop-holes in case of need. The
principal room on the master's side of the house has a bench
of clay, and leads into a dark closet where stores and merchandise are placed. There are separate lodgings for the
harem, and the domestic slaves live in barracoons or in their
own outhouses. This form of Tembe is perhaps the dullest
habitation ever invented by man. The exterior view is carefully removed from sight, and the dull, dirty courtyard, often
swamped during the rains, is ever before the tenant's eyes; the
darkness caused by want of windows painfully contrasts with
the flood of sunshine pouring in through the doors, and at
night no number of candles will light up its gloomy walls of
grey or reddish mud. The breeze is either excluded by careless frontage, or the high and chilling winds pour in like torrents; the roof is never water-tight, and the walls and rafters

harbour hosts of scorpions and spiders, wasps and cock-roaches. The Arabs, however, will expend their time and trouble in building rather than trust their goods in African huts, exposed to thieves and to the frequent fires which result from barbarous carelessness: everywhere, when a long halt is in prospect, they send their slaves for wood to the jungle, and superintend the building of a spacious Tembe. They neglect, however, an important precaution, a sleeping-room raised above the mean level of malaria.

Another drawback to the Arab's happiness is the failure of his constitution: a man who escapes illness for two successive months boasts of the immunity; and, as in Egypt, no one enjoys robust health. The older residents have learned to moderate their appetites. They eat but twice a-day – after sunrise, and at noon – the midday meal concluded, they confine themselves to chewing tobacco or the dried coffee of Karagwah. They avoid strong meats, especially beef and game, which are considered heating and bilious, remaining satisfied with light dishes, omelets and pillaus, harisah, firni, and curdled milk, and the less they eat the more likely they are to escape fever. Harisah, in Kisawahili "boko-boko," is the roast beef – the plat de resistance – of the Eastern and African Arab. It is a kind of pudding made with finely shredded meat, boiled with flour of wheat, rice, or holcus, to the consistence of a thick paste, and eaten with honey or sugar. Firni, an Indian word, is synonymous with the muhallibah of Egypt, a thin jelly of milk-and-water, honey, rice-flour, and spices, which takes the place of our substantial northern rice-pudding. The general health has been improved by the importation from the coast of wheat, and a fine white rice, instead of the red aborigen of the country, of various fruits, plantains, limes, and papaws; and of vegetables, brinjalls, cucumbers, and tomatos, which relieve the indigenous holcus and maize, manioc and sweet-potato, millet and phaseoli, sesamum and ground-nuts. They declare to having derived great benefit from the introduction of onions, – an antifebral, which flourishes better in Central than in Maritime Africa. The onion, so thriving in South Africa, rapidly degenerates upon the island of Zanzibar into a kind of houseleek. In Unyamwezi it is of tolerable size and flavour. It enters into a variety of dishes, the most nauseous being probably the sugared onion-omelet. In consequence of general demand, onions are expensive in the interior; an indigo-dyed shukkah will purchase little more than a pound. When the bulbs fail, the leaves chopped into thin circles and fried in clarified butter with salt, are eaten as a relish with meat. They are also inserted into marak or soups, to disguise the bitter and rancid taste of stale ghee. Onions may be sown at all seasons except during the wet monsoon, when they are liable to decay. The Washenzi have not yet borrowed this excellent and healthy vegetable from the Arabs. Garlic has also been tried in Unyanyembe, but with less success; moreover, it is considered too heating for daily use. As might be expected, however, amongst a floating population with many slaves, foreign fruits and vegetables are sometimes allowed to die out. Thus some enterprising merchant introduced into Unyanyembe the date and the mkungu, bidam, or almond-tree of the coast: the former, watered once every third day, promised to bear fruit, when, in the absence of the master, the Wanyamwezi cut up the young shoots into walking-sticks. Sugar is imported: the water-wanting cane will not thrive in arid Unyanyembe, and honey must be used as a suceedaneum. Black pepper, universally considered cooling by Orientals, is much eaten with curry-stuffs and other highly-seasoned dishes, whereas the excellent chillies and bird-pepper, which here grow wild, are shunned for their heating properties. Butter and ghee are made by the wealthy; humbler houses buy the article, which is plentiful and good, from the Wanyamwezi. Water is the usual beverage. Some Arabs drink togwa, a sweet preparation of holcus; and others, debauchees, indulge in the sour and intoxicating pombe, or small-beer.

The market at Unyanyembe varies greatly according to the quantity of the rains. As usual in barbarous societies, a dry season, or a few unexpected caravans, will raise the prices, even to trebling; and the difference of value in grain before and after the harvest will be double or half of what it is at par. The price of provisions in Unyamwezi has increased inordinately since the Arabs have settled in the land. Formerly a slave-boy could be purchased for five fundo, or fifty strings of beads: the same article would now fetch three hundred. A fundo of cheap white porcelain-beads would procure a milch cow; and a goat, or ten hens its equivalent, was to be bought for one khete. In plentiful years Unyanyembe is, however, still the cheapest country in East Africa, and, as usual in cheap countries, it induces the merchant to spend more than in the dearest. Paddy of good quality, when not in demand, sells at twenty kayla (120 lbs.) for one shukkah of American domestics; maize, at twenty-five; and sorghum, here the staff of life, when in large stock, at sixty. A fat bullock may be bought for four domestics, a cow costs from six to twelve, a sheep or a goat from one to two. A hen, or its equivalent, four or five eggs, is worth one khete of coral or pink porcelain beads. One fundo of the same will purchase a large bunch of plantains, with which mawa or plantain-wine, and siki or vinegar are made; and the Wanyamwezi will supply about a pint of milk every morning at the rate of one shukkah per mensem. A kind of mud-fish is caught by the slaves in the frequent pools which, during the cold season, dot the course of the Gombe Nullah, lying three miles north of Kazeh; and return-caravans often bring with them stores of the small fry, called Kashwa or Daga'a, from the Tanganyika Lake.

From Unyanyembe twenty marches, which are seldom accomplished under twenty-five days, conduct the traveller to Ujiji, upon the Tanganyika. Of these the fifth station is Msene, the great Bandari of Western Unyamwezi. It is usually reached in eight days; and the twelfth is the Malagarazi River, the western limit of the fourth region.

The traveller, by means of introductory letters to the Doyen of the Arab merchants at Kazeh, can always recruit his stock of country currency, – cloth, beads, and wire, – his requirements of powder and ball, and his supply of spices, comforts, and drugs, without which travel in these lands usually ends fatally. He will pay, it is true, about five times their market-value at Zanzibar: sugar, for instance, sells at its weight in ivory, or nearly one-third more than its weight in beads. But though the prices are exorbitant they preserve the buyer from greater evils, the expense of porterage, the risk of loss, and the trouble and annoyance of personally superintending large stores in a land where "vir" and "fur" are synonymous terms.

And now comfortably housed within a stone-throw of my new friend Shaykh Snay bin Amir, I bade adieu for a time to the march, the camp, and the bivouac. Perhaps the reader may not be unwilling to hear certain details concerning the "road and the inn" in Eastern Africa; he is familiar from infancy with the Arab Kafilah and its host of litters and camels, horses, mules, and asses, but the porter-journeys in Eastern Africa have as yet escaped the penman's pen.

Throughout Eastern Africa made roads, the first test of progress in a people, are unknown. The most frequented routes are foot-tracks like goat-walks, one to two spans broad, trodden down during the travelling season by man and beast, and during the rains the path in African parlance "dies," that is to say, it is overgrown with vegetation. In open and desert places four or five lines often run parallel for short distances. In jungly countries they are mere tunnels in thorns and under branchy trees, which fatigue the porter by catching his load. Where fields and villages abound they are closed with rough hedges, horizontal tree-trunks, and even rude stockades, to prevent trespassing and pilferage. Where the land is open, an allowance of one-fifth must be made for winding: in closer countries this must be increased to two-fifths or to one-half, and the traveller must exercise his judgment in distributing the marches between these two extremes. In Uzaramo and K'hutu the tracks run through tall grasses, which are laid by their own weight after rains, and are burned down during the hot seasons: they often skirt cultivated lands, which they are not allowed to enter, miry swamps are spanned, rivers breast-deep, with muddy bottoms and steep slippery banks, are forded, whilst deep holes, the work of rodents and insects, render them perilous to ridden cattle. In Usagara the gradients are surmounted either by beds of mountain torrents or by breasting steep and stony hills, mere ladders of tree-root and loose stones: laden animals frequently cannot ascend or descend them. The worst paths in this region are those which run along the banks of the many streams and rivulets, and which traverse the broken and thorny ground at the base of the hills. The former are "thieves' roads," choked with long succulent grass springing from slushy mud; the latter are con-tinued rises and falls, with a small but ragged and awkward watercourse at every bottom. From Usagara to Western Unyamwezi the roads lead through thick thorn-jungle, and thin forests of trees blazed or barked along the track, without hill, but interrupted during the rains by swamps and bogs. They are studded with sign-posts, broken pots and gourds, horns and skulls of game and cattle, imitations of bows and arrows pointing towards water, and heads of holcus. Some-times a young tree is bent across the path and provided with a cross-bar; here is a rush gateway like the yoke of the ancients, or a platform of sleepers supported by upright trunks; there a small tree felled and replanted, is tipped with a crescent of grass twisted round with bark, and capped with huge snail shells, and whatever barbarous imagination may suggest. Where many roads meet, those to be avoided are barred with a twig or crossed by a line drawn with the foot. In Western Uvinza and near Ujiji, the paths are truly vile, combining all the disadvantages of bog and swamp, river and rivulet, thorn-bush and jungle, towering grasses, steep inclines, riddled sur-face, and broken ground. The fords on the whole line are temporary as to season, but permanent in place: they are rarely more than breast-deep; and they average in dry weather a cubit and a half, the fordable medium. There are but two streams, the Mgeta and the Ruguvu, which are bridged over by trees; both could be forded higher up the bed; and on the whole route there is but one river, the Malagarazi, which requires a ferry during the dry season. Cross roads abound in the populous regions. Where they exist not, the jungle is often impassable, except to the elephant and the rhinoceros: a company of pioneers would in some places require a week to cut their way for a single march through the network of thorns and the stockade of rough tree-trunks. The directions issued to travellers about drawing off their parties for safety at night to rising grounds, will not apply to Eastern Africa; it would be far easier to dig for themselves abodes under the surface.

It is commonly asserted in the island of Zanzibar that there are no caravans in these regions. The dictum is true if the term be limited to the hosts of camels and mules that traverse the deserts and the mountains of Arabia and Persia. It is erroneous if applied to a body of men travelling for commercial purposes. From time immemorial the Wanyamwezi have visited the road to the coast, and though wars and blood-fends may have temporarily closed one line, another necessarily opened itself. Amongst a race so dependent for comfort and pleasure upon trade, commerce, like steam, cannot be compressed beyond a certain point. Until a few years ago, when the extension of traffic induced the country people to enlist as porters, all merchants traversed these regions with servile gangs hired on the coast or island of Zanzibar, a custom still prevailing on the northern and southern routes front the sea-board to the lakes of Nyanza and Nyassa. Porterage, on the long and toilsome journey, is now considered by the Wanyamwezi a test of manliness, as the Englishman deems a pursuit or a profession necessary to clear him from the charge of effeminacy. The children imbibe the desire with their milk, and at six or seven years old they carry a little tusk on their shoulders – instinctive porters, as pointer-pups are hereditary pointers. By premature toil their shinbones are sometimes bowed to the front like those of animals too early ridden. "He sits in hut egg-hatching," is their proverbial phrase to express one more elegant

"Home-keeping youth have ever homely wits."

And they are ever quoting the adage that men who travel not are void of understanding – the African equivalent of what was said by the European sage: "The world is a great book, of which those who never leave home read but a page." Against this traditional tendency reasons of mere hire and rations, though apparently weighty, are found wanting. The porter will bargain over his engagement to the utmost bead, saying that all men are bound to make the best conditions for themselves: yet, after two or three months of hard labour, if he chance upon a caravan returning to his home, a word from a friend, acting upon his innate debility of purpose, will prevail upon him to sacrifice by desertion all the fruits of his toil. On these occasions the porters are carefully watched; open desertion would, it is true, be condemned by the general voice, yet no merchant can so win the affections of his men that some will not at times disappear. Until the gangs have left their homes far behind, their presence seems to hang by a thread; at the least pretext they pack up their goods and vanish in a mass. When approaching their settlements – at the frontier districts of Tura and Mfuto, for instance – their cloth and hire are taken from them, packed in the employer's bales, and guarded by armed slaves, especially at night, and on the line of march. Yet these precautions frequently fail, and, once beyond the camp limits, it is vain to seek the fugitive. In the act of desertion they show intelligence: they seldom run away when caravans first meet, lest their employer should halt and recover them by main force, and, except where thieves and wild beasts are unknown, they will not fly by night. The porter, however, has one point of honour; he leaves his pack behind him. The slave, on the other hand, certainly robs his employer when he runs away, and this, together with his unwillingness to work and the trouble and annoyance which he causes to his owner, counterbalances his superior dexterity and intelligence.

Caravans, called in Kisawahili safari (from the Arab safar, a journey) and by the African rugendo orlugendo, "a going," are rarely wanting on the main trunk-lines. The favourite seasons for the upward-bound are the months in which the greater and the lesser Masika or tropical rains conclude – in June and September, for instance, on the coast – when water and provisions are plentiful. Those who delay till the dry weather has set in must expect hardships on the march; the expense of rations will be doubled and trebled, and the porters will frequently desert. The down-caravans set out in all seasons except the rainy; it is difficult to persuade the people of Unyanyembe to leave their fields between the months of October and May. They will abandon cultivation to the women and children, and merrily take the footpath way if laden with their own ivory, but from the merchant they will demand exorbitant wages, and even then they will hesitate to engage themselves.

Porterage varies with every year and in every caravan. It knows but two limits: the interest of the employer to disburse as little as possible by taking every advantage of the necessities of his employee, and the desire of the employee to extract as much as he can by presuming upon the wants of his employer. In some years there is a glut of porters on the coast; when they are rare quarrels take place between the several settlements, each attempting a monopoly of enlistment to the detriment of its neighbours, and a little blood is sometimes let. When the Wanyamwezi began to carry, they demanded for a journey from the coast to their own country six to nine dollars' worth of domestics, coloured cloths, brass-wires, and the pigeon's-egg bead called sungomaji. The rate of porterage then declined; the increase of traffic, however, has of late years greatly increased it. In 1857 it was 10 dollars, and it afterwards rose to 12 dollars per porter. In this sum rations are not included; the value of these – which by ancient custom are fixed at 1 kubabah (about 1.5 lbs.) of grain per diem, or, that failing, of manioc, sweet potatoes, and similar articles, with the present of a bullock at the frontier – is subject to greater variations, and is even less reducible to an average than the porter's pay. It is needless to say that the down-journey is less expensive than the up-march, as the carriers rely upon a fresh engagement on the coast. The usual hire from Unyanyembe would be nine cloths, payable on arrival at the sea-port, where each is worth 25 cents, or about 1 shilling. The Arabs roughly calculate – the errors balancing one another – that, rations included, the hire of a porter from the coast to the Tanganyika Lake and back amounts to a total of 20 dollars = 4l. 3s. From the coast, Wanyamwezi porters will not engage themselves for a journey westward of their own country; at Unyanyembe they break up, and a fresh gang must be enlisted for a march to the Tanganyika or to the Nyanza Lake.

It is impossible to average the numbers of an East African caravan, which varies from half a dozen to 200 porters, under a single Mundewa or merchant. In dangerous places travellers halt till they form an imposing force; 500 is a frequent figure, and even bodies of 1000 men are not rare. The only limit to the gathering is the incapability of the country to fill more than a certain number of mouths. The larger caravans, however, are slow and cumbrous, and in places they exhaust the provision of water.

Caravans in East Africa are of three kinds. The most novel and characteristic are those composed only of Wanyamwezi; secondly, are the caravans directed and escorted by Wasawahili freemen or fundi (slave fattori), commissioned by their patrons; and, lastly, those commanded by Arabs.

The porter, called pagazi or fagazi – the former is the African, the latter the ridiculous Arabised form of the word –

corresponds with the carregador of West Africa. The Wan-yamwezi make up large parties of men, some carrying their own goods, others hired by petty proprietors, who for union and strength elect a head Mtongi, Ras Kafilah, or leader. The average number of these parties that annually visit the coast is far greater than those commanded by stranger-merchants. In the Unyamwezi caravan there is no desertion, no discontent, and, except in certain spots, little delay. The porters trudge from sunrise to 10 or 11 A.M., and sometimes, though rarely, they will travel twice a day, resting only during the hours of heat. They work with a will, carrying uncomplainingly huge tusks, some so heavy that they must be lashed to a pole between two men – a contrivance technically called mziga-ziga. Their shoulders are often raw with the weight, their feet are sore, and they walk half or wholly naked to save their cloth for displays at home. They ignore tent or covering, and sleep on the ground; their only supplies are their country's produce, a few worn-down hoes, intended at times to pur-chase a little grain or to be given as blackmail for sultans, and small herds of bullocks and heifers that serve for similar pur-poses if not lost, with characteristic African futility, upon the road. Those who most consult comfort carry, besides their loads and arms, a hide for bedding, an earthen cooking pot, a stool, a kilindo or bark-box containing cloth and beads, and perhaps a small gourd full of ghee. They sometimes suffer severely from exposure to a climate which forbids long and hard work upon short and hard fare. Malignant epidemics, especially smallpox, often attack caravans as they approach the coast; generally, however, though somewhat lean and haggard, the porters appear in better condition than might be expected. The European traveller will repent accompanying these caravans: as was said of a similar race, the Indians of Guiana, "they will not deviate three steps from the regular path."

Porters engaged by Arab Mtajiri or Mundewa – the former is the Kisawahili, the latter is the Inner African term for a merchant or travelling trader – are known by their superior condition; they eat much more, work much less, and give far greater trouble to their commanders. They expend part of the cloth and beads which they have received as hire to procure for themselves occasional comforts; and on the down-journey they take with them a few worn-down hoes to retain the power of desertion without starving. The self-willed wretches demean themselves with the coolest impudence; reply imperiously, lord it over their leaders, regulate the marches and the halts, and though they work they never work without loud complaints and open discontent. Rations are a perpetual source of heart-burning: stinted at home to a daily mess of grain-porridge, the porters on the line of march devote, in places where they can presume, all their ingenuity to extort as much food as possible from their employers. At times they are seized with a furore for meat. When a bullock is slaughtered, the Kirangozi or guide claims the head, leaving the breast and loin to the Mtongi or principal proprietor, and the remainder is equally portioned amongst the khambi or messes into which the gang divides itself. As has been remarked, the Arab merchant, next to the Persian, is the most luxurious traveller in the East; a veteran of the way, he well knows the effects of protracted hardship and scarcity upon a wayfarer's health. The European traveller, however, will not enjoy the companionship of the Arab caravan, which marches by instinct rather than by reason. It begins by dawdling over the preliminaries; it then pushes hurriedly onwards till arrested by epidemic or desertion; and finally it lingers over the end of the journey, thus loosing time twice. This style of progress is fatal to observation; moreover, none but a special caravan, consisting of slaves hired for the purpose in the island of Zanzibar or on the coast, and accompanied by their own Ahbab or patron – without whom they will obey no employer, however generous or energetic – will enable the explorer to strike into an unbeaten path, or to progress a few miles beyond the terminus of a main trunk-road. The most enterprising of porters will desert, leaving the caravan-leader like a water-logged ship.

Between these two extremes are the trading parties directed by the Wasawahili, the Wamrima, and the slave Fundi – the Pombeiros of West Africa – kindred souls with the Pagazi, understanding their languages and familiar with their habits, manners, and customs. These "Safari" are neither starved like those composed of Wanyamwezi, nor pampered like those headed by the Arabs. There is less fatigue during the march, and more comfort at the halting-place, consequently there are fewer cases of disease and death. These semi. African Mtongi, hating and jealousing Arabs and all strangers, throw every obstacle in their way, spread reports concerning their magical and malevolent powers which are dangerous amongst the more superstitious barbarians, they offer a premium for desertion, and in fine, they labour hard though fruitlessly, to retain their ancient monopoly of the profits derived from the interior.

I will now describe the day's march and the halt of the East African caravan.

At 3 A.M., all is silent as the tomb, even the Mnyamwezi watchman nods over his fire. About an hour later the red-faced apoplectic chanticleer – there are sometimes half-a-dozen of them – the alarum of the caravan, and a prime favourite with the slaves and porter, who carry him on their banghy-poles by turns, and who drench him with water when his beak opens under the sun, – flaps his wings and crows a loud salutation to the dawn: he is answered by every cock and cockerel within ear-shot. I have been lying awake for some time, longing for the light, and when in health, for an early breakfast. At the first paling of the East, the torpid Goanese are called up to build a fire, they tremble with the cold – thermometrically averaging 60° F. – and they hurry to bring food. Appetite somewhat difficult at this hour, demands a frequent change of diet, we drink tea or coffee when procurable, or we eat rice-milk and cakes raised with whey, or a porridge not unlike water-gruel. Whilst we are so engaged, the Baloch chanting the spiritual songs which follow prayers, squat round a cauldron placed upon a roaring fire, and fortify the inner man with boiled meat and grain, with toasted pulse and tobacco.

About such time, 5 A.M., the camp is fairly roused, and a little low chatting becomes audible. This is a critical moment. The porters have promised overnight, to start early, and to make a long wholesome march. But, "uncertain, coy, and hard to please," they change their minds like the fair sex, the cold morning makes them unlike the men of the warm evening, and perhaps one of them has fever. Moreover, in every caravan there is some lazy, loud-lunged, contradictory and unmanageable fellow, whose sole delight is to give trouble. If no march be in prospect, they sit obstinately before the fire warming their hands and feet, inhaling the smoke with everted heads, and casting quizzical looks at their fuming and fidgety employer. If all be unanimous, it is vain to attempt them, even soft sawder is but "throwing comfits to cows." We return to our tent. If, however, there be a division, a little active stimulating will cause a march. Then a louder conversation leads to cries of Kwecha! Kwecha! Pakia! Pakia! Hopa! Hopa! Collect! pack! set out! Safari! Safari leo! a journey, a journey to-day! and some peculiarly African boasts, P'hunda! Ngami! I am an ass! a camel! accompanied by a roar of bawling voices, drumming, whistling, piping, and the braying of Barghumi, or horns. The sons of Ramji come in a body to throw our tents, and to receive small burdens, which, if possible, they shirk; sometimes Kidogo does me the honour to inquire the programme of the day. The porters, however, hug the fire till driven from it, when they unstack the loads piled before our tents and pour out of the camp or village. My companion and I, when well enough to ride, mount our asses, led by the gunbearers, who carry all necessaries for offence and defence; when unfit for exercise, we are borne in hammocks, slung to long poles, and carried by two men at a time.

The Baloch tending their slaves hasten off in a straggling body, thinking only of escaping an hour's sun. The Jemadar, however, is ordered to bring up the rear with Said bin Salim, who is cold and surly, abusive and ready with his rattan. Four or five packs have been left upon the ground by deserters, or shirkers, who have started empty-handed, consequently our Arab either double-loads more willing men, or persuades the sons of Ramji to carry a small parcel each, or that failing, he hires from some near village a few porters by the day. This, however, is not easy, the beads have been carried off, and the most tempting promises without pre-payment, have no effect upon the African mind.

When all is ready, the Kirangozi or Mnyamwezi guide rises and shoulders his load, which is ever one of the lightest. He deliberately raises his furled flag, a plain blood-red, the sign of a caravan from Zanzibar, much tattered by the thorns, and he is followed by a privileged Pagazi, tom-toming upon a kettle-drum much resembling a European hour-glass. The dignitary is robed in the splendour of scarlet broadcloth, a narrow piece about six feet long, with a central aperture for the neck, and with streamers dangling before and behind; he also wears some wonderful head-dress, the spoils of a white and black "tippet-monkey," or the barred skin of a wild cat, crowning the head, bound round the throat, hanging over the shoulders, and capped with a tall cup-shaped bunch of owl's feathers, or the gorgeous plumes of the crested crane. His insignia of office are the kipungo or fly-flapper, the tail of some beast which he affixes to his person as if it were a natural growth, the kome, or hooked iron spit, decorated with a central sausage of parti-coloured beads, and a variety of oily little gourds containing snuff, simples, and "medicine," for the road, strapped round his waist. He leads the caravan, and the better to secure the obedience of his followers he has paid them in a sheep or a goat, the value of which he will recover by fees and superiority of rations – the head of every animal slaughtered in camp and the presents at the end of the journey are exclusively his. A man guilty of preceding the Kirangozi is liable to fine, and an arrow is extracted from his quiver to substantiate his identity at the end of the march. Pouring out of the kraal in a disorderly mob, the porters stack their goods at some tree distant but a few hundred yards, and allow the late, the lazy, and the invalids to join the main body. Generally at this conjuncture the huts are fired by neglect or mischievousness. The khambi, especially in winter, burns like tinder, and the next caravan will find a heap of hot ashes and a few charred sticks still standing. Yet by way of contrast the Pagazi will often take the trouble to denote by the usual sign-posts to those following them that water is at hand. Here and there a little facetiousness appears in these erections, a mouth is cut in the tree-trunk to admit a bit of wood, simulating a pipe, with other representations still more waggish.

After the preliminary halt, the caravan, forming into the order of march, winds, like a monstrous land-serpent, over hill, dale, and plain. The Kirangozi is followed by an Indian file, those nearest to him, the grandees of the gang, are heavily laden with ivories: when the weight of the tusk is inordinate, it is tied to a pole and is carried palanquin-fashion by two men. A large cowbell, whose music rarely ceases on the march, is attached to the point which is to the fore; to the bamboo behind is lashed the porter's private baggage, – his earthen cooking-pot, his water-gourd, his sleeping-mat, and his other necessaries. The ivory-carriers are succeeded by the bearers of cloth and beads, each man, poising upon either shoulder, and sometimes raising upon the head for rest, packs that resemble huge bolsters, six feet long by two in diameter, cradled in sticks, which generally have a forked projection for facility of stacking and reshouldering the load. The sturdiest fellows are usually the lightest loaded: in Eastern Africa, as elsewhere, the weakest go to the wall. The maximum of burden may be two farasilah, or seventy pounds, avoirdupois. Behind the cloth bearers straggles a long line of porters and slaves, laden with the lighter stuff, rhinoceros-teeth, hides, salt-cones, tobacco, brass wire, iron hoes, boxes and bags, beds and tents, pots and water-gourds, mats and private stores. With the Pagazi, but in separate parties, march the armed slaves, who are never seen to quit their muskets, the women, and the little toddling children, who rarely fail to carry something, be it only of a pound weight, and the asses neatly laden with saddle-bags of giraffe or buffalo-hide. A "Mganga" almost universally accompanies the caravan, not disdaining to act as a common porter. The "parson" not only claims, in virtue of his sacred calling, the lightest load; he is also a stout, smooth, and sleek-headed man, because, as usual with his class, he eats much and he works little. The rear is brought up by the master or the masters of the caravan, who often remains far behind for the convenience of walking and to prevent desertion.

All the caravan is habited in its worst attire, the East African derides those who wear upon a journey the cloth which should be reserved for display at home. If rain fall they will doff the single goatskin hung round their sooty limbs, and, folding it up, place it between the shoulder and the load. When grain is served out for some days' march, each porter bears his posho or rations fastened like a large "bussel" to the small of his back. Upon this again, he sometimes binds, with its legs projecting outwards, the three-legged stool, which he deems necessary to preserve him from the danger of sitting upon the damp ground. As may be imagined, the barbarians have more ornament than dress. Some wear the ngala, a strip of zebra's mane bound round the head with the bristly parti-coloured hair standing out like a saint's "gloria:" others prefer a long bit of stiffened ox-tail, rising like a unicorn's horn, at least a foot above the forehead. Other ornaments are the skins of monkeys and ocelots, rouleaus and fillets of white, blue, or scarlet cloth, and huge bunches of ostrich, crane, and jay's feathers, crowning the head like the tufts of certain fowls. Their arms are decorated with massive ivory bracelets, heavy bangles of brass or copper, and thin circlets of the same metal, beads in strings and bands, adorn their necks, and small iron bells, a "knobby" decoration, whose incessant tinkling harmonises, in African ears, with the regular chime-like "Ti-ti! Ti-ti! tang!" of the tusk-bells, and the loud broken "Wa-ta-ta!" of the horns, are strapped below the knee or round the ankle by the more aristocratic. All carry some weapon; the heaviest armed have a bow and a bark-quiver fill of arrows, two or three long spears and assegais, a little battle-axe borne on the shoulder, and the sime or dudgeon.

The normal recreations of a march are, whistling, singing, shouting, hooting, horning, drumming, imitating the cries of birds and beasts, repeating words which are never used except on journeys – a "chough's language, gabble enough and good enough" – and abundant squabbling; in fact perpetual noise which the ear however, soon learns to distinguish for the hubbub of a halt. The uproar redoubles near a village, where the flag is unfurled and where the line lags to display itself. All give vent to loud shouts, "Hopa! hopa! – go on! go on! Mgogolo! – a stoppage! Food! food! Don't be tired! The kraal is here – home is near! Hasten, kirangozi – Oh! We see our mothers! We go to eat!" On the road it is considered prudent as well as pleasurable to be as loud as possible, in order to impress upon plunderers an exaggerated idea of the caravan's strength; for equally good reasons silence is recommended in the kraal. When threatened with attack and no ready escape suggests itself, the porters ground their loads and prepare for action. It is only self-interest that makes them brave; I have seen a small cow, trotting up with tail erect, break a line of 150 men carrying goods not their own. If a hapless hare or antelope cross the path, every man casts his pack, brandishes his spear, and starts in pursuit; the animal never running straight is soon killed, and torn limb from limb, each negroid helluo devouring his morsel raw. Sometimes a sturdy fellow "renowns it" by carrying his huge burden round and round, like a horse being ringed, and starts off at full speed. When two bodies meet, that commanded by an Arab claims the road. If both are Wanyamwezi, violent quarrels ensue, but fatal weapons, which are too ready at hand, are turned to more harmless purposes, the bow and spear being used as whip and cudgel. These affrays are not rancorous till blood is shed. Few tribesmen are less friendly for so trifling an affair as a broken head; even a slight cut or a shallow stab is little thought of; but, if returned with interest, great loss of life may arise from the slenderest cause. When friendly caravans meet, the two Kirangozis sidle up with a stage pace, a stride, and a stand, and with sidelong looks prance till arrived within distance; then suddenly and simultaneously "ducking," like boys "giving a back," they come to logger-heads and exchange a butt violently as fighting rams. Their example is followed by all with a rush and a crush, which might be mistaken for the beginning of a faction, but it ends, if there be no bad blood, in shouts of laughter. The weaker body, however, must yield precedence and offer a small present as blackmail.

About 8 A.M, when the fiery sun has topped the trees and a pool of water, or a shady place appears, the planting of the red flag, the braying of a Barghumi, or koodoo's horn, which, heard at a distance in the deep forests, has something of the charm which endears the "Cor de Chasse" to every wood-man's ear, and sometimes a musket-shot or two, announces a short halt. The porters stack their loads, and lie or loiter about for a few minutes, chatting, drinking, and smoking tobacco and bhang, with the usual whooping, screaming cough, and disputing eagerly about the resting-place for the day. On long marches we then take the opportunity of stopping to discuss the contents of two baskets which are carried by a slave under the eye of the Goanese.

If the stage be prolonged towards noon, the caravan lags, straggles, and suffers sorely. The heat of the ground, against which the horniest sole never becomes proof, tries the feet like polished-leather boots on a quarter-deck in the dog-days near the Line, and some tribulation is caused by the cry M'iba hapa! – thorns here! The Arabs and the Baloch must often halt to rest. The slaves ensconce themselves in snug places; the porters, propping their burdens against trees, curl up, dog-like, under the shade; some malinger; and this, the opportunity preferred for desertion, is an anxious hour to the proprietor; who, if he would do his work "deedily," must be the last in the kraal. Still the men rarely break down. As in Indian marching, the African caravan prefers to end the day, rather than to begin it, with a difficulty – the ascent of a hill, or the fording of a stream. They prefer the strip of jungle at the further end of a district or a plantation, for safety as well as for the comfort of shade. They avoid the vicinity of rocks; and on desert plains they occupy some slightly rising ground, where the night-cold is less severe than in the lower levels.

At length an increased hubbub of voices, blended with bells, drums, fifes, and horns, and sometimes a few musket-shots, announce that the van is lodged, and the hubbub of the halt confirms the pleasing intelligence that the journey is shortened by a stage. Each selfish body then hurries forward to secure the best boothy in the kraal, or the most comfortable hut in the village, and quarrels seem serious. Again, however, the knife returns home guiltless of gore, and the spear is used only as an instrument for sound belabouring. The more energetic at once apply themselves to "making all snug" for the long hot afternoon and the nipping night; some hew down young trees, others collect heaps of leafy boughs; one acts architect, and many bring in huge loads of firewood. The East African is so much accustomed to house-life, that the bivouac in the open appears to him a hardship; he prefers even to cut out the interior of a bush and to squat in it, the portrait of a comfortable cynocephalus. We usually spread our donkey-saddles and carpets in some shade, awaiting the arrival of our tents, and its erection by the grumbling sons of Ramji; if we want a hut, we draw out the man in possession like a badger, – he will never have the decency to offer it. As a rule, the villagers are more willing to receive the upward-bound caravans, than those who, returning, carry wealth out of instead of into the country. Merchants, on account of their valuable out-fits, affect, except in the safest localities, the khambi rather than the village; the latter, however, is not only healthier, despite its uncleanliness in miasmatic lands, but is also more comfortable, plenty and variety of provisions being more readily procured inside than outside. The Arab's khaymah is a thin pole or ridge-tent of flimsy domestics, admitting sun and rain, and, like an Irish cabin, permitting at night the occupant to tell time by the stars; yet he prefers it, probably for dignity, to the boothy which, in this land of verdure and cool winds, is a far more comfortable lodging.

The Wamrima willingly admit strangers into their vil-lages; the Wazaramo would do the same, but they are con-stantly at feud with the Wanyamwezi, who therefore care not to avail themselves of the dangerous hospitality. In K'hutu caravans seize by force the best lodgings. Throughout Eastern Usagara travellers pitch tents in the clear central spaces, sur-rounded by the round huts of the peasantry, under whose low and drooping caves the pagazi find shelter. In the western regions, where the Tembe or square village prevails, kraals form the nighting-place. In Ugogo strangers rarely enter the hamlets, the hovels being foul, and the people dangerous. Throughout Eastern and Central Unyamwezi caravans defile into the villages without hesitation. Some parties take posses-sion of the Iwanza or public-house; others build for them-selves tabernacles of leafy boughs, which they are expected to clear away before departure, and the headman provides lodg-ings for the Mtongi. In Western Unyamwezi the doors are often closed against strangers, and in Eastern Uvinza the peo-ple will admit travellers to bivouac, but they will not vacate their huts. In Western Uvinza, a desert like Marenga and Mgunda Mk'hali, substantial khambi occur at short intervals. At Ujiji, the Sultan, after offering the preliminary magubiko or presents, provides his guests with lodgings, which, after a time sufficient for enabling them to build huts, they must vacate in favour of new comers. In the other Lake Regions the reception depends mainly upon the number of muskets in a caravan, and the character of the headman and his people.

The khambi or kraal everywhere varies in shape and material. In the eastern regions, where trees are scarce, wattle frames of rough sticks, compacted with bark-fibre, are disposed in a circle; the forked uprights, made higher behind and lower in front, to form a sloping roof, support horizontal or cross poles, which are overlaid with a rough thatch of grass or grain-cane. The central space upon which the boothies open is occupied by one or more huts for the chiefs of the party; and the outer circle is a loose fence of thorn branches, flimsy, yet impassable to breech-less legs, unshod feet, and thin loose body-garments. When a kraal must be built, rations are not served out till enclosures made round the camp secure the cattle; if the leader be dilatory, or unwilling to take strong measures, he may be a serious loser. The stationary kraals become offensive, if not burnt down after a few months. The Masika-kraal, as it is called, is that occupied only during the rainy monsoon, when water is everywhere found. The vicinity and the abundance of that necessary are the main considerations in selecting the situation of encampments. The bark-kraals commence in Uvinza, where trees abound, and extend to the Tanganyika Lake; some are substantial, as the temporary villages, and may be a quarter of a mile in circumference. The Lakist population carry with them, when travelling, Karagwah or stiff mats of reed and rush; these they spread over and fasten to a firmly-planted framework of flexible boughs, not unlike a bird's nest inverted, or they build a cone of strong canes, in the shape of piled muskets, with the ends lashed together. It is curious to see the small compass in which the native African traveller can contract himself: two, and even three, will dispose their heads and part of their bodies – leaving their lower limbs to the mercy of the elements – under a matting little more than a yard square.

When lodgings in the kraal have been distributed, and the animals have been off-packed, and water has been brought from the pit or stream, all apply themselves to the pleasant toil of refection. Merrily then sounds the breathless chant of the woman pounding or rubbing down grain, the song of the cook, and the tinkle-tinkle of the slave's pestle, as he bends over the iron mortar from which he stealthily abstracts the coffee. The fireplaces are three stones or clods, placed trivet-wise upon the ground, so that a draught may iced the flame, they are far superior to the holes and trenches of our camps and pic-nics. The tripod supports a small black earthen pot, round which the khambi or little knot of messmates persever-ingly squat despite the stinging sun. At home where they eat their own provisions they content themselves with a slender meal of flour and water once a day. But like Spaniards, Arabs, and all abstemious races, they must "make up for lost time." When provisions are supplied to them, they are cooking and consuming as long as the material remains; the pot is in per-petual requisition, now filled to be emptied, then refilled to be re-emptied. They will devour in three days the rations pro-vided for eight, and then complain loudly that they are starved. To leave a favourable impression upon their brains, I had a measure nearly double that generally used, yet the per-verse wretches pleading hunger, though they looked like aldermen by the side of the lean bony anatomies whom they met on the road, would desert whenever met by a caravan. After a time there will, doubtless, be a re-action; when their beards whiten they will indulge in the garrulity of age; they will recount to wondering youth the prodigality of the Muzungu, in filling them with grain, even during the longest marches, and they will compare his loads of cloth and beads with the half dozen "shaggy" cows and the worn-out hoes, the sole outfit for presents and provisions carried by caravans of "Young Africa." If there be any delay in serving out provi-sions, loud cries of Posho! p'hamba! rations! food! – resound through the camp; yet when fatigued, the porters will waste hours in apathetic idleness rather than walk a few hundred yards to buy grain. Between their dozen meals they puff clouds of pungent tobacco, cough and scream over their jungle-bhang, and chew ashes, quids, and pinches of red earth, probably the graves of white ants. If meat be served out to them, it is eaten as a relish; it never, however, interferes with the consumption of porridge. A sudden glut of food appears to have the effect of intoxicating them. The Arabs, however, avoiding steady rations, alternately gorge and starve their porters, knowing by experience that such extremes are ever most grateful to the barbarian stomach. The day must be spent in very idleness; a man will complain bitterly if told to bring up his pack for opening; and general discontent, with hints concerning desertion, will arise from the mortification of a muster. On such occasions he and his fellows will raise their voices, – when not half-choked by food – and declare that they will not be called about like servants, and crouch obstinately round the smoky fire, the pictures of unutterable disgust; and presently enjoy the sweet savour of stick-jaw dough and pearl-holcus like small shot, rat stews, and boiled weeds, which they devour till their "bulge" appears like the crop of a stuffed turkey. Sometimes when their improvidence has threatened them with a Banyan-day, they sit in a melancholy plight, spitefully smoking and wickedly eyeing our cooking-pots; on these occasions they have generally a goat or a bullock in store, and, if not, they finesse to obtain one of ours. I always avoid issuing an order to them direct, having been warned by experience that Kidogo or the Kirangozi is the proper channel; which sorely vexes Valentine and Seedy Bombay, whose sole enjoyment in life is command. I observed that when wanted for extra-work, to remove thorns or to dig for water, that the false alarm of Posho! (rations!) summons them with a wonderful alacrity. Moreover, I remarked that when approaching their country and leaving ours – the coast – they became almost unmanageable and vice versa as conditions changed.

My companion and I pass our day as we best can, sometimes in a bower of leafy branches, often under a spreading tree, rarely in the flimsy tent. The usual occupations are the diary and the sketch-book, added to a little business. The cloth must be doled out, and the porters must be persuaded, when rested, to search the country for rations, otherwise – the morrow will be a blank. When a bullock is killed one of us must be present. The porters receive about a quarter of the meat, over which they sit wrangling and screaming like hyaenas, till a fair division according to messes is arrived at. Then, unless watched, some strong and daring hand will suddenly break through the ring, snatch up half a dozen portions and disappear at a speed defying pursuit; others will follow his example, with the clatter and gesture of a troop of baboons, and the remainder will retire as might be expected, grumbling and discontented. Dinner at 4P.M. breaks the neck of the day. Provisions of some kind are mostly procurable, our diet, however, varies from such common doings as the hard holcus-scone, the tasteless bean-broth and the leathery goat-steak, to fixings of delicate venison, fatted capon, and young guinea-fowl or partridge, with "bread sauce," composed of bruised rice and milk. At first the Goanese declined to cook "pretty food," as pasties and rissoles, on the plea that such things were impossible upon the march; they changed their minds when warned that persistence in such theory might lead to a ceremonious fustigation. Moreover, they used to serve us after their fashion, with a kind of "portion" on plates; the best part, of course, remained in the pots and digesters; these, therefore, were ordered to do duty as dishes. When tea or coffee is required in a drinkable state, we must superintend the process of preparing it, the notions of the Goanese upon such subjects being abominable to the civilised palate. When we have eaten our servants take their turn; they squat opposite each other over a private "cooking-pot" to which they have paid unremitting attention; they stretch forth their talons and eat till weary, not satiated, pecking, nodding, and cramming like two lank black pigeons. Being "Christians," that is to say, Roman Catholics, they will not feed with the heathenry, moreover a sort of semi-European dignity forbids. Consequently Bombay messes with his "brother" Mabruki, and the other slaves eat by themselves.

When the wells ahead are dry the porters will scarcely march in the morning; their nervous impatience of thirst is such that they would exhaust all their gourds, if they expected a scarcity in front, and then they would suffer severely through the long hot day. They persist, moreover, upon eating before the march, under the false impression that it gives them strength and bottom. In fact, whenever difficulties as regards grain or drink suggest themselves, the African requires the direction of some head-piece made of better stuff than his own. The hardships of the tirikeza have already been described: they must be endured to be realised.

Night is ushered in by penning and pounding the cows, and by tethering the asses – these "careless Æthiopians" lose them every second day, – and by collecting and numbering the loads, a task of difficulty where every man shirks the least trouble. When there has been no tirikeza, when provisions have been plentiful, and when there is a bright moonshine, which seems to enliven these people like jackals, a furious drumming, a loud clapping of hands, and a general droning song, summon the lads and the lasses of the neighbouring villages to come out and dance and "make love." The performance is laborious, but these Africans, like most men of little game, soon become too tired to work, but not too tired to play and amuse themselves. Their style of salutation is remarkable only for the excessive gravity which it induces; at no other time does the East African look so serious, so full of earnest purpose. Sometimes a single dancer, the village buffoon, foots a *pas seul*, featly, with head, arms, and legs, bearing strips of hair-garnished cow-skin, which are waved, jerked, and contorted, as if dislocation had occurred to his members. At other times, a line or a circle of boys and men is formed near the fire, and one standing in the centre, intones the song solo, the rest humming a chorus in an undertone. The dancers plumbing and tramping to the measure with alternate feet, simultaneously perform a treadmill exercise with a heavier stamp at the end of every period: they are such timists, that a hundred pair of heels sound like one. At first the bodies are slowly swayed from side to side, presently as excitement increases, the exercise waxes severe: they "cower down and lay out their buttocks," to use pedantic Ascham's words, "as though they would shoot at crows;" they bend and recover themselves, and they stoop and rise to the redoubled sound of the song and the heel-music, till the assembly, with arms waving like windmills, assumes the frantic semblance of a ring of Egyptian Darwayshes. The performance often closes with a grand promenade; all the dancers being jammed in a rushing mass, a *galop infernale*, with the features of satyrs, and gestures resembling ought but the human. When the fun threatens to become too fast and furious, the song dies, and the performers, with loud shouts of laughter, throw themselves on the ground, to recover strength and breath. The greybeards look on with admiration and sentiment, remembering the days when they were capable of similar feats. Instead of "bravo," they ejaculate "Nice! nice! very nice!" and they wonder what makes the white men laugh. The ladies prefer to perform by themselves, and perhaps in the East, ours would do the same, if a literal translation of the remarks to which a ball always gives rise amongst Orientals, happened by misfortune to reach their refined ears.

When there is no dancing, and the porters can no longer eat, drink, and smoke, they sit by their fires, chatting, squabbling, talking and singing some such "pure nectar" as the following. The song was composed, I believe, in honour of me, and I frequently heard it when the singers knew that it was understood. The Cosmopolitan reader will not be startled by the epithet "Mbaya," or wicked, therein applied to the Muzungu. A "good white man," would indeed, in these lands, have been held an easy-going soul, a natural, an innocent, like the "buona famiglia," of the Italian cook, who ever holds the highest quality of human nature to be a certain facility for being "plucked without 'plaining," and being "flayed without flinching." Moreover, despite my "wickedness," they used invariably to come to me for justice and redress, especially when proximity to the coast encouraged the guide and guards to "bully" them.

"Muzungu mbaya" (the wicked white man) goes from the shore, (Chorus) Puti! Puti! (I can only translate it by "grub! grub!")
We will follow "Muzungu mbaya."
Puti! Puti!
As long as he gives us good food!
Puti! Puti!
We will traverse the hill and the stream,
Puti! Puti!
With the caravan of this great mundewa (merchant).
Puti! Puti! &c., &c.

The Baloch and the sons of Ramji quarrel, yell, roar, and talk of eating – the popular subject of converse in these lands, as is beer in England, politics in France, law in Normandy, "pasta" at Naples, and to say no more, money everywhere – till a late hour. About 8 P.M., the small hours of the country, sounds the cry lala! lala! – sleep! It is willingly obeyed by all except the women, who must sometimes awake to confabulate even at midnight. One by one the caravan sinks into torpid slumber. At this time, especially when in the jungle-bivouac, the scene often becomes truly impressive. The dull red fires flickering and forming a circle of ruddy light in the depths of the black forest, flaming against the tall trunks and defining the foliage of the nearer trees, illuminate lurid groups of savage men, in every variety of shape and posture. Above, the dark purple sky, studded with golden points, domes the earth with bounds narrowed by the gloom of night. And, behold! in the western horizon, a resplendent crescent, with a dim, ash-coloured globe in its arms, and crowned by Hesperus, sparkling like a diamond, sinks through the vast of space, in all the glory and gorgeousness of Eternal Nature's sublimest works. From such a night, methinks, the Byzantine man took his device, the Crescent and the Star.

The rate of caravan-marching in East Africa greatly varies. In cool moonlit mornings, over an open path, the Pagazi will measure perhaps four miles an hour. This speed is reduced by a quarter after a short "spurt," and under normal, perhaps favourable, circumstances, three statute miles will be the highest average. Throughout the journey it is safe to reckon for an Indian file of moderate length – say 150 men – 2.25 English miles, or what is much the same, 1.75 geographical miles per hour, measured by compass from point to point. In a clear country an allowance of 20 per cent. must be made for winding: in closer regions 40 – 50 per cent., and the traveller must exercise his judgment in distributing his various courses between these extremes. Mr. Cooley (Inner Africa Laid Open, p. 6) a "resolute," and I may add a most successful "reducer of itinerary distances," estimates that the ordinary day's journey of the Portuguese missionaries in West Africa never exceeded six geographical miles projected in a straight line, and that on rare occasions, and with effort only, it may have extended to 10 miles. Dr. Lacerda's porters in East Africa were terrified at the thought of marching ordinarily 2.50 Portuguese leagues, or about 9.33 statute miles per day. Dr. Livingstone gives the exceedingly high maximum of 2.50 to 3 miles an hour in a straight line, but his porters were lightly laden, and the Nakololo are apparently a far "gamer" race, more sober and industrious, than the East Africans. Mr. Petheriek, H.M.'s Consul at Khartum, estimates his gangs to have marched 3.50 miles per hour, and the ordinary day's march at 8 hours. It is undoubted that the negro races north of the equator far surpass in pedestrian powers their southern brethren; moreover the porters in question were marching only for a single day; but as no instruments were used, the average may fairly be suspected of exaggeration. Finally Mr. Galton's observation concerning Cape travelling applies equally well to this part of Africa, namely, that 10 statute or 6 rectilinear geographical miles per diem is a fair average of progress, and that he does well who conducts the same caravan 1,000 geographical miles across a wild country in six months.

I will conclude this chapter with a succinct account of the inn, that is to say the village in East Africa.

The habitations of races form a curious study and no valueless guide to the nature of the climate and the physical conditions to which men are subject.

Upon the East African coast the villages, as has been mentioned, are composed of large tenements, oblongs or squares of wattle and dab, with eaves projecting to form a deep verandah and a thatched pent-roof, approaching in magnitude that of Madagascar.

Beyond the line of maritime land the "Nyumba" or dwelling-house assumes the normal African form, the circular hut described by every traveller in the interior: Dr. Livingstone appears to judge rightly that its circularity is the result of a barbarous deficiency in inventiveness. It has, however, several varieties. The simplest is a loose thatch thrown upon a cone of sticks based upon the ground, and lashed together at the apex: it ignores windows, and the door is a low hole in the side. A superior kind is made after the manner of our ancient bee-hives; it is cup-shaped with bulging sides, and covered with neat thatch, cut in circles which overlap one another tile-fashion: at a distance it resembles an inverted bird's nest. The common shape is a cylindrical framework of tall staves, or the rough trunks of young trees planted in the earth, neatly interwoven with parallel and concentric rings of flexible twigs and withies: this is plastered inside and outside with a hard coat of red or grey mud; in the poorer tenements the surface is rough and chinked, in the better order it is carefully smoothed and sometimes adorned with rude imitations of life. The diameter averages from 20 to 25, and the height from 7 to 15 feet in the centre, which is supported by a strong roof-tree, to which all the stacked rafters and poles converge. The roof is subsequently added, it is a structure similar to the walls, interwoven with sticks, upon which thick grass or palm-fronds are thrown, and the whole is covered with thatch tied on by strips of tree-bark. It has eaves which projecting from two to six feet – under them the inhabitants love to sit or sun shade themselves – rest upon horizontal bars, which are here and there supported by forked uprights, trees rudely barked. Near the coast the eaves are broad and high: in the interior they are purposely made so low that a man must creep in on all fours. The door-way resembles the entrance to an English pig-sty, it serves, however, to keep out heat in the hot season, and to keep in smoke and warmth during the rains and the cold weather: the threshold is garnished with a horizontal log or board that defends the interior from inundation. The door is a square of reeds fastened together by bark or cord, and planted upright at night between the wall and two dwarf posts at each side of the entrance: there is generally a smaller and a secret door opposite that in use, and jealously closed up except when flight is necessary. In the colder and damper regions there is a second wall and roof outside the first, forming in fact one house within the other.

About Central Usagara the normal African haystack-hut makes place for the "Tembe" which extends westward, a little beyond Unyanyembe. The Tembe, though of Hamitic origin, resembles the Utum of the ancients, and the Hishan of the modern Hejaz, those hollow squares of building which have extended through Spain to France and even to Ireland: it was, probably, suggested to Africa and to Arabia by the necessity of defence to, as well as lodging for, man and beast. It is to a certain extent, a proof of civilisation in Eastern Africa: the wildest tribes have not progressed beyond the mushroom or circular hut, a style of architecture which seems borrowed from the indigenous mimosa tree.

Westward of Unyamwezi in Uvinza and about the Tanganyika Lake the round hovel again finds favour with the people; but even there the Arabs prefer to build for themselves the more solid and comfortable Tembe.

The haystack-hut has been described by a multitude of travellers: the "Tembe," or hollow village, yet awaits that honour.

The "Tembe" wants but the addition of white-wash to make it an effective feature in African scenery: as it is, it appears from afar like a short line of raised earth. Provided with a block-house at each angle to sweep dead ground where fire, the only mode of attack practised in these regions, can be applied, it would become a fort impregnable to the Eastern African. The form is a hollow square or oblong, generally irregular, with curves, projections, and semicircles; in the East African Ghauts, the shape is sometimes round or oval to suit the exigencies of the hill-sides and the dwarf cones upon which it is built. On the mountains and in Ugogo, where timber is scarce, the houses form the continued frontage of the building, which, composed of mimosa-trunks, stout stakes, and wattle and dab, rarely exceeds seven feet in height. In the southern regions of Usagara where the Tembe is poorest, the walls are of clods loosely put together and roofed over with a little straw. About Msene where fine trees abound, the Tembe is surrounded by a separate boma or palisade of young unbarked trunks, short or tall, and capped here and there with cattle-skulls, blocks of wood, grass-wisps, and similar talismans; this stockade, in damper places, is hedged with a high thick fence, sometimes doubled and trebled, of peagreen milk-bush, which looks pretty and refreshing, and is ditched outside with a deep trench serving as a drain. The cleared space in front of the main passage through the hedges is often decorated with a dozen poles, placed in a wide semicircle to support human skulls, the mortal remains of ill-conducted boors. In some villages the principal entrance is approached by long, dark and narrow lanes of palisading. When the settlement is built purely for defence, it is called "Kaya," and its headman "Muinyi Kaya," the word, however, is sometimes used for "Boma" or "Mji," a palisaded village in general. In some parts of Unyamwezi there is a Bandani or exterior boothy, where the men work at the forge, or sit in the shade, and where the women husk, pound, and cook their grain.

The general roof of the Tembe is composed of mud and clay heaped upon grass thickly strewed over a framework of rafters supported by the long walls. It has, usually, an obtuse slope to the front and another to the rear, that rain may not lie; it is, however, flat enough to support the bark-bins of grain, gourds, old pots, firewood, water-melons, pumpkins, manioc, mushrooms, and other articles placed there to ripen or dry in the sun. It has no projecting eaves, and it is ascended from the inside by the primitive ladder, the inclined trunk of a tree, with steps formed by the stumps of lopped boughs, acting rings. The roof, during the rains, is a small plot of bright green grass: I often regretted not having brought with me a little store of mustard and cress. In each external side of the square, one or two door-ways are pierced; they are large enough to admit a cow, and though public they often pass through private domiciles. They are jealously closed at sunset, after which hour not a villager dares to stir from his home till morning. The outer doors are sometimes solid planks, more often they are three or four heavy beams suspended to a cross-bar passing through their tops When the way is to be opened they are raised from below and are kept up by being planted in a forked tree-trunk inside the palisade: they are let down when the entrance is to be closed, and are barred across with strong poles.

The tenements are divided from one another by party-walls of the same material as the exterior. Each house has, usually, two rooms, a "but" and a "ben," which vary in length from 20 to 50 feet, and in depth from 12 to 15: they are partitioned by a screen of corn-canes supported by stakes, with a small passage left open for light. The "but," used as parlour, kitchen, and dormitory, opens upon the common central square; the "ben" receives a glimmer from the doors and chinks, which have not yet suggested the idea of windows: it serves for a sleeping and a store room; it is a favourite place with hens and pigeons that aspire to be mothers, and the lambs and kids in early infancy are allowed to pass the night there. The inner walls are smeared with mud: lime is not procurable in Eastern Africa, and the people have apparently no predilection for the Indian "Gobar:" the floor is of tamped earth, rough, uneven, and unclean. The prism-shaped ceiling is composed of rafters and thin poles gently rising from the long-walls to the centre, where they are supported by strong horizontals, which run the whole length of the house, and these again rest upon a proportionate number of pillars, solid forked uprights, planted in the floor. The ceiling is polished to a shiny black with smoke, which winds its way slowly through the door – smoke and grease are the African's coat and small clothes, they contribute so much to his health and comfort that he is by no means anxious to get rid of them – and sooty lines depend from it like negro-stalactites.

The common enceinte formed by the houses is often divided into various courts, intended for different families, by the walls of the tenements, or by stout screens, and connected by long wynds and dark alleys of palisade-work. The largest and cleanest square usually belongs to the headman. In these spaces cattle are milked and penned; the ground is covered with a thick coat of the animals' earths, dust in the hot weather and deep viscid mud during the rains: the impurity must be an efficacious fomite of cutaneous and pectoral disease. The villagers are fond of planting in the central courts trees, under whose grateful shade the loom is plied, the children play, the men smoke, and the women work. Here, also, stands the little Mzimu, or Fetiss-hut, to receive the oblations of the pious. Places are partitioned off from the public ground, near the houses, by horizontal trunks of trees, resting on forks, forming pens to keep the calves from the cows at night. In some villages huge bolsters of surplus grain, neatly packed in bark and corded round, are raised on tall poles near the interior doors of the tenements. Often, too, the insides of the settlements boast of pigeon-houses, which in this country are made to resemble, in miniature, those of the people. In Unyamwezi the centre is sometimes occupied by the Iwanza, or village "public-house," which will be described in a future chapter.

In some regions, as in Ugogo, these lodgings become peculiarly offensive if not burnt after the first year. The tramping of the owners upon the roof shakes mud and soot from the ceiling, and the rains wash down masses of earth-work heavy enough to do injury. The interior is a menagerie of hens, pigeons, and rats, of peculiar impudence. Scorpions and earwigs fall from their nests in the warm or shady rafters. The former, locally termed "Nge," is a small yellow variety, and though it stings spitefully the pain seldom lasts through the day; as many as three have dropped upon my couch in the course of the week. In Ugogo there is a green scorpion from four to five inches long, which inflicts a torturing wound. According to the Arabs the scorpion in Eastern Africa dies after inflicting five consecutive stings, and commits suicide if a bit of stick be applied to the middle of its back. The earwig is common in all damp places, and it haunts the huts on account of the shade. The insect apparently casts its coat before the rainy season, and the Africans ignore the superstition which in most European countries has given origin to its trivial name. A small xylophagus with a large black head rains a yellow dust like pollen from the riddled woodwork; house-crickets chirp from evening to dawn; cockroaches are plentiful as in an Indian steamer; and a solitary mason-wasp, the "Kumbharni," or "potter's wife" of western India – a large hymenopter of several varieties, tender-green, or black and yellow, or dark metallic blue – burrows holes in the wall, or raises plastered nests, and buzzes about the inmates' ears; lizards, often tailless after the duello, tumble from the ceilings; in the darker corners spiders of frightful hideousness weave their solid webs; and the rest of the population is represented by tenacious ticks of many kinds, flies of sorts, bugs, fleas, mosquitoes, and small ants, which are, perhaps, the worst plagues of all. The Riciniae in Eastern Africa are locally called Papazi, which probably explains the "Pazi bug," made by Dr. Krapf a rival in venom to the Argas Persicus, or fatal "bug of Miana." In Eastern Africa these parasites are found of many shapes, round and oval, flat and swollen; after suction they vary in size from microscopic dimensions to three-quarters of an inch; the bite cannot poison, but the constant irritation caused by it may induce fever and its consequences. A hut infested with Papazi must be sprinkled with boiling water, and swept clean for many weeks, before they will disappear. In the Tembe there is no draught to disturb the smaller occupants, consequently they are more numerous than in the circular cottage. Moreover, the people, having an aversion to sleeping in the open air, thus supply their co-inhabitants with nightly rations, which account for their fecundity.

The abodes, as might be expected, are poorly furnished. In Unyamwezi, they contain invariably one or more "Kitanda." This cartel, or bedstead, is a rude contrivance. Two parallel lines of peeled tree-branches, planted at wide intervals, support in their forks horizontal poles: upon these is spread crosswise a layer of thick sticks, which forms the frame. The bedding consists of a bull-hide or two, and perhaps a long, coarse, rush-mat. It is impossible for any one but an African to sleep upon these Kitanda, on account of their shortness, the hardness of the material, and the rapid slope which supplies the want of pillows, and serves for another purpose which will not be described. When removed, a fractured pole will pour forth a small shower of the foul cimex: this people of hard skins considers its bite an agreeable titillation, and, what may somewhat startle a European, esteems its odour a perfume. Around the walls depend from pegs neatly-plaited slings of fibrous cord, supporting gourds and "vil-indo" – neat cylinders, like small band-boxes, of tree bark, made to contain cloth, butter, grain, or other provisions. In the store-roomy propped upon stones, and plastered over with clay for preservation, are Lindo, huge corn-bins of the same material; grain is ground upon a coarse granite slab, raised at an angle of 25°, about one foot above the floor, and embedded in a rim of hard clay. The hearth is formed of three "Mafiga," or truncated cones of red or grey mud, sometimes two feet high, and ten inches in diameter at the base: they are disposed triangularly, with the apex to the wall, and open to the front when the fire is made. The pot rests upon the tripod. The broom, a wisp of grass, a bunch of bamboo splints, or a split fibrous root, usually sticks in the ceiling; its work is left to the ants. From the rafters hang drums and kettle-drums, skins and hides in every process, and hooked twigs dangling from strings support the bows and arrows, the spears and assegais. An arrow is always thrust into the inner thatch for good luck: ivory is stored between the rafters, hence its dark ruddy colour, which must be removed by ablution with warm blood; and the ceiling is a favourite place for small articles that require seasoning – bows, quivers, bird-bolts, knob-sticks, walking-canes, reed-nozzles for bellows, and mi'iko or ladles, two feet long, used to stir porridge. The large and heavy water-pots, of black clay, which are filled every morning and evening by the women at the well, lie during the day empty or half empty about the room. The principal article of luxury is the "Kiti," or dwarf stool, cut out of a solid block, measuring one foot in height by six inches in diameter, with a concave surface for convenience of sitting: it has usually three carved legs or elbows; some, however, are provided with a fourth, and with a base like the seat, to steady them. They are invariably used by the Sultan and the Mganga, who disdain to sit upon the ground: and the Wamrima ornament them with plates of tin let into the upper concaves. The woods generally used for the Kiti, are the Mninga and the Mpingu. The former is a tall and stately tree, which supplies wood of a dark mahogany colour, exuding in life a red gum, like dragon's blood: the trunk is converted into bowls and platters, the boughs into rafters, which are, however, weak and subject to the xylophagus, whilst of the heart are made spears, which, when old and well-greased, resemble teak-wood. The Mpingu is the Sisam of India, (*Dalbergia Sissoo*) here erroneously called by the Arabs Abnus – ebony. The tree is found throughout Eastern Africa. The wood is of fine quality, and dark at the core: the people divide it into male and female; the former is internally a dark brick-dust red, whilst the latter verges upon black: they make from it spears and axe-handles, which soon, however, when exposed to the air, unless regularly greased, become brittle. The massive mortar, for husking grain, called by the people "Mchi," is shaped exactly like those portrayed in the interior-scenes of ancient Egypt: it is hewn out of the trunk of the close-grained Mkora tree. The huge pestle, like a capstan-bar, is made of the Mkorongo, a large tree with a fine-grained wood, which is also preferred to others for rafters, as it best resists the attacks of insects.

Such, gentle reader, is the Tembe of Central Africa. Concerning village life, I shall have something to say in a future page. The scene is more patent to the stranger's eye in these lands than in the semi-civilised regions of Asia, where men rarely admit him into their society.

Chapter 11

WE CONCLUDE THE TRANSIT OF UNYAMWEZI

I was detained at Kazeh from the 8th November to the 14th December, 1857, and the delay was one long trial of patience.

It is customary for stranger-caravans proceeding towards Ujiji to remain six weeks or two months at Unyanyembe for repose and recovery from the labours which they have, or are supposed to have, endured: moreover, they are expected to enjoy the pleasures of civilised society, and to accept the hospitality offered to them by the resident Arabs. In Eastern Africa, I again suggest, six weeks is as the three days' visit in England.

On the morning after our arrival at Kazeh, the gang of Wanyamwezi porters that had accompanied us from the coast withdrew their hire from our cloth-bales; and not demanding, because they did not expect, bakhshish, departed, without a sign of farewell, to their homes in Western Unyamwezi. The Kirangozi or guide received a small present of domestics: his family being at Msene, distant five marches ahead, he fixed, after long haggling, the term of fifteen days as his leave of absence, after which he promised to join me with a fresh gang for the journey to Ujiji.

The rest of the party apparently considered Unyanyembe, not Ujiji, the end of the exploration; it proved in effect a second point of departure, easier than Kaole only because I had now gained some experience.

Two days after our arrival, the Baloch, headed by their Jemadar, appeared in full toilette to demand a "Hakk el Salamah," or reward for safe-conduct. I informed them that this would be given when they had reached the end of the up-march. The pragmatical Darwaysh declared that without bakhshish there would be no advance; he withdrew his words, however, when my companion was called in to witness their being committed to paper – a proceeding always unpalatable to the Oriental. The Baloch then subsided into begging for salt and spices, and having received more than they had probably ever possessed in their lives, they privily complained of my parsimony to Said bin Salim. They then sent for tobacco, a goat, gunpowder, bullets – all which they obtained. Their next manoeuvre was to extract four cloths for tinning their single copper pot and for repairing the matchdogs and stocks of two old matchlocks. They then sold a keg of gunpowder committed to their charge. They had experienced every kindness from Snay bin Amir, from Sallum bin Hamid, in fact, from all the Arab merchants of Kazeh. They lodged comfortably in Musa Mzuri's house, and their allowance, one Shukkah of domestics per diem, enabled them to buy goats, sheep, and fowls – luxuries unknown in their starving huts at Zanzibar. Yet they did not fail, with their foul tongues, ever ready, as the Persians say, for "spitting at Heaven," to charge their kind hosts with the worst crime that the Arab knows – niggardness.

On the 8th November, I had arranged with Kidogo, as well as with the Kirangozi, to resume the march at the end of a fortnight. Ten days afterwards I again sent for him to conclude the plans concerning the journey: evidently something lay deep within his breast, but the difficulty was to extract it. He began by requiring a present for his excellent behaviour – he received, to his astonishment, four cloths. He next demanded leave to visit his Unyamwezi home for a week, and was unpleasantly surprised when it was granted. He then "hit the right nail on the head." The sons of Ramji, declaring that I had promised them a bullock on arrival at Kazeh, had seized, hamstrung, and cut up a fine fat animal sent to me by Sallum bin Harold; yet, Kidogo averred that the alleged promise must be fulfilled to them. When I refused, he bluntly informed me that I was quite equal to the task of collecting porters for myself; I replied that this was his work and not mine. He left the house abruptly, swearing that he would not trouble himself any longer, and, moreover, for the future that his men should not carry the lightest load, nor assist us even in threading beads. At last, on the 27th November, I sent for Kidogo, and told him that the march was positively fixed for the next week. After sitting for a time "cupo concentrato," in profound silence, the angry slave arose, delivered a volley of rattling words with the most theatrical fierceness, and rushed from the room, leaving the terrified Said bin Salim gazing upon vacancy like an idiot. Accompanied by his followers, who were shouting and laughing, he left the house, when – I afterwards heard – they drew their sabres, and waving them round their heads, they shouted, for the benefit of Arabs, "Tumeshinda Wazungu" – "We have conquered the Whites!" I held a consultation with my hosts concerning the advisability of disarming the recreant sons of Ramji. But Sallum bin Hamid, the "papa" of the colony, took up the word, and, as usual with such deliberative bodies, the council of war advised peace. They informed me that in Unyamwezi slaves and muskets are the stranger's sole protection, and as they were unanimous in persuading me to temporise, to "swallow anger" till after return, I felt bound, after applying for it, to be guided by their advice. At the consultation, however, the real object which delayed the sons of Ramji at Kazeh oozed out: their patroon, Mr. Rush Ramji, had written to them that his and their trading outfit was on its way from the coast; consequently, they had determined to await, and to make us await, its arrival before marching upon Ujiji.

On the 14th November, the Masika or wet season, which had announced its approach by premonitory showers and by a final burst of dry heat, set in over the Land of the Moon with torrents of rain and "rain-stones," as hail is here called, and with storms of thunder and lightning, which made it more resemble the first breaking of an Indian than the desultory fall of a Zanzibar wet-monsoon. I was still under the impression that we were encountering the Choti Barsat or Little Rains of Bengal and Bombay; and curious to say, the Arabs of Unyanyembe one and all declared, even after the wet-monsoon had reached its height, that the Masika in Unyamwezi is synchronous with that of the island and the coast, namely, in early April.

The Rains in Eastern Africa are, like the summer in England, the only healthy and enjoyable season: the contrast between the freshness of the air and the verdure of the scenery after the heat, dust, and desolation that preceded the first showers, was truly luxurious. Yet the Masika has many disadvantages for travellers. The Wanyamwezi, who were sowing their fields, declined to act porters, and several Arab merchants, who could not afford the expenditure required to hire unwilling men, were halted perforce in and near Unyanyembe. The peasants would come in numbers; offer to accompany the caravan; stand, stare, and laugh their vacant laughs; lift and balance their packs; chaffer about hire; promise to return next morning, and definitively disappear. With the utmost exertion Snay bin Amir could collect only ten men, and they were all ready to desert. Moreover, the opening of the Masika is ever unhealthy; strangers suffer severely from all sudden changes of temperature; Unyamwezi speedily became

"As full of agues as the sun in March."

Another cause of delay became imminent; my companion was comparatively strong, but the others were prostrated by sickness. Valentine first gave in; he was nearly insensible for three days and nights, the usual period of the Mukunguru or "Seasoning" of Unyamwezi – a malignant bilious remittent –

which left him weaker and thinner than he had ever been before. When he recovered, Gaetano fell ill, and was soon in the happy state of unconsciousness which distinguished all his fevers. The bull-headed slave Mabruki also retired into private life, and Bombay was laid up by a shaking ague, whilst the Baloch and the sons of Ramji, who had led a life so irregular that the Arabs had frequently threatened them with punishment, also began to pay the penalty of excess.

Snay bin Amir was our principal doctor. An adept in the treatment, called by his countrymen "camel-physic," namely, cautery and similar counter-irritants, he tried his art upon me when I followed the example of the party. At length, when the Hummah, or hot fit, refused to yield to its supposed specific, a coating of powdered ginger, he insisted upon my seeing a Mganga, or witch, celebrated for her cures throughout the country-side. She came, a wrinkled old beldame, with a greasy skin, black as soot, set off by a mass of tin-coloured pigtails: her arms were adorned with copper bangles like manacles, and the implement of her craft was, as usual, a girdle of small gourds dyed red-black with oil and use.

After demanding and receiving her fee in cloth, she proceeded to search my mouth, and to inquire anxiously concerning poison. The question showed the prevalence of the practice in the country, and indeed the people, to judge from their general use of "Mithri-dates," seem ever to expect it. She then drew from a gourd a greenish powder, which was apparently bhang, and having mixed it with water, she administered it like snuff, causing a convulsion of sneezing, which she hailed with shouts and various tokens of joy. Presently she rubbed my head with powder of another kind, and promising to return the next day, she left me to rest, declaring that sleep would cause a cure. The prediction, however, was not fulfilled, nor was the promise. Having become wealthy, she absconded to indulge in unlimited pombe for a week. The usual consequences of this "seasoning," distressing weakness, hepatic derangements, burning palms, and tingling soles, aching eyes, and alternate thrills of heat and cold, lasted, in my case, a whole month.

Our departure from Kazeh had now been repeatedly deferred. The fortnight originally fixed for the halt had soon passed in the vain search for porters. Sickness then delayed the journey till the 1st December, and Snay bin Amir still opined that want of carriage would detain me till the 19th of that month; he would not name the 18th, which was an unlucky day. When they recovered from their ailments, the Jemadar and the Baloch again began to be troublesome. All declared that a whole year, the term for which they had been sent by their Prince, had elapsed, and therefore that they had now a right to return. The period was wholly one of their own, based perhaps upon an answer which they had received from Lieut.-Col. Hamerton touching the probable duration of the Expedition, "a year or so." Even of that time it still wanted five months, but nothing from myself or from Said bin Salim could convince men who would not be convinced, of that simple fact. Ismail, the Baloch, who was dying of dysentery, reported himself unable to proceed: arrangements were made to leave him and his "brother" Shahdad – the fearful tinkling of whose sleepless guitar argued that the sweet youth was in love – under the charge of Shay bin Amir, at Kazeh. Greybeard Mohammed was sulking with his fellows. He sat apart from them; and complaining that he had not received his portion of food, came to me for dismissal, which was granted, but not accepted. The Jemadar required for himself and the escort a porter per man. When this was refused, he changed his tactics, and began to lament bitterly the unavoidable delay. He annoyed me with ceaseless visits, which were spent in harping upon the one string, "When do we march?" At last I forbade all allusion to the subject. In wrath he demanded leave, declaring that he had not come to settle in Africa, and much "excessiveness" to the same effect. He was at last brought to his senses by being summarily turned out of the house for grossly insulting my companion.

A reaction then ensued; the Baloch professed penitence, and all declared themselves ready to march or to halt as I pleased. Yet, simulating impatience to depart, they clung to the pleasures of Kazeh; they secretly caused the desertion of the porters, and they never ceased to spread idle reports, vainly hoping that I might be induced to return to the coast.

Finally, Said bin Salim fulfilled at Kazeh Lieut.-Col. Hamerton's acute prophecy. The Bukini blood of his mother – a Malagash slave – got the better of his Omani descent. I had long reformed my opinion concerning his generosity and kindheartedness, hastily concluded during a short cruise along the coast. "Man's heart," say the Arabs, "is known only in the fray, and man's head is known only on the way." But though high-flown sentiment and studied courtesy had disappeared with the first days of hardship and fatigue, he preserved for a time the semblance of respectability and respect. Presently, like the viler orders of Orientals, he presumed upon his usefulness, and his ability to forward the Expedition; the farther we progressed from our "point d'appui," the coast, the more independent became his manner, – of course it afterwards subsided into its former civility, – and an overpowering egotism formed the motive of his every action. I had imprudently allowed him to be accompanied by the charming Halimah. True to his servile origin, he never seemed happy except in servile society, where he was "king of his company." At Kazeh, jealous of my regard for Snay bin Amir, and wearied by long evening conversations, where a little "ilm" or knowledge in the shape of history and divinity used to appear, – his ignorance and apathy concerning all things but A. bin B., and B. bin C., who married his son D. to the daughter or E., prevented his taking part in them, – he became first sulky, and then "contrarious." Formerly he was wont, on the usual occasions, to address a word of salutation to my companion: this ceased, and presently he would pass him as if he had been a bale of cloth. He affected in society the indecorous posture of a European woman stretched upon a sofa, after crouching for months upon his shins, – in fact he was, as the phrase is, "trailing his jacket" for a quarrel.

Through timidity he had been profuse in expending the goods entrusted to his charge, and he had been repeatedly reproved for serving out, without permission, cloth and beads to his children. Yet, before reaching Unyanyembe, I never had reason to suspect him of dishonesty or deceit. At Kazeh, however, he was ordered to sell a keg of gunpowder, before his slaves could purloin the whole. He reported that he had passed on the commission to Shay bin Amir. I also forbade him to issue hire to porters for a return-march from the Lake, having been informed that such was the best way to secure their desertion; and the information proved true enough, as twenty-five disappeared in a single night, tie repeatedly affirmed that he had engaged and paid them for the up-march only. When he stood convicted of a double falsehood, he had not spoken about the gunpowder, and he had issued whole hire to several of the porters, I improved the occasion with a mild reproach. The little creature became vicious as a weasel, screamed like a hyaena, declared himself no tallab or "asker," but an official under his government, and poured forth a torrent of justification. I cut the same short by leaving the room – a confirmed slight in these lands – and left him to rough language on the part of Snay bin Amir. Some hours subsequently he recovered his temper, and observed that "even husband and wife must occasionally have a gird at each other." Not caring, however, for a repetition of such puerilities, I changed the tone of kindness in which he had invariably been addressed, for one of routine command, and this was preserved till the day of our final parting on the coast.

The good Shay bin Amir redoubled his attentions. His slaves strung in proper lengths, upon the usual palm-fibre, the beads sent up loose from Zanzibar; and he distributed the bales in due proportions for carriage. Our lights being almost exhausted, he made for us "dips," by ladling over wicks of unravelled "domestics" the contents of a cauldron filled with equal parts of hot wax and tallow. My servant, Valentine, who, evincing uncommon aptitude for cooking, had as yet acquired only that wretched art of burlesquing coarse English dishes which renders the table in Western India a standing mortification to man's palate, was apprenticed to Mama Khamisi, a buxom housekeeper in Snay's establishment. There, in addition to his various Goanese accomplishments – making curds and whey, butter, cheese, and ghee; potting fish, pickling onions and limes, and preparing jams and jelly from the pleasant and cooling rosel, – he learned the art of yeasting bread with whey or sour bean-flour (his leathery scones of coarse meal were an abomination to us); of straining honey, of preparing the favourite "Kawurmeh," jerked or smoked meat chipped up and soused in ghee; of making Firni, rice-jelly, and Halwa, confectionery, in the shape of "Kazi's luggage," and "hand-works:" he was taught to make ink from burnt grain; and last, not least, the trick of boiling rice as it should be boiled. We, in turn, taught him the various sciences of bird-stuffing, of boiling down isinglass and ghee, of doctoring tobacco with plantain, heeart, and tea leaves, and of making milk-punch, cigars, and guraku for the hookah. Snay bin Amir also sent into the country for plantains and tamarinds, then unprocurable at Kazeh, and he brewed a quantity of beer and mawa or plantain-wine. He admonished the Baloch and the sons of Ramji to be more careful, as regards conduct and expenditure. He lent me valuable assistance in sketching the outlines of the Kinyamwezi, or language of Unyamwezi, and by his distances and directions we were enabled to lay down the Southern limits, and the general shape of the Nyanza or Northern Lake, as correctly – and the maps forwarded from Kazeh to the Royal Geographical Society will establish this fact – as they were subsequently determined, after actual exploration, by my companion. He took charge of our letters and papers intended for home, and he undertook to forward the lagging gang still expected from the

Coast: as the future will prove, his energy enabled me to receive the much wanted reserve in the "nick of time."

At length, it became apparent that no other porters were procurable at Kazeh, and that the restiff Baloch and the sons of Ramji disdaining Caesar's "ite," required his "venite." I therefore resolved to lead them, instead of expending time and trouble in driving them, trusting that old habit, and that the difficulties attending their remaining behind would induce them to follow me. After much murmuring, my companion preceded me on the 5th December, and "made a Khambi," at Zimbili, a lumpy hill, with a north and south lay, and conspicuous as a landmark from the Arab settlements, which are separated from it by a march of two hours. On the third day I followed him, in truth, more dead than alive, – the wing of Azrael seemed waving over my head, – even the movement of the Manchila was almost unendurable. I found cold and comfortless quarters in a large village at the base of Zimbili, no cartel was procurable, the roof leaked, and every night brought with it a furious storm of lightning, wind, and rain. By slow degrees, the Baloch began to drop in, a few of the sons of Ramji, and the donkey-men followed, half-a-dozen additional porters were engaged, and I was recovering strength to advance once more, when the report that our long-expected caravan was halted at Rubuga, in consequence of desertion, rendered a further delay necessary. My companion returned to Kazeh, to await the arrival of the reserve-supplies, and I proceeded onwards to collect a gang for the journey westwards.

At 10 A.M., on the 15th December, I mounted the Manchila, carried by six slaves, hired by Snay bin Amir, from Khamis bin Salim at the rate of three pounds of white beads each, for the journey to Msene. After my long imprisonment, I was charmed with the prospect, a fine open country, with well-wooded hills rolling into blue distance on either hand. A two hours' ride placed me at Yombo, a new and picturesque village of circular tents, surrounded by plantains and wild fruit-trees. The Mkuba bears an edible red plum, which, though scanty of flesh, as usual, where man's care is wanting, was found by no means unpalatable. The Metrongoma produces a chocolate-coloured fruit, about the size of a cherry: it is eaten, but it lacks the grateful acid of the Mkuba. The gigantic Palmyra or Borassus, which failed in the barren platform of Ugogo, here re-appears, and hence extends to the Tanganyika Lake.

I halted two days at Yombo: the situation was low and unhealthy, and provisions were procurable in homeopathic quantities. My only amusement there was to watch the softer part of the population. At eventide, when the labours of the day were past and done, the villagers came home in a body, laden with their implements of cultivation, and singing a kind of "dulce domum," in a simple and pleasing recitative. The sunset hour, in the "Land of the Moon," is replete with enjoyments. The sweet and balmy breeze floats in waves, like the draught of a fan; the sky is softly and serenely blue; the fleecy clouds, stationary in the upper firmament, are robed in purple and gold, and the beautiful blush, crimsoning the west, is reflected by all the features of earth. At this time, all is life. The vulture soars with silent flight, high in the blue expanse; the small birds preen themselves for the night, and sing their evening hymns; the antelopes prepare to couch in the bush; the cattle and flocks frisk and gamble, whilst driven from their pastures; and the people busy themselves with the simple pleasures that end the day. Every evening there is a smoking party, which particularly attracts my attention. All the feminine part of the population, from wrinkled grandmother to the maiden scarcely in her teens, assemble together, and sitting in a circle upon dwarf stools and logs of wood, apply themselves to their long black-bowl'd pipes.

> *"Saepe illae long-cut vel short-cut flare tobacco*
> *Sunt solitae pipos."*

They smoke with an intense enjoyment, slowly and deeply inhaling the glorious weed, and exhaling clouds from their nostrils; at times they stop to cool the mouth with slices of raw manioc, or cobs of green maize roasted in the ashes; and often some earnest matter of local importance causes the pipes to be removed for a few minutes, and a clamour of tongues breaks the usual silence. The pipe also requires remark: the bowl is of imperfect material – the clay being half-baked – but the shape is perfect. The African tapering cone is far superior to the European bowl: the former gives as much smoke as possible whilst the tobacco is fresh and untainted, and as little when it becomes hot and unpleasant; the latter acts on the contrary principle. Amongst the fair of Yombo, there were no less than three beauties – women who would be deemed beautiful in any part of the world. Their faces were purely Grecian; they had laughing eyes, their figures were models for an artist, with

> *"Turgide, brune e ritondette mamme,"*

like the "bending statue that delights the world" cast in bronze. The dress – a short kilt of calabash fibre, – rather set off than concealed their charms, and though destitute of petticoat or crinoline they were wholly unconscious of indecorum. It is a question that by no means can be positively answered in the affirmative, that real modesty is less in proportion to the absence of toilette. These "beautiful domestic animals" graciously smiled when in my best Kinyamwezi I did my devoir to the sex; and the present of a little tobacco always secured for me a seat in the undress circle.

After hiring twenty porters – five lost no time in deserting – and mustering the Baloch, of whom eleven now were present, I left Yombo on the 18th December, and passing through a thick green jungle, with low, wooded, and stony hills rising on the left hand, to about 4000 feet above sea-level, I entered the little settlement of Pano. The next day brought us to the clearing of Mfuto, a broad, populous, and fertile rolling plain, where the stately tamarind flourished to perfection. A third short march, through alternate patches of thin wood and field, studded with granite blocks, led to Irora, a village in Western Mfuto, belonging to Salim bin Salih, an Arab from Mbuamaji, and a cousin of Said bin Mohammed, my former travelling companion, who had remained behind at Kazeh. This individual, a fat, pulpy, and dingy-coloured mulatto, appeared naked to the waist, and armed with bow and arrows: he received me surlily, and when I objected to a wretched cow-shed outside his palisade, he suddenly waxed furious: he raved like a madman, shook his silly bow, and declared that he ignored the name of the Sayyid Majid, being himself as good a "Sultan" as any other. He became pacified on perceiving that his wrath excited nothing but the ridicule of the Baloch, found a better lodging, sent a bowl of fresh milk wherein to drown differences, and behaved on this and a subsequent occasion more like an Arab Shaykh, than an African headman.

On the 22nd December my companion rejoined me, bringing four loads of cloth, three of beads, and seven of brass wire: they formed part of the burden of the twenty-two porters who were to join the Expedition ten days after its departure from the coast. The Hindus, Ladha Damha and Mr. Rush Ramji, after the decease of Lieut.-Colonel Hamerton, had behaved with culpable neglect. The cloth was of the worst and flimsiest description; the beads were the cheap white and the useless black – the latter I was obliged to throw away; and as they sent up the supply without other guard than two armed slaves, "Mshindo" and "Kirikhota," the consequence was that the pair had plundered ad libitum. No letters had been forwarded, and no attention had been paid to my repeated requests for drugs and other stores. My companion's new gang, levied at Kazeh, affected the greatest impatience. They refused to halt for a day, – even Christmas day. They proposed double marches, and they resolved to proceed by the straight road to Msene. It was deemed best to humour them. They arrived, however, at their destination only one day before my party, who travelled leisurely, and who followed the longer and the more cultivated route.

We left Irora on the 23rd December, and marched from sunrise till noon to the district of Eastern Wilyankuru. There we again separated. On the next day I passed alone through the settlement called Muinyi Chandi, where certain Arabs from Oman had built large Tembe, to serve as barracoons and warehouses. This district supplies the adjoining countries with turmeric, of which very little grows in Unyanyembe. After this march disappeared the last of the six hammals who had been hired to carry the hammocks. They were as unmanageable as wild asses, ever grumbling and begging for "kitoweyo," – "kitchen;" – constitutionally unfitted to obey an order; disposed, as the noble savage generally is, to be insolent; and, like all porters in this part of the world, unable to carry a palanquin. Two men, instead of four, insisted upon bearing the hammock; thus overburdened and wishing to get over the work, they hurried themselves till out of breath. When one was fagged, the man that should have relieved him was rarely to be found, consequently two or three stiff trudges knocked them up and made them desert. Said bin Salim, the Jemadar, and the Baloch, doubtlessly impressed with the belief that my days were numbered, passed me on the last march without a word – the sun was hot, and they were hastening to shade – and left me with only two men to carry the hammock, in a dangerous strip of jungle where, shortly afterwards, Salim bin Masud, an Arab merchant of Msene, was murdered.

On Christmas day I again mounted ass, and passing through the western third of the Wilyankuru district, was hospitably received by a wealthy proprietor, Salim bin Said, surnamed, probably on account of his stature, Simba, or the Lion, who had obtained from the Sultan Mrorwa permission to build a large Tembe. The worthy and kind-hearted Arab exerted himself strenuously to promote the comfort of his guest. He led me to a comfortable lodging, placed a new cartel in the coolest room, supplied meat, milk, and honey, and spent the evening in conversation with me. He was a large middle-aged man, with simple, kindly manners, and an honesty of look and words which rendered his presence exceedingly prepossessing.

After a short and eventless march, on the 26th December, to Masenge, I reached on the following day the little clearing of Kirira. I was unexpectedly welcomed by two Arabs, Masud ibn Musallam el Wardl, and Hamid bin Ibrahim el Amuri. The former, an old man of the Bent Bu All clan, and personally familiar with Sir Lionel Smith's exploits, led me into the settlement, which was heaped round with a tall green growth of milkbush, and placed me upon a cartel in the cool and spacious barzah or vestibule of the Tembe. From my vantage-ground I enjoyed the pleasant prospect of those many little miseries which Orientals – perhaps not only Orientals – create for themselves by "ceremony" and "politeness." Weary and fagged by sun and dust, the Baloch were kept standing for nearly half an hour before the preliminaries to sitting down could be arranged and the party could be marshalled in proper order, – the most honourable man on the left hand of the host, and the "lower class" off the dais or raised step; – and, when they commenced to squat, they reposed upon their shins, and could not remove their arms or accoutrements till especially invited to hang them up. Hungry and thirsty, they dared not commit the solecism of asking for food or drink; they waited from 9 A.M. till noon, sometimes eyeing the door with wistful looks, but generally affecting an extreme indifference as to feeding. At length came the meal, a mountain of rice, capped with little boulders of mutton. It was allowed to cool long before precedence round the tray was settled, and ere the grace, "Bismillah," – the signal to "set to," – was reverentially asked by Said bin Salim. Followed a preparation of curdled milk, for which spoons being requisite, a wooden ladle did the necessary. There was much bustling and not a little importance about Hamid, the younger host, a bilious subject twenty-four or twenty-five years old, who for reasons best known to himself assumed the style and title of Sarkal, – Government servant. The meal concluded with becoming haste, and was followed by that agreeable appearance of repletion which is so pleasing to the Oriental Amphitryon. The Baloch returned to squat upon their shins, and they must have suffered agonies till 5 P.M., when the appearance of a second and a more ceremonious repast enabled them once more to perch upon their heels. It was hard eating this time; the shorwa, or mutton broth, thickened with melted butter, attracted admiration; the guests, however, could only hint at its excellences, because in the East if you praise a man's meat you intend to slight his society. The *plat de resistance* was, as usual, the pillaw, or, as it is here called, pulao, – not the conventional mess of rice and fowl, almonds and raisins, onion-shreds, cardomoms, and other abominations, which goes by that name amongst Anglo-Indians, but a solid heap of rice, boiled after being greased with a handful of ghee –

I must here indulge in a little digression. For the past century, which concluded with reducing India to the rank of a British province, the proud invader has eaten her rice after a fashion which has secured for him the contempt of the East. He deliberately boils it, and after drawing off the nutritious starch or gluten called "conjee," which forms the perquisite of his Portuguese or his Pariah cook, he is fain to fill himself with that which has become little more nutritious than the prodigal's husks. Great, indeed, is the invader's ignorance upon that point. Peace be to the manes of Lord Macaulay, but listen to and wonder at his eloquent words! – "The Sepoys came to Clive, not to complain of their scanty fare, but to propose that all the grain should be given to the Europeans, who required more nourishment than the natives of Asia. The thin gruel, they said, which was strained away from the rice would suffice for themselves. History contains no more touching instance of military fidelity, or of the influence of a commanding mind." Indians never fail to drink the "conjee." The Arab, on the other hand, mingles with his rice a sufficiency of ghee to prevent the extraction of the "thin gruel," and thus makes the grain as palatable and as nutritious as Nature intended it to be.

– and dotted over with morsels of fowl, so boiled that they shredded like yarn under the teeth. This repast again concluded with a bowl of sweetened milk, and other entremets, for which both hosts amply apologised; the house had lately been burned down, and honey had been used instead of sugar. The day concluded with prayers, with a seance in the verandah and with drinking fresh milk out of gourds – a state of things which again demanded excuses. A multitude of "Washenzi" thronged into the house, especially during the afternoon, to gaze at the Muzungu. I was formally presented to the Sultan Kafrira, a tall and wrinkled elder, celebrated for ready wits and spear. The sons of Ramji had often looked in at the door whilst preparations for feeding were going on, but they were not asked to sit down: the haughty host had provided them with a lean goat, in return for which they privily expressed an opinion that he was a "dog." Masud, boasting of his intimacy with the Sultan Msimbira, whose subjects had plundered our portmanteau, offered on return to Unyanyembe his personal services in ransoming it. I accepted with joy; but the Shaykh Masud, as afterwards proved, nearly "left his skin" in the undertaking.

The climate of Kirira is called by the Arabs a medicine. They vaunt its virtues, which become apparent after the unhealthy air of Kazeh, and after a delicious night spent in the cool barzah, I had no reason to question its reputation. I arose in the morning wonderfully refreshed, and Valentine, who had been prostrated with fever throughout the day, became another man. Yet the situation was apparently unpropitious; the Gombe Nullah, the main drain of this region, a line of stagnant pools, belted with almost impassable vegetation, lies hard by, and the background is an expanse of densest jungle.

Three short and eventless marches through thick jungle, with scattered clearings, led me, on the 30th December, to the district of Msene, where the dense wild growth lately traversed suddenly opens out and discloses to the west a broad view of admirable fertility. Before entering the settlements, the caravan halted, as usual, to form up. We then progressed with the usual pomp and circumstance; the noise was terrific, and the streets, or rather the spaces between the houses, were filled with Negroid spectators. I was led to the Tembe of one Saadullah, a low-caste Msawahili, and there found my companion looking but poorly. Gaetano, his "boy," was so excited by the scene, that he fell down in a fit closely resembling epilepsy.

Msene, the chief Bandari of Western Unyamwezi, may be called the capital of the Coast Arabs and the Wasawahili, who, having a natural antipathy to their brethren of Oman, have abandoned to them Unyanyembe and its vicinity. Of late years, however, the Omani merchants, having been driven from the neighbouring districts by sundry murders into Msene, may at times be met there to the number of four or five. The inhabitants are chiefly Wasumbwa, a subtribe of the Wanyamwezi race.

There is, however, besides Arabs and Wasawahili, a large floating population of the pastoral clan called Watosi, and fugitives from Uhha. In 1858 the chief of Msene was the Sultan Masanza. Both he and Funza, his brother, were hospitable and friendly to travellers, especially to the Arabs, who but a few years ago beat off with their armed slaves a large plundering party of the ferocious Watuta. This chief has considerable power, and the heads of many criminals elevated upon poles in front of his several villages show that he rules with a firm hand. He is never approached by a subject without the clapping of hands and the kneeling which in these lands are the honours paid to royalty. He was a large-limbed, gaunt, and sinewy old man, dressed in a dirty Subai or Arab check, over a coating of rancid butter, with a broad brass disk, neatly arabesqued, round his neck, with a multitude of little pigtails where his head was not bald, and with some thirty sambo or flexible wire rings deforming, as if by elephantiasis, his ankles. Like the generality of sultans, he despises beads as an article of decoration, preferring coils of brass or copper. He called several times at the house occupied by the Expedition, and on more than one occasion brought with him a bevy of wives, whose deportment was, I regret to say, rather naive than decorous.

Msene, like Unyanyembe, is not a town, but a mass of detached settlements, which are unconscious of a regular street. To the northwards lie the villages of the Sultan – Kwihanga and Yovu. These are surrounded with a strong stockade, a deep moat, and a thick milk-bush hedge, intended for defence. The interior is occupied by thatched circular huts, divided by open squarelike spaces, and wynds and alleys are formed by milk-bush hedges and palisades. There are distinct places for the several wives, families, and slaves. The other settlements – Mbugani ("in the wild") and Mji Mpia ("new town"), the latter being the place affected by the Wasawahili – cluster in a circle, separated by short crossroads, which after rain are ankle-deep in mud, from Chyambo, the favourite locale of the Coast Arabs. This settlement, which contained in 1858 nine large Tembe and about 150 huts, boasts of an African attempt at a soko or bazar, a clear space between the houses, where, in fine weather, bullocks are daily slaughtered for food, and where grain, vegetables, and milk are exposed for sale. At Msene a fresh outfit of cloth, beads, and wire can be procured for a price somewhat higher than at Unyanyembe. The merchants have small stores of drugs and spices, and sometimes a few comforts, as coffee, tea, and sugar. The latter is generally made of granulated honey, and therefore called sukari zi asali. The climate of Msene is damp, the neighbouring hills and the thickly-vegetated country attracting an abundance of rain. It is exceedingly unhealthy, the result doubtless of filth in the villages and stagnant waters spread over the land. The Gombe Nullah, which runs through the district, about six hours' march from the settlements, discharges after rain its superfluous contents into the many lakelets, ponds, and swamps of the lowlands. Fertilised by a wet monsoon, whose floods from the middle of October to May are interrupted only by bursts of fervent heat, the fat, black soil manured by the decay of centuries, reproduces abundantly anything committed to it. Flowers bloom spontaneously over the flats, and trees put forth their richest raiment. Rice of the red quality – the white is rare and dear – grows with a density and a rapidity unknown in Eastern Unyamwezi. Holcus and millet, maize and manioc, are plentiful enough to be exported. Magnificent palmyras, bauhinias and sycomores, plantains, and papaws, and a host of wild fruit-trees, especially the tamarind, which is extensively used, adorn the land. The other productions are onions, sweet potatoes, and egg-plants, which are cultivated; turmeric, brought from the vicinity; tomatos and bird-pepper, which grow wild; pulse, beans, pumpkins, water-melons, excellent mushrooms, and edible fungi. Milk, poultry, honey, and tobacco are cheap and plentiful. The currency at Msene in 1858 – the date is specified, as the medium is liable to perpetual and sudden change, often causing severe losses to merchants, who, after laying in a large outfit of certain beads, find them suddenly unfashionable, and therefore useless – was the "pipe-stem," white and blue porcelain-beads, called soft in the string, and individually msaro. Of these ten were sufficient to purchase a pound of beef. The other beads in demand were the sungo-maji, or pigeon-egg, the red-coral, the pink-porcelain, and the shell-decorations called kiwangwa. The cheaper varieties may be exchanged for grain and vegetables, but they will not purchase fowls, milk, and eggs. At this place only, the palmyra is tapped for toddy; in other parts of East Africa the people are unable to climb it. The market at Msene is usually somewhat cheaper than that of Unyanyembe, but at times the prices become very exorbitant.

The industry of Msene is confined to manufacturing a few cotton cloths, coarse mats, clay pipeheads, and ironmongery. As might be expected from the constitution of its society, Msene is a place of gross debauchery, most grateful to the African mind. All, from sultan to slave, are intoxicated whenever the material is forthcoming, and the relations between the sexes are of the loosest description. The drum is never silent, and the dance fills up the spare intervals of carouse, till exhausted nature can no more. The consequence is, that caravans invariably lose numbers by desertion when passing through Msene. Even household slaves, born and bred upon the coast, cannot tear themselves from its Circean charms.

There was "cold comfort" at Msene, where I was delayed twelve days. The clay roof of the Tembe was weed-grown like a deserted grave, and in the foul patio or central courtyard only dirty puddles set in black mud met the eye. The weather was what only they can realise who are familiar with a "Rainy Monsoon." The temptations of the town rendered it almost impossible to keep a servant or a slave within doors; the sons of Ramji vigorously engaged themselves in trading, and Muinyi Wazira in a debauch, which ended in his dismissal. Gaetano had repeated epileptic fits, and Valentine rushed into the room half-crying to show a white animalcule – in this country called Funza – which had lately issued from his "buff." None of the half-caste Arabs, except I'd and Khalfan, sons of Muallim Salim, the youths who had spread evil reports concerning us in Ugogo and elsewhere, called or showed any civility, and the only Arab at that time resident at Msene was the old Salim bin Masud. I received several visits from the Sultan Masanza. His first greeting was, "White man, what pretty thing hast thou brought up from the shore for me?" He presented a bullock, and received in return several cloths and strings of beads, and he introduced to us a variety of princesses, who returned the salutes of the Baloch and others with a wild effusion. As Christmas-day had been spent in marching, I hailed the opportunity of celebrating the advent of the New Year. Said bin Salim, the Jemadar, and several of the guard, were invited to an English dinner on a fair sirloin of beef, and a curious succedaneum for a plum-pudding, where neither flour nor currants were to be found. A characteristic trait manifested itself on this occasion. Amongst Arabs, the remnants of a feast must always be distributed to the servants and slaves of the guests; – a "brass knocker" would lose a man's reputation. Knowing this, I had ordered the Goanese to do in Rome as the Romans do; and being acquainted with their peculiarities, I paid them an unexpected visit, where they were found so absorbed in the task of hiding, under pots and pans, every better morsel from a crowd of hungry peerers that the interruption of a stick was deemed necessary.

At length, on the 10th January, 1858, I left Msene with considerable difficulty. The Kirangozi, or guide, who had promised to accompany me, had sent an incompetent substitute, his brother, a raw young lad, who had no power to collect porters. The sons of Ramji positively refused to lend their aid in strengthening the gang. One of Said bin Salim's children, the boy Faraj, had fled to Kazeh. The bull-headed Mabruki was brought back from flight only by the persuasion of his brother "Bombay," and even "Bombay," under the influence of some negroid Neaera, at the time of departure hid himself in his hut. All feared the march westwards. A long strip of blue hill lying northwards ever keeps the traveller in mind of the robber Watuta, and in places where the clans are mixed, all are equally hostile to strangers. Villages are less frequented and more meanly built, and caravans are not admitted beyond the faubourgs – the miserable huts outlying the fences. The land also is most unhealthy. After the rain, the rich dark loam becomes, like the black soils of Guzerat and the Deccan, a coat of viscid mire. Above is a canopy of cumulus and purple nimbus, that discharge their loads in copious day-long floods. The vegetation is excessive, and where there is no cultivation a dense matting of coarse grass, laid by wind and water and decayed by mud, veils the earth, and from below rises a clammy chill, like the thaw-cold of England, the effect of extreme humidity. And, finally, the paths are mere lines, pitted with deep holes, and worn by cattle through the jungle.

After an hour and thirty minutes' march I entered Mb'hali, the normal cultivator's village in Western Unyamwezi; — a heap of dwarf huts like inverted birds' nests surrounding a central space, and surrounded by giant heaps of euphorbia or milk-bush. Tall grasses were growing almost up to the door-ways, and about the settlement were scattered papaws and plantains; the Mwongo, with its damson-like fruit, the Mtogwe or wood-apple tree, and the tall solitary Palmyra, whose high columnar stem, with its graceful central swell, was eminently attractive. We did not delay at Mb'hali, whence provisions had been exhausted by the markets of Msene. The 11th January led us through a dense jungle upon a dead flat, succeeded by rolling ground bordered with low hills and covered with alternate bush and cultivation, to Sengati, another similar verdure-clad village of peasantry, where rice and other supplies were procurable. On the 12th January, after passing over a dead flat of fields and of the rankest grass, we entered rolling ground in the vicinity of the Gombe Nullah, with scattered huts upon the rises, and villages built close to the dense vegetation bordering upon the stream. Sorora or Solola is one of the deadliest spots in Unyamwezi; we were delayed there, however, three long days, by the necessity of collecting a two months' supply of rice, which is rarely to be obtained further west.

The non-appearance of the sons of Ramji rendered it necessary to take a strong step. I could ill afford the loss of twelve guns, but Kidogo and his men had become insufferable: moreover, they had openly boasted that they intended to prevent my embarking upon the "Sea of Ujiji." Despite therefore the persuasions of the Jemadar and Said bin Salim, who looked as if they had heard their death-warrants, I summoned the slaves, who first condescended to appear on the 13th January – three days after my departure, – informed them that the six months for which they were engaged and paid had expired, and that they had better return and transact their proprietor's business at Kazeh. They changed, it is true, their tone and manner, pathetically pleaded, as an excuse for their ill conduct, that they were slaves, and promised in future to be the most obedient of servants. But they had deceived me too often, and I feared that, if led forwards, they might compromise the success of the exploration. They were therefore formally dismissed, with a supply of cloth and beads sufficient to reach Kazeh, a letter to their master, and another paper to Snay bin Amir, authorising him to frank them to their homes. Kidogo departed, declaring that he would carry off perforce, if necessary, the four donkey-drivers who had been engaged and paid for the journey to the "Sea of Ujiji" and back: as two of these men, Nasibu and Hassani, openly threatened to desert, they were at once put in irons and entrusted to the Baloch. They took oaths on the Koran, and, by strong swearing, persuaded Said bin Salim and their guard to obtain my permission for their release. I gave it unwillingly, and on the next march they "levanted," carrying off, as runaway slaves are wont to do, a knife, some cloth, and other necessaries belonging to Sangora, a brother donkey-driver. Sangora returning without leave, to recover his goods, was seized, tied up, and severely fustigated by the inexorable Kidogo, for daring to be retained whilst he himself was dismissed.

The Kirangozi and Bombay having rejoined at Sorora, the Expedition left it on the 16th January. Traversing a fetid marsh, the road plunged into a forest, and crossed a sharp elbow of the Gombe Nullah, upon whose grassy and reedy banks lay a few dilapidated "baumrinden" canoes, showing that at times the bed becomes unfordable. Having passed that night at Ukungwe, and the next at Panda, dirty little villages, where the main of the people's diet seemed to be mushrooms resembling ours and a large white fungus growing over the grassy rises, on the 18th January we entered Kajjanjeri.

Kajjanjeri appeared in the shape of a circle of round huts. Its climate is ever the terror of travellers: to judge from the mud and vegetation covering the floors, the cultivators of the fields around usually retire to another place during the rainy season. Here a formidable obstacle to progress presented itself. I had been suffering for some days: the miasmatic air of Sorora had sown the seeds of fresh illness. About 3 P.M., I was obliged to lay aside the ephemeris by an unusual sensation of nervous irritability, which was followed by a general shudder as in the cold paroxysm of fevers. Presently the extremities began to weigh and to burn as if exposed to a glowing fire, and a pair of jack-boots, the companions of many a day and night, became too tight and heavy to wear. At sunset, the attack had reached its height. I saw yawning wide to receive me

> *"those dark gates across the wild*
> *That no man knows."*

The whole body was palsied, powerless, motionless, and the limbs appeared to wither and die; the feet had lost all sensation, except a throbbing and tingling, as if pricked by a number of needle points; the arms refused to be directed by will, and to the hands the touch of cloth and stone was the same. Gradually the attack seemed to spread upwards till it compressed the ribs; there, however, it stopped short.

This, at a distance of two months from medical aid, and with the principal labour of the Expedition still in prospect! However, I was easily consoled. Hope, says the Arab, is woman, Despair is man. If one of us was lost, the other might survive to carry home the results of the exploration. I had undertaken the journey in the "nothing-like-leather" state of mind, with the resolve either to do or die. I had done my best, and now nothing appeared to remain for me but to die as well.

Said bin Salim, when sent for, declared, by a "la haul!" the case beyond his skill; it was one of partial paralysis brought on by malaria, with which the faculty in India are familiar. The Arab consulted a Msawahili Fundi, or caravan-guard, who had joined us on the road, and this man declared that a similar accident had once occurred to himself and his little party in consequence of eating poisoned mushrooms. I tried the usual remedies without effect, and the duration of the attack presently revealed what it was. The contraction of the muscles, which were tightened like ligatures above and below the knees, and those luta gounata, a pathological symptom which the old Greek loves to specify, prevented me from walking to any distance for nearly a year; the numbness of the hands and feet disappeared even more slowly. The Fundi, however, successfully predicted that I should be able to move in ten days – on the tenth I again mounted my ass.

This unforeseen misfortune detained the caravan at Kaj-janjeri till porters could be procured for the hammock. On the 21st January four men were with difficulty persuaded to carry me over the first march to Usagozi. This gang was afterwards increased to six men, who severally received six cloths for the journey to Ujiji; they all "bolted" eight days after their engagement, and before completing half the journey. These men were sturdier than the former set of Hammals, but being related to the Sultan of Usagozi, they were even more boister-ous, troublesome, and insolent. One of them narrowly escaped a pistol bullet; he ceased, however, stabbing with his dagger at the slave Mabruki before the extreme measure became necessary.

Usagozi was of old the capital province of Unyamwezi, and is still one of its principal and most civilised divisions. Some authorities make Usagozi the western frontier of Unyamwezi, others place the boundary at Mukozimo, a few miles to the westward; it is certain, however, that beyond

Usagozi the Wanyamwezi are but part-proprietors of the soil. The country is laid out in alternate seams of grassy plains, dense jungle, and fertile field. The soil is a dark vegetable humus, which bears luxuriant crops of grain, vegetables, and tobacco; honey-logs hang upon every large tree, cattle are sold to travellers, and the people are deterred by the aspect of a dozen discoloured skulls capping tall poles, planted in a semicircle at the main entrance of each settlement, from doing violence to caravans. When I visited Usagozi it was governed by "Sultan Ryombo," an old chief "adorned with much Christian courtesy." His subjects are Wakalaganza, the noble tribe of the Wanyamwezi, mixed, however with the Watosi, a fine-looking race, markedly superior to their neighbours, but satisfied with leaky, ragged, and filthy huts, and large but unfenced villages. The general dress of the Wakalaganza is bark-cloth, stained a dull black.

We halted three days on the western extremity of the Usagozi district, detained by another unpleasant phenomenon. My companion, whose blood had been impoverished, and whose system had been reduced by many fevers, now began to suffer from "an inflammation of a low type, affecting the whole of the interior tunic of the eyes, particularly the iris, the choroid coat, and the retina;" he describes it as "an almost total blindness, rendering every object enclouded as by a misty veil." The Goanese Valentine became similarly afflicted, almost on the same day; he complained of a "drop serene" in the shape of an inky blot – probably some of the black pigment of the iris deposited on the front of the lens – which completely excluded the light of day; yet the pupils contracted with regularity when covered with the hand, and as regularly dilated when it was removed. I suffered in a minor degree; for a few days webs of flitting muscae obscured smaller objects and rendered distant vision impossible. My companion and servant, however, subsequently, at Ujiji, were tormented by inflammatory ophthalmia, which I escaped by the free use of "camel-medicine."

Quitting Usagozi on the 20th January, we marched through grain fields, thick jungle-strips, and low grassy and muddy savannahs to Masenza, a large and comfortable village of stray Wagara or Wagala, an extensive tribe, limiting Unyamwezi on the S. and S.E., at the distance of about a week's march from the road. On the 27th January, after traversing cultivation, thick jungles, and low muddy bottoms of tall grass chequered with lofty tamarinds, we made the large well-palisadoed villages of the Mukozimo district, inhabited by a mixture of Wanyamwezi, with Wagara from the S.E. and Wawende from the S.W. The headman of one of these inhospitable "Kaya," or fenced hamlets, would not house "men who ride asses." The next station was Uganza, a populous settlement of Wawende, who admitted us into their faubourg, but refused to supply provisions. The 29th January saw us at the populous and fertile clearing of Usenye, where the mixed races lying between the Land of the Moon eastward, and Uvinza westward, give way to pure Wavinza, who are considered by travellers even more dangerous than their neighbours.

Beyond Usenye we traversed a deep jungle where still lingered remains of villages which had been plundered and burned down by the Wawende and the Watuta, whose hills rose clearly defined on the right hand. Having passed the night at Rukunda, or Lukunda, on the 31st January we sighted the plain of the Malagarazi River. Northwards of the road ran the stream, and the low level of the country adjoining it had converted the bottoms into permanent beds of soft, deep, and slippery mire. The rest of the march was the usual country — jungle, fields, and grasses – and after a toilsome stretch, we unpacked at the settlement of Wanyika.

At Wanyika we were delayed for a day by the necessity of settling Kuhonga, or blackmail, with the envoys of Mzogera. This great man, the principal Sultan of Uvinza, is also the Lord of the Malagarazi River. As he can enforce his claims by forbidding the ferrymen to assist strangers, he must be carefully humoured. He received about forty cloths, white and blue, six Kitindi or coil bracelets, and ten Fundo (or 100 necklaces) of coral beads. It is equivalent in these lands to 50l. in England. When all the items had been duly palavered over, we resumed our march on the 2nd February. The road, following an incline towards the valley of the river, in which bush and field alternated with shallow pools, black mud, and putrid grass, led to Unyanguruwwe, a miserable settlement, producing, however, millet in abundance, sweet potatoes, and the finest manioc. On the 3rd February we set out betimes. Spanning cultivation and undulating grassy ground, and passing over hill-opens to avoid the deeper swamps, we debouched from a jungle upon the river-plain, with the swift brown stream, then about fifty yards broad, swirling through the tall wet grasses of its banks on our right hand, hard by the road. Upon the off side a herd of elephants, forming Indian file, slowly broke through the reed-fence in front of them: our purblind eyes mistook them for buffaloes. Northwards lay an expanse of card-table plain, over which the stream, when in flood, debords to the distance of two miles, cutting it with deep creeks and inlets. The flat is bounded in the far offing by a sinuous line of faint blue hills, the haunts of the Watuta; whilst, westward and southward, rises the wall-shaped ridge, stony and wooded, which buttresses the left bank of the river for some days' journey down the stream. We found lodgings for the night in a little village, called from its district Ugaga; we obtained provisions, and we lost no time in opening the question of ferryage. The Sultan Mzogera had sold his permission to cross the river. The Mutware, or Mutwale, the Lord of the Ferry, now required payment for his canoes.

Whilst delayed at Ugaga by the scabrous question of how much was to be extracted from me, I will enter into a few geographical details concerning the Malagarazi River.

The Malagarazi, corrupted by speculative geographers to Mdjigidgi, – the uneuphonious terminology of the "Mombas Mission Map," – to "Magrassie" and to "Magozi," has been wrongly represented to issue from the Sea of Ujiji. According to all travellers in these regions, it arises in the mountains of Urundi, at no great distance from the Kitangure, or River of Karagwah; but whilst the latter, springing from the upper counterslope, feeds the Nyanza or Northern Lake, the Malagarazi, rising in the lower slope of the equatorial range, trends to the south-east, till it becomes entangled in the decline of the Great Central African Depression – the hydrographical basin first indicated in his Address of 1852 by Sir Roderick I. Murchison, President of the Royal Geographical Society of London.[10] Thence it sweeps round the southern base of Urundi, and, deflected westwards, it disembogues itself into the Tanganyika. Its mouth is in the land of Ukaranga, and the long promontory behind which it discharges its waters, is distinctly visible from Kawele, the head-quarters of caravans in Ujiji. The Malagarazi is not navigable; as in primary and transition countries generally, the bed is broken by rapids. Beyond the ferry, the slope becomes more pronounced, branch and channel-islets of sand and verdure divide the

---

10.   The following notice concerning a discovery which must ever be remembered as a triumph of geological hypothesis, was kindly forwarded to me by the discoverer: –

"My speculations as to the whole African interior being a vast watery plateau-land of some elevation above the sea, but subtended on the east and west by much higher grounds, were based on the following data:-

"The discovery in the central portion of the Cape colony, by Mr. Bain, of fossil remains in a lacustrine deposit of secondary age, and the well-known existence on the coast of loftier mountains known to be of a Palaeozoio or primary epoch and circling round the younger deposits, being followed by the exploration of the Ngami Lake, justified me in believing that Africa had been raised from beneath the ocean at a very early geological period; and that ever since that time the same conditions had prevailed. I thence inferred that an interior network of lakes and rivers would be found prolonged northwards from Lake Ngami, though at that time no map was known to me showing the existence of such central reservoirs. Looking to the west as well as to the east, I saw no possibility of explaining how the great rivers could escape from the central plateau-lands and enter the ocean except through deep lateral gorges, formed at some ancient period of elevation, when the lateral chains were subjected to transverse fractures. Knowing that the Niger and the Zaire, or Congo, escaped by such gorges on the west, I was confident that the same phenomenon must occur upon the eastern coast, when properly examined. This hypothesis, as sketched out in my 'Presidential Address' of 1852, was afterwards received by Dr. Livingstone just as he was exploring the transverse gorges by which the Zambesi escapes to the east, and the great traveller has publicly expressed the surprise he then felt that his discovery should have been thus previously suggested."

stream, and as every village near the banks appears to possess one or more canoes, it is probably unfordable. The main obstacle to crossing it on foot, over the broken and shallower parts near the rock-bars, would be the number and the daring of the crocodiles.

The Lord of the Ferry delayed us at Ugaga by removing the canoes till he had extracted fourteen cloths and one coil-bracelet, – half his original demand. Moreover, for each trip the ferryman received from one to five khete of beads, according to the bulk, weight, and value of the freight. He was as exorbitant when we returned; then he would not be satisfied with less than seven cloths, a large jar of palm oil, and at least three hundred khete. On the 4th February we crossed to Mpete, the district on the right or off bank of the stream. After riding over the river plain, which at that time, when the rains had not supersaturated the soil, was hard and dry, we came upon the "Ghaut," a muddy run or clearing in the thicket of stiff grass which crossed the stream. There we found a scene of confusion. The Arabs of Kazeh had described the canoes as fine barges, capable of accommodating fifty or sixty passengers. I was not, however, surprised to find wretched "baumrinden" – tree-rind – canoes, two strips of "myombo" bark, from five to seven feet in length, sown together like a doubled wedge with fibres of the same material. The keel was sharp, the bow and stern were elevated, and the craft was prevented from collapsing by cross-bars – rough sticks about eighteen inches long, jammed ladder-wise between the sides. When high and dry upon the bank, they look not unlike castaway shoes of an unusual size. We entered "gingerly." The craft is crankier than the Turkish caique, and we held on "like grim death" to the gunwale with wetted fingers. The weight of two men causes these canoes to sink within three or four inches of water-level. An extra sheet of stiff bark was placed as a seat in the stern; but the interior was ankle-deep in water, and baling was necessary after each trip. The ferryman, standing amidships or in the fore, poled or paddled according to the depth of the stream. He managed skilfully enough, and on the return-march I had reason to admire the dexterity with which he threaded the narrow, grass-grown and winding veins of deep water, that ramified from the main trunk over the swampy and rushy plains on both sides. Our riding asses were thrown into the river, and they swam across without accident. Much to my surprise, none of the bales were lost or injured. The ferrymen showed decision in maintaining, and ingenuity in increasing, their claims. On the appearance of opposition they poled off to a distance, and squatted, quietly awaiting the effect of their decisive manoeuvre. When the waters are out, it is not safe to step from the canoe before it arrives at its destination. The boatman will attempt to land his passenger upon some dry mound emerging from deep water, and will then demand a second fee for salvage.

THE NARRATIVE PRESS
FIRST PERSON ACCOUNTS OF ADVENTURE & EXPLORATION

The Narrative Press prints only true, first-person accounts of adventures — explorations, circumnavigations, shipwrecks, jungle treks, safaris, mountain climbing, spelunking, treasure hunts, espionage, polar expeditions, and a lot more.

Some of the authors are famous (Ernest Shackleton, Kit Carson, Sir Richard Burton, Francis Chichester, Henry Stanley, T. E. Lawrence, Buffalo Bill). Some of the adventures are scientifically or historically important. Every one of these stories is fascinating.

All of our books are available as high-quality, lifetime softcover paper books. Each is also available as an electronic ebook, ready for viewing on your desktop, laptop, or handheld computer.

Visit our on-line catalog today, or call or write to us for a free copy of our printed catalogue.

THE NARRATIVE PRESS
P.O. BOX 2487, SANTA BARBARA, CALIFORNIA 93120 U.S.A.
(800) 315-9005
www.narrativepress.com

Printed in the United States
2755